Praise for *American Founders*

American Founders offers an extraordinary new narrative of the African role in creating the Americas of the Western Hemisphere. From hundreds of sources Christina Proenza-Coles has gathered the stories of people of African descent — politicians, soldiers, poets, journalists, doctors, teachers, and entrepreneurs — who laid the foundations of the New World. Briskly and vividly told, this important work illuminates both the past and the present.

— Henry Wiencek, author of *The Hairstons: An American Family in Black and White*, winner of the National Book Critics Circle Award

Erudite and balanced, Christina Proenza-Coles traces a complicated and arresting history with scholarly skill and finesse. She compellingly makes the case that the story of greater America is a deeply interconnected history where people of African descent played a more comprehensive, indelible, and sweeping role than once thought. Emerging from her story is a hopeful vision of a common past that links us more than it divides. Her book builds a framework for a new understanding of freedom, and expands the pantheon of freedom's founders and its defenders in the articulation of the idea of America. A feat of synthesis and hemispheric understanding.

— Ben Vinson III, George Washington University, Dean of Columbian College of Arts and Sciences

American Founders offers a sweeping history of African-descended people in the Americas that not only centers them in the fight for their own freedom, but also positions them as the intellectual progenitors and central actors in freedom struggles throughout the Americas. *American Founders* makes plain that the possibility of freedom was conceptualized and enacted by black people throughout the Americas, sometimes in conjunction with European and Native actors, but often by themselves.

— Elizabeth Stordeur Pryor, Smith College, Associate Professor of History, author of *Colored Travelers: Mobility and the Fight for Citizenship before the Civil War*

Christina Proenza-Coles gives us a stirring and sweeping history that shows how appreciation of the freedom struggles of African-descended people changes the whole story of national histories.
— DAVID ROEDIGER, University of Kansas, Foundation Professor of American Studies, author of *The Wages of Whiteness: Race and the Making of the American Working Class*

American Founders illuminates the myriad ways by which individuals of African descent fought for their freedom in the Americas — through maroon communities and military service, journalism and political organization, court petitions and club movements. It can stand as a model of a new kind of hemispheric history, a counternarrative to help guide historical change.
— JOEL DINERSTEIN, Tulane University, Clark Chair of American Civilization, author of *Swinging the Machine: Modernity, Technology, and African American Culture between the World Wars*

American Founders is a much needed, well researched, original contribution to studies of Africans in the Americas. The book's breadth of time and place reveals the largely unknown, indomitable, and courageous struggles for freedom of African-descended peoples and their enormous contributions to the arts and sciences and the wealth of the Americas. Most important, this book convincingly argues that we are all one, both biologically and culturally.
— GWENDOLYN MIDLO HALL, Rutgers University, Professor Emeritus of Latin American and Caribbean Studies, author of *Slavery and African Ethnicities in the Americas: Restoring the Links*

In this kaleidoscopic narrative, *American Founders* tackles the long history of people of African descent in the Western Hemisphere. The book shows how Americans of African origin have been central to our country's history and served as active agents in pushing for their freedom and the freedom of others. Proenza-Coles writes well, her mining of her sources is impressive, her argument cogent. A passionate work of history with a clear point of view.
— KIRKUS REVIEWS

AMERICAN FOUNDERS

AMERICAN FOUNDERS

How People of African Descent
Established Freedom
in the New World

CHRISTINA PROENZA-COLES

FOREWORD BY EDWARD L. AYERS

NEWSOUTH BOOKS

Montgomery

NewSouth Books
105 S. Court Street
Montgomery, AL 36104

Library of Congress Cataloging-in-Publication Data

Names: Proenza-Coles, Christina, author. | Ayers, Edward L., 1953- , writer of foreword.
Title: American founders : how people of African descent established freedom in the new world / Christina Proenza-Coles ; Foreword by Edward L. Ayers.
Description: Montgomery, AL : NewSouth Books, [2019] | Includes bibliographical references and index.
Identifiers: LCCN 2018047640 (print) | LCCN 2018050598 (ebook) | ISBN 9781603064385 (Ebook) | ISBN 9781588383310 (hardcover)
Subjects: LCSH: African Americans—History. | United States—History.
Classification: LCC E185 (ebook) | LCC E185 .P76 2019 (print) | DDC 973/.0496073—dc23
LC record available at https://lccn.loc.gov/2018047640

Design by Randall Williams

Printed in the United States of America

For Kitty

Contents

Foreword / IX

Preface / XI

Acknowledgments / XIII

Introduction / XV

1 The Rise of Atlantic Slavery in a World Historical Context / 3

2 Sixteenth-Century Afro-American Conquistadores / 25

3 Seventeenth-Century Afro-American Colonials / 53

4 Eighteenth-Century Afro-American Revolutionaries / 87

5 Nineteenth-Century Afro-American Patriots and Liberators / 147

6 Nineteenth-Century Afro-American Nationals / 187

7 Twentieth-Century Afro-American Freedom Fighters / 245

Conclusion: New World History / 293

Appendix: Eighteenth-Century Uprisings for Freedom / 298

Bibliography / 301

Sources of Illustrations / 330

Index / 334

Foreword

EDWARD L. AYERS

Christina Proenza-Coles has written a remarkable book. It combines one of the oldest traditions in histories of people of African descent with the newest advances in scholarship. The combination is powerful.

American Founders, in the older tradition, establishes people in places where they have been excluded from our understanding. We are introduced to African conquistadores and gentlemen painted in striking portraits in Ecuador in 1599, to black landowners and settlers in Manhattan and Virginia, to African American scientists, writers, and political leaders in the nineteenth and twentieth centuries. The portrayals exert a powerful cumulative effect, giving faces and names and histories to people too often reduced to generalizations and abstractions, to passive roles in other people's histories. In this way, Proenza-Coles sustains a proud and useful legacy.

Even as it draws on that older tradition, *American Founders* mines the last several decades of scholarship, in which the geographic and chronological range of history has expanded exponentially. By building on histories of the ancient world and the modern Atlantic world, Proenza-Coles shows that Africa and Africans helped shape global history at every turn. The continent and its peoples appear in the great dramas of world history, from war and conquest to music and literature.

The two perspectives in *American Founders* intersect with particular power in the history of United States. Proenza-Coles's hemispheric vision reveals surprises for North American history, as when she points out that maroons established the first settlement on the continent in Georgia eighty years before Jamestown and that in Virginia the first legal case contesting the legal boundaries of permanent servitude was waged between an owner and an enslaved man, both of African ancestry.

Proenza-Coles focuses ever more intently on the United States in the nineteenth and twentieth centuries as the cumulative force of her story lays a historical understanding for the black freedom struggles of the 1950s and 1960s. That moral revolution of the United States becomes comprehensible in a new way after reading *American Founders*, for we understand just how deep the roots extend into the history of the nation, the continent, the hemisphere, and the world.

Thanks to this book, we can see the largest patterns of history embodied in the lives of individuals with accomplishments born of their particular time in history. We see that American genealogies weave together, that the conventional divisions of history into racial and regional categories artificially separate our story. That perspective, at once broad and humane, is a rare gift.

Historian Edward L. Ayers, a recipient of the National Humanities Medal, is Tucker-Boatwright Professor of the Humanities and President Emeritus of the University of Richmond.

Preface

*A*merican *Founders* is filled with studiously documented facts, but it
is not an academic endeavor; it is a window onto a more complete
understanding of our interconnected past with implications for
our present. This is a history of all Americans because our heritage is fundamentally entwined, African and European, slave and free, Anglo and Latin.
Multiculturalism is not a contemporary artifact of political correctness; it
is the demographic reality of the founding and development of America.

Growing up in the Southern, Caribbean, and Latin kaleidoscope of
Miami, and spending summers in the American South, the Bahamas, and
Cuba, among other places, I was understandably curious about the dynamic
cultures around me. That is why I pursued any course and any opportunity, regardless of discipline, that could help me unpack the complexities
of race and ethnicity in the Americas. I had excellent teachers of literature,
philosophy, psychology, biology, anthropology, classical and urban sociology, political science, and comparative history who helped me to see the
connections among seemingly disparate traditions and prepare for a joint
doctorate in history and sociology.

As an assistant professor of the African Diaspora and the Atlantic World
in the profoundly historic town of Petersburg, Virginia, I had the invaluable opportunity to research and teach about the issues I care most deeply
about—how we created America—and then ponder them as I crossed the
James River on my commute. I came to this project while teaching world
history, U.S. history, Latin American history, and Atlantic World history; I
continually encountered examples of Americans of African descent whose
remarkable actions fundamentally shaped history, undermined the standard narratives of slavery, and, ultimately, revealed a deeper understanding
of American democracy. The wide-ranging contributions of the many

hundreds of individuals compiled here make a single argument: black men and women were central to the founding of the Americas, the establishment of New World nations, the dismantling of slavery, and the rise of freedom in the Americas.

American Founders invites readers to re-examine their understanding of freedom and what it means to be an American. It is a compilation of remarkable people and events that have profoundly shaped our contemporary world, based on a synthesis of a very large body of scholarship. I am beholden to these American founders and to the scholars who wrote about them. I have amassed all of this research, not for a specialized scholastic reader, but to share the verity of our common origins and our interconnected, Afro-descended, pan-American roots. This account does not aim to displace or erase our more conventional conceptions of America's founders, but rather to engage, enrich, and expand them. This book is meant to be an inspiration to gather deeper understandings of our shared American history and identity.

Acknowledgments

I am indebted to and inspired by too many people to name. My teachers at Ransom-Everglades school were outstanding, as were my professors at Swarthmore College. I feel especially grateful for my experience with the New School for Social Research Graduate Faculty whose full time and visiting scholars (with whom I spent a decade) were exceptional. I would like to offer particular acknowledgement and profound thanks to Dirk Philipsen and my colleagues and students at Virginia State University with whom I collaborated from 2004 to 2011 and from whose insights I benefitted immeasurably. The research programs supported by the National Endowment for the Humanities, specifically *Petersburg and the Atlantic World* and *Slaves, Soldiers, Rebels: Currents of Black Resistance in the Tropical Atlantic, 1760–1888,* as well as those developed by the CubaNOLA Arts Collective, brought together constellations of dedicated scholars and individuals whose ideas profoundly shaped this work. Without my good friend and intellectual mentor, the distinguished historian Paul Gaston, this book might still exist only on my hard drive. Without the talent and perspicacity of my editor, Randall Williams, and my unofficial editors, Heather Roberson Gaston and Stuart Horwitz, it might be unreadable. The vision and indefatigable work ethic of NewSouth's editors Beth Marino, Kelsie Kato, and Matthew Byrne and publisher Suzanne La Rosa have been vital to this project. To my extraordinary husband and children, family and friends, whose steadfast support has been essential, the depth of my gratitude is infinite.

Introduction

In the simplest version of our national narrative, Africans came to the United States as slaves and worked on plantations until they were liberated by Lincoln's Emancipation Proclamation. In this telling of history, slavery was an unfortunate aberration—limited to the American South—in the country's principal pursuit of democratic nation building. Among the implications of our national Black History Month is that African American history is an important but separate and not quite equal subset of American history. Popular history tends to suggest that black people stepped onto the stage of American history as plantation slaves in the nineteenth century and entered the political arena in the 1950s. These misconceptions have profound consequences not only for how we understand the past, but also for how we understand ourselves as Americans in the present.

Historical narratives shape how we imagine our place in the world. Much of American historiography has limited African Americans to a few roles, usually related to slavery or the civil rights movement, and gives the impression that mainstream history is the patrimony of white people. However, if we turn up the lights on our history, it becomes evident that people of color were there at every point, and not just as passive observers. The distinction between American history and African American history is imaginary.

This book explores three themes that refigure traditional conventions of American history. First, slaves were Americans—irrespective of whether their citizenship rights were recognized by the state—who participated widely and meaningfully in the ordinary and the watershed events that comprise the history of the Americas. Enslaved individuals were instrumental to the initiation and course of virtually every major New World historical event before the demise of slavery, itself an epic, multifaceted revolution in which slaves played substantial roles. Second, in the era that preceded the formal abolition of American slavery, not all black people were slaves. Despite the ubiquity of slavery, free people of color (i.e., they were born free, won freedom because of military service or familial relationships, purchased their own freedom, secured it in the courts, or, most commonly, liberated themselves through flight) abounded throughout the Americas and contributed greatly to their development in myriad ways. The third theme undergirds the first two: black and white Americans not only share the same New World history, they share the same ancestry. Enslaved and free people of color frequently had European relatives whose descendants became both black and white Americans.

Slavery is no aberration of American history; it is the foundation of American history. However, American history and African American history, though inextricable and founded on slavery, cannot be simply reduced to slavery. Africans and their descendants preceded the English in settling what would become the United States. People of African descent have been in the Americas since well before the English attempted the Roanoke colony, much less Jamestown, and have been risking their lives to advance freedom ever since. This book chronicles many of the ways in which Afro-American men and women helped to found and develop not just the United States but the Americas as a whole by forming communities, continually undermining and ultimately eradicating New World slavery, and championing universal citizenship.

Until 1820 Africans outnumbered Europeans coming to the New World by a ratio of four to one. In the early sixteenth century, people of African descent accompanied European expeditionaries in virtually every exploratory and military New World campaign from Canada to Chile, inaugurating a long and continuous tradition of black military service in the Americas. Seventeenth-century Afro-Americans continued to establish, develop, and defend towns and settlements throughout the Americas as explorers, soldiers, settlers, cowboys, pirates, priests, proprietors, agents, artisans, rebels, and maroons. While revolts against slavery, from armed uprisings to legal challenges, began in the 1500s, the early eighteenth century saw significant military and legal actions for freedom; these black democratic insurgents paved the way for and shaped the national independence wars that started at the end of the century and continued into the next. In the nineteenth century, Afro-Americans actively negotiated the terms of republicanism and citizenship during this critical period of nation building as military leaders, soldiers, lawyers, medical professionals, entrepreneurs, educators, journalists, artists, and as local and international activists. In the early twentieth century, Afro-Americans continued to champion the American ideals of universal rights, equality, justice, and civic engagement through their endeavors and innovations in politics, law, academia, science, engineering, mathematics, medicine, business, journalism, and art.

The events included here cover virtually all of the modern period and the Americas as a hemispheric whole. The fact that people of African descent were omnipresent and integral to the history of the New World means that each chapter covers a wide range of times and places. In an effort to convey how events and individuals connect to larger historical forces—colonialism, revolution, republicanism, and nation building—the chapters proceed chronologically and endeavor to provide a pan-American vantage point. By framing each chapter within a particular century, I hope to give the reader an overarching sense of the progression of American history; I ask the reader's forbearance in navigating the manifold sites, dates, and examples. Some examples exceed their origins in a particular century to make thematic connections across time. The vast number of individuals included here is overwhelming and deliberate; I encourage the reader to let the sheer weight of their number, and their intricate connections to global currents of history, compel us to rethink our own history, our national narrative, and our creation myths. These black men and women are not exceptions; they are our founders.

Slavery, the institution, is transhistorical—as soon as we humans came together in civilization, we enslaved each other. Slavery was part of virtually every civilization in the ancient world. But New World slavery was a novel institution quite distinct from traditional slavery. The Atlantic system that developed after 1500 was on a scale unprecedented in human history: it created modern capitalism; it invented the social fact of race. While xenophobia and ethnic intolerance are transhistorical, the idea of discrete races of white and black people is a wholly modern phenomenon born of the contradictions of Enlightenment ideology and the realities of the twin birth of capitalism and Atlantic plantation slavery. European and Euro-descended theologians, philosophers, planters, politicians, scientists, and academics invented and reinforced hierarchical concepts of race in attempts to rationalize the contradictions between the ideals of Christian and civic virtues on the one hand and the realities of colonialism, slavery, and, eventually, the American class system on the other.

The variant of New World slavery created by our European founding fathers in the United States was unique. Elsewhere in the Americas, modern slavery was built upon a traditional legal foundation reaching back to the Justinian code and ancient Rome. In the Spanish, French, and Portuguese colonies, these traditional legal protections for slaves and the strength of the Catholic brotherhood, of which slaves were members, provided legal and customary protections for enslaved persons (which could be discarded by individual planters). However, in the U.S., our founding fathers in Virginia, themselves individual planters, created slave laws which were suited to their interests, with no oversight from crown or church. This system of race-based slavery not only advantaged the planters who reaped wealth from it, it also greatly advantaged anyone on either side of the Atlantic who benefited from ancillary industries like banking, insurance, transportation, manufacture, or merchandising. One did not have to actually own slaves to benefit from their exploitation, then or now.

All who live in the Americas today, regardless of genealogy or country of origin, navigate societies shaped by the demographic, economic, social, cultural, and political realities that Atlantic slavery created. Even the lives of the most recent immigrants are shaped by slavery's consequences. For those of us who are designated as white, those consequences have been advantageous; for those of us designated as non-white, those consequences have largely been disadvantageous. These advantages and disadvantages are economic, structural, institutional, educational, cultural, social, political, psychological, and intergenerational. As W. E. B. Du Bois pointed out almost a century ago, whiteness provides a psychological and social wage in terms of imagined status and potential opportunities to even its poorest claimants.[1]

The systematic degradation of black people (many of whom had European

ancestry) and its necessary corollary, the systematic elevation of people regarded as white, did end not with abolition 150 years ago. This system was
perpetuated and indeed intensified with Jim Crow, convict labor schemes,
so-called medical programs [*see* page xiv], and terrorism—including lethal
anti-black riots, of which there were 25 in 1919 alone.[2] This system has been
perpetuated with post-war government policies, like federal housing loans
and interstate highway construction and school funding, which dovetailed
with banking and real estate practices that supported and advantaged a white
middle class and disadvantaged and decimated what was and what could
have been the black middle class.[4] The prison industrial complex picked up
where Jim Crow left off, just as Jim Crow had picked up where slavery left
off; these three continuous regimes were part of an institutionalized system
orchestrated to exploit, eliminate, and degrade black people. Black degradation was, and continues to be, a conscious or unconscious psychological
wage for many whites.

The ideology of black degradation and its intended corollary, white
valorization, attempted to rationalize race-based exploitation. In the United
States the privileges of whiteness were offered to palliate class inequality
among whites in a nominal democracy. This bifurcated conceptualization
of race also endeavored to forge a fixed color line in a society where covert
exogamy made the idea of insular racial categories a fiction. How do we
reconcile Thomas Jefferson extolling equality in his Declaration and deni-
grating black people in his *Notes on Virginia* with his being the father of
six enslaved children with African ancestry? Strom Thurmond was surely
not the only segregationist white Southerner to father a black child in the
twentieth century. It is no wonder that we have historical amnesia.

Throughout the history of the Americas, people of African descent negotiated, risked their lives for, and realized their own freedom and that of
others in myriad ways. Black women and men used the courts to petition
for their own freedom on both sides of the Atlantic; in doing so, they challenged and altered the legal frameworks of the institution of slavery. Afro-
Americans consistently capitalized on political instability and the outbreak
of conflict to undermine slavery. This can be said of the many thousands of
black militia members who earned their freedom and/or pursued upward

African American Medical Pioneers

The tragic Tuskegee Syphilis Study, where six hundred African American men with the disease were left untreated for forty years by the U.S. Public Health Service, ultimately prompted Congress to pass the 1974 National Research Act. Ironically, the most effective and widely used medical protocols regarding syphilis were developed by an African American, Dr. William Hinton (right), starting around 1927 and were endorsed by the U.S. Public  *Health Service in 1934. Hinton, the son of former slaves, earned his medical degree from Harvard in 1912, where he served as a professor for 27 years. He was a renowned physician, clinical pathologist, laboratory director, and textbook author in the 1930s. Hinton collaborated in his pioneering work on syphilis with another African American pathologist: Dr. Ruth Easterling, who earned her medical degree from Tufts in 1921. They jointly researched tuberculosis and published their findings in 1939. Easterling had her own private practice and served at the Tuskegee Veterans Administration Hospital before becoming director of laboratories at the Cambridge Massachusetts City Hospital. Another African American doctor, Solomon Carter Fuller, trained doctors at the VA Hospital in Tuskegee to diagnose black veterans with syphilis even before the experiment began in 1932. Fuller was the grandson of a Virginia slave who had purchased his and his wife's freedom and migrated to Liberia. Fuller was born in Liberia and earned his medical degree at Boston University in 1897. Fuller, an esteemed neuropsychiatrist as well as a medical researcher and educator, was invited by Alois Alzheimer to conduct research at the University of Munich in 1904, leading to data still lauded as recently as 2000.*[3]

mobility for their families in Latin American and Caribbean units. This can be said of the thousands of maroon rebels (fugitive slaves) who seized and defended their freedom militarily as well. Black conquistadores and black pirates, on opposite ends of the colonial spectrum, both escaped slavery and claimed freedom and material advancement. People of color served in every military engagement throughout the Americas (including North America), in many cases gaining freedom for themselves (if they were not already free) and eroding the political economy of slavery.

As Africans in the Americas undermined slavery, negotiated rights, and pursued citizenship, they helped to establish freedom in the Americas. The roots of the American Revolution and the legal erosion of institutional slavery in the West may arguably be traced to James Somerset, who won a watershed freedom suit in England in 1772. The court's decision determined that slavery was illegal in England and called into question the legality of slavery in Britain's colonies. North American planters may have been more concerned to protect their livelihoods based on slavery than to challenge taxes when they sought independence from England.

The American Revolution itself may be seen as part of a centuries long process of emancipation in the United States where African Americans sought freedom on both sides of the conflict. Thousands joined the Patriot army, including James Armistead, an enslaved American whose services as a double agent helped to foster the Yorktown victory and the British surrender. Many more African Americans recognized the promise of freedom offered to those who served in Loyalist companies. The vast ranks of men and women who left plantations to aid the British in exchange for their freedom made the American Revolution among the largest slave revolts in American history.[5]

The American Revolution did not result in the abolition of slavery on a federal level, but it undermined the institution. Freedom suits brought by African American plaintiffs engendered the legal termination of slavery in northern states. Freedom suits and manumissions throughout the South helped to strengthen the free black population. In Virginia, manumission acts in 1782 and 1783 granted freedom to thousands of slaves and specifically acknowledged that enslaved veterans of the Patriot army "contributed toward the establishment of American liberty and independence."[6] Free black communities in the North and South immediately organized churches, schools, businesses, mutual aid societies, and literary and civic organizations that advocated democracy. Despite its practical and ideological challenges to slavery, the American Revolution did not establish a democracy but rather left one-fifth of the U.S. population legally enslaved.[7]

It was the New World's second independent nation that established the first free republic in the Americas: Haiti. The American, French, and Haitian Revolutions were grounded in Enlightenment philosophy and driven by the political, economic, and social concerns that sprang from the entwined development of capitalism and slavery. Saint Domingue was a linchpin of the Age of Revolution. The colony's immense profits allowed the French state to underwrite the American Patriots; many have argued the American Revolution would not have succeeded without the financial and military aid of France. France put boots on the ground, including Afro-Haitian volunteers, to fight alongside the American revolutionaries; among them were some of Haiti's soon-to-be founding fathers, including Henri Christophe, Haiti's first elected president.

While Saint Domingue impacted the American Revolution and the American Revolution influenced Saint Domingue, Haiti's subsequent revolution profoundly altered the entire Atlantic world. Soundly defeating Napoleon Bonaparte's military, overturning slavery, and establishing an independent black republic, Haiti terrified those who supported and were supported by slavery and inspired Afro-Americans and abolitionists by signaling to all the limits of Atlantic slavery. From Virginia to Venezuela, revolutionaries like Gabriel Prosser and Simón Bolívar looked to Haiti and recognized that republican political economy required the end of slavery. This was not the case simply because these institutions were contradictory but because the wars of independence in Latin America and "the second war of independence" in North America—the American Civil War—could not be won without the support of Afro-Americans.

Abraham Lincoln understood that were it not for the military service of African Americans, the Union would not have prevailed during the American Civil War. Yet the president initially rejected arming African Americans in favor of protecting the tenuous union with slave-holding border states. However, once many hundreds of thousands of enslaved Americans had liberated themselves by fleeing plantations and flooding Union lines, Lincoln was left little choice. U.S. slavery was irreversibly undermined by African Americans' mass flight from plantations, and ambitious generals had already accepted the volunteers in combat, despite Lincoln's qualms. By the time the Emancipation Proclamation was issued, abolition was a *fait accompli*. From this vantage point, one could argue that African Americans brought an end to slavery and established democracy in the United States.

In Latin America and the Caribbean, the military and political actions of Afro-Americans also served to undermine slavery, even if formal abolition lagged behind. Still, these efforts led to de jure abolition throughout the Americas well before Lincoln's 1863 proclamation, with the exception of Cuba and Brazil. While Brazil did not have a war for independence, Cuba's late nineteenth-century independence wars were not only fought by Afro-Americans but also led by them. Like Brazil, the British Caribbean did not experience independence wars in the nineteenth century, but massive uprisings orchestrated by Afro-Americans in the 1820s and '30s, such as those in Demerara and Jamaica, compelled the British to unequivocally abolish slavery in 1838.

Abolition, however, was not equivalent to freedom, and Afro-Americans throughout the Atlantic world fought to advance the latter throughout the twentieth century. While Cuba and Brazil were the last nations to officially terminate slavery in the 1880s, they were the first to see the formation of independent black political parties in 1908 and 1931. Early twentieth-century precursors of the American civil rights movement were extremely prolific during this period as professionals and activists who created organizations and media to advance democratic principles; they built upon the scaffolding of previous generous and generated momentum for a movement that reached its political and emotional peak in the 1960s. The civil rights movement in turn inspired freedom movements as far away as South Africa and India.

People of African descent not only championed the Enlightenment ideals of liberty, equality, and natural rights, they helped to define these very ideals. It was precisely because of the development of the association between blackness and slavery in the modern period that people of color were continually seeking ways to achieve, assert, and protect their rights and those of others. The men and women who challenged slavery and discrimination in battle, in courts, in their writings, and in their actions, laid the foundation for the universal citizenship upon which democracy relies.

Afro-Americans did not share a uniform racial or political consciousness. Readers need not feel surprised, outraged, or exonerated by examples of Afro-Americans who owned slaves. Black slaveholders were a small but hardly monolithic group. Some Afro-American planters relied on enslaved labor for their livelihoods and enjoyed some of the economic and social privileges of their white counterparts, such as the prosperous free colored planters of Saint-Domingue and Louisiana. In other cases, black slave-owners purchased loved ones as a means to liberate them. (During the period when Virginia imposed laws requiring freed slaves to leave the state, black slave-holders might choose not to manumit loved ones to prevent their deportation.) In still other cases, Afro-Americans acquired slaves to assist in their small businesses as apprentices. In all of these scenarios, one could argue, the Atlantic slave system was undermined. New World slavery came to rely on a violent distinction between free whites and black slaves and the policing of Afro-American agency—therefore black slave-owners, by definition, contested and destabilized that system.

Free people of color, including the small minority who owned slaves, not only challenged the inequities of New World colonialism and slavery by definition but also by design. A colored planter in the French Caribbean and a free black artisan in the urban U.S. South might, like their white counterparts, own slaves and still be very engaged in the republican discourse of rights and devoted to the Enlightenment principles of liberty and equality. Compared to their white counterparts, these Afro-Americans would have been especially invested in the significance of those rights since their racial status made them more precarious. Free colored Haitians from slave-owning families served alongside the Patriots in the American Revolution and were directly engaged in French revolutionary politics to advance freedom. Tens of thousands of African Americans, on the other hand, opposed the American Patriots (whose leadership was composed of slave-owners and whose ranks included 5,000 African American Patriots) and joined the British forces for the love of freedom as well.

Afro-Americans' engagement in the Age of the Revolution preceded—and, in some ways, paved the way for—the Declaration of Independence of 1776. Slave revolts and maroon communities were a continuous and considerable part of American life, de facto political movements that shaped the larger events of the Age of Revolution. South Carolina's Stono Rebellion and Jamaica's First Maroon War, for instance, were their own declarations of independence that reverberated far beyond their locales. Throughout the history of the Americas, Afro-Americans took up arms, both for and against the state, as Patriots and Royalists, maroons and militia, rebel slaves and regular army officers, to stake claims to rights.

Afro-Americans sought to advance freedom in highly variable and sometimes conflicting and violent ways. Individuals of African descent were not consistently victims or heroes; they were Americans navigating particular cultures and contexts with individual motives, allegiances, ambiguities, and concerns. What this panoply of historical actors had in common was that slavery and the racial oppression that it generated "was a powerful orientation to the ideologies of liberty and justice."[8] What unites the disparate endeavors of Afro-Americans described here—individuals from different epochs and distinctive regions, each with particular bearings and circumstances—was that their "major loyalty was not [necessarily] to a place or a people, but to a principle:"[9] freedom.

The fact that black and white Americans have an extensive shared ancestry is another fundamental way in which the traditional distinction between American and African American history is illusory. Our nation's founding families included both white and black Americans. Martha Jefferson owned her own half sister, Sally Hemings—the mother of Thomas Jefferson's six black children after Martha's death. The union of Martha Jefferson's father with Sally Hemings's mother, Elizabeth, produced six half-siblings to Martha—one of whom was sold as a slave to James Monroe—and ultimately seventy-five descendants born into slavery at Monticello. Our first First Lady, Martha Washington, likely owned her own half-sister. George and Martha Washington had progeny among their servants as well.

Fathers of Our Country, In More Ways Than One

More than a fourth of U.S. presidents owned slaves. Thomas Jefferson placed an ad for a fugitive "Mulatto" with "light complexion" named Sandy in 1769. Newspaper advertisements seeking the return of self-liberated slaves were very common. An advertisement for Ona Judge—who liberated herself from George and Martha Washington by walking out of the Executive Mansion while the first couple was eating dinner—described her as

RUN away from the subscriber in *Albemarle*, a Mulatto slave called *Sandy*, about 35 years of age, his stature is rather low, inclining to corpulence, and his complexion light; he is a shoemaker by trade, in which he uses his left hand principally, can do coarse carpenters work, and is something of a horse jockey; he is greatly addicted to drink, and when drunk is insolent and disorderly, in his conversation he swears much, and in his behaviour is artful and knavish. He took with him a white horse, much scarred with traces, of which it is expected he will endeavour to dispose; he also carried his shoemakers tools, and will probably endeavour to get employment that way. Whoever conveys the said slave to me, in *Albemarle*, shall have 40 s. reward, if taken up within the county, 4 l. if elsewhere within the colony, and 10 l. if in any other colony, from
THOMAS JEFFERSON.

"light mulatto." Descriptions of light-skinned and mulatto slaves abound in ledgers, legal papers, travelogues, and memoirs. This is the case because countless Afro-Americans had white ancestry. Racial conventions have trained us to regard black and white as separate categories, but in reality racial boundaries were permeable. White Americans often owned other Americans with significant white ancestry. In many cases, Americans (including the Jeffersons and the Washingtons) owned their own kin.

Thomas Jefferson's father-in-law had six children with his slave Elizabeth Hemings. More than 75 of Elizabeth's descendants were enslaved at Monticello, including Sally Hemings. Sally's enslaved brother, James, led Martha Jefferson and her daughters to safety during the American Revolution and

WILLIAM MONROE TROTTER

accompanied Thomas Jefferson to France. Sally's sister, Thenia, was sold, along with her five daughters, to James Monroe. One of Sally Hemings's and Thomas Jefferson's daughters, Harriet, was an enslaved cotton worker. According to her brother, Madison, Harriet found freedom through flight and married a "white man of good standing" in Washington, D.C., where she raised a family that passed as white. In the 1930s, William Monroe Trotter, a Hemings descendent, excelled as a

FREDERICK MADISON ROBERTS

brilliant Harvard student, newspaper founder, and democracy activist. While Trotter descended from Monticello's enslaved community on his mother's side, his father, James Monroe Trotter, was the son of an enslaved mother and their owner (who freed James and his mother). James Monroe Trotter worked as a teacher and eventually for the U.S. government; during the Civil War, he served as a lieutenant in the U.S. Army.

Frederick Madison Roberts was the first African American elected to the California State Assembly, in 1918, where he served for almost two decades, helped to establish UCLA and other public schools, and proposed civil rights measures. A businessman and educator, Roberts also published a weekly newspaper. He was an associate of Marcus Garvey, a friend of Governor Earl Warren, and a great-grandson of Sally Hemings and Thomas Jefferson (Roberts descended from their child, Madison Hemings, whose own sons fought in the Civil War, one as a white soldier and one among the United States Colored Troops). Roberts was killed in an accident before he could assume a diplomatic post offered to him by President Eisenhower.

Afro-Americans and the Washingtons

This is a portrait of the Washington family by Edward Savage circa 1789. The identity of the black gentleman on the right is uncertain. Some have speculated that it is William Lee or Christopher Sheels, both of whom assisted George Washington as a valet. Others speculate that John Riley, a free person who assisted the American ambassador to London, may have served as a model. It is interesting to note that people of African descent accompanied the political elite at every historical turn throughout the Age of Revolution. Afro-Americans were witnesses to the writing of the Declaration of Independence as well as the diplomacy after the American Revolution. Sam Fraunces, widely known as "Black Sam," operated a tavern that served as Washington's headquarters in New York; he prepared the meal for Washington's negotiations with Sir Guy Carleton after the British surrender.

Some of the slaves at Mount Vernon were kin to the Washingtons. While George and Martha Washington never had children, George became the guardian of two of Martha's grandchildren (with her late first husband, Daniel Parke Custis) after the death of their father. George and Martha raised Martha's grandchildren; George Washington Parke Custis—along with his sister Eleanor—is depicted in the accompanying Washington family portrait.

George Washington Parke Custis is believed to have fathered enslaved children with at least two enslaved women from Mount Vernon. Custis eventually granted his daughter, Maria Carter Syphax, freedom and property in 1826, along with her children. Custis likely fathered another daughter, Lucy Branham, who remained in slavery. (Custis's only surviving "legitimate" child married Robert E. Lee.) Thus, two of Martha Washington's great-granddaughters were born into slavery; they were, in effect, Robert E. Lee's sisters-in-law. Historians have also suggested that Martha Washington and her servant Ann Dandridge shared paternity.

Another fair-skinned Mount Vernon slave, West Ford (who may have been George Washington's grandnephew—the grandson of Washington's brother), was eventually freed and granted property. West Ford's great-grandson, Major George Ford, served alongside Teddy Roosevelt as a Buffalo Soldier during the Spanish-American War and collaborated with W. E. B. Du Bois in the Niagara Movement, the forerunner of the NAACP.

MOUNT VERNON

West ford

A great number of the Americans who advanced democracy, as described in the following chapters, were the descendants of slaves and slave owners.[10] In addition to the countless Americans and their progeny who are literally the descendants of slaves and slave owners, all Americans, regardless of ancestry, are inheritors of the interrelations between slaves and slave own-ers—culturally, economically, politically, and socially. American history is not black or white, free or slave; it is both, we are both, and this realization will help us to better understand our past and our present.

Barack Obama has been identified as the eleventh great-grandson of John Punch, the Virginia colony's first slave. The genealogical link between the first African American president of the United States and the nation's first African American slave is through Obama's maternal lineage. In the 1630s, Punch had a son with a European woman who passed on her free status and racial designation to their progeny, at least one of whom fought in the Confederate Army. Obama's mother, Ann Dunham, a white woman born in Kansas, descended from this line. (Another of Punch's descendants, Ralph Bunche, was a political scientist, diplomat, and, in 1950, the first African American to win the Nobel Peace Prize.) African Americans are not only our founding fathers and mothers metaphorically; they are, though often unrecognized, our genetic ancestors as well. If ten million Africans came to the Americas via the Middle Passage, outnumbering Europeans by a factor of four until 1820, it should not be surprising that Americans have African ancestry.[11]

Barack Obama has been called the first African American president, but that distinction belongs to Joseph Jenkins Roberts, a free black entrepreneur from Virginia who served as the first president of the nation of Liberia starting in 1848. (Roberts was raised by his stepfather—a successful free black entrepreneur in Virginia—and his mother, who had been born into slavery but eventually freed. Roberts's biological father was likely his mother's former owner.) At least eleven Afro-Americans—people of known African descent—have served as presidents in Latin American nations.

This book is not a hagiography, nor is it a chronicle of the extreme brutality that inhered in the Atlantic system. The focus on the agency and achievements of free people of color and enslaved individuals may obscure the profound violence of plantation societies and the omnipresent oppression and danger that Afro-Americans had to navigate in slave- and post-slave societies. This book presupposes a working knowledge of that pervading violence as it endeavors to reframe well-known historical events and recover lesser-known ones.

Among the novel elements of American slavery that made it so radically different from earlier forms of slavery was that it came to rely on the severe and systematic curtailing of the rights of people of African descent, both enslaved *and* free. The denial of rights to black Americans was rationalized by an increasingly elaborate ideology of white supremacy that was in turn reinforced and reified by the denial of rights to people regarded as non-white. This book is less concerned with trying to adjudicate which individuals, black or white, were on the "right side" of this complex history than with demonstrating that our understanding of how black people participated in and shaped Western history, from the mundane trajectories of daily life to the critical turning points of major historical events, has been severely limited. I also hope to show that our very conceptualizations of racial categories have been severely limited—and limiting—as well.

The ways in which we conceptualize race are embedded in and shaped by language and terminology. Because this work examines the ubiquity of African-descended people in the making of American history, I generally refrain from inserting racial qualifiers except to indicate when an individual was not black (the inverse of the convention that assumes universal terms like "person" or "American" refers to white people). However, I use the term *African American* to refer specifically to people from the United States and *Afro-American* to include black people throughout the Americas as a hemispheric whole. These terms describe people of known African ancestry who were considered "negro" or "mulatto" by law and custom, despite the fact that many black people had European and Native American ancestry as well. I use the term *white* to refer to individuals throughout the New World who were predominantly (though rarely exclusively) of European ancestry.

Racial categories are the products of politics and culture, not biology and nature. The idea that there are discrete, organic categories of black people and white people has been revealed by history and science to be a total fiction. To underscore this point, consider the fact that Lucia Stanton has documented ten descendants from the enslaved community of Thomas Jefferson's Monticello—eight connected by blood to Elizabeth Hemings (and thus to Martha Jefferson) and two by marriage—who served in Federal military units during the Civil War. Four of them served in white units.[12]

The history recounted here pertains not only to Afro-Americans; it is the history of all Americans. In recent generations, mainstream scholarship, art, and media have become more diverse, inclusive, and nuanced. Yet, in many circumstances, we remain ensnared by deep-seated habits of thought about who fits into American history and how. If the accomplishments and actions of some of the individuals here are surprising, it shows us how attached we have been to assumptions about how people of African descent figure into American history. This book is not attempting to incorporate African American history into the dominant narrative; it aims to transform the narrative itself by recognizing and restoring our shared history.

NOTES FOR INTRODUCTION

1. W. E. B. Du Bois, *Black Reconstruction in America, 1860–1880* (New York: The Free Press, 1992 [1935]).

2. In the late nineteenth century and the first half of the twentieth century, authorities pursued countless black men for incarceration and impressment into convict labor programs. From Alabama's coal mines and Mississippi's penitentiary to the Tuskegee Experiment and forced sterilizations, state sponsored programs targeted, tortured, and killed innocent African American individuals, as did the state sanctioned vigilante violence perpetrated during riots, lynching, Klan activities, and general voter and residential intimidation. Douglas Blackmon, *Slavery By Another Name: The Re-Enslavement of Black Americans from the Civil War to World War II* (New York: Anchor Books, 2008); David Oshinsky, *Worse Than Slavery: Parchman Farm and the Ordeal of Jim Crow Justice* (New York: Simon & Schuster, 1997); James H. Jones, *Bad Blood: The Tuskegee Syphilis Experiment* (New York: Free Press, 1993); Gregory Michael Dorr, *Segregation's Science: Eugenics and Society in Virginia* (Charlottesville: University of Virginia Press, 2008); Cameron McWhirter, *Red Summer: The Summer of 1919 and the Awakening of Black America* (New York: Henry Holt, 2011); Philip Dray, *At the Hands of Persons Unknown: The Lynching of Black America* (New York: Random House, 2002); Amy Louise Wood, *Lynching and Spectacle: Witnessing Racial Violence in America, 1890–1940* (Chapel Hill: University of North Carolina Press, 2009).

3. M. Kaplan and A. R. Henderson. "Solomon Carter Fuller, M.D. (1872–1953): American Pioneer in Alzheimer's Disease Research." *Journal of the History of the Neurosciences* 9, no. 3 (2000): pp. 250–261.

4. Federal highway construction and redevelopment schemes routinely destroyed black

businesses and neighborhoods. Black Americans were also denied access to the low-interest loans and real estate appreciation that propelled many white Americans and their children and grandchildren into the middle class after World War II. Melvin Oliver and Thomas Shapiro, *Black Wealth/White Wealth* (New York: Routledge, 2006 [1995]).

5. Gary Nash, *The Forgotten Fifth: African Americans in the Age of Revolution* (Cambridge: Harvard University Press, 2006).

6. William Hening, *The Statutes at Large* (New York: Bartow, 1823), 308.

7. The majority of the free population was excluded from voting in the wake of the American Revolution, as neither women nor property-less men could vote.

8. Paul Gilroy, *The Black Atlantic: Modernity and Double Consciousness* (Cambridge: Harvard University Press, 1993), 13.

9. Benjamin Quarles, *The Negro in the American Revolution* (Chapel Hill: University of North Carolina Press, 1996 [1961]), xx.

10. Many notable African Americans were fathered by their owners. In addition to Elizabeth and Sally Hemings, a highly selective list includes Frederick Douglass, Booker T. Washington, Elizabeth Keckley, John Mercer Langston, William Wells Brown, West Ford, Moses Roper, George Latimer, Anna Julia Cooper, Alonzo Herndon, John Roy Lynch, Joseph Jenkins Roberts, Lucy Quarles, Ellen Craft, Lewis Clark, Sidney Morgan, James M. Trotter, James W. Mason, James Crawford, Robert Church, John Day, P. B. S. Pinchback, John Bathan Vashon, Stephen Smith, Henry Bibb, and Archibald Grimké. Dr. James McCune Smith had an anonymous white father. Artist Laura Wheeler Waring descended from a union between an enslaved Jamaican woman named Barbara Wheeler and the grandson of Philip Livingston, a signer of the Declaration of Independence. Inventor Garrett Morgan descended from a Confederate colonel. Likewise, democracy advocates Pauli Murray and Ella Baker descended from enslaved grandmothers and the unwelcomed license of their owners.

11. The Trans-Atlantic Slave Trade Database of Emory University puts the figure of enslaved Africans who landed in the New World between 1500 and 1875 at 10.7 million. Another two million individuals died during the Middle Passage. Between 1830 and 1875, enslaved Africans continued to arrive in massive numbers (two million people), though they did not outnumber European immigrants during this period. http://www.slavevoyages.org (7/7/2016).

12. Lucia Stanton, *"Those Who Labor for My Happiness": Slavery at Thomas Jefferson's Monticello* (Charlottesville: University of Virginia, 2012).

AMERICAN FOUNDERS

～ TIMELINE ～

B.C.E.

3500 Rise of world's first civilization, Sumer; 50 percent of the population is enslaved

3100 Nubian civilization begins in what is today Sudan (more pyramids than Egypt)

800 Homer's *Iliad* refers to "noble Ethiopians"

700 Nubia conquers Egypt

500 Height of Classical Greece; 25 percent of population enslaved

C.E.

200 Afro-Roman emperor Septimius Severus oversees Roman Empire from Scotland to Sudan

500 Fall of Roman Empire, start of European Dark Ages

550 Teotihuacan (in what will be known as Mexico) is among world's largest cities

600 Bilal the African, friend of Mohammad, serves as Islam's first muezzin

711–1492 Moors conquer Spain: North African Muslims bring arts & sciences to southern Europe

800–1200 House of Wisdom: Baghdad academy compiles science & scholarship from China to Africa

1000 Serfdom eclipses slavery in England; slavery persists in southern Europe & Mediterranean

1250–1350 Pax Mongolica: Mongols control largest contiguous empire in history (Eurasia)

1300 Marco Polo's book circulating (hand-copied before Gutenberg)

1312 Malocello lands in Canary Islands (after Vivaldi brothers left Italy 1291)

1324 Mansa Musa rules empire of Mali; Timbuktu and Jenné renowned centers of learning

1405–1433 Chinese international naval expeditions reach at least as far as Africa

1453 Ottoman Turks conquer Constantinople (first decisive use of gunpowder; end of Byzantium as the medieval extension of the Roman Empire and axis of trade between Europe and Asia)

1460 Madeira is largest producer of sugar in the world (start of Atlantic plantation system)

1500–1800 one million Europeans enslaved in North Africa by "Barbary pirates"

1

The Rise of Atlantic Slavery
in a World Historical Context

Until about two hundred years ago, most people were unfree. Throughout human history, the vast majority of the population was bound to some authority as subjects, vassals, supplicants, serfs, or slaves, perhaps indentured, impressed, or apprenticed. Indeed, before the 1800s, "personal bondage was the prevailing form of labor in most of the world."[1] Preceding the advent of the Enlightenment notions of individualism, equalitarianism, liberty, republicanism, and rights, which guided the aims (if not always the outcomes) of the American, French, Haitian, and Latin American revolutions, the modern concept of personal freedom was essentially nonexistent.

It can be tempting to read history backwards and impose our contemporary values on actors from very different epochs. We may feel that the moral repugnance of slavery is self-evident, but throughout most of world history, it was freedom that was extraordinary. Slavery was considered a legitimate fate for vanquished rivals and natural underlings. To legitimize their dominion, religious and political authorities depended on ideologies that framed social hierarchy as ordained and subservience as natural. Until the social and political transformations associated with what historians now call the Age of Revolution, the word *revolution* simply meant making a complete turn around an axis.[2] The abolition of slavery was a revolution in the modern sense—a fundamental and historic break with the past.

Another tempting aspect of reading history backwards is that it encourages us to perceive an inevitability of outcome. In the way we tell the stories that comprise history, there is a great potential to give the impression that history was bound to turn out as it did. Even the most seemingly judicious narratives of modern western history can be freighted with the unspoken assumption that Europe was destined to dominate and Africa was destined to be dominated. However, Europe, like many of the great civilizations that preceded it, was dominated and disorganized before it became an imperial power. In fact, conquering Africans, who occupied southern Europe for 800 years, brought arts and science to the continent during the Dark Ages. Moreover, the institution of slavery was hardly unique to sub-Saharan Africans; slavery had a transhistorical and global reach and "almost all peoples have been both slaves and slaveholders at some point in their histories." Between 1500 and 1800, roughly one million Europeans were enslaved in North Africa.[3]

Many associate the historical modern period—roughly 1500 to today—with European ascendancy and its attendant cultural hegemony. Yet the rise of Europe as the dominant power in the early modern period was not inescapable. Narratives that imply Europeans were the principal architects of the most advanced features of civilization fail to recognize that Europe's political, economic, and technological advance after 1500 was contingent on myriad factors and the complex civilizations that preceded it. European hegemony was not inevitable; nor was the Atlantic system that relied on the expropriation of African labor and American land. This chapter offers a brief overview of traditional forms of slavery, earlier civilizations that aided Europe's modern ascension, and the emergence of the novel system of slavery that developed in the Atlantic world after 1500.

THE ANCIENT WORLD

Slavery began with the dawn of human civilization around 3500 BCE, about 5,000 years before the concept of race emerged. In Mesopotamia's ancient Sumer, approximately fifty percent of the population was enslaved. In classical Athens, the birthplace of the concept of democracy, about a quarter of the population was enslaved. In ancient Roman society, the percentage of persons enslaved was considerably higher—close to forty percent—and included more than two million individuals. The Greeks enslaved barbarian foreigners considered outsiders to Greek culture, while the Romans enslaved their vanquished rivals from France, Spain, and North Africa. Ancient slavery had nothing to do with race.

With the formation of cities, humans initiated several new systems of political, economic, and social organization to manage the needs of densely populated urban communities: this is the rise of civilization. Among these new systems—including centralized government, bureaucracy, record keeping, and economic specialization—slavery emerged in all of the earliest and ancient civilizations, including China, India, Persia, Egypt, Sudan, Mexico, and Peru, as well as the aforementioned ancient Sumer (Iraq) and classical Greco-Roman world. Slaves were typically prisoners of war and often served as tribute laborers or in some cases for ritual sacrifice; others served as civil servants, administrators, concubines, cooks, domestics, musicians, guards, soldiers, artisans, and tutors.

While genomics indicate that everyone on the planet is descended from a woman who lived in East Africa about 150,000 years ago, human migration and mutation fostered populations with different phenotypes (traits of appearance) well before the ancient period.[4] For most of history, human difference was understood largely in terms of tribe and culture. Slavery was governed by the rules of war and religion. In the ancient and medieval periods, phenotypic population differences were gradual and geographic, perhaps less stark and less relevant to individuals traveling overland. The earliest references to human "races" originated when some Europeans tried to square their transoceanic encounters with populations previously unknown to them based on an Old Testament understanding of natural history. Broadly speaking, the concept of race first emerged during Europe's Age of Exploration in the 1500s, and it developed, gradually and unevenly, from an imprecise folk classification to a pliant legal and scientific category to a persistent social fact.

During the ancient period, Europe, along with North Africa and western Asia, was conquered and colonized by the Roman Empire. By way of their imperial centralized state, Romans (some of whose cultural roots can be directly traced to classical Greece, whose can be directly traced to ancient Egypt, whose can be directly traced to the Sudan)[5] introduced many features of civilization—trade, hygiene, engineering—to the "barbaric" tribes of ancient Europe. Under Afro-Roman emperor Septimius Severus, Roman soldiers reconstructed Hadrian's Wall in Great Britain to keep the barbarians at the gate. Several Afro-Roman soldiers were among them, just as African soldiers had been enlisted by earlier imperial regimes, including ancient Egypt, Persia, and Greece.

Rome's fall towards the end of the ancient period (roughly 500 CE) left Europe in the political and economic vacuum known as the Dark Ages. However, Spain and Portugal (Iberia) were centers of culture and learning because of their occupation by North African Muslims for eight centuries, from 711 to 1492. The African Moors brought with them the philosophy, astronomy, engineering, mathematics, and medicine that Muslim scholars were mining from ancient cultures, including classical Greece and Rome, and thereby helped lay the foundations of the Renaissance that eventually lifted the whole of Europe out of its intellectual quiescence. Tenth-century Cordoba was the most sophisticated city in Europe and among the most advanced cities in the world. Under Islamic rule, Christians, Jews, and Muslims collaborated in political and intellectual life. Cordoba boasted several universities, a robust economy, and a sophisticated infrastructure, and it was the home of scientific pioneers like the Arab surgeon Al-Zahrawi, whose definitive thirty-volume encyclopedia informed medicine throughout the Islamic world and Europe for five hundred years.

In the medieval period, as most of Europe struggled in the Dark Ages, expanding Muslim networks generated a cosmopolitan vanguard. In the two centuries after the death of Mohammad in 632, Islam spread from the Arabian peninsula to north and west Africa, southern Europe, and east India. Far from the conservative, anti-intellectualism associated with contemporary fundamentalist Islamic culture, the rise of Islam in this golden age linked people across the globe in a web of transcontinental trade, intellectual and scientific collaboration and innovation, as well as shared ideology and culture.

Through Islam, the broad dissemination of technology, goods, and ideas connected scholarship from west Africa to China and ushered in a new era: the internationalization of civilization. Muslim scholars in the newly established capital of Baghdad invited scholars from Christian Byzantium (including Jews), Hindu India, and Zoroastrian Persia to share, preserve, and synthesize their ancient scholarship. From about 800 to the Mongol conquest in 1245, Baghdad's House of Wisdom was an international scholarly academy with the world's largest library. It housed approximately 400,000 volumes that included humanities and sciences from ancient Greece to China as well as original Arabic knowledge like algebra and optometry.

In an era when most European libraries were fortunate to have a few dozen books, substantial libraries and universities were established in western Africa as well as southern Spain. From about 1200 to 1500, West Africa's Mali (which succeeded the empire of Ghana that began in 300) was among the largest, richest, and most powerful empires on the planet; its cities Timbuktu and Jenné were widely known for their academies of scholarship and thriving book trade. In the Middle Ages—in stark contrast to the mythology of the Dark Continent that Europeans would construct in the modern period—one was more likely to encounter someone who had read Plato and Aristotle in Timbuktu than a Parisian who could read.

Baghdad served as the intellectual center of this erudite international Islamic universe until its sack by the Mongols in 1245. Over the next century, the Mongols controlled the largest contiguous empire in history, from the Pacific Ocean to the Danube River. The Mongolian empire connected Asia, Europe, and Africa in a complex economic and cultural network of which the Middle East was the fulcrum and during which time Asian civilizations, far more advanced than Europe, had the hegemonic advantage.[6]

In retrospect, the century 1250–1350 was a point in history in which the balance of East and West could have tipped in either direction. The century was also known as the *Pax Mongolica* because, for the first time since the armies of Alexander the Great traveled to India a millennium before, westerners could safely travel east. It was said that in Mongol-controlled Eurasia, a maiden could ride bare-breasted from Europe to China, unmolested. At least two Venetian merchants traveled from Europe to China unmolested, the father and uncle of the better-known Marco Polo. While Polo may not have been the first European to see China, the publication of his book around 1300 made him the first European to describe China in print to a western audience. His book accurately described Mongol-controlled Chinese cities as far more populous, wealthy, and technologically sophisticated than any in Europe. Ancient China had greatly outpaced Europe in terms of technology and scholarship, and medieval China continued to do so with running water, heating systems, mass-produced books, paper currency, and gunpowder.[7]

Several factors brought the thriving economic networks of the *Pax Mongolica* to an end: the pandemic of the Bubonic plague (initially spread by Mongol horsemen), the breakdown of the Mongol empire, and, ultimately, the dismantling of the powerful Chinese navy. Between 1405 and 1433, China's navy, led by the Chinese Muslim admiral Zeng He, pursued voyages of exploration throughout Indonesia, India, the Arabian Peninsula, and East Africa. The Chinese navy's absence left Asian waters wide open once Portuguese explorer Bartolomeu Dias rounded Africa's Cape of Good Hope in 1498. Six Africans accompanied Dias's historic expedition. The balance began to tip in favor of Europe.

Arab traders had introduced to Europe a type of Indian wheat that helped to swell Europe's food production and thus its population. This helped revive towns, cities, and trade—the rise of urban forms commonly called civilization. As for the scholarly and technological aspects of civilization, Muslims had preserved, synthesized, and built upon the arts and sciences of the ancient Greeks, Iranians, and Indians, and had spread science, medicine, and technology from East to West. Not only did the Islamic scholars preserve the classical Greco-Roman humanities and sciences that stimulated the European Renaissance, but they also spread the technology of paper-making and book-making from China to Europe.

In addition to contributing to the origins of the European Renaissance, Islamic civilization helped to set western Europe on its course of expansion and colonization. The extensive reach of Muslim civilization stimulated a European desire to Christianize outlying lands to curtail the spread of Islam and to establish Europe's own trade networks with the East. Returning European Crusaders brought home new consumer items from the Islamic trade, including sugar. In the eighteenth century, sugar would stimulate the rise of modern slavery and capitalism, but in the fourteenth century it was used sparingly for food preservation (its first appearance in English cookbooks was in this period as a spice) and sometimes as medicine by the elite.[8] In the 1300s, many Europeans were eager to establish their own outposts in the lucrative Muslim-dominated spice trade; they could not have anticipated the impact sugar would have on world history, how it would shape a New World.

Atlantic Slavery

Fourteenth-century Europe was a uniquely rich arena for boatbuilding research and development. Geographically, Europe was a small peninsula protruding from the large landmass of Asia, surrounded by seas. Northern Europeans had long gained experience with sea-faring vessels in the North and Baltic seas. Scandinavians dominated the North Atlantic waters from the eighth through the eleventh centuries, capturing Europeans, whom they sold in Mediterranean slave markets. These conquering Scandinavian sailors, also known as Vikings, established an enduring colony in Greenland and made several expeditions to—and some short-lived settlements on—the northeast coast of mainland North America during this period.

Southern Europeans had long experience sailing in the Mediterranean, which benefited from boatbuilding technology developed in the Islamic world, like Arabic sails, and the introduction of the compass, invented in China. When the grain trade along Europe's Atlantic coast began to link shipbuilding techniques from the Mediterranean with those of the North and Baltic seas, the synthesis was a prodigious boon to maritime engineering. As John Thornton observed, "Not only did the needs of this seaborne trade between the Mediterranean and northern Europe serve as a stimulus to Iberian shipbuilding and interest in the interregional trade, but the fairly large number of ships involved increased the potential of accidental voyages of discovery."[9] By contrast, Africa was an enormous continental landmass with numerous rivers and an ancient overland trade route across the Sahara—the Gambia, Senegal, and Niger rivers connected easily with the "desert ships" (camels)—that had linked West Africa's gold to the rest of the world since Roman times. In 1324, Mansa Musa, the ruler of Mali, traveled by caravan to the Arabian peninsula with his entourage and spent so much gold that it altered the currency's market value.[10]

Winds and currents off the western coast of Africa made it easy to sail south but impossible for African, Arabic, or European craft to return north. Because of geography, coastal currents, and extant trade routes, fourteenth-century West Africans specialized in boats for river passages. West Africans did not generally pursue seafaring in the open Atlantic nor did they settle several of the islands along the Atlantic coast. Mansa Musa's predecessor as emperor of Mali, Abubakari II, was an exception; in 1311, he organized an exploratory sea-faring fleet for an expedition that may have made landfall in Recife, Brazil, the following year. Scholars have long speculated over the evidence of Africans in pre-Columbian America; recent findings suggest that Africans in Brazil may have predated Asian migration across the Bering Strait.[11]

While Abubakari II and other West Africans may have orchestrated exploratory expeditions across the Atlantic, it was Europe's short-range missions for expanded trade networks that led them to pioneer the navigation of the return. Just as Africa's geography and robust trade networks may have inhibited their development of transoceanic navigation, Europe's geography may have played a role in its motivation for expansion. With limited land and resources, Europeans were compelled to look abroad for trade and market opportunities. While European expansion began with "accidental voyages of discovery," ultimately the prospect of a sea route to West Africa's gold fields prompted a collaboration of Iberian, Italian, French, and English people, vessels, and capital in the pursuit of short-range maritime exploration along the West African coast. At their closest points, Spain is separated from Africa by fewer than eight miles of water. It was during these short-range, trial-and-error voyages that Europeans encountered the Atlantic islands off the coast of northwest Africa and, incidentally, set the Atlantic world system in motion.

One could say that the Atlantic world began when Genoan merchant Lancelotto Malocello came across the Canary Islands in 1312. (Some believe that Malocello's expedition was searching for the Vivaldi brothers, who had set out from Genoa in 1291 to sail to India but were never heard from again.) Malocello helped establish an outpost and remained in the Canaries for almost twenty years until he fled during an uprising of the island's original inhabitants. The Canaries and other nearby Atlantic islands became the first sites of Iberian trading and slave raiding as well as the first sites of Iberian colonization and the start of the Atlantic sugar plantation system. The Canaries also proved to be the key that allowed Europeans to unlock the puzzle of wind and current that had prevented easy sailing for the return trip from West Africa.

In 1402, Castile sponsored the first permanent colonization of the Canaries with Norman (French) colonists. In the following century, the Canary Islands produced sugar, wine, sheep, and cattle. Because the islands were a source of profit for Europeans, much attention was devoted to their navigation, shipping south of the Strait of Gibraltar increased, and raiding and commercial activity expanded further south. The Canaries served as a base for the development of additional European raiding and trading along the African coast as well as for the colonization of uninhabited Atlantic islands to the south (Cape Verde) and north (the Azores and Madeira). In the fifteenth century, Madeira and the Canaries began to export large quantities of wheat (cultivated by locals and indentured laborers from Europe) to consumers in Portugal and Africa. Madeira also produced wine, though the cultivation of sugar would become its most profitable venture.

The Rise of Sugar Plantations

Sugar cultivation originated in Southwest Asia during the ancient period and gradually spread westward to Persia. In the twelfth and thirteenth centuries, Arab traders brought sugar cultivation to the Mediterranean, where the first plantation system emerged. Mediterranean merchants imported bond laborers from the eastern Mediterranean, North Africa, and southern Russia—Slavs, from whom the English word *slave* derives—to produce sugar for an elite European market. By the fourteenth century, Cyprus produced large quantities of sugar with the labor of Syrian and Arab slaves, and the plantation system of coerced labor, large land units, and long-range commerce moved still further west, to Sicily.

Sicilian sugar plantations served as models for the Iberian colonies in the Atlantic islands, and, in 1420, Portugal's Prince Henry sent for cane plantings and sugar technicians to be brought from Sicily. The Atlantic islands offered a favorable climate and soil, and nearby West African sources came to provide a ready supply of laborers. The trial-and-error processes that shaped these endeavors is captured in Robin Blackburn's account:

The islands of the Canaries, Madeira, Cape Verde, and the Azores were the first sites of Iberian raiding, trading, and colonization in the Atlantic. When they imported the sugar cane planting techniques that Arabs had developed in the Mediterranean with Slavic slaves and turned to nearby West Africa for bond laborers, the Atlantic plantation system was born. These Atlantic islands were the stepping stones that would bring sugar and slaves from the Old World to the New World, not only because they were models of sugar production, but also because their navigation allowed the Iberians to unlock the patterns of wind and current that had prevented earlier sailors from making round trips in the Atlantic Ocean.

> In 1441 a Portuguese expedition on the West African coast captured
> two nobles; some gold was acquired by handing them back . . . In 1444 a
> cargo of 235 captives, comprising both 'whites' (Berbers) and 'blacks,' were
> seized in another Portuguese raid . . . However, the Portuguese captains
> soon discovered that they could, with less trouble and expense, also buy
> slaves and sell them to those involved in settling the [Atlantic] islands . . .[12]

The beginnings of the market for West African slaves arose from these incipient negotiations originating with ransomed nobles. As a result of this preliminary shift to procuring West African bond labor, almost all of the Atlantic islands experienced sugar booms in the fifteenth and sixteenth centuries. By the 1460s, Madeira was the largest sugar producer in the world.

In the fifteenth century, the Atlantic islands off the coast of southern Europe and northwest Africa were a model and launching ground for New World sugar cultivation, which combined the techniques of the Mediterranean plantation system with West African sources of labor. The region's successful exploitation prompted European explorers to seek additional islands further west in the Atlantic Ocean. It was the prospect of finding new Atlantic islands as well as the aspiration of reaching India (encouraged by Marco Polo's book) that motivated Christopher Columbus's initial voyage.

With funding from the Spanish Crown, Columbus set out in 1492 from Palos, Spain, with his three famous caravels and Africans in his crew. Written accounts describe the captain of the *Nina* on that expedition, Alonso Pietro, as "negro." Several free persons of African descent accompanied Columbus's second voyage. Records clearly show that a young African named Diego accompanied Columbus on his fourth voyage in 1502. Dental records from graves at the sites of Columbus's first settlements in Hispaniola also confirm that Africans accompanied his New World expeditions.[13]

The first landing of Columbus's original caravel was in the Canary Islands. The second was on Watlings Island in the Bahamas. A few days later, the ship landed in Cuba and then Hispaniola (the island composed of the contemporary nations of Haiti and the Dominican Republic), where Columbus—and the Africans and Europeans who accompanied him—established the first New World settlements in the Americas. Columbus had trained in the Madeira sugar trade as a young man and married the daughter of a founder of Portugal's Madeira colony. He brought his plantation experience to the New World on his second voyage in 1493 when he introduced sugar cane plantings to the Caribbean.

In the following centuries, the immense profits of sugar plantations in the Americas prompted the expansion of a uniquely modern form of slavery that was vastly different from its pre-modern predecessors. The eighteenth-century "sugar revolution" was the single most important element in the growth of the Atlantic World.[14] To produce this consumer commodity on a large scale, the plantation slavery that developed was unprecedentedly massive and brutal, novel in its global mass consumption, and singularly profitable. This pioneering system fostered the advent of capitalism and ultimately invented the concept of race for its justification. However, as illustrated above, its origins were neither race-based nor the result of a comprehensive European strategy.

The first Europeans in West Africa did not overwhelm locals with force but rather established commercial ties through diplomatic relations. When the Portuguese knight Nuño Tristão landed in the mouth of the Gambia River in 1446, the waiting West African armies decimated his crew. According to European sources, only two Portuguese survived the attack. Prince Henry the Navigator was devastated by the loss of Tristão, his favorite captain, and the expeditions he sent to West Africa the following year suffered heavy casualties as well. Even when Europeans were able to defeat West and West Central Africans in combat, the costs were much higher than alliance-based peaceable trade would have been. European merchants came to rely on an intricate diplomacy of mercantilism where they were required to pay taxes and provide offerings along what became known as the Slave Coast. As a 1655 Dutch commercial guide described, the "'prospective buyer of slaves and cloth . . . had to present a complex series of presents to dancers, food sellers, linguists, brokers . . . nobles, and the king himself, both upon arrival and upon departure.'"[15]

West African societies had long relied on a system of domestic and im-perial slavery that, like most pre-modern slave systems, provided a certain amount of social flexibility and mobility. Household and domestic slavery was often a temporary or transitional status. Prisoners of war and enemies of the state were fair game for trade; the further away they could be channeled, the safer the state. "By the fifteenth century it is likely that residents of [West Africa] were just as eager as Europeans to find access to greater and more direct participation in the expanding market of the world system."[16] Among the resources these West African states could offer for trade were foreign slaves. Just as European nations could view each other as foreign rivals and potential slaves—as in the Roman Empire described above—so did West African nations. The idea that the vast number of ethnic, religious, and linguistic groups on the continent of Africa could be regarded as a uniform group of "blacks" is a fiction.

While the original forays of exploring Europeans in West Africa sought to build trade relationships on diplomacy, their negotiations ultimately benefited from the use of gunpowder weapons, another technology advanced by Islamic civilization. Islamic Ottomans first combined Chinese gunpowder and European metallurgy to create an empire.[17] While the Mongols experimented with gunpowder, their dominance of Eurasia in the thirteenth and fourteenth centuries was grounded in their exceptional horsemanship; not until the 1500s did the "Islamic gunpowder empires" (India's Mughals, Iran's Safavids, and the Ottoman Turks) employ explosive weapons decisively. While the Mongols and Chinese had used bamboo and other vessels to detonate gunpowder since the Chinese invented it around 1000 CE, European metalsmiths, especially those who cast large church bells, were able to craft more durable bronze and brass bombards. The Ottoman sultan Mehmet used Transylvanian smiths to make the cannons that defeated Constantinople (and the thousand-year reign of Byzantium and its antecedent, the Roman Empire) in 1453, an event that, for many historians, signaled the start of the modern period. /

In the sixteenth century, the Ottomans were the most powerful state in the West, controlling much of the Near East, North Africa, and eastern Europe. In 1529, the Ottomans were poised to take western Europe, or at least its cultural capital, Vienna, until unusually heavy spring rains stymied Suleiman's European campaign; the mud broke camels' legs and bogged down heavy artillery. The Ottomans' military strength stemmed not only from their superior weapons, but also from their reliance on the famous Janissary infantry composed of eastern European slaves. The Ottomans also employed African slaves as soldiers; however, slavery in the Islamic world was quite unlike its modern variant in the Americas.[18]

Islamic slavery was more a matter of conspicuous consumption than coerced labor. Whereas Atlantic slavery functioned to generate enormous profits for a new European elite, Islamic slavery functioned to demonstrate the wealth and power of an established elite. One tenth-century Baghdad caliph, for example, had 11,000 slaves in his palace. These slaves were often treated as well-kept ornaments rather than as beasts of burden. Like slaves in the ancient world, Islamic slaves served as administrators, soldiers, guards, concubines, cooks, and musicians. Also, as with slaves in the ancient world, the status of the enslaved individual in the medieval Islamic world was malleable and offered room for mobility.

> The Ottoman sultan commonly married off his daughters and sisters to slaves, and in this and many other Islamic regimes, slaves or former slaves reached astonishingly high positions. Baybars, a former Turkish slave, led an army that defeated a Mongol invasion of Egypt in 1260; there were other slave generals as well. An Ethiopian slave became vizier to the sultan of Delhi and later governor of a province. A caliph who ruled in Egypt for most of the eleventh century was the son of a black slave concubine. A Slavic slave—not all slaves were Africans—was governor of Valencia in Islamic Spain.[19]

Africans, both free and enslaved, contributed to the rise and spread of Islamic civilization as soldiers, administrators, clergy, and poets. Bilal ibn Rabah, friend of Mohammad and Islam's first muezzin, was born to an enslaved African woman in Mecca. He was purchased and freed by Mohammad's father-in-law, who was moved by Bilal's sacrifices for his faith. Mohammad himself chose Bilal to pioneer the crucial role of calling the community to prayer.

NEW WORLD SLAVERY

In the modern period, the growing demand for sugar fundamentally altered the nature of slavery. In the 1660s, when England sent the East India companies to India, where tea was grown, and the Portuguese Catherine de Braganza came to the English throne with a taste for drinking it, tea (along with African coffee and American chocolate) joined sugar as an elite consumer item. In the early 1700s, sugar went from a ceremonial item and an upper-class status display to a daily food item and necessity for a new industrial working class. Sugar became the first item of mass consumption for an emerging population of wage earners.[20]

As English men, women, and children were pulled out of the agrarian countryside where they had produced and prepared their own food, whole families were introduced to the unyielding industrial schedule of factory life, and sugar, especially hot tea with sugar, became the world's first fast food. For sugar to become the world's first mass-produced product, it needed wage-earning consumers, which were provided by the burgeoning English working class; their exploitation made the exploitation of African sugar producers in the Americas so profitable.

It is unlikely that the Europeans who first engaged in trading captive people from West Africa could envision the scale or the consequences of the eighteenth-century Atlantic plantation regime. Nor could the West Africans who raided and traded rivals. Certainly the African and European agents who colluded in kidnapping people and imprisoning them in ship holds so they could be sold on another continent were engaged in brutality. But they may not have foreseen that the typical eighteenth-century American would be an enslaved woman on a Jamaican sugar plantation.

Sugar production was the most lucrative and lethal of all the New World plantation systems. Sugar cane had to be processed immediately upon harvest, requiring huge numbers of people to coordinate cutting and boiling on a continuous schedule at an unrelenting pace; the production itself was dangerous, the discipline barbaric, and the unprecedented profits rendered workers expendable. More than half of the captive Africans in the New World were trapped on sugar plantations. "As black slave labor . . . enabled Europeans to prosper throughout the Americas, it powered a massive engine

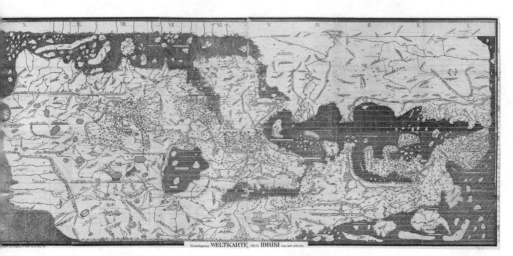

The Tabula Rogeriana was created by Mohammad al-Idrisi, a Muslim scholar who was born in Ceuta in North Africa and educated in Cordoba. Al-Idrisi worked on the map, commissioned by Sicily's King Roger II in 1138, at the Sicilian court in Palermo for fifteen years until its completion in 1154. The most accurate map of its time, Al-Idrisi's work formed the basis of geography for the next three centuries and inspired explorers like Columbus and Vasco de Gama. Note the dominance of Africa in Al-Idrisi's depiction of the world. Of course, modern viewers will need to stand on their heads, since the map is drawn upside down by modern perspectives.

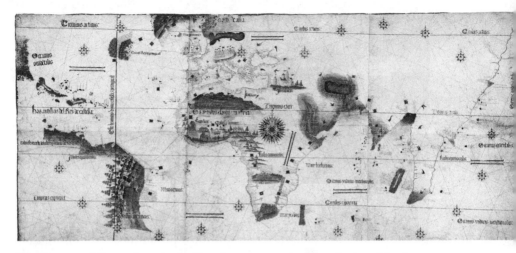

The Cantino Planisphere is the first known map to have depicted both the old and new worlds. It was named for Alberto Cantino, who was enlisted by an Italian duke to determine Portugal's exploratory reach. Cantino seems to have either commissioned or intercepted the map from a Portuguese mapmaker with access to classified royal records; he smuggled it from Portugal to Italy in 1502. The Planisphere shows the peninsula of Florida eleven years before Ponce de Leon—and the Afro-Iberian conquistador, Juan Garrido—"discovered" it in 1513. Theirs was the first old world expedition known to have made landfall in what would become the United States. The Cantino Planisphere was slightly preceded by Juan de la Cosa's World Chart, compiled in 1500. Cosa was a veteran of the Columbus voyages; it was not clear if his chart was depicting the Americas or Asia. While Cosa's map did not recognize the Florida peninsula, it did depict Cuba as an island despite the fact that Cosa had signed an affidavit, demanded by Columbus of the crew during his second voyage, that he believed Cuba to be a part of the mainland of Asia.

of wealth—and of death."[21] Many New World planters found they could extract the greatest financial return by providing minimum sustenance while demanding maximum labor from enslaved persons. As investments in sugar brought bigger and bigger returns, plantations got larger and larger. Africans increasingly outnumbered Europeans in many parts of the Americas, and slavery evolved into a New World nightmare where it became more "efficient" to work people to death and buy replacements, and "safer" to torture, mutilate, and terrorize individuals to control the population.

Yet, despite the extreme brutality of American plantation systems, New World slavery did not begin as a regime in which African-descended people were disposable. The earliest New World settlements, like the earlier European expeditions of exploration, were often the products of ad hoc decisions and experimental approaches. In 1505, when the king of Spain wrote the governor of Hispaniola about the first few hundred African slaves mining for New World gold, he advised, "'promise them ease if they work well,'" and, in 1511, "'take much care of them.'" However, even the earliest African slaves in the Americas insisted on freedom; the Hispaniola governor urged the king to stop sending slaves because "they fled among the Indians and taught them bad customs and never would be captured."[22]

Slavery in the Americas preceded the New World encounters of Europeans and Africans. The people who originally inhabited Mexico and Peru established complex urban civilizations in the ancient and medieval periods, and slavery was part of their elaborate imperial states. By 500 CE, Mexico's Teotihuacan was the sixth largest city in the world. Present-day Mexico City was founded on the original Aztec city of Tenochtitlan, itself founded in 1325. It has been estimated that in 1492, when Europeans and Africans began to arrive, the Native population of the Americas ranged between 35 and 45 million people; the empires of the Aztec and the Inca would have had the highest population densities. Tenochtitlan and Cuzco were significantly larger than any of Spain's cities at the time, and many of the conquistadores reported being awestruck by them.[23]

The Spanish were acquainted both as slaves and as masters with traditional slavery prior to the rise of the Atlantic plantation complex. In eastern and southern Europe, lively slave trades thrived during the ancient and medieval periods. After the fall of the Roman Empire, the enslavement of western Europeans persisted for roughly the next five centuries.[24] In England, slavery was eclipsed by serfdom after about 1000 CE. (In 1086, King William I's survey of England, the Domesday Book, recorded that slaves comprised ten percent of the population.) Serfs were bound to a master, but they could not be sold separately from a parcel of land. Indentured servants, however, were contractually bound to a master for a finite period of time. In the seventeenth century, nearly two-thirds of English settlers in the Americas arrived as indentured servants. Some French settlers arrived in the Americas as indentured servants (*engagés*) as well.

At the start of the colonization of the New World, the Spanish used Native American slaves to mine for gold and silver (often with African overseers), and the English used European indentured servants to grow tobacco. But by the 1700s, large-scale sugar cultivation—brought to the Caribbean by the Dutch, who had perfected it in Brazil—was absurdly profitable because of African slaves. The forced labor of Europeans and Native Americans, while it continued until the end of the eighteenth century, became a trickle amidst a massive demographic shift that flooded the Americas with the modern African Diaspora.

The factors and actors that came together to shape the rise of Atlantic slavery were legion. Portugal's Prince Henry did not single-handedly bring about a revolution in shipbuilding and ocean navigation in the fifteenth century. What would become known as Europe's Age of Exploration was a centuries-long process of trial and error and an international endeavor. A number of technical and geographic factors combined to make western Europeans the most likely people to explore the Atlantic and develop its commerce. This Atlantic commerce would eventually depend on a uniquely modern slave system unprecedented in human history.

Traditionally, slavery had nothing to do with race, and enslavement was not a condition unique to African and African-descended populations. The institution of slavery emerged with the dawn of human civilization and was practiced in societies across the globe and throughout history. However, the form of slavery that developed, gradually and unevenly, in the Americas after 1500 was a radically novel institution that violently exploited circumscribed populations on an unprecedented scale, grossly advantaged others on an unparalleled scale, and invented an elaborate ideology of race and racism to justify itself. The forms taken by American slavery were not preordained but were variable and contingent on various circumstances; New World slavery ranged from improvised, small-scale enterprises to brutal systematic regimes.

NOTES FOR CHAPTER 1

1   Seymour Drescher, *From Slavery to Freedom: Comparative Studies in the Rise and Fall of Atlantic Slavery* (London: Macmillan Press, 1999), 158.

2   Raymond Williams, *Culture and Society* (New York: Columbia University Press, 1958), 84. Williams outlined several "revolutionary" changes in meaning occurring at the close of the eighteenth century and the first half of the nineteenth; in addition to the term *revolution*, the significance of the terms *culture, class, industry*, and *art* transformed during this period as well.

3   David Eltis, *The Rise of African Slavery in the Americas* (New York: Cambridge University Press, 2000), xiii; Robert Davis, *Christian Slaves, Muslim Masters* (New York: Palgrave, 2003).

4   Steve Olsen, *Mapping Human History* (New York: Mariner Books, 2003).

5   Christopher Ehret, *Sudanic Civilization* (American Historical Association, 2003).

6   Janet Abu-Lughod, *Before European Hegemony* (New York: Oxford University Press, 1991).

7   A variation of the bare-breasted maiden saying is "a virgin carrying a gold urn filled with jewels could walk from one end of the empire to another without being molested," found in Timothy May, *The Mongol Conquests in World History* (London: Reaktion Books, 2012), 109. Among the reasons that scholars like Frances Wood (1995) believe that Marco Polo did not travel to China but instead based his reporting on the tales of other merchants are the features of Chinese civilization that his account omits, such as tea drinking, foot binding, the Great Wall, and chopsticks. For a western European, chopsticks would have been remarkable since at this point, around 1300, Europeans still ate with their hands. Forks were first used by Islamic royals in the seventh century and from there they spread to Byzantium. Italian elites adopted the use of forks in the sixteenth century, and Catherine de Medici brought the practice to France when she married its future king. An English traveler to Italy returned with forks in the early seventeenth century, but the practice was eschewed for years. The fork gained popularity in the United States in the nineteenth century.

8   Sidney Mintz, *Sweetness and Power: The Place of Sugar in Modern History* (New York: Penguin Books, 1985).

9   John Thornton, *Africa and Africans in the Making of the Atlantic World, 1400–1800* (New York: Cambridge University Press, 1998), 23.

10 David C. Conrad, *Empires of Medieval West Africa: Ghana, Mali, and Songhay* (New York: Chelsea House Publishers, 2010), 47.

11 Joan Baxter, "Africa's Greatest Explorer," BBC News Online, December 13, 2000;

Simon Romero, "Discoveries Challenge Beliefs on Human Arrivals in the Americas," *New York Times*, March 27, 2014.

12   Robin Blackburn, *The Making of New World Slavery* (New York: Verso, 1997), 102.

13   Hugh Thomas, *The Slave Trade* (New York: Simon & Schuster, 1997), 87–91; Kari Lyderson, "Dental Studies Give Clues About Christopher Columbus's Crew," *The Washington Post*, May 18, 2009.

14   For an overview of the concept of the sugar revolution in scholarly literature see B. W. Higman, "The Sugar Revolution," *Economic History Review* LIII, no. 2 (2000): 213–236.

15   Thornton, *Africa and Africans*, 67.

16   Donald R. Wright, *The World and a Very Small Place in Africa* (New York: M. E. Sharpe, 1997), 40.

17   William McNeil, *Age of Gunpowder Empires* (Washington DC: American Historical Association, 1990).

18   Ronald Segal, *Islam's Black Slaves* (New York: Farrar, Straus & Giroux, 2001). In the context of internecine political rivalries, foreign slaves were often considered more loyal collaborators.

19   Adam Hothschild, "Human Cargo," *New York Times*, March 4, 2001.

20   Mintz, *Sweetness and Power,* 130.

21   Vincent Brown, *The Reaper's Garden: Death and Power in the World of Atlantic Slavery* (Cambridge: Harvard University Press, 2008), 24.

22   R. R. Wright, "Negro Companions of the Spanish Explorers," *American Anthropologist* 4, no. 2 (1902): pp. 219.

23   Matthew Restall, *Seven Myths of the Spanish Conquest* (New York: Oxford University Press, 2003), xiii; Mark Burkholder and Lyman Johnson, eds., *Colonial Latin America* 6th edition (New York: Oxford University Press, 2008), 23.

24   In 642 an Anglo-Saxon slave named Balthild married the Frankish King Clovis II; after the king's death in 657, Balthild ruled as a regent, became a candidate for sainthood, and was succeeded by her royal children.

❧ TIMELINE ❧

1478 & 1495 Afro-Spaniards Johanna and Ursula win their freedom in Valencia, Spain

1492 Afro-Portuguese Alonso Pietro pilots *Nina* for Columbus's expedition

1502 Free Afro-Spaniard Juan Garrido lands in New World with Cortez

1502 First enslaved Africans arrive in New World

1503 Reports of first independent maroon community (fugitive slaves) in New World

1513 Nuflo de Olan & Balboa are first African & European to see America's West Coast

1521 Enslaved Africans rise up on Hispaniola plantation; more revolts in Colombia 1529, Panama 1531, Cuba 1533, Mexico 1537, Honduras 1548, and Peru 1553

1524 Spain commissions Afro-Portuguese navigator Esteban Gomez to explore Hudson Valley

1526 St. Benedict born in Sicily to enslaved African parents

1526 Africans resist Allyón settlement in Georgia, become first permanent trans-Atlantic settlers in North America

1526 Domingo Bioho founds first free Afro-American town, San Basilio, Colombia

1528 Esteban Dorantes is among first Old World explorers to see American Southwest

1529 Spanish authorities arm Africans to defend Cuba, create official troops by close of century

1532 Afro-Italian Alessandro de Medici becomes Duke of Florence

1534 Afro-Spaniards Juan and Anton are among founders of Quito, Ecuador

1535 Margarita Almagro in expedition to Chile; will gain freedom, open shop in Peru

1536 Enslaved Africans help to found Buenos Aires, Argentina

1538 Enslaved Africans help to found Bogota, Colombia

1544 Former slave Maestre António is granted license for surgery in Oporto, Portugal

1546 Enslaved Juan Valiente helps to found Santiago, Chile; is granted land and title

1550 Spanish report almost half of population of Merida (Mexico) of African descent

1559 Tomé Vasquez's petition for land is granted by Santiago de Chile's town council

1566 Juan Latino becomes a professor in Granada, Spain, publishes books of poetry

1572 Maroon population in Panama is roughly 3,000; Francis Drake allies with "valiant negroes" to defeat Spanish in Peru

1586 Alonso de Illescas petitions Quito court; maroon community is granted independence in Ecuador in 1600

1593 Parish records estimate majority population of Lima, Peru, is of African descent

2

Sixteenth-Century Afro-American Conquistadores

frican American history began simultaneously with European American history; both Africans and Europeans crewed on Columbus's first voyage. In 1494, on Columbus's second voyage, the crew established the New World's first planned colonial town: the settlement of La Isabella in the Dominican Republic. Excavations of the site have unearthed the remains of seven individuals with isotopes in their tooth enamel from West African bedrock. Scientists believe these remains are of Africans, and historians believe these Africans were free.[1] In fact, many of the first Africans in the Americas were free. People of African descent formed sizeable communities in Iberia's early modern trading and port cities and were active participants in voyages of exploration and conquest. Despite historical narratives that suggest all Africans arrived in the New World as slaves, contemporary records show that in the sixteenth century "a good many black freedmen from Seville and elsewhere found passage on westward bound ships" to the New World.[2]

The first Africans in the Americas, many of whom were not slaves, were vital contributors to the imperial endeavors to navigate, settle, and secure the lands of the Western Hemisphere. Africans participated in the New World campaigns as soldiers, seamen, settlers, artisans, agents, linguists, laborers, overseers, and rebels. Africans not only accompanied and assisted all of the Iberian conquests, they also were instrumental in creating New World settlements and were regularly called upon to defend them. It would have been "impossible for the Spaniards and the Portuguese to colonize the Americas without . . . Africans as soldiers."[3] The Latin tradition of African soldiering had ancient precedent in the Roman Empire, but its medieval roots lay in the conquest wars of Iberia.

Africans in Iberia

The North African Muslims (Moors) who controlled southern Spain and Portugal for almost eight centuries (711–1492) brought the arts and sciences of civilization—preserved and perpetuated in medieval Islamic culture—to a Europe otherwise mired in the Dark Ages. They also brought sub-Saharan Africans as soldiers to Spain and Portugal to serve in the occupying armies; during these eight hundred years, West Africans served on both sides of the countless *Reconquista* battles between the Iberians and the North Africans. Elaborate networks integrated Iberian and African residents, especially under Almoravid rule, when West Africans "travelled north freely to work or fight" in Islamic Spain.[4] The Moors also brought West Africans as slaves for domestic service or manual labor, if not military duties.

Slavery had long been established in Spain, beginning with the conquering Romans in the ancient period. In the Middle Ages, the captives taken in Spain's numerous wars and the eastern European and Baltic slaves of Italian merchants created a large, multi-ethnic institution. African slaves joined a diverse enslaved community in Spain that included Egyptians, Syrians, Lebanese, Sardinians, Greeks, Russians, Bulgarians, and Guanches from the Canary Islands.[5] Spaniards, too, were potential slaves in medieval Spain; they, along with the other "barbarian" tribes of western Europe, had been enslaved in the ancient Roman Empire.

"Just as all slaves in Spain were not Africans, not all Africans were slaves."[6] Some Africans entered Iberia as free persons on trade or diplomatic missions, while a few—the sons of the West African and Ethiopian elite—came for study or to enter the folds of religion or state in Rome or Lisbon. In addition to the Africans who had arrived as free men, Iberia had a population of freedmen—those who had come to southern Europe via the trans-Saharan and, later, the Atlantic slave trade but had negotiated their freedom. These also included freedwomen such as Ursola and Johana, who, in 1478 and 1495, respectively, pled their cases in Valencia's governor's court to win their liberty. Hence, even before slavery was established in the Americas, these fifteenth-century Afro-Spanish women set a precedent for the panoply of Afro-Americans' freedom suits in the following centuries whereby individuals secured their own freedom and, in several cases, altered legal doctrine and the course of history.[7]

In medieval Spain, Africans worked in foundries, stables, and bakeries and as builders, vendors, and butchers. In Portugal, Maestre António, a former slave, was licensed in 1544 to practice surgery. In Lisbon, some Africans served in royal households as musicians, cooks, and apothecary attendants, and, in the case of Domingo de Florença, as a confectioner and pastry chef to the queen.[8]

Members of the Portuguese royal family were themselves of African descent, specifically those descended from the fifteenth-century noblewoman Margarita de Castro e Sousa. Her lineage has been traced to a union between Portugal's King Afonso III and a Moorish woman, Madalena Gil, that produced a son in 1249. Historian Mario de Valdez y Cocom argues that this mixed-race royal was the progenitor of several lines of European nobility, six of which converged in England's eighteenth-century Queen Charlotte, who was variously described and depicted as "mulatto" by contemporaries and as a direct descendant of Margarita de Castro e Sousa. The mixed-race ancestries that would shape New World families had many precursors in the Old World.[9]

In the decades immediately prior to the Columbus expeditions—especially after 1479, when Spain authorized Portuguese merchants to sell West African slaves—most Africans who populated Iberia's southern cities were enslaved. Yet some Afro-Iberians enjoyed a high social status. Licenciado Ortiz was a lawyer of the Spanish Royal Court; Cristobal de Menses was a Dominican priest; and Catalina de Soto was a renowned embroiderer attended by white servants. At least three Africans—Luis Peres, D. Pedro da Silva, and João de Sá de Panasco—were granted knighthood in Portugal's Order of Santiago in the 1500s.[10]

A striking case was that of Juan Latino, who was liberated from slavery in sixteenth-century Spain, became a professor of Latin, and was the "first person of sub-Saharan African descent to publish a book of poems in a Western language."[11] Born in Africa, the young Juan had served in the household of the Spanish Count of Cabra as a page and companion to the count's son. However, when Latino accompanied his young master to

Right: Alessandro de Medici became the first duke of Florence in 1532. The son of an enslaved African mother and a father from the Medici dynasty (possibly Pope Clement VII), Alessandro ruled Florence from 1532 to 1537 and fathered two children.

Below: Portrait of the Afro-Spanish artist Juan de Pareja from 1649. Painted by Diego Velazquez (one of the masters of the Baroque period) for an exhibition in Rome, the portrait is now in the Metropolitan Museum of Art. Pareja lived and worked with Velazquez in Madrid and was officially freed by Velazquez in 1650. Pareja's own paintings are on display throughout Spain, including in the Museo del Prado.

school, the servant's gift for scholarship was so evident that he was enrolled and eventually freed.[12]

Latino's social circle eventually comprised other literary as well as socially and politically prominent figures. The opening poem of *Don Quixote*, a foundational work of Western literature published in the early 1600s, refers to Latino as "black Juan." The personage of Juan Latino was also the subject and hero of an early seventeenth-century Spanish play; he was one of several Afro-Spanish protagonists in early modern Spanish theater.[13]

By the fifteenth and sixteenth centuries, people of African descent formed sizeable communities in southern Spanish cities, where they participated actively in civic and religious life as "*vecinos* [neighbors/townspeople] and as members of parishes and religious brotherhoods called *cofradías*."[14] (The tradition of black *cofradías* and *cabildos*, religious and secular confraternities, would cross the Atlantic to Cuba in the 1500s and become a crucial part of Afro-American civic life throughout Latin America, from St. Augustine in North America to Buenos Aires in South America.) In fifteenth- and sixteenth-century Spain, the Afro-Spanish population grew to the extent that Queen Isabel and King Ferdinand appointed Juan de Valladolid, "a royal servant . . . 'of noble lineage among Blacks,' to regulate Seville's large black population and serve as its 'Chief and Judge.'"[15] Intermarriage was not proscribed in the Iberian Peninsula, and by 1550 Lisbon was said to have more people with mixed-race African ancestry than people of exclusively European descent.[16] The political, cultural, and demographic impact of Africans in Iberia was captured in the adage often attributed to Napoleon: "Africa begins at the Pyrenees." While the Pyrenees range has long served as a natural border between northern Spain and France, southern Spain is separated from Africa by the Strait of Gibraltar—a mere 7.7 nautical miles across.

BLACK EXPLORERS AND CONQUISTADORES

Because African-descended peoples formed sizeable communities in southern Spain and Portugal, it should not be surprising that many accompanied—and sometimes commanded—the Iberian-sponsored expeditions of exploration and conquest in the New World from Columbus on. As noted in the previous chapter, six Africans accompanied Bartolomeu Dias to the Cape of Good Hope. At least two men of African descent accompanied Magellan's global exploration. Esteban Gomez, an explorer of Afro-Portuguese descent who was part of Magellan's fleet, ultimately secured his own funding from Spain to lead expeditions in pursuit of the Northwest Passage in 1524. Sixteenth-century maps describe the northeastern edge of what is now the United States as "Tierra de Esteban Gomez."

According to the contemporary records of the Spaniard Cabeza de Vaca, Esteban "el Negro" Dorantes was, like Esteban Gomez, among the first explorers of North America. Dorantes was born in sub-Saharan Africa around 1500, purchased by a Spanish conquistador in Seville in 1522, and landed in Tampa with the ill-fated expedition of Pánfilo Narváez in 1528. Dorantes was among the four men who survived the mission and journeyed from Florida to Mexico, making them the first Old World explorers to see the American Southwest.[17] Dorantes's linguistic skills allowed him to serve as the principal intermediary and diplomat between the Spanish and the Native Americans they encountered. Hernan Cortez and the viceroy of New Spain met Dorantes and his party when they arrived in Mexico City, where "Esteban el Negro" was officially granted his freedom for his service to the Crown.

Africans also accompanied French forays to the New World, including Mathieu da Costa, a highly sought-after translator from Benin who assisted French expeditions in Canada around 1600. Da Costa, an experienced seaman as well as a linguist, led French expeditions in the region of Lake Champlain. Like Jan Rodriguez, the Afro-Portuguese sailor and linguist who settled in Manhattan in 1613 as an intermediary between the native New Yorkers and the Dutch, Da Costa facilitated communication and trade between the residents of Nova Scotia and the French.

A century earlier, Nuflo de Olan "discovered" the Pacific Ocean in 1513 after crossing Panama overland. According to Matthew Restall, "the first two men from the Old World to see the Pacific Ocean were Nuflo de Olan, an enslaved black conquistador, and his owner . . . Balboa—who subsequently brought thirty black workers to build ships on the Pacific coast." Restall also observed that "wherever Spaniards set foot in the Americas as members

Well after the "Age of Discovery," Matthew Henson continued in the tradition of black explorers at the turn of the 20th century. Henson, an explorer and seaman (starting at age 12), pursued a series of expeditions from Nicaragua to the Arctic with Robert Peary. The two men, who were accompanied by four Inuit companions, are recognized as the first to reach the North Pole in 1909; National Geographic maintains that Henson preceded Peary. In 1986, the

U.S. Postal Service issued a commemorative stamp to honor the pair. While Henson was given little recognition in the wake of the discovery, he was ultimately honored by Congress, two presidents, the Explorers Club, and the National Geographic Society as well as by the various schools, the naval vessel, and the national Earth Conservation Center that bear his name. Henson and his wife are buried in Arlington National Cemetery.

of conquest companies they were accompanied by black conquistadores."[18]

In the New World "few conquests were accomplished without African participation."[19] The Africans and Afro-Spaniards who came to the Americas as voluntary expeditioners and involuntary colonists were a "ubiquitous and pivotal part of Spanish conquest campaigns in the Americas."[20] They included free Iberians of African descent; mixed-race, enslaved Africans and Afro-Spaniards who garnered their freedom by serving as soldiers and translators; and enslaved Africans and Afro-Spaniards who remained servants but often operated with surprising autonomy.

The best documented of these black conquistadores was Juan Garrido, a free man of African descent. Although it is not clear whether he was born in Africa or Portugal, Garrido traveled from Lisbon to Seville around 1496 and shortly thereafter joined a voyage to Hispaniola. In 1494, Columbus and the Africans and Europeans in his crew established the first New World settlement in the Americas in Hispaniola; approximately eight years later, another free black adventurer, Juan Garrido, arrived in its capital, Santo Domingo.

Garrido's arrival around 1502 places him among the earliest Africans in the New World. He served with Hernan Cortez in the conquest of the Aztec in Mexico. Earlier he had served with Ponce de Leon in the exploration of Florida and Puerto Rico and had fought in "pacification campaigns" against the Amerindian defenders of Cuba, Dominica, and Guadeloupe. Garrido originally lived in Puerto Rico between campaigns but ultimately settled in Mexico City, where he was granted land and an official post, raised a family, ran a gold mine, introduced the cultivation of wheat, and continued to assist campaigns in Mexico and Baja, California.

Garrido served alongside other Afro-Spaniards in these campaigns. In 1533, Cortez's Baja mission included three hundred Africans. Cortez referenced particular Afro-Spaniards in Mexico, including Pedro de Alvarado, who served as first lieutenant, and Francisco de Eguia, who may have introduced smallpox to Mexico. Ponce de Leon took a number of "armed Africans" to conquer Puerto Rico in 1508, including Juan Gonzales who, along with Garrido, temporarily settled in Puerto Rico to pursue gold mining. In Puerto Rico, Francisco Mejias, another free person of color, served as "Indian collector and overseer" and established several of the New World's first ranches. Other documents refer to a group of African men and women who herded cattle outside of Lima, Peru, in 1547. "As large-scale ranching began to develop in the 1550s, whole teams of blacks worked at cattle herding."[21] In sixteenth-century Veracruz, Mexico, the majority of residents on cattle ranches were black, and some were listed as the major-domos in charge of ranching operations—at least one, Benito el Negro, was a ranch owner.[22] In the following centuries, many Afro-Spaniards manned ranches from Argentina to Venezuela to Texas. U.S. culture depicts American cowboys as quintessentially white, but in fact the Americas' original cowboys were typically of African and Afro-Latin descent. In the mid-1600s, "enslaved black vaqueros [cowboys] from the Americas" first demonstrated the use of a lasso from horseback to a rapt audience in Madrid. Seventeenth-century Afro-Mexican cowboys are believed to have adapted traditional West African horsemanship into what became the American lasso and the Western saddle.[23]

In addition to serving as the Americas' first explorers, settlers, soldiers, miners, ranchers, and cowboys, Africans were among the New World's first slave owners. For his service in the conquest of Chile, Afro-Spaniard Juan Beltran was made a Spanish captain and granted an *encomienda*—a legal technique used by the Crown to grant conquistadores "responsibility" for and tribute labor from the Native Americans who inhabited conquered lands. While the roots of the institution lay in the Spanish *Reconquista* practice of exacting tribute from Muslims and Jews, the New World variant devolved into the enslavement of indigenous laborers. Beltran was a free mixed-race person who had been born in the Americas to African and Indian parents. At least four additional Afro-Spaniards received similar awards for their service in Chile.

African-born Juan Valiente (John Brave) was made a Spanish captain and ultimately granted an estate with laborers for his service in the conquest of Chile. After assisting Almagro's expeditions in Guatemala and Peru (along with two hundred black soldiers), Valiente, still technically a slave, signed on for a 1535 Chilean campaign. In 1540, he was promoted to captain, and in 1546 he helped to found Santiago de Chile. For his heroic service and "central role in the conquest of Chile,"[24] Valiente was awarded with an *encomienda* and land, where he settled with his wife Juana de Valdivia, a former slave of the governor. After Valiente's death during a campaign in the Andes, his titles and properties were officially passed down to his son.[25] The fact that a former African slave was awarded an estate with Indian bond labor highlights the fluidity of race and slavery in the early Americas; the fact that Valiente had a recognized heir underscores his role, figuratively and literally, as a founding father.

Women of African descent participated in the conquest and settlement of the Americas. In addition to Valiente's wife, Juana de Valdivia, records indicate that an enslaved woman named Margarita assisted in New World conquests when she accompanied Diego de Almagro on his expeditions from Panama through Chile until he was imprisoned and executed by his former ally, Pizarro. Margarita's loyalty has led some to speculate that she was Almagro's lover; upon his death, she was liberated by his will, took his surname, and founded a convent chaplaincy to preserve his memory. She ultimately settled in Cuzco, Peru, where she established a presumably quite successful shop—records show she lent money to the Spanish Crown.[26]

According to James Lockhart, "the conquest of Peru was carried out by an equal partnership" among Spaniards and Africans.[27] "Africans . . . were a factor of absolutely first importance in Peru in the conquest period [and] an organic part of the enterprise of occupying Peru from its inception."[28] Thousands of Afro-Spaniards, both free and enslaved, served in the Peruvian campaigns. Pizarro's expeditions included many black soldiers and at least one black captain between 1524 and 1528. Free mixed-race Spaniards like Juan Garcia and Miguel Ruiz were rewarded with gold and silver for their service in Peru. After serving with Cortez, Afro-Spaniard Pedro de Alvarado led several expeditions in Peru and Central America that enlisted large numbers of slaves. In 1593, the Archbishop of Lima used parish records to estimate that a little over half of the overall population was composed of people of African descent.

In addition to the communities of Africans and their descendants who helped to establish settlements in sixteenth-century Mexico, Peru, Hispaniola, Cuba, Puerto Rico, Florida, California, and Chile, many accompanied the campaigns in Costa Rica, Panama, Honduras, Guatemala, Venezuela, Argentina, and Trinidad. Juan Bardales, for example, was an African-born slave who "participated in the conquests of Panama and Honduras, for which services he was granted his freedom and a modest pension."[29] In an official estimate made in 1630, Africans outnumbered Europeans in Panama ten to one.[30]

Africans were crucial to New World colonization not only as soldiers and builders of fortifications, but also as producers of military materiel. "Black artisans manufactured harquebuses, swords, and lances, and an African woman was commissioned to supply . . . rosaries."[31] James Lockhart observed that "'black artisans . . . blacksmiths and swordsmiths . . . made the whole Spanish conquest and occupation possible.'"[32] The same might be said of the earliest settlements in Brazil where the Portuguese initially brought Africans as soldiers, artisans, and agricultural workers prior to importing enslaved plantation laborers.[33]

MAROONS AND SLAVE REVOLTS

While many of the first Africans in the Americas shaped New World history as free subjects, slaves played foundational roles as well. For some, service to the Spanish Crown offered a promise of freedom; for others, direct resistance to the institution of slavery itself was the most accessible, if perilous, path. The history of Afro-American resistance to slavery began with the inception of Afro-American slavery. When the first African slaves were brought to Hispaniola in 1502, several were reported to have liberated themselves and joined Native communities in 1503. After that, the earliest slave revolt recorded in the Americas dates to 1522 and involved laborers on the Hispaniola plantation of Christopher Columbus's son, Diego Colon. In 1527, self-liberated Africans rose up against the Spanish and settled with Taino residents in Puerto Rico. In Colombia's first New World settlement, Santa Marta, slaves rebelled in 1530 (five years after its founding); Afro-Colombians rose up again in 1548 and 1550. Enslaved Africans rebelled in Venezuela in 1532 and again in 1552. Rebellions also occurred in Panama in 1531, Cuba in 1533, Mexico in 1537, Honduras in 1548, and Peru in 1553. In 1598, Colombia experienced another rebellion when some 4,000 slaves rose up and could not be subdued until the following year. [34]

Preceding their arrival on terra firma, enslaved men and women regularly resisted their captors on the ships of the Middle Passage. The first recorded shipboard uprising in 1509 was unsuccessful, but Africans gained their freedom through maritime revolts in 1532 and 1571. Eric Robert Taylor has documented nearly five hundred incidents of shipboard rebellion during the Middle Passage. David Richardson estimated that perhaps one in ten slave ships experienced some form of insurrection. Shipboard insurgencies that resulted in enslaved individuals disembarking as free persons occurred in at least twenty-three recorded events. While the odds of achieving freedom were long for those imprisoned on ships, even the vastly more numerous unsuccessful revolts, which resulted in the deaths of an estimated 100,000 individuals, served to undermine the trade.[35]

Everywhere slaves arrived in the Americas, self-liberated renegades established independent communities; in English, these individuals were called maroons. The Spanish reported the establishment of maroon societies in their earliest settlements starting in 1503, a year after the king had agreed to the importation of slaves to Hispaniola. Archeological evidence from the Dominican Republic revealed remnants of maroon pottery and metallurgy, including copper and iron jewelry, tools, and weapons.[36] In other cases, maroon communities traded with colonists or pirates for supplies, and in still other cases, European government treaties awarded regular tribute (including weapons) to these micro-states.

"These new societies ranged from tiny bands that survived less than a year to powerful states encompassing thousands of members and surviving for generations or even centuries."[37] Because maroon communities were living advertisements for alternatives to slavery and because maroons could—and did—ally with rival states, they were a central concern for colonial authorities. In places like Ecuador, Panama, Colombia, Mexico, Jamaica, Suriname, Cuba, and Florida, colonial powers (which could include militias with Afro-descended soldiers) were unable to subdue maroon societies militarily; these governments negotiated with maroon leaders and recognized the rights of these free black communities.

Maroons were the first permanent New World settlers in what is now the United States. In 1526, Spanish sugar planter Lucas Vázquez de Allyón set out from Hispaniola with six hundred colonists, an unspecified number of enslaved Africans, supplies, and livestock to establish the colony of San Miguel de Guadeloupe on the coast of what is today Georgia. The effort was beset with a series of disasters, including Allyón's death. The enslaved Africans mutinied, enacting perhaps the earliest slave revolt in North America, and fled the Spanish colony before it disbanded to Hispaniola. Settling with the Native population in eastern Georgia, these Africans established the first maroon community in what would become the United States, more than sixty years before the English attempted the Roanoke settlement and about eighty years before Jamestown. In contrast to narratives that celebrate the

English as the first American settlers, Africans—self-liberated slaves—were the first transatlantic immigrants to permanently reside in what is today the United States, a century before the Mayflower arrived.

Around the time of these pioneering black settlers in North America, Domingo Bohio, a former African ruler, established San Basilio, the first free black town in South America. San Basilio originated as a maroon settlement in northern Colombia around 1526. Under the title King Benkos, Bohio negotiated a peace treaty with the governor of Cartagena. The maroon settlement thrived and included more than three thousand inhabitants under independent rule until 1686. The area is now known as San Basilio de Palenque, or simply Palenque (*palenque* or "palisade" in Spanish, came to serve as a common term for the fortified settlements of maroons), and has 3,500 residents today. It is recognized by UNESCO as the oldest continuous free black town in the Americas and as the only site in the world where a unique creole of Bantu and Spanish is spoken. In the 1970s, Palenque resident Antonio "Pambelé" Cervantes became a world champion of boxing. In 1994, a statue of Palenque's founder, Domingo Bohio, was included among several Colombian national heroes honored in a Cartagena memorial.[38]

Hispaniola (now known as the Dominican Republic) was the site of the first New World settlement, including the first arrivals of free and enslaved Africans; it was also the site of the Americas' earliest maroon community—and among its most formidable. In 1542, a Spanish official estimated that the maroon population of Hispaniola (2,000–3,000) outnumbered the European population (1,200) and that the enslaved population greatly outnumbered them both (25,000–30,000). Another mid-sixteenth-century estimate numbered the maroon inhabitants of Hispaniola at 7,000.[39]

During the 1540s, the Spanish spent considerable resources resisting attacks from African freedom fighters like Lemba (whom the Spanish described as "extremely knowledgeable and very able"), Diego Guzman, Diego Ocampo, and Juan Vaquero (which translates as "John Cowboy") during what became known as Hispaniola's Maroon Wars.[40] In fact, at least thirty enslaved Africans were recruited by Spanish colonials and granted freedom in exchange for defending the colony against Lemba and his followers.

For about fourteen years, self-liberated Africans and Taino Indians resisted Spanish domination and plantation slavery by attacking sugar plantations; "outnumbered and beleaguered Spanish settlers were restricted to the capital of Santo Domingo."[41] Far from passive underlings tangential to American history, slaves had a tremendous impact on the lives of European settlers and Native Americans, both as supporters and resisters.

While "beleaguered Spaniards" (and some Africans) fought against maroons in the Dominican Republic, early Mexico, like Hispaniola, had a majority African population and was home to approximately 2,000 maroons. Africans soon outnumbered Europeans on Mexico's west coast, and the area became a refuge for fugitive slaves. "Fugitives founded maroon camps that evolved into towns and eventually became incorporated under Spanish law. Royal authorities, tacitly admitting their inability to disband runaway communities, tried to win them over through legalization."[42] Maroon settlements "mushroomed" throughout Mexico during the sixteenth century, encompassing about twenty specific sites.[43]

In 1549, enslaved pearl divers liberated themselves and formed a maroon community on the island of Margarita off the coast of Venezuela. Several enslaved Africans worked as pearl divers off Colombia and Venezuela in the 1500s; it was a dangerous occupation, but fortunates who found exceptionally large pearls could purchase their freedom. A few years later, on Venezuela's mainland, "King Miguel" led some eight hundred gold miners in a revolt that became the foundation of a large *palenque* organized under an independent government. In 1545, the governor of Lima moved against "some 200 cimarrones, who had entrenched themselves in a well-organized settlement . . . accumulated large quantities of Spanish weapons and armor, and were rumored to have allies among the city's slave population."[44]

In 1553, seventeen enslaved African men and six enslaved African women overpowered their Spanish captors while gathering provisions on the coast of Ecuador, seized their ship, liberated the remaining enslaved crew, and sailed south to establish a town in the Andean foothills. They allied themselves with the Native population and were governed by Anton, one of the mutineers. After Anton's death, the ten surviving Africans and the locals founded a community: Esmeraldas. "The early Esmeraldas, although ruled by Africans and their descendants, was thus a multiracial settlement to which many cultural-linguistic groups contributed."[45]

By the 1570s, another African man, Alonso de Illescas, governed an independent Afro-Indian society on the northwest coast of Ecuador; the society was recognized by the Spanish Crown. Illescas, who had previously assisted an important Spanish merchant in Seville and the Caribbean, governed a community in Esmeraldas that produced timber, ships, agricultural products, and metal goods. Illescas built a powerful patronage system and gained the allegiance of Native American elites as well as Spanish missionaries. In 1586, he sent a petition to the colonial court in Quito threatening retaliation should Spanish settlers trespass. Illescas's petition, like the siege of Santo Domingo's colonists described above, is an example of how "Spanish authority was limited, indeed stymied, by maroon independence."[46] While the petition was initially rejected, the Spanish government ultimately granted this community freedom. In 1600, the colonial Audencia "recognized the Maroons' dominance in the region, granted them their freedoms and liberties . . . Illescas did not survive long enough to witness this victory of Maroon diplomacy, but his sons and daughters lived to receive their legally recognized freedom. . ."[47] (In 1997, Ecuador declared Antonio Illescas a national hero.)

Maroons shaped American history not only by challenging European imperial schemes but, in some cases, by supporting them. Sir Francis Drake successfully allied his English crew with Panamanian maroons to defeat a Spanish force which also had soldiers of African descent, including "an entire unit of free blacks under a black captain."[48] By 1572, Panama contained a maroon society of about three thousand individuals. While black soldiers had been an integral part of Spanish forces since the early 1500s, this was likely the first time the British enlisted people of African descent for military aid in the Americas. Drake described "the Cimaroones" (the English *maroon* is derived from the Spanish *Cimarron*) as "a black people, which about eighty years past, fled from the Spaniards their masters, by reason of their cruelty, and are since grown into a Nation, under two Kings of their own."[49]

The maroons provided Drake and his crew invaluable support in terms of intelligence, supplies, and labor during raids and for simple survival on the Spanish Main. In his writings, Drake, once an active slave trader, described these formerly enslaved men as courageous, astute, and skillful. He detailed the manifold ways in which the Cimarrons "did us continually very good service . . . no less valiant than industrious, and of good judgment."⁵⁰ Drake was initially introduced to the Cimarrons by a close aide, Diego. Described as a negro fluent in both Spanish and English, Diego became Drake's loyal companion after defecting from the Spanish during a raid. Drake built a fort in Panama that he named in Diego's honor. Diego served alongside Drake until Diego was killed in Chile in 1579, along with much of Drake's crew, in a surprise attack by Native Americans. In 1593, the Panamanian maroons signed a treaty with the Spanish "that allowed them local autonomy under a Spanish protectorate, settling in two towns, Santa Cruz la Real and Santiago del Principe."⁵¹

While enslaved Africans inaugurated a long, continuous tradition of revolt and maroons established their own independent societies, numerous free and enslaved Africans and mixed-race Afro-Latins asserted their independence and rights as Spanish subjects in the colonial period. While the accomplishments of maroons and black soldiers attest that not all Afro-Americans were slaves, the achievements of some Afro-American slaves illustrate degrees of independence and agency that challenge prevailing assumptions about American slavery.

NEW WORLD SETTLERS

Despite the inherent oppression of legal enslavement, Africans in the New World faced a wide array of conditions; some were able to carve out a sphere of relative autonomy like other colonial subjects. In sixteenth-century Spanish America, before the rise of the plantation economy and while indigenous people were pressed into service in mining, agricultural, and domestic labor, enslaved persons of African descent were often highly skilled and conducted endeavors that conferred independence and responsibility. Their efforts were instrumental to the development of the early Americas. While many of the individuals were enslaved, they often had more in common with free colonists than we have previously imagined.

In the 1500s, Guatemala's Santiago came to serve as a regional entrepôt. Enslaved and free people of color played vital roles in the economic, cultural,

Three Gentlemen of Esmeraldas. This 1599 portrait from Ecuador is the oldest known signed and dated painting from the Americas. The maroon leader (center) and his sons are depicted with the honorific title "Don": Don Francisco Arobe, Don Pedro, and Don Domingo. The artist was of native Ecuadoran descent. Maroon communities (independent societies of fugitive slaves) were prevalent throughout the Americas from 1503 onward. Several became officially recognized as free black settlements and towns in Ecuador, Panama, Mexico, Colombia, Jamaica, Cuba, Suriname, Guyana, and Florida.

and social development that propelled "the growth of Santiago from little more than a village to an important center of colonial commerce."[52] Legally enslaved Africans operated as de facto administrators of mines, agricultural enterprises, and small businesses, often supervising indigenous workers. Ana Martel, for example, "administered a cacao grove . . . and apparently acted with autonomy from her owners."[53] In the 1570s, "Domingo the black mason" supervised the construction of a wheat mill and fifteen Native workers. Records indicate that other enslaved Africans worked as millers, cobblers, aides to barber surgeons, bakers, household managers, and muleteers. Moreover, "black slaves could and did own real estate in early Santiago."[54] In 1559, the town council of another town named Santiago, Santiago de Chile, granted the real estate petition of a "Negro" named Tomé Vasquez.[55]

In Peru, records show that two enslaved black artisans ran a shop in 1550. In another case, an enslaved Afro-Peruvian carpenter, Andres de Llerena, "entered into a company with a Spanish carpenter on equal terms, or indeed as the senior partner."[56] In 1550, Afro-Peruvian freedman Juan de Frenegal provided a substantial dowry for his daughter's marriage, presumably from his earnings from masonry and real estate. Several records show Afro-Peruvians as property owners, landlords, and entrepreneurs. In the 1540s–50s, a free Afro-Peruvian woman, Catalina de Zorita, owned a bakery in Lima that was staffed by slaves. She married a Spaniard, as did their daughter. In 1576, Francisco de Marchena, a free Afro-Peruvian slave owner, successfully petitioned Lima's city council for permission to build an inn and the use of *encomienda* indigenes to staff it. Throughout the early mining enterprises in Peru and Mexico, it was not uncommon for African and Afro-Spanish overseers to supervise indigenous laborers.[57]

As in Peru, immigration to Cuba was often more African than European. In 1532, one official estimated that Cuba's colonial population comprised three hundred Europeans and five hundred Africans.[58] Some enslaved Cubans found sanctioned routes to freedom, such as Catalina Garay, a former slave who signed the deed for her first urban parcel of land in 1559 and rented out a number of properties. Freedman Diego de Rojas was granted permission to establish a pig farm in 1577, for which he was able to secure increasing amounts of land in addition to the urban properties he owned. Other Afro-Cubans may have been born to freedom, like Domingo de Quejo, a mulatto blacksmith who operated a Havana foundry in 1573.[59]

Some enslaved individuals in sixteenth-century Havana owned property, including slaves, while other enslaved Afro-Cubans operated businesses.[60] In the late sixteenth century and on into the seventeenth, well before the domination of Cuba's sugar plantation economy in the early nineteenth century, Havana's main commercial activity was as a port, servicing the Spanish fleets returning to Europe with Mexican and Peruvian silver and gold. People of color dominated this seaport economy; free people of color and urban slaves (whom authorities complained often lived like free people) and even some rural slaves took advantage of the economic opportunities in provisioning and entertaining the Spanish fleets as porters, merchants, cooks, laundresses, and keepers of taverns and inns. Women of African descent were frequently tavern owners in early Cuba and in late medieval Spain as well. Their incomes and businesses helped to further expand Havana's free black population.

By the end of the sixteenth century, there was a significant free black population in Cuba that would play foundational roles in the economy and security of the island. Afro-Americans were vital to Cuba's military from its inception. Black auxiliaries, including Juan Garrido, accompanied Diego Velazquez in the Spanish conquest of Cuba in 1511–12. In 1529, Cuban colonists organized a force of Africans, Spaniards, and Native Americans to defend against Cubeño Indians. In the 1550s, when French corsairs attacked Havana, they were aided by enslaved Africans to whom they had offered freedom; in response, the Spanish raised a force to defend the city that was overwhelmingly of African descent.[61] Before the close of the sixteenth century, an official black militia was established—at the close of the nineteenth century, Afro-Cuban soldiers would be essential to the nation's wars for independence.

Africans founded and populated towns throughout Spanish America in the sixteenth century. In 1534, two free black men, Juan and Anton, were among those inscribed on Quito's cathedral wall as the city's founders.[62] In 1536, enslaved black laborers helped to found Buenos Aires, and in 1538 enslaved black laborers assisted the founding of Bogota in Colombia.[63] Juan Valiente, as observed above, was awarded by the Crown for his service in the founding of Santiago de Chile. Significant black populations were instrumental to the development of Hispaniola, Cuba, Peru, and Brazil during this period. However, it was Mexico, or what Spanish colonials called "New Spain," that cultivated the largest population of Afro-Americans in the sixteenth century.

In 1553, the governor of New Spain estimated the colony's black population at twenty thousand individuals, including two thousand maroons. (At its height in 1795, New Spain encompassed all of Central America except Panama, most of North America—everything west of the Mississippi as well as Florida—as well as the western Caribbean and the Philippines, but its core population centered around what is today Mexico.) Africans "surpassed

European populations in the colony at large from the sixteenth through the eighteenth centuries."[64] Fifty years after the conquest of Tenochtitlan, Mexico's African population not only outnumbered the Spanish population, but "by 1570, Mexico City was home to the largest African population in the Americas." [65]

Afro-Americans helped to found another Mexican city, Merida; these black conquistadores, among them Sebastian Toral, fought in campaigns against the Maya in the Yucatan. An ecclesiastical report from 1550 suggested that Afro-Spaniards comprised almost half of Merida's population. Other documents show that Toral, who was granted his freedom and exemption from tribute, raised a family and lived well into the century in Mexico. Merida was only one of several New Spain towns with a large and, in some cases, majority-black population.[66]

Following Esteban's route, the Spaniard Coronado's 1540–1542 expedition of two thousand people from Mexico to New Mexico included numerous persons of African descent, many of whom settled in regions that would become the United States. From 1535, when Spain established a colonial government in Mexico, until the treaty of the Mexican-American War in 1848, Mexico included what are today the U.S. states of Texas, New Mexico, Colorado, Wyoming, Arizona, Utah, Nevada, and California. Virtually all of the Spanish attempts to conquer and populate North America from the American Southwest to Florida included people of African descent.

In 1565, free and enslaved people of African descent accompanied the Spanish colonial mission that founded St. Augustine, Florida—the oldest official town in the United States. Catholic parish registers record the birth of an African American child in St. Augustine in 1606, a year before the first settlers arrived in Jamestown and fourteen years before the Mayflower landed in Massachusetts. In 1687, fugitive slaves from the English colonies were formally granted sanctuary in Spanish Florida. In addition to the African Americans who settled in St. Augustine, the free black settlement two miles north was officially sanctioned by the Spanish governor of Florida in 1738, making Gracia Real de Santa Teresa de Mosé (today known as Fort Mosé and designated as a National Historic Landmark) the first legally recognized free black town in what would become the United States.[67]

In the French colonies, "as in Spanish and Portuguese America, the early settlers found African slaves valuable military allies."[68] This was especially true in areas defended by Native residents. Accounts of the seventeenth-century settlement of French Guyana "mention frequent use of *negres* to fight the local Carib inhabitants."[69] The Dutch and the English legislated the arming of slaves against Native Americans in mainland North America during the seventeenth century. European powers often armed slaves and free people of color to defend against competing colonial claims.

As WE HAVE SEEN, people of African descent, both free and enslaved, were integral to the early colonization of the Americas. Africans accompanied the transatlantic voyages of Christopher Columbus and were among the earliest New World settlers. The fact that Africans and their descendants in the Americas might be enslaved or free, that they might be allied with or against Europeans, or with or against the Native population, or with or against each other, indicates a tremendous fluidity in racial identities, social statuses, and political alliances in the earliest centuries of New World settlement. People of African descent were conquered and conquerors, allies and enemies. Africans and Afro-Americans were central to the building of the New World as laborers and artisans as well as intermediaries, administrators, and linguists negotiating between Europeans and Amerindians. Black conquistadores established a permanent institution of Afro-American community and military service in alliance with the state. Black soldiers played critical roles in the defense of all of the New World colonies throughout the colonial period and were pivotal during the nineteenth-century wars for independence throughout the hemisphere.

Maroons, on the other hand, inaugurated a continuous tradition of Americans who realized liberty through insurgency and negotiation. In many cases, maroons gained additional power by allying with a colonial state; all European powers sought support from self-liberated slaves at one time or another. For example, while the English depended militarily on maroons in their contests with Spain in the sixteenth century, they would again rely heavily on the service of fugitive slaves in their contests with British colonists in 1776 and 1812. Spain depended on maroon soldiers to defend Florida and Jamaica from the English in the seventeenth and eighteenth centuries and offered sanctuary to maroons from the Danish Caribbean during that period as well.

Maroons played major roles in the military and political history of the Americas, and the sixteenth century saw the establishment of the first maroon communities of self-liberated former slaves in the New World—in the Dominican Republic, the Southeastern U.S., Mexico, Panama, Ecuador, Colombia, and Venezuela. In the seventeenth and eighteenth centuries, powerful maroon communities developed in Brazil, Suriname, Guyana, Jamaica, Haiti, Cuba, and Florida. Because of the potential threats maroons posed to colonial slavery and the inability of colonial states to subdue them, the authority of maroon leaders and the autonomy of maroon societies were often recognized by European powers. Many of these independent communities of freedom-seekers, developed and defended by self-emancipated slaves and their progeny, evolved into officially sanctioned free black towns in the sixteenth, seventeenth, and eighteenth centuries.

Colonial militias and maroon communities were not the only routes to freedom and founding for Afro-Americans. Black people, enslaved and free, played critical roles in conquering, settling, and defending colonies throughout the New World. Colonial slavery and imperial authority could be so amorphous during this pioneering period that some enslaved individuals were able to procure freedom, officially and unofficially. Free and enslaved Africans and their descendants accompanied the Spanish in virtually every New World expedition and participated widely in the earliest American settlements as explorers, soldiers, settlers, servants, artisans, proprietors, business managers, merchants' agents, colonial agents, slave-owners, shop owners, ranchers, cowboys, miners, and overseers of indigenous workers. While the status of individuals of African descent varied widely in the sixteenth century, people of color were omnipresent and instrumental in the founding of the Americas.

NOTES FOR CHAPTER 2

1   Kari Lyderson, "Dental Studies Give Clues About Christopher Columbus's Crew," *Washington Post*, May 18, 2009; Shanta Barley, "Graveyard DNA Rewrites African American History," *New Scientist*, September 16, 2010. Scientists Douglas Price of the University of Wisconsin-Madison and Hannes Schroeder of the University of Copenhagen, Denmark, found that dental isotopes and mitochondrial DNA indicate that at least seven of the individuals in this first New World settlement were likely from West Africa. Archaeologist Kathleen Deagan of the University of Florida, a scholar of La Isabella, found that contemporary Spanish historians who were well acquainted with that expedition did not indicate that it carried slaves.

2   Peter Gerhard, "A Black Conquistador in Mexico," *Hispanic American Historical Review* 58, no. 3 (1971), 451.

3   Aba Karam, "The Origins of the West India Regiments," *Science and Society* 35 (Spring 1971), 59, as cited in Peter M. Voelz, *Slave and Soldier: The Military Impact of Blacks in the Colonial Americas* (New York: Garland Publishing, 1993), 3.

4   Andrew Sluyter, *Black Ranching Frontiers: African Cattle Herders of the Atlantic World, 1500–1900* (New Haven: Yale University Press, 2012), 39.

5   Jane Landers, *Black Society in Spanish Florida* (Champaign: University of Illinois, 1999), 283 footnote 4.

6   Landers, *Black Society in Spanish Florida*, 8.

7   Lerone Bennett, *Before the Mayflower* (New York: Penguin, 1982), 33–34; Deborah Blumenthal, "'La Casa de Negres': Black African Solidarity in Late Medieval Valencia," in *Black Africans in Renaissance Europe*, eds., T. F. Earle and K. J. P. Lowe (New York: Cambridge University Press, 2005), 232–235. Watershed freedom suits include those of John Casor in 1655, James Somerset in 1772, Elizabeth Freeman in 1781, and George Latimer in 1843; they and others are described in subsequent chapters.

8   A. Saunders, *A Social History of Black Slaves and Freedmen in Portugal, 1441–1555* (New York: Cambridge University Press, 1982), 146; Annemarie Jordan, "Images of Empire: Slaves in the Lisbon Household Court of Catherine de Austria," in *Black Africans in Renaissance Europe*, 159.

9   In addition to the six distinct royal lines that connected Margarita de Castro y Sousa and Queen Charlotte, from whom the current British royal family descends, Italy's Medici dynasty also had mixed-race ancestry. Alessandro de Medici, who became the Duke of Florence in 1532, was the son of Cardinal Giulio de Medici, a future Pope, and Simonetta da Collavechio, an African member of the Cardinal's household staff. Alessandro de Medici's descendants went on to populate the noble houses of Italy as well as the Hapsburg lineages of Europe. Louise Marie-Thérèse (1664–1732) was a French nun of African ancestry (her portrait hangs in the Bibliotheque Saint Genevieve in Paris) who was thought to be the daughter of the French queen, Maria Theresa of Spain, the first wife of King Louis XI. Adolf Badin, who had been born into slavery on Danish St. Croix, became a member of the Swedish court and a multilingual book collector who accompanied and represented Queen Louisa Ulrika of Sweden (r. 1751–1771) on diplomatic missions. In 1850, England's Queen Victoria adopted Sarah Forbes Bonetta, a Nigerian princess orphaned during a slave raid, as her god-daughter and sponsored the private education of the young girl, who was known for

her intellectual gifts. Eventually Sarah's daughter, Victoria, was granted an annuity by the English queen, who was also her godmother and namesake.

10   Aurelia Martin Casares, "Free and Freed Black Africans in the Spanish Renaissance," in *Black Africans in Renaissance Europe*, 259; Francis A. Dutras, "A Hard Fought Struggle for Recognition: Manuel Gonçalves Doria, First Afro-Brazilian to Become a Knight of Santiago," *The Americas* 56, no. 1 (July, 1999): 91–113; Joanteh Spicer, ed., *Revealing the African Presence in Renaissance Europe* (Baltimore: The Walters Art Museum, 2012).

11   Henry Louis Gates Jr. and Maria Wolff, "An Overview of Sources on the Life and Work of Juan Latino, the 'Ethiopian Humanist,'" *Research in African Literatures* 29, no. 4 (1998): 14. In 1566, Juan Latino became a professor of Latin at the Cathedral in Grenada. He published his first book of poetry, *Austriad*, in 1573 and two subsequent volumes in 1576 and 1585.

12   Publius Terentius Afer was a Roman playwright whose Latin works were first performed in the second century BCE. Like Juan Latino, Terence the African was a slave owned by a political elite—in his case a Roman senator—who granted him freedom because of his talent.

13   Annette Ivory, "Juan Latino: The Struggle of Blacks, Jews, and Moors in Golden Age Spain," *Hispania* 62, no. 4 (December 1979): 613.

14   Jane Landers, "Cimarron and Citizen," in *Slaves, Subjects, and Subversives: Blacks in Colonial Latin America*, eds., Jane Landers and Barry Robinson (Albuquerque: University of New Mexico, 2006), 112–113.

15   Landers, "Cimarron and Citizen," 113; Jorge Cañizares-Esguerra, Matt D. Childs, and James Sidbury, *The Black Urban Atlantic in the Age of the Slave Trade* (Philadelphia: University of Pennsylvania Press, 2013), 90.

16   Oscar Reiss, *Blacks in Colonial America* (Jefferson, NC: McFarland, 1997), 23–24.

17   Irene Aloha Wright, *The Early History of Cuba, 1492–1586* (New York: Macmillan, 1916), 164; *Robert Goodwin, Crossing the Continent, 1527–1540: The Story of the First African American Explorer of the American South* (New York: HarperCollins, 2008).

18   Matthew Restall, "Black Conquistadores: Armed Africans in Early Spanish America," *The Americas* 57, no. 2 (October 2000): 183, 175.

19   John Thornton, *African and Africans in the Making of the Atlantic World, 1400–1800* (New York: Cambridge University Press, 1998), 140.

20   Restall, "Black Conquistadores," 172.

21   James Lockhart, *Spanish Peru, 1532–1560: A Social History* (Madison: University of Wisconsin Press, 1994 [1968]), 211.

22   Sluyter, *Black Ranching Frontiers*, 44, 55.

23   Sluyter, *Black Ranching Frontiers*, 51–57. The English word *buckaroo* comes from the Mexican *vaquero*, itself rooted in the Spanish word for cow (*vaca*) and literally meaning cow-man. The vaqueros were the *mestizo* (mixed-race people of Indian, Spanish, and African descent) horse-riding hands who drove the cattle of New Spain's *caballeros* (the Spanish term for horseman, knight, and gentlemen), starting with the conquistadores who brought horses and cattle to the New World. The Oñate expedition from Mexico City to Santa Fe that included Isabel de Olvera (described in the next chapter) intro-duced horses to the American West in 1600. Much of the vernacular associated with

American cowboy culture derives from Mexican Spanish: *bronco, burro, canyon, chaps, corral, coyote, desperado, lariat, lasso, hombre, jerky, macho, mesa, mesquite, mustang, pronto, ranch, renegade, rodeo, stampede, tobacco, tornado, vamoose, vigilante.* The best derivation might be the "ten gallon" hat, which emerged from *tan galán* or "very gallant." For more on Afro-American cowboys, see Chapter Five.

24 Restall, "Black Conquistadores," 183.

25 Michael Conniff and Thomas Davis, *Africans in the Americas: A History of the Black Diaspora* (Caldwell, NJ: Blackburn Press, 1994), 119.

26 Susan Migden Socolow, *The Women of Colonial Latin America* (New York: Cambridge, 2000), 131; Frederick P. Bowser, *The African Slave in Colonial Peru* (Stanford, CA: Stanford University Press, 1974), 7–8.

27 James Lockhart, *Spanish Peru 1532–1560: A Colonial Society* (Madison: University of Wisconsin Press, 1994 [1968]), 224.

28 Bowser, *The African Slave in Colonial Peru*, 339.

29 Restall, "Black Conquistadores," 183.

30 Conniff and Davis, *Africans in the Americas*, 114.

31 Bowser, *The African Slave in Colonial Peru*, 9.

32 Lockhart, *Spanish Peru*, 206.

33 Conniff and Davis, *Africans in the Americas*, 90.

34 Jose L. Franco, "Maroons and Slave Rebellions in the Spanish Territories," in *Maroon Societies: Rebel Slave Communities in the Americas*, ed., Richard Price (Baltimore: Johns Hopkins University Press, 1996), 35–37. George Reid Andrews, *Afro-Latin America, 1800-2000* (New York: Oxford University Press, 2004), 37.

35 Eric Robert Taylor, *If We Must Die: Shipboard Insurrections in the Era of the Atlantic Trade* (Baton Rouge: Louisiana State University Press, 2009); Marcus Rediker, *The Slave Ship: A Human History* (New York: Penguin, 2007); David Richardson, "Shipboard Revolts, African Authority and the Atlantic Slave Trade," *William and Mary Quarterly* 58, no. 1 (2001): 69–92; David Eltis, *The Rise of African Slavery in the Americas* (Cambridge: Cambridge University Press, 2000), 232.

36 Landers, "Cimarron and Citizen," 115.

37 Richard Price, *Maroon Societies: Rebel Slave Communities in the Americas* (Baltimore: Johns Hopkins University Press, 1996 [1979]), 1.

38 Jane Landers, "Central Africans in Haiti and Spanish America," in *Central Africans and Cultural Transformation in the American Diaspora*, ed., Linda Heywood (New York: Cambridge University Press, 2002), 239; Ana Lucia Araujo, *Shadows of the Slave Past: Memory, Heritage, and Slavery* (New York: Routledge, 2014), 196.

39 Jane Landers, "Maroon Women in Spanish Colonial America," in *Beyond Bondage: Free Women of Color in the Americas*, eds., David Gaspar and Darlene Hine (Chicago: University of Illinois Press, 2004), 5.

40 Landers, "Central Africans in Haiti and Spanish America," 234.

41 Alvin O. Thompson, *Flight to Freedom: African Runaways and Maroons in the Americas* (Kingston, Jamaica: University of the West Indies Press, 2006), 266–267; Landers, "Cimarron and Citizen," 119.

42 Conniff and Davis, *Africans in the Americas*, 112.

43 Thompson, *Flight to Freedom*, 115.

44 Leslie Rout, *The African Experience in Spanish America* (Princeton: Markus Wiener Publishers, 2003 [1976]), 78; Herbert Klein, *African Slavery in Latin America and the Caribbean* (New York: Oxford University Press, 1986), 202; Bowser, *The African Slave in Colonial Peru*, 188.

45 Conniff and Davis, *Africans in the Americas*, 118; Landers, "Maroon Women in Spanish Colonial America," 7.

46 Charles Beatty-Medina, "The Spanish-African Maroon Competition for Captive Indian Labor in the Region of Esmeraldas During the Late Sixteenth and Early Seventeenth Centuries," *The Americas* 63, no. 1 (2006): 113–136.

47 Charles Beatty-Medina, "Maroon Chief Alonso de Illescas' Letter to the Crown, 1586," in *Afro-Latino Voices: Narratives from the Early Modern Ibero-Atlantic World, 1550–1812*, eds., Kathryn McKnight and Leo Garofalo (Indianapolis: Hackett Publishing Company, 2009), 33.

48 Klein, *African Slavery in Latin America and the Caribbean*, 202: Voelz, *Slave and Soldier*, 16, quoting Kenneth Andrews, *The Spanish Caribbean Trade and Plunder, 1530–1630* (New Haven: Yale University Press, 1968), 144–145.

49 Philip Nichols, *Sir Francis Drake Revived* (New York: Collier & Son Company, 1910 [1623]), 7.

50 Nichols, *Sir Francis Drake Revived*, 40.

51 Walter Harte, *Sir Francis Drake* (New York: MacMillan, 1920), 13–15, 23–24; Voelz, *Slave and Soldier*, 16.

52 Robinson A. Herrera, "'Por Que No Sabemos Firmar': Black Slaves in Early Guatemala," *The Americas* 57, no. 2 (October 2000): 265.

53 Herrera, "'Por Que No Sabemos Firmar,'" 260.

54 Herrera, "'Por Que No Sabemos Firmar,'" 263.

55 R. R. Wright, "Negro Companions of Spanish Explorers," *American Anthropologist* 4, no. 2 (1902): 220.

56 Lockhart, *Spanish Peru*, 207–208.

57 Bowser, *The African Slave in Colonial Peru*, 317–318.

58 Wright, *Early History of Cuba*, 197; Restall, "Black Conquistadores," 182.

59 Alejandro de la Fuente, *Havana and the Atlantic in the Sixteenth Century* (Chapel Hill: University of North Carolina Press, 2008), 177, 176, 134. De la Fuente provides many more examples of successful free people of color in seventeenth century Havana.

60 Alejandro de la Fuente, "Slave Law and Claims-Making in Cuba: The Tannenbaum Debate Revisited," *Law and History Review* 22, no. 2 (Summer 2004): 340–369.

61 220 of African descent, compared to about 30 Spaniards and 80 Native Americans. Voelz, *Slave and Soldier*, 442; Wright, *Early History of Cuba*, 239.

62 Sherwin K. Bryant, "Finding Gold, Forming Slavery: The Creation of a Classic Slave Society, Popayan, 1600–1700," *The Americas* 63, no. 1 (July 2006): 81.

63 Howard Dodson, *Becoming American: The African American Journey* (New York: Sterling, 2009), 12.

64 Landers, "Cimarron and Citizen," 118.

65 Herman L. Bennett, *Colonial Blackness: A History of Afro-Mexico* (Bloomington: Indiana University Press, 2009), 4.

66 Restall, "Black Conquistadores," 181, footnote 27; Herman L. Bennett, *Africans in Colonial Mexico: Absolutism, Christianity, and Afro-Creole Consciousness, 1570–1640* (Bloomington: Indiana University Press, 2003), 2; Landers, "Cimmaron and Citizen," 118.

67 The personage of St. Augustine, for whom the historic Florida town was named, was born in North Africa in the fourth century and was one of the many saints of African descent recognized by the Roman Catholic Church.

68 Thornton, *Africa and Africans in the Making of the New World*, 149.

69 Ibid.

✥ TIMELINE ✥

1600   Isabel de Olvera files deposition in Mexico before setting out for New Mexico

1608   Antonio Vieira born in Portugal to mixed-race parents; in Brazil, he becomes renowned enlightened priest, philosopher, writer, orator, and diplomat

1613   Afro-Portuguese sailor, linguist Jan Rodriguez is first settler in what will become New York

1618   Gaspar Yanga's treaty with Spanish turns a 30-year-old maroon community near Veracruz, Mexico, into the officially recognized free black town of San Lorenzo

1621   Anthony Johnson arrives in Virginia from captured slave ship, becomes a successful planter

1628   Manuel Gonzales Doria is the first Afro-Brazilian to be knighted

1640   Runaway indentured servant John Punch (likely Obama ancestor) is sentenced to lifetime service (fellow European runaways receive only extra time)

1642   Mathias de Sousa is first African American to vote in a legislature (Maryland)

1644   "Dutch Negroes" sue sucessfully for freedom and land in New York

1654   Anthony Iland wins freedom in British court in Barbados

1655   Virginia court rules that John Casor is Anthony Johnson's servant for life

1656   Elizabeth Key successfully sues for her and her son's freedom in Virginia

1667   Physician Lucas Santomee granted land in lower Manhattan

1676   Armed black and white Virginians fight for freedom in Bacon's Rebellion

1677   Juan Moreno and other Afro-Cubans in Cobre, Cuba, petition Spain to recognize free black town (edict finally granted in 1800)

1680   Mixed-race population of New Mexico nears 3,000

1681   In Colombia, Domingo and Juana Padilla found maroon community of Matudere

1681   Brazilian-born Angolan Lourenco da Silva de Mendonça petitions Pope regarding slavery

1683   North America's first Afro-American militia formed (to defend Spanish Florida from English)

1685   France issues Code Noir, first New World slave code

1690   Brazil's maroon community, Palmares, may have as many as 20,000 residents

1693   Spain offers sanctuary, subjecthood, and land to fugitive slaves in Florida

1700   Afro-Cuban Juana Carvajal is deeded her former master's colonial mansion in Havana

3

Seventeenth-Century
Afro-American Colonials

Preceding the arrival of the first colonists in Jamestown, Isabel de Olvera helped to settle what would become the United States. In 1600 she participated in a Spanish expedition from Mexico to New Mexico. Predating the Enlightenment tracts that would fuel the Age of Revolution two centuries later, Olvera employed the language of citizenship and civil law to assert and defend her rights before setting out:

> As I am going on the expedition to New Mexico and have some reason to believe that I may be annoyed by some individual since I am a mulatto, and as it is proper to protect my rights in such an eventuality by an affidavit showing that I am a free woman, unmarried, and the legitimate daughter of Hernando, a negro, and an Indian named Magdalena, I therefore request your grace to accept this affidavit, which shows that I am free and not bound by marriage or slavery. I request that a properly certified and signed copy be given to me in order to protect my rights, and that it carry full legal authority. I demand justice.[1]

Olvera's deposition encapsulates several fundamental truths of American history. First, people of African descent were among the earliest settlers of the Americas, including what is today the United States.[2] Beginning before the arrival of the English, black people helped to found American towns from Santa Fe to St. Augustine, Manhattan to Los Angeles, and from Buenos Aires, Argentina, to Birchtown, Canada. Second, the roots of the twentieth-century American civil rights movement can be traced to the first Africans in the Americas and their succeeding generations throughout the hemisphere. Third, Olvera was of mixed race, as would be her descendants;

she embodies the demographic reality that American family trees are founded on mixed-race roots.

Afro-American slavery in the seventeenth century was still relatively small-scale, and as a legal, social, and racial status, slavery was quite variable and inchoate; thus, in the 1600s people of African descent, both free and bond, played a wide variety of roles in the establishment of American societies. Black settlers and soldiers continued to shape American development, and Afro-Americans were among the New World's earliest scholars, assemblymen, merchants, military officers, physicians, and planters. Like Olvera, many seventeenth-century Afro-Americans were freedom seekers. This chapter highlights some of their efforts as litigants and maroons to establish the rights of colonial subjects.

While Africans and their descendants were an important minority in nascent British America, Afro-Americans comprised a very significant proportion—sometimes the majority—of America's seventeenth-century capitals further south. In the 1600s, people of African descent were half or more of the populations of colonial centers like Mexico City, Veracruz, Havana, Lima, and Rio de Janeiro, and about half of these Afro-descended peoples were free.[3] New World colonies with limited European populations needed soldiers, skilled laborers, and subjects; therefore, Iberian-America encouraged "the rise of a large free Afro-American population . . . allowed to join the ranks of citizens and that a certain fluidity in racial definition be permitted."[4]

While free people of color participated widely in colonial American societies, enslaved individuals contributed to their communities as laborers and domestics and also as artisans and agents, property holders and entrepreneurs, parents and partners. Enslaved residents of seventeenth-century Virginia, Maryland, New York, South Carolina, Florida, Barbados, Mexico, Peru, Cuba, Colombia, Ecuador, and Brazil sought their rights to freedom and property with petitions in colonial courts, with appeals to and as clerical authorities, and in colonial militias. Maroons who established independence also challenged colonial authorities.

Afro-Americans formed enduring majorities in Caribbean colonies like Saint-Domingue and Jamaica, as these regions developed into centers of the sugar revolution that would transform modern slavery at the end of the 1600s. As in all of the American regions that came to rely on slavery, racial mixing resulted in significant free colored populations and African-descended elites. In the seventeenth century, Caribbean populations were largely comprised of enslaved Americans, many of whom regularly challenged slavery through organized revolt, establishing a tradition of armed initiatives for freedom that in the eighteenth century directly precipitated the end of slavery and the rise of freedom in the Americas.[5]

North American Settlement

Around 1650, Thomas Hobbes famously declared life nasty, brutish, and short. For the early seventeenth-century residents of the English colony of Virginia, most of whom had arrived from Europe as indentured servants, this was decidedly so. In England, where political policies displaced peasant farmers and targeted Irish Catholics, thousands of men and women were voluntarily or involuntarily bound as servants to New World planters for a finite term (usually three to seven years).[6] In British America, mortality rates initially were so high that it made more economic sense to spend a smaller amount for a temporary servant than to make a large investment in a lifetime slave. In Barbados, Britain's first plantation colony in the Americas, it was cheaper still to force kidnapped English and Irish indigents to grow tobacco.

The first Africans in Virginia were generally treated as indentured servants. While the 1600s would see the first attempts to define slavery as a legal category and black slaves would eventually displace white servants, European indentures were the primary source of labor in the mainland English colonies until the early 1700s. Indentured servitude and a small but steady trade in Native American slaves persisted into the eighteenth century. In 1671, one official estimated that Virginia had two thousand black slaves and six thousand "Christian servants."[7] In Maryland, English and Irish servants outnumbered African servants until the 1690s. Both Virginia and Maryland had free populations of color.

When "Antonio a Negro" arrived in the Virginia colony in 1621, he was among the first Africans in mainland British America. Jamestown, the first permanent English settlement in what would become the United States, was founded in 1607, a year after the first recorded birth of an Afro-American child in Spanish Florida. After serving a term of service alongside indentured servants from the British Isles, Anthony Johnson, as he had become known, married an African woman known as Mary, established five headrights (claims on land established by working it, typically by importing indentured servants), and acquired 250 acres.

Among the Johnsons' contemporaries of free, property-holding Afro-Virginians were men like Emmanuel Driggus and Francis Payne. "Indeed if the county clerk had not from time to time inserted the word 'Negro' next to their names, it would have been impossible to distinguish the Drigguses, Harmans, and Paynes of Northampton from a hundred other contemporary small planters."[8] By 1668, about 30 percent of the African population in Northampton County, Virginia, was free. Seventeenth-century Afro-Virginians could vote and hold office as well as own property and servants, white and black. In the 1650s, Anthony Johnson's sons John and Richard were granted headrights for five hundred and one hundred acres, respectively, presumably based on their purchase of indentured servants.[9]

When Anthony Johnson's white neighbor, Richard Parker, attempted to lay claim to Johnson's black servant John Casor, Johnson took the neighbor to court and won. The 1655 ruling in *Johnson v. Parker* determined Johnson to be John Casor's master "for life" and ordered Parker to make payment of all charges in the suit. In an epoch when the legal boundaries of permanent slavery and finite servitude were still amorphous, this was the first recorded case of a judicial determination of perpetual servitude as a legal status in a civil case (rather than as a punishment in a criminal one).

John Casor was, arguably, the nation's first slave, which would make the man once described as "Antonio a Negro" the first slaveholder in what would become the United States. In the court case, Casor argued unsuccessfully that he was an indentured servant who had completed his tenure and thus was free to make a contract with the neighbor; this makes Casor not only among the first lifetime slaves in English America but also one of the first to argue for his freedom in court.[10] Two years earlier in 1653, John Baptiste, an African-born indentured servant, had petitioned for and won his freedom in a Maryland court with the same argument.

While Afro-Virginians helped to establish the British colony in the south, in the north Afro-Americans established a settlement in Manhattan in 1626, preceding the English and the name New York.[11] Most of the first African men and women in New Amsterdam were owned by the Dutch West India Company, yet they were active members of the community who could sue in the courts, marry in the church, and receive wages. Until the close of the eighteenth century, they buried their loved ones in a graveyard that underlies about six acres of lower Manhattan; the African Burial Ground is now recognized as a national historic site.

In 1644, several of Manhattan's "Dutch Negroes" filed a petition for freedom from the Dutch West India Company, initiating perhaps the first black legal protest in North America. The protest was successful, for "the petition was granted by the Council of New Netherlands. . . . All received parcels in what is now Greenwich Village."[12] Black landowners came to possess some 130 acres around what is today Washington Square Park. According to a 1645 deed, lower Manhattan's Washington Square originally belonged to Anthony Portuguese, a former slave, and subsequently to his daughter, Susanna Anthony Roberts.[13] Lucas Santomee, the son of one of these original black freeholders, studied medicine in Holland and was granted permission to practice as a black physician in the New York colony in the 1660s.[14] For his service to the colony, Dr. Santomee was awarded a grant of land in 1667 (three years after the English took control).

One could say the founder of New Amsterdam's black settlement, and indeed the founding father of New York City, was Jan Rodriguez, born in Santo Domingo to an African mother and a Portuguese father. A sailor known for his linguistic abilities, Rodriguez was hired by a Dutch sea captain to serve as a translator on a mission to the Algonquin-controlled island of Manhattan. Arriving in 1613, Rodriguez chose to settle there, married a Rockaway Indian woman, and became a successful trader and intermediary for the Dutch.

Rodriguez is now recognized as the embodiment of many of New York's firsts: its first non-Native American settler, its first merchant, and, in retrospect, New York City's first Dominican immigrant. While Rodriguez may have been the first person of African descent to settle in what would become New York, he was not the first to see it—as noted earlier, Esteban Gomez, an Afro-Portuguese navigator commissioned by Spain to explore the Hudson Valley, arrived in 1525, almost a century before Henry Hudson.[15]

In 1642, Mathias de Sousa seems to have been the first African American to vote in a legislative assembly in the Americas. Arriving in Maryland in 1633, Sousa was described in contemporary documents as "a Molato" and as one of Maryland's original colonists. Nine years later, Sousa was listed as an attendee of the Maryland General Assembly. Sousa was a free man and "any free man could vote as a member of the General Assembly that session." In fact, the record for that session states that the laws "were passed by all [in attendance]."[16]

Bacon's Rebellion represents yet another American first; the 1676 uprising was a democratic precursor to the anti-colonial struggles of the American Revolution. Led by the Englishman Nathaniel Bacon, about four hundred African and European indentured servants and slaves took up arms against the colonial governor of Virginia in an organized, inter-racial protest for freedom. The revolt was ultimately quelled by British forces but not before a contingency of twenty whites and eighty African Americans refused to surrender. They were subsequently disarmed by royal troops; twenty-three of the rebels were hanged. From their earliest days in Jamestown, black servants and slaves agitated for freedom. As a flurry of statutes passed from 1660–1662 suggest and contemporary documents state, Afro-Virginians made many attempts to liberate themselves. Bacon's challenge to Virginia's colonial governor created a "crisis of political rule" and an opportunity for an organized bid for freedom. "It was this pattern of state crisis and the search for liberty in 1676 that anticipated numerous slave rebellions against colonial and American slavery in the subsequent two centuries."[17]

Edmund Morgan's classic analysis of Bacon's Rebellion argues that American freedom was the product of black enslavement. Seventeenth-century Virginia planters were unable to control the rising ranks of discontented European indentured servants who had completed their service until "the rights of Englishmen were preserved by destroying the rights of Africans."[18] By turning away from temporary European bond labor and toward permanent

West African captives, Virginia's leaders stemmed the tide of disgruntled former servants and reduced the restrictions the colony had imposed to control the European lower orders. This shift away from subjugating temporary and former European bond servants and toward permanently subjugated African bondsmen and women helped to establish a color line which distinguished, in every sense, the lower ranks of white laborers.

Afro-American Militaries

Just as Nathaniel Bacon had offered freedom to servants and slaves in exchange for their military service against the English, so too did Spanish officials in Florida. While Bacon's initiative was suppressed in Virginia, in Spanish Florida Afro-Americans who took up arms against the English were granted freedom and property. In 1683, an Afro-American militia was officially established to help defend the Spanish territory from English encroachment; this was the first black militia in what would become the United States.

Spain's European rivals and their pirate proxies stimulated the arming of Afro-Spaniards throughout the hemisphere. A roster from 1673 lists some two thousand African-descended soldiers serving in Central American infantries. The royal order to the governor of New Spain to create additional free black companies noted "the mulattos and blacks who defended [Spain's] circum-Caribbean realms were 'persons of valor' who fought with 'vigor and reputation.'"[19] Black militias were formed in Hispaniola, Veracruz, Campeche, Puerto Rico, Panama, Caracas, and Cartagena in addition to Florida. In many cases, these militias were called upon to subdue maroons, but in Florida, the Afro-Spanish soldiers *were* maroons.

The prospect of additional Afro-Spanish soldiers was a principal reason why, in 1693, Spain's Charles II offered sanctuary in Florida to fugitive slaves arriving from English colonies. The Spanish government freed these individuals, granted them homesteads, and endorsed the election of black political and military leaders. In the 1730s, the Spanish officially transformed this de facto maroon community into a sanctioned free black town outside of St. Augustine and recognized its free black leader, Francisco Menendez. The success of Menendez, a fugitive slave from South Carolina, and the powerful maroon communities of Florida contributed to the initiation of the 1739 Stono Revolt and the Age of Revolution.

In addition to Florida, Africans helped to populate and defend Spanish towns throughout the American Southwest. By 1680, eighty years after Isabel de Olvera's deposition, the African, Native American, and European mixed-race population of New Mexico had almost reached three thousand. One of these residents, the Angolan-born Sebastian Rodriguez Brito, served as a military drummer for two of New Spain's governors there in the 1690s; he ultimately became a man of means and one of the first property owners in colonial Santa Fe. Brito's son was among the twelve black founders of Las Trampas, New Mexico.[20] Afro-Americans were also among the original Spanish settlers and defenders of towns like Albuquerque and Tucson.

In the seventeenth century, numerous Afro-Brazilians endeavored to secure and advance freedom through their military service to the Portuguese Crown. During Brazil's wars to recover the region of Pernambuco from an eight-year Dutch occupation in the 1630s, a principal army was composed of free colored men and fugitive slaves under the leadership of the free Afro-Brazilian Henrique Dias. "So important was Dias and his *terco* [a military unit consisting of several companies] in the ensuing reconquest of Dutch territories . . . he and several of his Negro captains were rewarded with titles of nobility and admittance into Iberian military orders."[21]

In 1638, Dias received a letter from the King of Portugal and Spain promising to bestow a noble title and a knighthood. It appears Dias never received the promised knighthood; he was, however, granted the title of governor and received additional royal decorations and compensations. The military unit continued to bear his name—"Terco de Henrique Dias"—until the mid-nineteenth century. Domingo Rodriguez Carneiro, of Angolan parentage, was one of Dias's successors who served as a field commander and received a royal pension.[22] These were not the first Africans to receive high honors for military service from the Portuguese Crown. In 1628, Manuel Gonzales Doria was the first Afro-Brazilian to be awarded a knighthood, and as previously noted, three Africans were knighted in Portugal's Order of Santiago in the 1500s.[23]

The first Afro-American militia in Peru was formed in 1615 and consisted of five companies who played a "'necessary and important' role in . . . defense." [24] Afro-Peruvians also served as regular soldiers in various military expeditions. Juan de Valladolid Mogorán, an Afro-Peruvian who began his military career in 1631, was appointed lieutenant in 1645. In 1653, Valladolid traveled to Spain to petition the Crown for Maestre de Campo, an elite military position that was, according to royal decree, accompanied by eight halberd-wielding German soldiers wherever the Maestre went.

Free black soldiers played significant roles from Cuba's establishment in the 1500s through its independence wars at the end of the nineteenth century. Afro-Cubans built Cuba's fortifications and defended the island against competing European powers, pirates, and indigenous settlers; they also assisted campaigns in Florida, including aiding the Patriots during the American Revolution. "[F]rom the founding of the first militia companies in the late sixteenth century until the 1800s, the free colored community contributed even more than the free whites to the defense and military security of the island." [25]

In Saint Domingue, former slaves founded a black militia at the turn of the seventeenth century. The commercial port of Cap-Francais "launched a number of military expeditions in which slaves . . . won their liberty." [26] Several former slaves were granted freedom for their service during a French raid on Cartagena in 1697. Among them was Vincent Olivier, who was captured in battle and taken to Europe, ransomed, met the king of France, and fought with the French army in Germany. Returning to Saint Domingue, Olivier was appointed captain-general of the free black militia, dined with the governor, and was awarded a pension. Olivier's former colleague and business partner, Etienne Auba, was another prominent black militia captain, whose daughter married a lieutenant of Saint Domingue's black militia. Two of Olivier's grandsons fought in the American Revolution. [27] The service of Afro-Americans in colonial militias illustrates not only their role in defending the rights of American colonists around the hemisphere but also how they perceived their own claims to rights and citizenship. At the outset of the French Revolution, for example, "across Saint-Domingue in 1789, free people of color identified militia service as their most important contribution to colonial civil life." [28]

Black soldiers served in Spanish militias starting in the 1500s, and several black companies were formed in the 1600s. This image depicts members of the free black militia of the Spanish Colonial Army circa 1770. The military figure on the left is an officer from Veracruz, Mexico; on the right, a soldier from Havana, Cuba. Free men of color served widely in the colonial American militias of Spain, France, Portugal, England,

and the Netherlands, defending various territories in the Americas. Afro-Cuban and Afro-Mexican soldiers helped to shape United States history when they assisted the patriots in Florida during the American Revolution.

African American soldiers from what would become the United States served widely in the American Revolution as well as in all of the colonial contests that preceded it. In 1676, during King Philip's War, "Rhode Island required its surprisingly large slave population to muster in the militia and perform the same training as white Englishmen."[29] Many Africans fought and died alongside the English in this costly war between settlers and Amerindian residents led by the Wampanoag leader known as Philip. Almost a decade later in 1689, "Blacks fought and died in the colonial militia in King William's War," as well as in "Queen Anne's War (1702–1713) and in numerous campaigns against the Indians of various magnitude."[30] While African Americans have participated in virtually every military contest in U.S. history, their service was repeatedly constrained by law and/or custom. Regardless of official prohibitions, African Americans continually risked their lives to defend U.S. interests during wartime, despite the fact that their service to their country did not always confer the rights of citizenship.

In Latin America and the Caribbean, black militias offered a reliable and vital avenue of social mobility for countless Afro-Americans. In addition to the civic and social status afforded soldiers and their families, Afro-Americans could and did rise to positions of leadership and officer rank. Throughout Ibero-America, black officers were not uncommon and "as officers, these men exercised considerable influence in colonial government."[31] Wherever in the Americas there were relatively small European populations, free people of color were called on to perform highly skilled military and economic duties that were typically reserved for whites in the mainland British colonies. Nevertheless, "African Americans played important, although often overlooked, roles in the military operations that made Britain the greatest imperial power of the late eighteenth century."[32] From the earliest sixteenth-century contests of colonial conquest to the independence wars of the eighteenth and nineteenth centuries, Afro-Americans played substantial military roles in American settlement, defense, and nation-building throughout the hemisphere.

MAROONS AND PIRATES

When military service in defense of a colonial power could not offer a reliable route to freedom, many Afro-Americans found that taking up arms against the state could. Having fought for liberty and independence for decades, Gaspar Yanga, a powerful maroon leader of a fugitive slave community outside of Veracruz, Mexico, negotiated a treaty with the Spanish government in 1618. A predominantly black town, "officials in Veracruz often had to rely on the more numerous persons of color to fill roles normally held by Spaniards."[33] For three decades, Yanga had administered and defended a maroon community in multiple sites outside of the port city against colonial combatants (including Afro-Spaniards). The 1618 treaty between Yanga and the Spanish government established the first officially designated free black town in North America: San Lorenzo de los Negros de Cerralvo. With the roots of the town stretching back to the 1570s, some have deemed Yanga "the first liberator of the Americas."[34] In 1769, Afro-Mexican maroons were again granted the right to establish an independent town.[35]

Africans established independent maroon communities throughout New Granada—the regions that would become known as Venezuela, Ecuador, Panama, and Colombia, the latter being the colonial seat. Cartagena, a city that by the seventeenth century was home to significantly more Africans than Europeans, was surrounded by several maroon settlements or *palenques*. Among these was Matudere, founded around 1681 by fugitive slaves Domingo and Juana Padilla as a refuge for escaped slaves, Amerindians, and others. Though the settlement lasted only twelve years, "In its political, military, and social organization, Matudere resembled what Spaniards would have recognized as an ordered polity, and Domingo and Juana's authority over diverse ethnolinguistic factions within their camps was similar to that exercised by Spaniards in their own multicultural cities."[36] It was perhaps no accident that Juana insisted on being referred to as vice queen, a position unique to the viceroyalties of Peru and New Spain. At that time, New Granada's highest Spanish official was only a governor, who himself led the raid to destroy the maroon settlement in 1693.[37]

Spanning most of the seventeenth century, Brazil's Palmares was the largest independent maroon state in the Americas. Brazil received more enslaved Africans than anywhere else in the Americas—approximately four and a half million people. Fugitive communities began with the first arrivals of slaves in the 1530s, and Brazil was the last country in the Western Hemisphere to end institutional slavery in 1888. Most fugitive slave communities in Brazil (often called *macombos* or *quilombos*) were composed of tens or sometimes hundreds of residents, somewhat isolated though often with access to a larger commercial center. Some *quilombos* were relatively short-lived while others have endured, with the descendants of their founders, until the present; in 1988, Brazil's Constitution officially recognized quilombo land rights.

Founded in 1605, Palmares encompassed some 20,000 inhabitants at its peak. It was a unique political confederation of multiple maroon towns with elected officials, taxes, and a central government, where fugitive slaves, as well as some indigenous and European persons, found refuge. Ganga Zumba, a captured Angolan nobleman who freed himself from a sugar plantation, headed the confederation politically and militarily, alternately fighting and negotiating with the colonial state. His nephew, Zumbi, was born free in Palmares in 1655, kidnapped as a child, and placed with a missionary with whom he studied Portuguese and Latin. Zumbi was able to make his way back to Palmares at age fifteen and eventually succeeded his uncle. Legend has it that during a stalemate, the colonial state offered to recognize the runaway slaves in the confederation as free, but Zumbi refused the treaty because it did not free *all* Brazilians. After decades of continuous attempts to conquer the maroon state, Portuguese authorities raised a highly specialized army that ultimately defeated Palmares in 1695.[38] Although several smaller maroon settlements continued to survive in the region, the centralized state did not.

In 1677, legally enslaved residents of Cobre in eastern Cuba submitted the first of many petitions to the Spanish Crown to negotiate for the protection of their de facto free black town. El Cobre (Spanish for copper) began as a mining settlement worked by privately owned slaves. In 1670, when the Spanish government claimed ownership of the mine, the privately held slaves technically became royal slaves while in reality further settling and developing the region as free people and forming maroon settlements in the surrounding mountains. The 1677 petition submitted by "el negro criollo" (the American-born black) Juan Moreno on behalf of "todos los negros y mulatos criollos" of the mine set in motion a century of El Cobre's residents negotiating their rights in courts, with colonial governors, and ultimately a fifteen-year litigation in Madrid's highest court that resulted in an 1800 royal edict formally acknowledging their collective emancipation, legitimacy as a corporate community, and land rights.[39]

Maroons played significant roles in America's French colonies as well. In Martinique in 1665, a group of five hundred maroons led by Francisque Fabulé entered negotiations with the colony's Sovereign Council. A treaty mediated by an enslaved Martinican granted Fabulé his freedom and one thousand pounds of tobacco; his collaborators were pardoned. Nevertheless, a 1671 decree lamented that independent maroon organizations continued to thrive in the French colony. In Saint Domingue, massive maroon settlements near the boarder of Santo Domingo often sought refuge and collaboration with the Spanish, making the Haitian maroons of Le Maniel, in particular, impossible to subdue.[40] /

The origins of Jamaica's maroons can be traced to the early 1600s when half of the Spanish-controlled colony was composed of Africans and the other half were Spaniards of mixed descent. During this period, a quarter of the militia was composed of free Africans and Amerindians who were called upon to repel pirates. When the English wrested control of Jamaica in 1655, numerous slaves joined independent communities of color in the interior. One of these maroons, a "Spanish negro" named Juan Lubolo, agreed to aid British forces when his palenque was captured. Three years later, Jamaica's governor signed a proclamation that Lubolo and "'the negroes of his Palenque . . . shall have grants of land and enjoy all the privileges and liberties of Englishmen.'"[41] Furthermore, Lubolo was to be made captain of the black militia as well as magistrate. The proclamation was the first of several treaties England made with Jamaica's maroons. In the 1700s, the power and organization of Jamaica's maroon communities, as evidenced in two Maroon Wars, compelled English and American authorities to question the sustainability of slavery.

Maroons often collaborated with—and sometimes were—pirates in the Caribbean. Throughout the seventeenth century and into the early eighteenth, piracy offered an avenue to freedom for many enslaved individuals. Pirate crews that captured slave ships or raided port towns often enlisted African captives (or sold them), and fugitive slaves themselves sought out the pirate's life as an alternative to slavery. A self-liberated Cuban slave named Diego Grillo captained his own pirate crew and accompanied the famous 1671 British attack on Spanish Panama that was orchestrated by pirate captain Henry Morgan, who was knighted and made Jamaica's lieutenant governor by England's King Charles II as a result. In 1679, Peter Cloise, a slave in the Caribbean, was captured by the English buccaneer Edward Davis. The two became successful partners in piracy; some aver that their profits, captured by the British Crown, helped fund the College of William and Mary. In 1699, thirty slaves on St. Thomas escaped bondage by joining a pirate crew.

Black pirates typically began as enslaved individuals embracing an avenue to freedom, but sometimes they originated as professional sailors. For example, the Afro-Dutchman Hendrick Quintor sailed on a Spanish vessel that was captured by Sam Bellamy's crew, which Quintor then joined. Many among Bellamy's crew were former slaves. At the peak of Caribbean piracy, 25–30 percent of pirates were estimated to be of African descent.

Around 1710, a West African chieftain managed to escape captivity on a sinking slave ship during a hurricane; a white crewman joined him and the pair roamed the south Florida coast, using the boat with which they had made their escape to pose as shipwrecked sailors and lure targets. Black Caesar, as the African pirate became known, acquired a crew and accumulated the spoils of years of raiding in south Florida waters, based out of Elliot Key in Miami's Biscayne Bay. Caesar ultimately served as a lieutenant on Blackbeard's flagship *Queen Anne's Revenge* in the mid-Atlantic. Caesar's ancestry was not unique among Blackbeard's crews; in 1718, an account of Blackbeard's hundred-man crew included sixty of African descent.[42]

Afro-Americans both defended American colonial settlements and rebelled against their tyrannies. In a British settlement off the coast of Nicaragua, after resisting a Spanish invasion in 1640, "Providence Islanders . . . celebrated 'with due gratitude and wonder' the 'loyalty in adversity of the negroes who had often rebelled in prosperity.'"[43] The colonial settlement of the island (today a possession of Colombia) was composed mostly of British indentured servants and an international panoply of privateers—state-sanctioned pirates. Daniel Elfrith, an English privateer who was among the first British settlers of the island in 1629, invited Diego el Mulato (Martín), an Afro-Cuban colleague sponsored by the Dutch government, to make Providence Island his base of operations.

An account left by Thomas Gage, an English priest whose ship returning him to England from Mexico was captured by Diego el Mulato, characterized the Afro-Cuban Diego Martín as a gentleman privateer. A self-liberated former slave, Martín had found refuge among the Dutch after suffering "abuse" from the Spanish in Havana. In the shifting winds of colonial alliance, Diego Martín petitioned Havana officials in 1638, offering his services as a valiant soldier for the Spanish Crown. Officials in Spain granted Martín a pardon, an admiral's salary, and a royal commission.[44]

As evidenced by the Spanish Crown's willingness to pardon and promote Martín, pirates were a serious threat to Spain's American empire, and the Crown was more than willing to arm and promote Afro-Americans to defend against them. "Imperial officials, alarmed by repeated assaults on Spain's various American possessions by freebooters linked to rival European powers . . . turned increasingly for military support in places like New Spain, Peru, and the Central American Audencia of Guatemala to [men] of African origins."[45] Afro-American militias defended Cuba and Florida from buccaneers as well.

ECCLESIASTIC AND CIVIC CHALLENGES TO SLAVERY

Some Afro-Americans engendered freedom by taking up arms for the state and others by taking up arms against it; however, many people of color advanced the discourse and legal framework of rights by navigating the channels of religious and civic law. Antonio Vieira, for example, was a prolific Afro-Iberian scholar and priest whose publications and sermons were influential in Europe and Brazil. Born in Lisbon in 1608 to mixed-race parents, Vieira moved to Brazil in 1615 and entered a Jesuit college in Bahia. Soon after, Vieira began teaching at the college of Olina. His abundant political and ideological sermons, pamphlets, and books (such as *History of the Future*) were widely read and internationally respected. In the next century, Vieira's sermons would be described by Abbé Raynal, among the preeminent French Enlightenment figures, as "'perhaps the most extraordinary discourse ever heard from a Christian pulpit.'"[46]

Vieira made diplomatic missions to England, Holland, France, and Italy and was an advisor to both Portugal's King John IV and Sweden's Queen Christina (and was a member of her literary academy). He openly denounced slavery—which in early seventeenth-century Brazil was largely associated with Native Americans—and anti-Semitism. Vieira's promulgation of his enlightened views in print and in person incited a temporary imprisonment by Inquisitors. Exonerated by a papal bull, Vieira returned to Brazil in 1687, where he died a decade later. Vieira has been commemorated on stamps in both Portugal and Brazil.

Afro-Americans fostered civic participation through numerous religious and secular brotherhoods throughout the Americas. People of African descent were active in the Catholic church, the largest and oldest sect of Christianity, throughout the Iberian provinces. In 1526, Benedict da San Fratello, the future St. Benedict, was born in Sicily—then a Spanish-ruled province—to enslaved African parents. Benedict became a Franciscan friar, and upon his death in 1589, Spain's King Phillip III sponsored the construction of his tomb in a Palermo monastery. Records show that in 1540, in colonial New Spain, an Afro-Mexican man "had taken holy ecclesiastical orders" and that in 1542 "there were established . . . three brotherhoods of the True Cross, one of Spaniards, one of Indians, and one of Negroes."[47] Afro-Peruvian freedwoman Ursula de Jesús documented her life in a Lima convent in the mid 1600s; her devotion to Catholic spirituality and her negotiation of the power relations of clerical authority helped her transition from slave to subject.[48] During Mexico's struggles for sovereignty in the early 1800s, Afro-Mexican priest José María Morelos became a key revolutionary general and national hero of Mexican independence. The presence of Afro-Mexicans in positions of civic authority date back at least to the mid-1660s when Miguel Moreno de Andrade served as the acting mayor of Valladolid's town council.[49]

In a bold effort to appeal to the ultimate clerical authority for the protection of rights and the eradication of slavery, Afro-Brazilian Lourenço da Silva de Mendonça traveled to Rome to petition the Pope in 1681. Mendonça, a Brazilian-born descendant of the Angolan royal family, "introduced himself in Rome with recommendations from Madrid and Lisbon . . . that declared him the 'leading representative of all the *pardos* [people of color] in [the Portuguese] kingdom, in Castile, and in Brazil'" as well as the leader of an influential brotherhood of *pretos* [mixed-race people].[50] Mendonça sent these affidavits, along with two petitions, to the Pope, requesting a papal condemnation of the abuses of slavery—in particular that it was a perpetual condition passed on to descendants—and arguing for the excommunication of slave owners who perpetuated it. Pope Innocent XI concurred that Mendonça's petitions showed American slavery to be "a disgraceful offence against Catholic liberty."[51]

Afro-Americans again petitioned the Pope two centuries later when veterans of Cuba's independence wars requested that the Virgin of Charity be recognized as the country's patron saint. The maroons of Cobre described above not only created a historic black town but also a universally venerated religious shrine for *La Virgin de Caridad de Cobre*. According to Cuban culture, mixed-race fishermen discovered the figurine of the Virgin of Charity in Cuban waters in the early 1600s while praying for safety during a storm. Today, the Virgin of Charity is a national icon revered by black and white Cubans alike and recognized by Catholics as the nation's patron saint. Cobre, a settlement that began with collective organization and petitions for freedom initiated by slaves in the 1600s, is now the most important religious site in all of Cuba.

Seventeenth-century colonial Mexico, designated by the Spanish as "New Spain," encompassed the second-largest enslaved population (after Brazil) but also the largest free black population in the Americas. "Savvy in their quest for autonomy," Afro-Mexicans acquired "a legal consciousness composed of an awareness of rights and obligations . . . and the ability to initiate litigation . . . in the pursuit of justice." [52] Afro-Mexicans skillfully navigated the matrix of royal and clerical authority to assert their rights and modify their circumstances. This "legal consciousness was . . . instrumental in the decline of slavery and the growth of the free black population." [53]

Enslaved men and women in South America pursued rights and demanded freedom in courts throughout the 1600s, "long before concepts of abolition and independence were articulated." [54] Enslaved litigants in early Peru, Bolivia, and Chile brought numerous cases of "reclamation" demanding specific rights, including the right to liberty, in Spanish tribunals. Evidence abounds of slaves suing for freedom in Quito from "at least the 1590s, and over the centuries, slaves become more adept at legalese . . . and when to press the issue in court." [55] Free Afro-Ecuadorans used the courts to press for the freedom of enslaved loved ones as well. In 1675, Adán Pardo sued a local mayor claiming that his children were unlawfully pressed into the mayor's service. In 1690, Pedro de Silva sued his wife's owner, insisting that the conditions for her freedom (his offer of payment) had been met. [56]

As early as 1526, the Spanish Crown invited colonists to allow faithful slaves to purchase their own freedom and continually acknowledged the right of slaves to use the courts to that end.[57] Iberian slave codes, originating in the medieval Seven Part Code or *Siete Partidas*, offered many channels to freedom and "were firm in the state's role in supporting the transition from slave to free status."[58] Afro-Spaniards resolutely established the practice and ultimately the right of *coartacion*: a legal tactic whereby an enslaved individual could petition an official to set a fixed price so that one could make payments toward his or her own self-purchase.

Slaves used the courts to secure their freedom in British America as well. John Baptiste's 1653 petition to a Maryland court, noted above, was perhaps the earliest freedom suit in British America. The following year, Anthony Iland successfully petitioned for his freedom in a British court in Barbados. Iland argued for his liberty on the grounds that he arrived on the island as a free person of his own volition and therefore was being illegally detained by sugar planter William Leachy. The court agreed with Iland. Between 1650 and 1700, at least 124 enslaved Afro-Americans obtained their freedom in Barbados.[59]

In 1655, Afro-Virginian Elizabeth Key won her freedom in a Virginia court. The daughter of an Englishman and an enslaved African mother, Key argued that her English patrimony and Christian faith excluded her (and her young son) from permanent enslavement. Key thus brought the first successful freedom suit in colonial Virginia, establishing her own freedom and that of her progeny.[60]

SLAVERY, SEX, AND LAW:
CLASSIFICATIONS OF MIXED-RACE AMERICANS

In many parts of the Americas, "freedom . . . emerged from sexual contact between slaves and free people."[61] In English law, a child took on the freedom condition of the father, as evidenced in Elizabeth Key's successful argument. In the 1660s, however, colonial Virginia's legislative assembly broke with English tradition when it established that slave status followed the condition of the mother. This legal reversal signaled a remarkable shift in the British colonies whereby mixed-race children with enslaved mothers and white fathers could be denied their European patrimony. In the French and Iberian colonies, as well as in the British

Caribbean, mixed-race children continued to be able to inherit the free status of a European father.

By the 1620s, French settlers were encroaching on Hispaniola, and in 1697 Spain officially ceded to France what is today Haiti. In the 1670s, French colonists began experimenting with industrial tobacco cultivation and sought increasing numbers of laborers from Africa to assist a small number of French indentured servants on New World plantations. Large-scale sugar production would not begin until the eighteenth century; however, the French found some success in the 1680s with indigo production. In contrast to the piecemeal and sometimes contradictory statutes issued from the colonial assemblies in mainland British colonies, in 1685 French authorities issued the first explicit slave legislation in the Americas: the Code Noir.

Among the main preoccupations of the Code Noir was that slave-owners and slaves must be Catholics; the code also required the expulsion of Jews from the French colonies.[62] For medieval and early modern Europeans, religion was the principal paradigm for human identity and difference, a paradigm that would only gradually—and in some cases, only partially—be eclipsed by novel, malleable, and heterogeneous conceptions of race in the eighteenth and nineteenth centuries.

The Code outlined sanctioned punishments and policing for enslaved persons; yet, unlike the slave codes and practices that would be developed in the colonies that became the United States, the French colonies were expressly forbidden from separating enslaved parents and prepubescent children. The Code also protected slaves from being killed, mutilated, or tortured; it must be noted, however, that the necessity of forbidding such practices suggests their existence. Furthermore, it would have been difficult to enforce legal codes on individual plantations. Still, the regulations speak to how French authorities may have thought about enslaved individuals and their children as eligible for rights. Article IX of the Code urged that unmarried masters who fathered children with enslaved women marry the mothers and raise the children as "free and legitimate." The Code explicitly acknowledged that children produced by a slave and master could enjoy all the rights of natural citizens.

Kinship ties between Europeans, Africans, and Native Americans had begun with first contact. In the case of Iberians like Antonio Vieira, mixed-race ancestry might precede one's arrival in the New World where interethnic sexual unions, under varying degrees of coercion, exigency, and intimacy, were common. How mixed-race unions were perceived and how mixed-race children were incorporated into the community varied greatly across region, period, and individual circumstances. In an effort to highlight the variability of mixed-race unions and their contexts, this section outlines legal strictures established in the seventeenth century as well as draws upon some illustrative examples from across centuries.

In 1662, Virginia enacted its first racially discriminatory statute when it doubled the standard fine for sex outside of marriage for "'any christian [who] shall committ Fornication with a negro man or woman'" and further declared "'all children borne in this country shall be held bond or free only according to the condition of the mother.'"[63] A year earlier, Virginia enacted the first law punishing white men and women who married a "negro, mulatto, or Indian . . . bond or free"; the penalty was permanent banishment from the colony. Maryland, which in 1662 had tried to discourage "freeborn English" women from marrying slaves, prohibited unions between white men and black women in 1692. The colonies of Massachusetts, North Carolina, Pennsylvania, and Georgia followed suit in the first half of the eighteenth century.

However, anti-mixing legislation was not all-pervasive in colonial British America; seven of the thirteen mainland colonies did not enact statutes prohibiting intermarriage, nor did these laws declare interracial marriages null and void, as they would in the nineteenth century. Within the six British North American colonies that did penalize mixed marriages, "community feeling was not . . . monolithically arrayed against interracial union."[64] In 1696, and again in 1699, Virginians petitioned "'for the repeal of the Act of the Assembly, Against English peoples marrying with Negroes, Indians, or Mulattos.'"[65] In 1755, citizens petitioned the North Carolina assembly to repeal the laws in which "free Negroes and Mulattos Intermarrying with white women are obliged to pay taxes for their wives and families."[66] In 1770, Pennsylvania repealed its ban on interracial marriage.

As evidenced in court records of "miscegenation" as well as in colonial newspapers—fugitive servant notices in particular—interracial unions continued despite legal or social prohibitions. As the wife of a Confederate planter and former South Carolina senator observed as late as 1861, "Like the patriarchs of old our men live all in one house with their wives and their concubines, and the mulattos one sees in every family exactly resemble the white children."[67] While the mixed-race children of white fathers and black mothers were often confined to slavery in the Anglo-American South, the mixed-race children of white mothers were free. In fact, in Virginia and the Carolinas, "White servant women continued to bear children by African American fathers through the late seventeenth century and well into the eighteenth century . . . [these unions were] the primary source of the increase in the free African American population for this period."[68]

Many Americans descended from black slaves were eventually recognized as white. The Elizabeth Key noted above was sometimes referred to as Black Bess. Her son, John, whom she also freed through her 1655 lawsuit, was named for his father, John Grinstead, an English former indentured servant who was Elizabeth's lawyer; they had a second child and married. Two centuries later, one of Key's descendants, also named John Grinstead, was listed in the 1830 U.S. census as a white slave owner. In an ironic twist, this white descendant of an African slave "was appointed to serve on a committee to determine the willingness of free persons of color in [Virginia's Northumberland] county to immigrate to West Africa."[69]

Virginia's slave laws were enacted gradually and piecemeal starting in the 1660s. Prior to the late seventeenth century, the line between servants and slaves was especially hazy and has been the subject of scholarly debate. When John Casor lost his freedom suit in 1654, a year before Elizabeth Key won hers, Casor became the first American to be declared a servant for life in a civil case. However, some historians regard John Punch, who was sentenced to lifetime service as a criminal punishment, as the first slave in U.S. history.

Punch, described in contemporary records as "negro," ran away from his master along with two European indentured servants. In 1640, a Virginia court sentenced the Dutch and Scots servants each to additional years of indentured service while Punch was ordered to serve for life. Remarkably, a team of genealogists determined in 2012 that Barack Obama is likely John Punch's eleventh great-grandson. In the 1630s, John Punch fathered a child with a European woman in Virginia who passed on her free legal status to their son and her white racial status to his progeny.[70]

John Punch's son, John Bunch, who in turn fathered two sons, John Bunch II and Paul Bunch, was the progenitor of various mixed-race descendants who bifurcated into both white and black American families. "Some members of this Bunch family passed for white and stayed in Virginia—they are President Obama's ancestors." [71] The genealogical link is through Obama's white mother, a direct descendant of John Bunch II, a planter born in the seventeenth century, who, in 1704, was taxed on 100 acres of land in Virginia.

In 1705, John Bunch III and Sarah Slayden, "a white woman," petitioned the Council of Virginia to legally wed. Their parish minister had refused to perform the ceremony because he believed the groom to be a "mulatto" despite having a preponderance of white ancestors, by virtue of his African great-grandparent. Their petition prompted the Virginia court to issue a decree that defined the legal term mulatto to include "any person who had a black parent, grandparent, or great-grandparent." This legal definition, which would hold sway for the next two centuries of American history, "was the direct result of President Obama's ancestor [his eighth great-grandfather] attempting to receive the same legal benefit offered to white people."[72]

Another branch of the Bunch family moved from Virginia to the Carolinas, where they were "frequently recorded as 'mulatto' in early records" and continued to intermarry with racially mixed families.[73] This branch includes Ralph Bunche, the political scientist and diplomat who was the first African American to be awarded a Nobel Prize in the mid-twentieth century.

Colonial Virginia and surrounding colonies developed a unique convention of *hypodescent* whereby mixed-race children were typically assigned the racial status of the lower-status parent, regardless of their appearance (*hyperdescent* is the opposite convention, assigning children to the race of the higher-status parent). In 1691, a Virginia statute attempted to stamp out interracial unions and prevent the freeing of mixed-race slaves. Yet the manumission of light-complexioned slaves of obvious European heritage circumvented these restrictions. In his study of manumission in the Virginia cities of Petersburg and Richmond, Luther Jackson observed that many emancipated slaves were listed as "bright mulatto," "very light," "very bright in complexion," and sometimes, "almost white."[74] Enslaved relatives in some cases were given preferential treatment and ultimately granted freedom but were rarely acknowledged as kin. In one unusual case, the will of white Virginian John Stewart stipulated that his estate—which exceeded $20,000—go to Mary Vizzaneau, "my natural colored daughter."[75] These individuals may have been exceptions in light of the many documented cases in the U.S. South where the children of planters were kept, sold, and treated as slaves.

Outside the mainland colonies of Anglo-America, authorities did not prohibit interracial contact nor punish slaves for having sex with free persons.[76] Conventions and authorities in the French Caribbean and throughout Latin America generally encouraged that enslaved women who bore children to their masters were to be freed. Outside what would become the U.S., mixed-race children often inherited the status of the higher caste parent. In the dangerous contexts of slave societies and their attendant racial and gender violence, Afro-American women were sometimes able to advance their and their children's freedom through relationships with European men. While many if not most of these encounters were involuntary for enslaved women, some were less so.

Unions between French men and African women engendered a large, self-sustaining class of free people of color in colonies like Louisiana, Saint-Domingue, Guyana, Guadeloupe, and Martinique. In the seventeenth century, the Code Noir made no distinction between the rights of free people based on ethnicity, and in many cases mixed-race persons were simply regarded as whites. "The lines between free and slave, black and white were porous prior to the arrival of sugar. Intermarriage between well-placed free people of color and ambitious French nationals was common. Indeed, census takers, notaries, and other officials regularly elevated free people of color to white."[77]

In colonial Latin America, marriages between enslaved and free individuals, often of European or indigenous descent, were a crucial means, along with manumission and self-purchase, of generating free colored colonial subjects in Latin America. In late seventeenth-century eastern and southern Guatemala, for example, Afro-Guatemalans composed about 40 percent of the non-indigenous population. "Almost without exception, this African-descended population was largely free and identified as mulatto by the end of the seventeenth century."[78]

Latin American conceptualizations of race varied across place and time, but on the main, mixed unions were socially acceptable and mixed-race individuals assimilated. While Latin American conceptions of race were, like those of the rest of the West, embedded in the defective premise of white supremacy, traditional notions of class and station remained paramount. Social-status markers like wealth, education, lineage, marriage, and accomplishment could supplant color. Among the popular classes, racial mixing was normative. In Mexico, for example, Africans outnumbered Europeans from the sixteenth through the eighteenth centuries. These Afro-descended populations were gradually and largely incorporated into the larger Mexican culture, as they were throughout Latin America.

The demographics of colonial Latin America indicate that people of African descent were vital to its founding and to populating and building its infrastructure. Afro-descended people advanced Ibero-America's economies, assimilated, and intermarried with the Native and Spanish population. Throughout the Americas, indigenous populations had declined dramatically as the result of European expropriation and disease. However, in Mexico, Central America, and many parts of South America, Amerindian populations rebounded to become a dominant part of the culture and labor market; that demography encouraged assimilation through *mestizaje*—the process of blending ancestries.

In Latin America, the mixed-race children of Europeans and Africans were often treated as the legitimate children of what were in effect common-law unions. Alejandro de la Fuente's examination of manumission records in seventeenth-century Havana determined that at least half involved children under fifteen years, three-quarters of whom were listed as "mulato." Numerous petitions revealed the desire of Cuban slave owners to liberate pregnant slaves or request that offspring of "unknown" parentage be officially designated as their legitimate heirs. In Old Havana today, one can visit the magnificent historic home of Juana Carvajal, a *mulata* woman who was deeded the gracious colonial mansion as well as freedom by her former owner in 1700.[79] Today, Carvajal's beautiful home serves as Havana's Museum of Archeology.

While it might be difficult to imagine Thomas Jefferson deeding Monticello to Sally Hemings, Juana Carvajal had a North American counterpart in another Spanish-controlled colony. When Marie Therese Metoyer obtained her freedom in Louisiana in 1778, it was during a period of Spanish custody when the colony was loosely administered from Havana. (Many of the buildings in New Orleans's "French Quarter" were built during the Spanish colonial period, 1762–1802.) Marie Therese's freedom was purchased by her long time partner, a French merchant, with whom she reared ten children.

As a free woman, Coincoin, as Marie Therese was known, was an assiduous entrepreneur in Natchitoches and amassed roughly a thousand acres and several slaves. While a number of Coincoin's relatives technically remained in bondage, her progeny founded a famous creole community along the Cane River. Her son, Louis Metoyer, studied architecture in Paris before building Melrose Plantation, the largest plantation built and owned by African Americans in the U.S., today recognized as a National Historic Landmark. Another son of Coincoin, Nicolas Augustin Metoyer, donated the land for the St. Augustine Parish church and commissioned his brother Louis to build it, making it among the earliest of several eighteenth-century churches in the U.S. built by and for African Americans.[80]

Another famous example, also from the eighteenth century, of an enslaved woman who created an eminent family with a European man was Brazil's Chica da Silva. Francisca da Silva Oliveira, alternately known as Xica da Silva or Chica da Silva, was born into slavery in the Brazilian state of Minas Gerais in 1732. She had two sons with her first owner, both of whom took their father's surname and studied at university.

Francisca eventually gained fame as the powerful de facto wife of her subsequent master, João Fernandez de Oliveira, a diamond mine owner who was among the wealthiest men in colonial Brazil. Together, the couple had thirteen children; their four sons were granted titles of nobility by the Portuguese court. Because of her exceptional wealth and power, Chica da Silva's story has been mythologized in popular media. However, as scholars like Júnia Ferreira Furtado have shown, there were many instances whereby Afro-American women participated in colonial society by establishing recognized families with European men.[81]

While Coincoin and Chica da Silva became a part of the popular consciousness of Louisianans and Brazilians, respectively, a great deal of Afro-American women bore children with European men, as evidenced throughout these pages. Some of these unions were out-and-out rape, as in the case of Elizabeth Keckley, the author, dressmaker, and companion of First Lady Mary Todd Lincoln who was born in Virginia in 1818. Keckley's only child was the result of the unwelcomed advances of a white man; Keckley was herself the unacknowledged daughter of her master, Colonial Armistead Burwell. She was passed to the ownership of Burwell's son (her half-brother), from whom she purchased her freedom. Other unions may have been more consensual, like that of the parents of John Mercer Langston, the black lawyer and statesman born in Virginia in 1829. Langston was the fourth child of a white slave-holding father and an emancipated slave mother (who had been freed by his father when his eldest sibling was born). Upon his parents' untimely death, Langston received a large inheritance and moved to the free state of Ohio as his father had prearranged.

Mixed unions were a regular, pervasive fact of American life. How the children of those unions were treated varied across time, place, and individual circumstances. Keckley and Langston were living in nineteenth-century Virginia, where the novel convention of a "one-drop" rule—which classified as black anyone with any African ancestry, no matter how distant or visible—would be enshrined in law in the early twentieth century. Latin Americans took the opposite approach, developing a convention of "whitening" whereby racial mixture could transform black Americans into white ones over generations. Whether ascribing to the conventions of hypo-descent or hyper-descent, the societies of the Americas were founded with mixed-race families.

American Establishment

As we have seen, from New Mexico to New York, Florida to California, the Caribbean, Central, and South America, men and women of African descent founded some of the earliest settlements in the New World. They freed themselves and established independent maroon communities, some of which became officially incorporated as free black towns. They advanced freedom by fighting for and winning their and their progeny's liberty in colonial courts and through military service. They petitioned the Pope and propagated sermons for the rights of others. Free black populations proliferated throughout the hemisphere, and some were absorbed into and helped to compose the white population. Conversely, many mixed-race people, free and enslaved, passed along their European as well as their African ancestry to the next generation of enslaved and free people of color.

In the colonial period, people like settler Isabel de Olvera, scholar Antonio Vieira, planter Anthony Johnson, physician Dr. Lucas Santomee, trader Jan Rodriguez, assemblyman Mathias de Sousa, "the first American liberator" Yanga, the hero Zumbi, the anti-hero Black Caesar, the entrepreneur Coincoin, and many other individuals sought to expand their autonomy by litigating in the courts, by forming independent communities, or by negotiating with the colonial state. All those endeavors offer a window onto a world of people of African descent whose actions undermined slavery—and the traditional historical narrative of slavery—and underscored the Enlightenment ideals of justice and liberty, even before the Enlightenment made these ideals fashionable. As Peter Wood has observed, Isabel de Olvera's descendants—and those of all the early African arrivals—"live on in all the races of . . . America."[82]

NOTES FOR CHAPTER THREE

1   Quintard Taylor and Shirley Ann Wilson Moore, eds., *African American Women Confront the West, 1600–2000* (Norman, OK: University of Oklahoma Press, 2003), 32.

2   Olvera was not the first person of African descent to settle in New Mexico. After the black explorer, Esteban, encountered the region in 1538, African men and women accompanied the Coronado expedition of 1540–1542 as well as additional forays in 1593 and 1598. Bruce A. Glasrud, *African American History in New Mexico: Portraits from Five Hundred Years* (Albuquerque: University of New Mexico Press, 2013).

3   Robin Blackburn, *Paths to Freedom: Manumission in the Atlantic World*, eds., Rosemary Brana-Shute and Randy J. Sparks (Columbia: University of South Carolina Press, 2009), 3.

4   Robert J. Cottrol, "The Long Lingering Shadow: Law, Liberalism, and Cultures of Racial Hierarchy and Identity," *Tulane Law Review*, no. 76, Vol. 1 (2001): 34.

5   Claudius K. Fergus, *Revolutionary Emancipation: Slavery and Abolition in the British West Indies* (Baton Rouge: Louisiana State University Press, 2013).

6   England's Enclosure Acts displaced peasants from communal lands from the sixteenth century to the nineteenth as they privatized large tracts of property. In the sixteenth and seventeenth centuries, the English displaced Irish Catholics through a policy of colonization (known as plantation), whereby the English Crown confiscated Irish land and settled English migrants on it. Numerous English policies from this period, from prohibitions on marriage between English and Irish persons to restrictions on Irish literacy and mobility, presaged discriminatory legislation in British America.

7   William O. Blake, *The History of Slavery and the Slave Trade, Ancient and Modern. The Forms Slavery the Prevailed in Ancient Nations, particularly in Greece and Rome. The African Slave Trade and the History of Slavery in the United States* (Columbus, OH: H. Miller, 1853), 372.

8   T. H. Breen and Steven Innes, *Myne Owne Ground: Race and Freedom on Virginia's Eastern Shore, 1640–1676* (New York: Oxford University Press, 1980), 111.

9   Linda Heywood and John Thornton, *Central Africans, Atlantic Creoles, and the Foundation of the Americas, 1585–1660* (New York: Cambridge University Press, 2007), 327; Lerone Bennett, *Before the Mayflower: A History of Black America* (New York: Penguin Books, 1984), 37–38.

10 William J. Wood, "The Illegal Beginning of American Negro Slavery," *American Bar Association Journal* 56 (January 1970), 48.

11 Bennett, *Before the Mayflower*, 41.

12 Ibid.

13 Ira Berlin and Leslie Harris, eds., *Slavery in New York* (New York: The New York Historical Society and The New Press, 2005), 9; Joan H. Geismar, "Washing Square Park Monitoring," *Report Prepared for the New York City Department of Parks and Recreation* (April 2004), 6. In the 1820s, African American property owners would again settle a historic New York City neighborhood, Seneca Village, in an area that came to be Central Park in the second half of the nineteenth century.

14 W. Michael Byrd and Linda A. Clayton, *An American Health Dilemma: A Medical History of African Americans and the Problems of Race, Beginnings to 1900* (New York: Routledge, 2000), 202.

15 Howard Dodson, et al, *Becoming American: The African American Journey* (New York: Sterling Publishing, 2009), 11; Graham Russell Hodges, *Root and Branch: African Americans in New York and East Jersey, 1613–1863* (Chapel Hill: University of North Carolina Press, 1999), 6–7.

16 David S. Bogen, "Mathias de Sousa: Maryland's First Colonist of African Descent," *Maryland Historical Magazine* 96, no. 1 (2001): 68–85.

17 Jeffery Kerr-Ritchie, "'Their Hoped for Liberty': Slaves and Bacon's 1676 Rebellion," *Voices from Within the Veil*, eds., William Alexander et al. (Newcastle, UK: Cambridge Scholars Publishing, 2008), 79.

18 Edmund Morgan, *American Slavery, American Freedom* (New York: Norton, 2003 [1975]); Edmund Morgan, *The Challenge of the American Revolution* (New York: Norton, 1976), 166.

19   Jane Landers, "Turning Bondsmen into Vassals," *Arming Slaves: From Classical Times to the Modern Age*, eds., Brown and Morgan (New Haven, CT: Yale University Press, 2006), 125.

20   Taylor, *In Search of the Racial Frontier*, 35; Elizabeth West, *Sante Fe: Four Hundred Years, Four Hundred Questions* (Santa Fe, NM: Sunstone Press, 2012), 174.

21   Herbert Klein, *Neither Slave nor Free: The Freedmen of African Descent in the Slave Societies of the New World*, eds., David W. Cohen and Jack P. Green (Baltimore: Johns Hopkins University Press, 1972), 310.

22   Hebe Mattos, "'Pretos' and 'Pardos' Between the Cross and the Sword: Racial Categories in Seventeenth Century Brazil," *Revista Europea de Estudios Latinoamericanos y del Caribe* 80 (April 2006): 42–49.

23   Francis A. Dutras, "A Hard Fought Struggle for Recognition: Manuel Gonçalves Doria, First Afro Brazilian to Become a Knight of Santiago," *Americas* 56, no. 1 (July 1999): 91; Mattos, "'Pretos' and 'Pardos,'" 47.

24   Frederick Bowser, *The African Slave in Colonial Peru* (Stanford, CA: Stanford University Press, 1974), 309–310.

25   Herbert Klein, *Slavery in the Americas* (Chicago: University of Chicago, 1967), 195.

26   David Geggus and Norman Fiering, eds., *The World of the Haitian Revolution* (Bloomington: Indiana University Press, 2009), 57.

27   John Garrigus, "Catalyst or Catastrophe? Saint-Domingue's Free Men of Color and the Battle of Savannah, 1779–1782," *Revista/Review Ineramericana* 22, no. 1–2 (1992): 109; Stewart King, *Blue Coat or Powdered Wig: Free People of Color in Pre-revolutionary Saint Domingue* (Athens: University of Georgia Press, 2001), 253.

28   John D. Garrigus, *Before Haiti: Race and Citizenship in French Saint-Domingue* (New York: Palgrave Macmillan, 2006), 229.

29   Gene Allen Smith, *The Slaves' Gamble: Choosing Sides in the War of 1812* (New York: Palgrave Macmillan, 2013), 8.

30   Michael Lee Lanning, *The African American Soldier* (New York: Citadel Press, 2004 [1997]), 7.

31   Klein, *Neither Slave nor Free*, 311.

32   Smith, *Slaves' Gamble*, 10.

33   Landers, "Cimarron and Citizen," 121.

34   Charles Henry Rowell, "'El Primer Liberador de las Americas'/The First Liberator of the Americas: The Editor's Notes," *Callaloo* 31, no. 1 (Winter 2008): 1–11. In the twentieth century, the Mexican state officially designated the town as Yanga, Veracruz.

35   Ben Vinson III and Matthew Restall, eds., *Black Mexico: Race and Society from Colonial to Modern Times* (Albuquerque: University of New Mexico Press, 2009), 31–32.

36   Jane Landers, "The African Landscape of Seventeenth-Century Cartagena and its Hinterlands," in *The Black Urban Atlantic in the Age of the Slave Trade*, eds., Jorge Cañizares-Esguerra, Matt D. Childs, and James Sidbury (Philadelphia: University of Pennsylvania Press, 2013), 157.

37   Jane Landers, "Maroon Women in Colonial Spanish America," in *Beyond Bondage: Free*

Women of Color in the Americas, eds., David Barry Gaspar and Darlene Clark Hine (Chicago: University of Illinois Press, 2004), 8–9.

38 Zumbi is a revered national hero in Brazil, whose memory was commemorated in 1999 with the naming of Zumbi dos Palmares International Airport. R.K. Kent, "An African State in Brazil," *Journal of African History* 6, no. 2 (Cambridge University Press, 1965): 161–175; Richard Price, *Maroon Societies: Rebel Slave Communities in the Americas* (Baltimore: Johns Hopkins University Press, 1972).

39 Maria Elena Díaz, *The Virgin, the King, and the Royal Slaves of El Cobre: Negotiating Freedom in Colonial Cuba, 1670–1780* (Stanford, CA: Stanford University Press, 2000).

40 Timothy Lockley, *Maroon Communities in South Carolina: A Documentary Record* (Columbia: University of South Carolina Press, 2009), xii; Price, *Maroon Societies*, 108.

41 Michael Craton, *Testing the Chains: Resistance to Slavery in the British West Indies* (Ithaca: Cornell University Press, 1982), 70–71.

42 What is known today as Caesar's Creek was one of his main escape routes that was frequently used by smugglers associated with the Florida Keys in the centuries that followed. Marcus Rediker, *Villains of All Nations: Atlantic Pirates in the Golden Age* (Boston: Beacon Press, 2004), 54; Kenneth Kinkor, "Black Men Under the Black Flag," *Bandits at Sea: A Pirate Reader*, ed., C. R. Pennell (New York: New York University Press, 2001), 200; Kevin McCarthy, *Black Florida* (New York: Hippocrene Books, 1995), 144; W. Jeffrey Bolster, *Black Jacks: African American Seamen in the Age of Sail* (Cambridge: Harvard University Press, 1998), 14.

43 Michael Guasco, *Slaves and Englishmen: Human Bondage in the Early Atlantic World* (Philadelphia: University of Pennsylvania Press, 2014), 215.

44 Matthew Restall, *The Black Middle: Africans, Mayas, and Spaniards in Colonial Yucatan* (Stanford, CA: Stanford University Press, 2009), 125.

45 Paul Lokken, "Useful Enemies: Seventeenth-Century Piracy and the Rise of Pardo Militias in Spanish Central America," *Journal of Colonialism and Colonial History* 5, no. 2 (Fall 2004).

46 Hugh Chisholm, ed., *The Encyclopaedia Britannica* 11th Edition 28 (New York: The Encyclopaedia Britannica Company, 1911), 49.

47 Leo Wiener, *Africa and the Discovery of America* (Philadelphia: Innes and Sons, 1922), 158–159.

48 Lolita Gutierrez Brockington, "The African Diaspora in the Eastern Andes: Adaptation, Agency, and Fugitive Action, 1573–1677," *Americas* 52, no. 2 (October 2000): 222–223; Herbert S. Klein and Ben Vinson III, *African Slavery in Latin America and the Caribbean* (New York: Oxford University Press, 2007 [1986]); Nancy E. Van Deuson, *The Souls of Purgatory: The Spiritual Diary of a Seventeenth-Century Afro-Peruvian Mystic, Ursula de Jesús* (Albuquerque: University of New Mexico Press, 2004).

49 Restall, *Black Middle*, 142.

50 Mattos, "'Pretos' and 'Pardos,'" 49.

51 D'Maris Coffman et al., eds., *The Atlantic World* (New York: Routledge, 2015), 338.

52 Herman L. Bennett, *Africans in Colonial Mexico: Absolutism, Christianity, and Afro-Creole Consciousness, 1570–1640* (Bloomington: Indiana University Press, 2003), 1–2.

53 Ibid.

54 Brockington, "African Diaspora in the Eastern Andes," 222–223.

55 Herbert S. Klein and Ben Vinson III, *African Slavery in Latin America and the Caribbean* (New York: Oxford University Press, 2007 [1986]), 173.

56 Sherwin K. Bryant, *Rivers of Gold, Lives of Bondage: Governing Through Slavery in Colonial Quito* (Chapel Hill: University of North Carolina Press, 2014), 127.

57 Irene Aloha Wright, *The Early History of Cuba, 1492–1586* (New York: Macmillan, 1916), 198.

58 Klein and Vinson, *African Slavery in Latin America*, 166.

59 Guasco, *Slaves and Englishmen*, 215.

60 Ira Berlin, *Many Thousands Gone: The First Two Centuries of Slavery in North America* (Cambridge: Harvard University Press, 2000), 27.

61 Herman L. Bennett, *Colonial Blackness: A History of Afro-Mexico* (Bloomington: Indiana University Press, 2009), 162.

62 Camille Pissarro, the renowned Impressionist painter, was born to a French family that was part of a Jewish community on St. Thomas, a Protestant Danish colony that offered a New World refuge for Jews from Catholic Spain, Portugal, and France. Also, Jewish settlers were among the Protestant Dutch in Brazil in the 1620s, but when Portuguese rule was restored—with the aid of Henrique Dias and his regiments—these early Jewish Americans resettled in Dutch New York in 1654.

63 William Hening, *The Statutes at Large* (New York: Bartow, 1823), 267.

64 Winthrop Jordan, *White Over Black: American Attitudes Towards to the Negro, 1550–1812* (Chapel Hill: University of North Carolina Press, 1968), 139.

65 Kathleen Brown, *Good Wives, Nasty Wenches, and Anxious Patriarchs: Gender, Race, and Power in Colonial Virginia* (Chapel Hill: University of North Carolina Press, 1996), 202.

66 Jordan, *White Over Black*, 140.

67 C. Vann Woodward, ed., *Mary Chesnut's Civil War* (New Haven, CT: Yale University Press, 1981), 29.

68 Paul Heinegg, *Free African Americans of North Carolina, Virginia, and South Carolina, From the Colonial Period to about 1820, Volume I* (Baltimore, MD: Clearfield, 2005), 3.

69 Taunya Lovell Banks, "Dangerous Woman: Elizabeth Key's Freedom Suit—Subjecthood and Racialized Identity in Seventeenth Century Colonial Virginia," *Akron Law Review* (March 23, 2009): 836.

70 Ancestry.com's findings were based on genealogical records and DNA analysis, reviewed by a former president of the U.S. Board for the Certification of Genealogists, and reported in numerous major news outlets (CBS, ABC, *New York Times*, *LA Times*, and *USA Today*.)

71 Anastasia Harman, Natalie D. Cottrill, Paul C. Reed, and Joseph Shumway, "Documenting President Barack Obama's Maternal African-American Ancestry: Tracing His Mother's Bunch Ancestry to the First Slave in America," *Ancestry.com* (July 15, 2012): 1.

72   Ibid.

73   Ibid.

74   Luther P. Jackson, "Manumission in Certain Virginia Cities," *Journal of Negro History* 15, no. 3 (July 1930): 310.

75   James Hugo Johnson, *Race Relations in Colonial Virginia and Miscegenation in the South* (Amherst: University of Massachusetts Press, 1970), 193.

76   Bennett, *Colonial Blackness*, 162.

77   Berlin, *Many Thousands Gone*, 27.

78   Paul Lokken, "Marriage as Slave Emancipation in Seventeenth Century Guatemala," *Americas* 58, no. 2 (October 2001): 175–200.

79   Alejandro de la Fuente, "Slave Law and Claims-Making in Cuba: The Tannenbaum Debate Revisited," *Law and History Review* (Summer 2004): 43–44; in 1710, a white Nantucket widower, William Gayer, willed a large share of his property to "'Africa, a negro once my servant." Frances Karttunen, *The Other Islanders: The People Who Pulled Nantucket's Oars* (New Bedford, MA: Spinner Publication, Inc., 2005), 71.

80   Elizabeth Shown Mills, "Marie Therese Coincoin," in *Louisiana Women*, eds., Janet Allured and Judith F. Gentry (Athens: University of Georgia Press, 2009). In 1773 George Leile, David George, and Andrew Bryan, all of whom were former slaves, established a congregation (composed largely of enslaved individuals) in Silver Bluff, South Carolina, which became the basis of Savannah, Georgia's First African Baptist Church that was officially recognized in 1788. Free and enslaved African Americans established Petersburg, Virginia's First Baptist Church in 1774. In the late 1770s, an enslaved preacher named Gowen Pamphlet ministered to an African American population around Williamsburg, Virginia, that had grown to five hundred congregants when it was officially recognized in 1793.

81   Júnia Ferreira Furtado, *Chica da Silva: A Brazilian Slave of the Eighteenth Century* (New York: Cambridge University Press, 2009).

82   Peter Wood, *Strange New Land: Africans in Colonial America* (New York: Oxford University Press, 2003 [1996]), 12.

❧ TIMELINE ❧

1715   South Carolina, Yamasee War (Afro-Americans on both sides)

1733   St. John Revolt in the Caribbean (international Afro-Americans on both sides)

1734   Anton Wilhelm Amo earns doctorate from Germany's University of Wittenberg

1738   Fort Mosé founded in Spanish Florida

1739   Stono Revolt in South Carolina (Afro-Americans serve on both sides)

1739   Treaty of Jamaica's First Maroon War, Britain recognizes maroon rights/property

1756   Seven Years' War begins (many Afro-Americans serve British against France)

1760   Tacky's War in Jamaica (Afro-Americans serve on both sides)

1760   Briton Hammon publishes autobiography in U.S.

1768   Afro-Haitian Jean Point du Sable becomes first Chicago settler

1768   Wentworth Cheswell of New Hampshire, first African American elected to office

1770   Crispus Attucks becomes first martyr for U.S. independence in Boston Massacre

1772   Somerset's legal victory in England challenges the legitimacy of slavery

1773   African Americans petition Massachusetts to end slavery, extend rights

1775   Peter Salem, Prince Easterbrooks, fight in the Battles of Lexington, Concord

1775   Dunmore Proclamation (tens of thousands fight for freedom as Loyalists)

1775   Prince Hall, et al., initiated into Freemasonry, dedicated to Enlightenment ideals

1780   Elizabeth Freeman sues against slavery in Massachusetts causing its demise

1781   James Armistead aids Yorktown victory and establishment of the United States

1781   Los Angeles founded (in Spanish territory); half its settlers are of African-descent

1783   Birchtown founded in Canada, largest free black settlement in North America

1787   African Americans petition Massachusetts legislature for equal school facilities

1787   New York City's African Free School is founded

1787   Absalom Jones and Richard Allen found the Free African Society in Philadelphia

1789   Olaudah Equiano publishes politically influential autobiography

1790   Treaty of New York aims to reduce free black population in Florida

1791   Haitian Revolution initiates formation of the first free republic in the Americas

1791   Benjamin Banneker surveys Washington, D.C., helps to site U.S. capital

1792   Julien Raimond prompts Nat. Assembly to raise black units for French Revolution

1794   Jean-Baptiste Belley instigates vote ending slavery in French colonies

1795   Julien Fédon leads uprising on Grenada; Joseph Chatoyer on St. Vincent

1799   Absalom Jones, James Forten, et al., petition Congress re Fugitive Slave Act

4

Eighteenth-Century
Afro-American Revolutionaries

Most eighteenth-century Americans arrived in the New World as slaves. By 1750, just more than six and a half million Old World people had come to the Americas since 1492, and four and a half million of them were enslaved.[1] The 1700s were the apex of the Atlantic plantation system; the century accounted for over half of the involuntary migrations during the entire Atlantic slaving enterprise. Initially, American slavery revolved around small-scale domestic, agricultural, and artisanal work. That pattern continued in various places (e.g., New England, Central America). However, after about 1650, the plantation system based on the mass production of consumer items like sugar, coffee, and tobacco took hold throughout much of the Americas—the Chesapeake, the Caribbean, and Brazil.

Among the novel elements of the New World plantation system was that it came to rely on increasingly severe and systematic curtailment of the rights of people of African descent, both enslaved and free. Unlike traditional slavery, which was generally based on domestic or tribute labor, the plantation system was unique in its capitalistic aims and scale: mass production for mass consumption to yield the highest profit. The economics of the plantation system fundamentally shaped political and industrial development in the West and helped to usher in modern capitalism and nation-states. This new economy demanded a massive labor force, resulting in ever-larger enslaved African populations that in many New World scenarios outnumbered Europeans—on slave ships, on individual plantations, in particular regions, and in colonies at large. Dwarfed demographically, slave traders, owners, and overseers sought control through the use of deprivation and torture. In the sugar industry, which produced staggering, unprecedented profits, it could be more advantageous to destroy workers and replace them than to ensure their survival.[2]

The unprecedented brutality of the New World plantation regimes coupled with the large black populations that sustained them motivated planters and their agents to suppress black agency at all costs. Still, enslaved people continued to pursue their rights and resist these regimes in a variety of ways. In addition to individual strategies of resistance, they collectively took up arms to both defend and attack colonial powers as soldiers, sailors, rebels, pirates, and maroons. Free people of color continued to populate virtually all of the Americas, and in areas with black majorities such as the Caribbean, coastal areas in Latin America, and North American regions like South Carolina, Virginia, Maryland, and Louisiana, free colored populations grew even faster. Despite the rise of plantation economies and their violent exploitation and suppression of millions of Afro-Americans, sheer demographics as well as particular circumstances allowed many people of color to live independently. Free people of African descent countermanded the ideological and practical underpinnings of race-based slavery as they contributed to the development of the Americas and the eventual triumph of freedom as military leaders, professionals, intellectuals, missionaries, educators, artisans, and activists.

In addition to free people of color, enslaved Americans profoundly shaped the Age of Revolution and the development of freedom in the Americas in fundamental ways. The American, French, Haitian, and Latin American revolutions were fueled by the restiveness and aspirations of the new elite and emergent bourgeoisie who had grown prosperous from the economics of slavery—even if they did not directly own slaves. Moreover, the continual unrest of enslaved and self-liberated Americans themselves propelled the Age of Revolution as they defied and destabilized colonial regimes. In the first half of the eighteenth century, slave rebellions and other forms of protest persistently challenged the colonial state. As white colonists deliberated how to protect their interests, the specter and reality of revolutionary slaves demanding liberty were omnipresent. By the 1790s the Caribbean was experiencing roughly four rebellions led by black revolutionaries every year. By the close of the century, organized

Afro-American bids for freedom had emerged from virtually every corner of the Americas.

Slaves and former slaves initiated movements for liberty throughout the colonial period, but the 1700s saw significant and continual uprisings that caused many authorities to question the viability of slavery (See Appendix). South Carolina's Stono Rebellion and Tacky's War in Jamaica along with protracted maroon wars in Jamaica and Suriname threatened to undermine colonial stability as they resonated with Afro-Americans around the Atlantic who saw liberty as their natural right. These early democratic insurgencies for freedom led by enslaved and free people of color presaged widespread bids for freedom by both black and white Americans at the end of the eighteenth century and the start of the nineteenth.

Early Eighteenth-Century Declarations of Independence

South Carolina

By 1708 people of African descent were a majority in North America's Carolina colony. Slave revolts occurred there in 1711 and again in 1714; nonetheless, Carolina repeatedly relied on enslaved black militiamen to defend the colony against Native Americans. (Slaves were legally permitted to serve in the South Carolina militia until 1740, a year after the colony codified the practice of granting freedom to those who captured or killed enemy combatants.) In 1715, during a series of attacks by a Native American federation that came to be known as the Yamasee War, South Carolina officials raised a militia composed of 400 black men (and 600 whites) to defend the colony. Without these African American soldiers, "the Carolina whites would have been 'hard pressed' to win."[3]

However, while almost half of the colonial militia during the Yamasee War was comprised of enslaved black men who presumably fought to defend the English colony and perhaps win their own freedom, some slaves immediately liberated themselves during the conflict and allied with the Yamasee contingent. After the war, several of the fugitive slaves and Native allies found sanctuary in Spanish Florida where they were recognized as free subjects of the Spanish king. One of these fugitives and former combatants,

West African-born Francisco Menendez, became the captain of St. Augustine's black militia and in 1738 helped to found the free black town Gracia Real de Santa Teresa de Mosé.[4]

While many enslaved Carolinians continued to seek liberty in Spanish Florida, some free people of color in Carolina enjoyed rights in the early 1700s. In 1701 free black men voted in the Carolina General Assembly election. Free black men could bear arms and serve in the colonial militia. In 1731, a member of the South Carolina Commons House of Assembly "announced that several free colored men with their white wives had immigrated from Virginia." After meeting with these prosperous families, Governor Robert Johnson concluded, "they are not Negroes nor slaves but Free people."[5] In 1734, a successful white planter named Joseph Pendarvis manumitted an enslaved woman named Parthea and their children, who went on to become successful (slave-owning) planters themselves. In 1763, white residents in several counties petitioned to repeal a discriminatory tax on mixed-race couples initiated in 1723, stating that the people of color subject to the fine "contribute towards the discharge of every public Duty injoined them by Law."[6]

In addition to underscoring the fact of mixed-race American families, these examples illustrate that the lives of individual Afro-Americans in colonial Carolina, as in the rest of the hemisphere, could follow varying trajectories. Some men and women of African descent participated in and contributed to colonial American societies as free subjects. Highly skilled slaves in urban centers like Charleston were likely to experience relative degrees of autonomy. However, in the main, as the eighteenth century unfolded and the plantation system peaked, laws increasingly curtailed the rights of free people of color and enslaved persons, particularly in the wake of the Stono Rebellion.

In 1739, near the Stono River outside of Charleston, roughly one hundred enslaved South Carolinians organized an armed insurrection. Some scholars have speculated that these freedom-seekers were inspired by the earlier self-liberation of Francisco Menendez and his collaborators. In any case, Spain's proclamation of freedom was well known among Carolina's enslaved residents and "slave escapes to Florida had become common by the time of the [Stono] revolt."[7] Presaging the rallying cry of the American Revolution, the Stono revolutionaries chanted "liberty" as they rallied around an Angolan-born organizer named Jemmy.[8] According to a 1930s WPA interview with one of his descendants, another organizer called Cato was willing to give his life for the right of liberty. While the insurgency was quelled by the superior force of the colonial militia—which included black soldiers—some rebels were never recovered, and their call for freedom continued to reverberate up and down the Atlantic coast both by word of mouth and in print. South Carolina's official 1741 report of the rebellion described the enslaved insurgents as fighting for "liberty and life," and the event was widely reported in newspapers throughout the colonies, including the *Boston Gazette*. "Enslaved people throughout the New World rejected bondage and either ran away to, or fought for, liberty. Sometimes, as at Stono, they did both at once."[9]

Jamaica

In Jamaica, powerful maroon communities preceded English settlement in the mid-1600s. In 1739, unable to defeat the resilient maroon forces after many decades of combat, the English negotiated with their opponents to end Jamaica's First Maroon War and offered a treaty acknowledging the sovereignty of five maroons towns. The British government granted maroons legal status, land, and a quasi-autonomous state in exchange for their aid in tracking and returning fugitive slaves. While maroons were officially required to return fugitive slaves, the maroons were fugitive slaves. Thus, even when they complied with the colonial requirement, they were themselves living advertisements for successful slave resistance and their settlements were de facto alternatives to slavery.

Jamaica's maroons "were not a small rebel community [but rather a] complex polity. . . . a dominating factor in Jamaican politics and development."[10] These Afro-Jamaicans threatened to undermine the stability of the colonial state and the viability of slavery, not only in Jamaica but also in the minds of anxious planters in other parts of the Americas. In 1736, William Byrd II, the founder of Richmond, Virginia, wrote to John Percival, the president of the Georgia Board of Trustees, recommending the end of slave imports to the colonies, "lest they prove as troublesome and dangerous everywhere, as they have been lately in Jamaica."[11] (Around the same time, in 1735, a massive uprising in Cordoba, Mexico, prompted planters to complain that maroons were "pouring their damned ideas about liberty" into the slave quarters, and after two more rebellions in 1741 and 1749, Afro-Mexican maroons were petitioning for their rights in 1762.)[12] Jamaica's maroons directly impacted Dutch policy in Suriname. In the 1760s, through two separate treaties explicitly modeled on Jamaica's First Maroon Treaty, colonial authorities offered conditional sovereignty and tribute to the unvanquished maroon societies who were disrupting Suriname.[13]

The restiveness of Jamaicans who remained in bondage was coordinated into a 1742 revolt which maroon forces helped to suppress; in 1760, Jamaican maroons were called upon to quell an even larger rebellion: Tacky's War, in which masses of enslaved Afro-Jamaicans took up arms to liberate themselves. According to an eighteenth-century English observer, for the slave rebels "a principal inducement was the happy circumstance of the Marons [sic]; who . . . had acquired very comfortable settlements, and a life of freedom . . . by dint of their prowess."[14] The maroon militias that opposed the slave rebels were motived by pragmatism: "Not only were the established maroons concerned lest new groups challenge their hard-won lands and privileges, but they were never more secure or well rewarded than when there was a conflict between planters and their slaves."[15]

The intense guerrilla war pitted slave soldiers, maroon warriors, and British militia against "Tacky and his followers, who might eventually have numbered 30,000."[16] While Tacky was killed two months into the revolt, the rebellion was sustained for six months. Among the largest organized insurrections for freedom in the Americas to that date, the event changed currents of public and political opinion regarding the sustainability of slavery. "By taking up arms, the Afro-Jamaican rebels of 1760 and 1831 [see Chapter Five] took active measures to stake a claim to the rights of British subjects."[17] Tacky's War catalyzed a shift in mainstream public discourse where the amelioration of slavery in the British Empire and the aims of enslaved freedom seekers became sympathetic in the British press. "In terms of shock to the imperial system, only the American Revolution surpassed Tacky's Revolt."[18]

Black people throughout the Americas were fierce advocates of independence well before Thomas Paine and Thomas Jefferson penned their famous documents. Even as they aligned with different groups, the Afro-Americans who fought on both sides of the Yamasee War, the Stono Rebellion, and Tacky's War sought liberty. For the Carolina slaves who made it to Spanish Florida, the Jamaican maroons who signed treaties with the British, and the Afro-Americans who served in the colonial militias that opposed the rebels and rewarded loyalty, all of their choices had a potential for increased rights and independence.

St. John

Among the uprisings that presaged the categorical triumph of Haiti's slave revolution, one of the most challenging bids for independence took place on St. John. In 1733, some 150 African men and women wrested control of the island (now part of the U.S. Virgin Islands) and held it for six months against Danish, Dutch, English, and French forces. The leaders of the insurrection were Ghanaian-born individuals (several of whom were recognized as royals), recent arrivals who had liberated themselves from St. John's plantations and joined maroon communities in the mountains of the Danish colony. The entrenched maroons used drums to coordinate an armed mission for freedom that began with rebel slaves taking control of St. John's military fort and initiating an island-wide event with the signal of cannon fire.

Like the later American revolutionaries George Washington and Thomas Jefferson, the St. John rebels sought not to overturn the island's plantation system but to govern it. Had they succeeded in maintaining their freedom and been able to operate the plantations, they would have likely sought the coerced labor of other (perhaps non-royal, non-Ghanaian) people. This may in part explain why several enslaved American-born Afro-Americans alerted, protected, and even fought alongside their owners. While several slaves escaped with their owners to safety on St. Thomas, a contingent of about forty armed men, roughly half of whom were slaves, hunkered down on a single plantation as a base of resistance against the rebels. A Dutch planter from neighboring St. Thomas led a contingent of men, including armed slaves, to resist the rebels as well.

In addition to enslaved combatants, the Danish forces included St. Thomas' Free Negro Corps and its free black captain, Mingo Tamarin. The maroon troops secured ammunition and reinforcements from external sources and defended themselves for half a year against the English, to whom the Danish had appealed for support. Ultimately, the rebels' supplies dwindled, and they were outnumbered and overpowered by French forces from Martinique, which also included a free black corps. Some of the resisters took their own lives in lieu of surrender, famously diving off a cliff, while others were promised pardons but were tortured and executed instead.[19]

The Danish West Indian colonies, which encompassed the neighboring islands of St. Thomas and St. John, were joined by St. Croix in 1733. The Danes bought St. Croix from the French during the St. John revolt, in part to enlist their military support against the rebels. Many planters chose to resettle in St. Croix in the wake of the destruction wrought in St. John. However, slaves in St. Croix threatened rebellion in 1746 and again in 1759 under the leadership of a free man of color named William Davis. In the following century, black residents of St. Croix, enslaved and free, enacted widespread protests and petitions that brought slavery in the Danish West Indies to a definitive end.[20]

The free black population expanded dramatically throughout the Danish West Indies in the 1700s. In the case of Franz Claasen, his free status was a direct result of the St. John Revolt. Colonial records from 1738 offer that a "loyal negro" was given a parcel of land in return for "help during the Rebellion."[21] Based on this and another report from 1733, the St. John Historical Society contends that this individual was Franz Claasen, a slave who reported to the maroon forces as a ruse that he had already killed his owners, thus deflecting harm to them. Because of Claasen's intervention, the family was able to escape; ultimately the St. John plantation was deeded to Claasan. Wittingly or not, he gained freedom, security, and property as the result of his actions against the rebel cause. As in many uprisings for freedom in the Americas, the enslaved

In the eighteenth century, black missionary scholars endeavored to promote self-realization through education and Christianity. In St. Thomas, a freedwoman named Rebecca (above right) was witness to the bloody reprisals against the Ghanaian-

led movement for independence in St. John. In the 1730s, on the cusp of the evangelical movement known as the Great Awakening in British North America, Rebecca worked to make Christian education available to enslaved individuals throughout the Virgin Islands. In the 1740s, she accompanied Moravian missionaries to Germany, where she met her husband (above left) and was ordained as a deaconess. Christian Protten was born in Ghana to a West African royal and a Danish soldier; he was baptized in Denmark with the king, Frederick I, as his patron and godfather. The Prottens returned to the West Indies briefly and eventually settled to teach in Christiansborg, West Africa. Another Ghanaian, Anton Wilhelm Amo, grew up in the household of a German duke and, in 1734, earned a doctorate from Germany's University of Wittenberg. While he became a well-known philosopher, professor, and author in Germany, Amo was also an instructor of medicine and law (he wrote a dissertation on the "The Rights of Moors in Europe"). Whereas the Prottens' scholarship and visions of liberty were embedded in evangelical Christianity, Amo endeavored to resist clerical restrictions on academia and championed social and intellectual freedoms. Like Protten, Amo ultimately returned to Ghana. The Ghanaian, Jacobus Capitein, enrolled in the Netherlands' University of Leiden in 1737 and became one of the first Africans ordained as a minister in the Dutch Reformed Church. Capitein ultimately returned to Ghana as a missionary as well.

informants were granted freedom while the freedom-seeking rebels were punished with torture and death.

The 1733 St. John Revolt shows how some rebels who betrayed their colleagues for their own survival may have "recycled themselves" as veterans to organize additional resistance efforts. Will, a St. John rebel who escaped capture by Danish forces, perhaps by turning evidence, resurfaced in records during the Antigua revolt in 1736, where he was spared in return for testifying against co-conspirators. Will was ultimately executed for his leadership role in the 1741 conspiracy of New York. While the participation of the same individual in the resistance movements of St. John, Antigua, and New York was probably unusual, Will's case underscores the wider fact that throughout the Americas "rebellions fed upon one another—news of one inspired others hundreds of miles away."[22]

The free black militia members, black officers, and enslaved soldiers pressed into service to quell the rebellion on St. John point to yet another key avenue for freedom and social mobility in the Americas. As has been described, the participation of black soldiers in colonial forces was widespread. Enslaved soldiers were often granted freedom because of their service, while free black soldiers regularly enjoyed civic benefits and opportunities for advancement.

The St. John Revolt encapsulates the complex and contradictory trajectories along which Afro-Americans charted courses to liberty. African-born slaves created an independent maroon community that challenged the colonial state by coordinating armed rebel slaves ready to give their lives for freedom. Unlike many slave uprisings, but like many maroon revolts, colonial forces could not promptly overwhelm their opponents by force, and the rebels held the island for many months. Some of the royal-born leaders of the insurrection may have been, like the leaders of the American Revolution, seeking to control the slavocracy rather than dismantle it. A royal would have been steeped in the ideology of natural hierarchy that had traditionally justified slavery. The American-born Afro-Creoles who opposed them, on the other hand, would have grown up amid the novel circumstances and ideologies of race being cultivated in the Americas. While these racial ideologies were often designed to get around Enlightenment assertions of natural rights and nascent notions of republican egalitarianism, they engaged them nonetheless.

Florida

Maroons were pervasive throughout the American South and integral to its history.[23] In the Great Dismal Swamp between Virginia and North Carolina, fugitive slaves established a "community of blacks, who . . . won their freedom and established themselves securely" for about two hundred years starting in 1680.[24] Despite efforts spearheaded by George Washington to drain the swamp of its water and presumably its residents, self-liberated slaves, Native peoples, and free African Americans generated informal economies and autonomous communities in the Great Dismal Swamp that developed over generations. Records abound for maroons living independently in South Carolina and Louisiana. However, Florida's were the most politically potent maroon communities in the United States. While fugitive slaves from Ayllon's failed 1526 Georgia settlement initiated the first maroon community in the U.S., in the following centuries, fugitive slaves from the Carolinas and Georgia established enduring and powerful maroon communities in Florida.

Francisco Menendez and his cohorts who fled servitude in Carolina for freedom in Florida in 1715 were not the first to do so. "Long before Florida was a U.S. state, it was home to diverse freedom seekers who found refuge from slavery, established thriving communities, and prospered on Florida's frontier."[25] Florida's indigenous population had gone into epidemiological decline with the arrival of the Spanish explorers and their African expeditionaries in the 1500s. In 1689, slaves from South Carolina sought freedom in Spanish Florida; in 1693, the Spanish Crown officially sanctioned the fugitives' legal freedom; and by 1700, Spain was endeavoring to populate the peninsula by offering freedom, property, and protection to Native Americans and Africans from English territories to the north.

Enslaved men and women who made their way from the Carolina (and later the Georgia) colonies and embraced Catholicism were given the rights and privileges of Spanish subjects as well as weapons to defend those rights. Fugitive slaves made St. Augustine into a sanctuary and in 1738 the Spanish governor chartered nearby Fort Mosé as the first sanctioned free black settlement in what would become the United States. When Spain traded Florida to the British in 1763, many of Florida's residents, including several black militia members and their families, evacuated to Havana.

However, not all of the African Americans who sought freedom in Florida served in the Spanish militia and lived in Spanish settlements. Some established communities alongside Creek Indians who had migrated to Florida. The Creeks and other Native peoples who came to Florida starting around 1700 from what is today Alabama and Georgia became known as the Seminoles, a transmutation of the Spanish term for maroon: *cimmaron*. During England's brief control of Florida (1763–1783), British agents gifted slaves to Seminole leaders in the hopes of engaging their allegiance. Seminoles may also have purchased slaves, though many African Americans sought out the Seminole communities voluntarily. In any case, "the distinction between purchased slaves and runaways—if it ever existed—blurred and essentially vanished. . . . [yielding among Native people and African-descended people] a primitive democratic feudalism, with basically no personal inequality."[26]

Native Americans traditionally considered prisoners of war as legitimate slaves who were eligible for incorporation into the community; with the arrival of the British, some tribes became involved in an indigenous slave trade. However, the Seminoles of Florida appear to have regarded their African American slaves as vassals and allies (as U.S. General Edmund Gaines—for whom Gainesville, Florida, is named—once described them). Black Seminole communities were largely independent of Native Seminole communities; they maintained their own lands and weapons and paid tribute in the form of agricultural surplus and military service.

With the outbreak of the American Revolution, many enslaved African Americans escaped to Florida, some joining established Black Seminole communities and others forming additional, separate maroon communities. The presence of a large population of free and armed African Americans in Florida prompted George Washington to engineer the new United States' first treaty, the 1790 Treaty of New York; Article III nominally required Creeks and Seminoles in Florida to return fugitive slaves. This spoke to the significance of Florida's maroons but did little to reduce their independence.

In fact, Black Seminole and maroon populations increased substantially during the nineteenth century and were sources for formidable soldiers during the War of 1812, the Seminole Wars (1817, 1835, 1855), and as Buffalo Soldiers in the 1880s.

THE AMERICAN REVOLUTION

While some eighteenth-century African Americans sought freedom in Florida, especially during the upheaval of the American Revolution, many thousands of African Americans, free and enslaved, were crucial participants in and witnesses to virtually every aspect of the American war for independence. Black men and women recognized the possibilities for their freedom that inhered in the conflict between England and the American colonies as well as the contradictions between the revolution's rhetoric and its aims. Americans of African descent capitalized on the possibilities, pursuing and advancing freedom as Patriots and Loyalists, soldiers and spies, petitioners and litigants, martyrs and migrants.

In 1770, Crispus Attucks, as the first American killed in the Boston Massacre, became the original martyr of the American Revolution. In the trial of the British soldiers who had opened fire on a group of Boston sailors, the future U.S. president John Adams asserted that Attucks led a defiant contingent of "saucy boys, Negroes, and mulattoes, Irish Teagues, and outlandish Jack-Tars."[27] Attucks, the son of an African father and a Native American mother, had liberated himself from slavery and joined the multiracial ranks of northeastern mariners. While some scholars contend that Attucks "risked life and limb not for an ideology but in the cause of sailors' and workingmens' rights,"[28] the context of his protest and his death made him a crucial symbol of Patriot sacrifice. As the African American historian George Washington Williams wrote in 1883, "Significant indeed that a Negro was the first to open the hostilities between the colonies and Great Britain, —the first to pour out his blood as a precious libation on the altar of a people's rights."[29] In 1772, Aaron, a Rhode Islander described as mulatto, helped to burn the British customs ship during the infamous *Gaspee* Affair that further heightened tensions between American colonists and British officials.[30]

James Somerset was another African American and former slave who instigated the American Revolution. Insisting on his freedom in a London court in 1772, his case became a watershed that signaled the beginning of the legal unraveling of Atlantic slavery. Somerset's victory had a broad impact on the American colonies and prompted Southern planters to see an urgent need for American independence from Britain.

The outcome of Somerset's case "represented the clear emergence of an idea of freedom in English law."[31] Kidnapped from West Africa as a child in 1749 and sold as a slave in Norfolk, Virginia, Somerset became an enslaved personal servant to James Stewart, a Boston customs official. Stewart and Somerset resettled in England, where Somerset ran away. Stewart arranged for slave-catchers to recapture Somerset and imprison him on a ship bound for the Caribbean. With the support of British anti-slavery advocates, Somerset sued for his freedom in court.

Numerous slaves had won their freedom in the French courts and Somerset's was not the first such instance in England.[32] In previous cases, judges were able to persuade slave owners to free the litigants and thus avoided ruling on the larger issue of the legality of slavery in the metropole. But when Somerset's owner refused to manumit him, Chief Justice Lord Mansfield was forced to rule on the legality of the institution. Mansfield decided that since England did not have positive law to enforce slavery, slavery was therefore not legal.

Somerset's victory had an enormous impact on both sides of the Atlantic. Some judges and journalists interpreted the ruling to mean that Mansfield had liberated England's 14,000 enslaved residents and that anyone who entered the country was entitled to natural rights, while others viewed the ruling more narrowly. Whatever Mansfield's intent, still debated by historians, his determination that slavery was "odious" and that England lacked positive law to support it, meant that both pro- and anti-slavery contemporaries recognized the Somerset decision as a powerful moral and legal contestation of slavery, especially in British North America where the case was widely publicized and discussed. As one journalist put it, the "late decision with regard to Somerset . . . will occasion greater ferment in America . . . than the Stamp Act," because, as another newspaper declared, its "consequences [could be] detrimental to those Gentlemen whose estates chiefly consist in Slaves."[33]

Slave owners in British colonies like Virginia and South Carolina saw the Somerset decision as a serious threat to the institution of slavery and, therefore, an impetus to break away from British control. The case had different implications for Britain's Caribbean colonies, observed historian Douglas Egerton, where "sugar planters . . . surrounded by black majorities on each island, fretted about the dangers of life without British military might."[34] But in British North America, where as late as 1775 only a third of American colonists supported independence, the fallout from Somerset's case weighed on southern planters and their decision to ally with the northern colonies in the First Continental Congress in 1774. In the wake of Somerset's and other Atlantic bids for freedom that were stoking abolitionism in England, many American planters sought total independence as a means to protect slavery.[35]

While Somerset's victory encouraged some colonists to perceive an urgent need to break with Britain, enslaved Americans and abolitionists were inspired by the ruling. Night watches were established in Williamsburg, Virginia, to quell "slave restiveness" that followed the news of the case. In 1773, the *Virginia Gazette* posted a notice for fugitive slaves Amy and Bacchus. The aggrieved author who claimed to be their owner stated, "I have some Reason to believe that they will endeavor to get . . . to Britain, where they imagine they will be free (a Notion now too prevalent upon the Negroes. . . .)" In 1774, another notice seeking a self-liberated Afro-Virginian opined, "He will probably . . . attempt to get on Board some Vessel bound for Great Britain, from the Knowledge he has of the late Determination of Somerset's case."[36]

Somerset's case spurred individuals to resist slavery in the northern colonies as well. In 1773, the governor and legislature of Massachusetts were served with the first known petition composed by enslaved African Americans. The petition, arguing for the end of slavery and pointing to the Somerset case as precedent, was published and circulated as a pamphlet shortly thereafter. While the petition did not immediately end slavery, it prompted the legislature to debate the topic. A few months later, a second petition referenced the aforementioned Spanish practice of *coartacion*, again

Phillis Wheatley was the second American woman to publish a book. This engraving of Wheatley by Scipio Morehead, an African American artist in Boston, was included in the frontispiece of Wheatley's 1773 publication, with an inscription to the artist from the author—both of whom were enslaved. Her poems gained international acclaim and fueled abolitionist politics. In a period when slavery's proponents posited African intellectual inferiority as a rationale to defend the institution, Thomas Clarkson seized on the poet's prodigious intellectual gifts to argue in front of the British Parliament, "if [Wheatley] was designed for slavery, *as the [pro-slavery] argument must confess, the greater part of the inhabitants of Britain must lose their claim to freedom."*[37] *Wheatley, who was named for the slave ship* Phillis *that transported her from West Africa at the age of seven (a journey on which many of her fellow captives perished), may have also authored the first known petition by African Americans in English North America. The petition, submitted to the Massachusetts legislature in 1773, called for the end of slavery based on James Somerset's watershed freedom suit in England. Earlier examples of African-descended poets in Western letters include Terrence the African, the second-century Roman poet, and Juan Latino, a professor in sixteenth-century Spain. Lucy Prince Terry authored the earliest known poem by an African American in 1746, "Bars Fight," but while her ballad was widely recited, it was not published until 1855.*

demonstrating a larger Atlantic sensibility. These and a third petition failed to motivate legislators to abolish slavery; however, the legislature did vote to abolish the slave trade. Some scholars believe that Phillis Wheatley assisted in the writing of the petitions.[38]

Wheatley "literally wrote her way to freedom."[39] Her 1773 London-published book, *Poems on Various Subjects, Religious and Moral*, garnered attention on both sides of the Atlantic and engaged eminences including George Washington, Benjamin Franklin, Thomas Paine, Thomas Jefferson, and Voltaire. Wheatley was born in West Africa, grew up enslaved in the home of a white Boston family in the midst of the American Revolution (the Stamp Act riots and the Boston Massacre, both with African American participants, took place down the street from her front door), and was granted her freedom as a young adult.[40] Wheatley's work addressed religious themes as well as some revolutionary ones; however, considering that the support of her owners was instrumental to her education and publication, it may not be surprising that one of her early poems lauds them and that only a few of her poems addressed slavery. Yet, the caliber and reach of Wheatley's work not only prompted her own liberation but also was influential and inspiring for both white and black individuals with democratic affinities. For many, the public display of "genius" by an African vitiated the rationalizations of slavery buttressed with a newly emerging discourse of biological white supremacy.[41]

Like Wheatley, Jupiter Hammon was an enslaved American who engaged in the politics of the revolutionary period. In 1761, the year that Wheatley survived the Middle Passage on the ship for which she was named, Jupiter Hammon became the first African American to publish a poem. In 1784, he delivered an address before the New York African Society with the message that "bondage and all human injustices were defenseless before God."[42] Jupiter Hammon's widely-circulated address helped to inspire the formation of similar black organizations in Philadelphia, Boston, and Newport in the 1780s and 1790s.

No relation to Jupiter Hammon, Briton Hammon published his autobiography in 1760, initiating a long tradition of slave narrative and prose. Two decades earlier, Britton Hammon's owner in Massachusetts had granted him permission to crew on a ship bound for Jamaica. Hammon's book re-counted the ship's wreck, his captivity among Native Americans in Florida, imprisonment in Cuba, and, ultimately, his experience in the Royal Navy during the Seven Years' War. Hammon, who served the British forces for several years before being wounded and honorably discharged, was but one of several African Americans who served in the Seven Years' War.

The Seven Years' War—known on the U.S. front as the French and Indian War—was a "conflict that reshaped the map of the Americas and rendered the [American] Revolution inevitable."[43] The British victory included enor-mous territorial gains in North America; however, tensions mounted over frontier policy and who should bear the brunt of the cost of the war in its wake. Some black Americans who served in the French and Indian War—for example, Barzillai Lew, Garshom Prince, and David Lamson—went on to serve in the American Revolution, a conflict that called many thousands of African Americans to military service.[44]

"Proportionate to their number, African American males—and some females—were more likely to join the fray [of the American Revolution] than white Americans."[45] Roughly 5,000 African Americans served the Patriots as soldiers and sailors. Free black men were enlisted early on and enslaved individuals followed. Guyana-born Cuffee Wells, for example, was the slave of an apothecary; his service at the Danbury hospital and at Valley Forge as a surgeon's assistant and pharmacist earned him the moniker "Dr. Cuffee" and his freedom.[46] Black soldiers fought in the battles of Lexington, Concord, and Trenton, among others, and were present at Valley Forge. Nearly 150 African American Patriots fought at Bunker Hill. Most black soldiers served in integrated units; however, the Bucks of America was one of four all-black military companies, with black leaders, celebrated for patriotic service. At the end of the war, Massachusetts Governor John Hancock presented a silk flag bearing the Bucks of America emblem "as a tribute to their courage and devotion in the cause of American Liberty."[47]

Wentworth Cheswell was a Revolutionary War hero who served the cause of American democracy throughout his life. Cheswell's grandfather Richard, a former slave, purchased property in New Hampshire in 1717. Cheswell's father Hopestill was a successful carpenter and substantial property owner (who built the home of another Revolutionary War hero: John Paul Jones). Hopestill sent his son to study at the Dummer Academy, a refined institution to which few Americans, regardless of ancestry, would have had access during the colonial period. In 1768, Wentworth Cheswell, by then a large property holder in his own right, was elected town constable, making him the first known African American elected to office in what would become the United States.

As a dispatch rider and member of the Committee for Public Safety, Cheswell, like Paul Revere, made an all-night ride to warn of the impending British invasion in 1775. The following year, Cheswell, along with African American George Blanchard, signed New Hampshire's Association Test, officially pledging his support of the Patriot cause. In 1777, Cheswell joined the Patriot military as a private and served in the Saratoga campaign, the first major Patriot victory of the war.

After the Revolution, Cheswell enjoyed a successful public career in Newmarket, New Hampshire, until his death in 1817. He was elected to numerous posts, including Justice of the Peace. In addition to his service as an elected official, Cheswell was the first historian of Newmarket and established the town's first library. In a Congressional debate over the Missouri Compromise in 1820, Cheswell's contributions to American civic life were lauded posthumously on a national stage. The senator from New Hampshire invoked the late Cheswell's achievements when he spoke in opposition to proposed legislation that would deny mulattos state citizenship. Despite their patrimony in slavery, many of Cheswell's descendants were regarded as white Americans.[48]

Several other Revolutionary War veterans were the sons of African Americans of some renown. The brothers Caesar and Festus Prince enlisted in the Continental Army. Their mother, Lucy Terry Prince, had been kidnapped in Africa, enslaved in Massachusetts, and liberated when her prosperous free black husband (a veteran of the French and Indian War) purchased her liberty. Writing about a 1746 Indian raid of Deerfield, Lucy Terry Prince is now recognized as the author of the earliest known poem by an African American in North America, "Bars Fight." (While "Bars Fight" became widely known and recited as a ballad, it was not published until

1855, leaving the aforementioned Jupiter Hammon as the first published African American poet in 1761.)

Lucy Terry Prince also used her exceptional oratory to defend the rights of her family. In one instance, she appealed to Vermont's governor for protection from a threat of expropriation from white neighbors; in another she argued before the trustees of Williams College regarding the admission of her son. She successfully argued to protect her family's property in the state supreme court against the future chief justice of Vermont. While scholar Gretchen Gerzina was unable to find documentary evidence to confirm the legend that the Honorable Samuel Chase had declared that Lucy Terry Prince "made a better argument than he had heard from any lawyer of the bar of Vermont,"[49] her findings supporting Prince's remarkable ingenuity and resilience inspired her conclusion that "the Princes and their children are at the heart of what it means to be an American."[50]

Like Prince's sons, Cuff Smith was a free young man of color who enlisted in the Continental Army. His father, Venture Smith, had been taken prisoner in West Africa, was enslaved in Massachusetts, and after many years purchased his own liberty. As a freeman, Venture Smith worked tirelessly as a farmer and businessman to purchase his two sons, his daughter, and his pregnant wife, rendering his entire family free by 1775. In 1798, when Venture Smith's autobiography was recorded and printed, the author of the preface compared Smith to "a Franklin or a Washington."[51]

In 1777, Agrippa Hull, a Massachusetts freeborn man of African descent, enlisted in the Continental Army. He served for over six years, earning a badge of honor. However, his contributions to history extended beyond his wartime service. "Hull's influence on shaping the abolitionist thought of Tadeuz Kosciuszko, a Polish military engineer for whom he served as an orderly for the last fifty months of the war, is the hidden importance of the young black patriot."[52] Hull's service inspired the great Polish patriot to instruct Thomas Jefferson to use Kosciuszko's estate to free and educate Jefferson's slaves upon Kosciuszko's death—a promise which Jefferson did not fulfill. After the war, Hull received a veteran's pension signed by George Washington and returned to Stockbridge. Hull's neighbor and friend in Stockbridge was an enslaved widow known as "Mum Bett." Taking the name Elizabeth Freeman, Bett's earnings as a midwife and nurse allowed her to purchase about twenty acres in Stockbridge, making her one of the few women of that era to pay taxes.

In 1780, Elizabeth Freeman filed the first freedom suit to test Massachusetts' newly established constitution. The Massachusetts legislature had never passed a law outlawing slavery but the Bill of Rights of the Constitution of Massachusetts declared all men free and equal. "Freeman used this language to challenge the constitutionality of slavery in Massachusetts; her struggle remains one of the great attempts to put the ideals of inalienable rights into practice."[53] *Brom and Bett v. Ashley* not only won Freeman her freedom but also led to the abolition of slavery in the state when it was cited as precedent for another freedom suit filed in 1783 by Quock Walker.

During the American Revolution, Freeman's husband "had fallen on a Massachusetts battlefield [and made a] blood sacrifice for the emerging nation."[54] Thousands of African Americans risked their lives for American freedom during the war. The 1st Rhode Island Regiment was a majority black force established by former slaves in 1778. These soldiers assisted in the Patriot victory at Yorktown in 1783. Salem Poor fought so bravely at the Battle of Bunker Hill that fourteen officers recommended him for commendation.[55] His commanders wrote that he "behaved like an experienced officer as well as an excellent soldier," and Poor received commendation as "a brave and gallant soldier."[56] Peter Salem was another African American soldier at Bunker Hill who served throughout the war and was best known for felling a British general. Nero Hawley was awarded "extraordinary pay" in 1778 and was among the many black soldiers at Valley Forge. Among them, Oliver Cromwell, who "marched with troops on the historic Christmas crossing of the Delaware" and fought in the battles of Trenton, Princeton, Brandywine, Monmouth, and Yorktown, ultimately received a badge of merit and an honorable discharge signed by George Washington.[57]

Lemuel Haynes enlisted as a militiaman in 1774 at twenty-one years of age. Haynes's father was born in Connecticut "of unmingled African extraction" while his mother was "a white woman of respectable ancestry in New England."[58] Haynes served in combat in Lexington and Boston as well as with Ethan Allen's Green Mountain Boys in Ticonderoga. After his service, Haynes authored an ode to freedom in a ballad-poem titled *The Battle of Lexington*. Following his ordination as a minister in 1785, Haynes's numerous sermons and treatises on freedom and citizenship captured the attention not only of his many congregants but also of colleges like Yale, whose president invited Haynes to speak, and Middlebury, which conferred on Haynes an honorary master's degree. The author of political discourses like *The Nature and Importance of True Republicanism*, Haynes was lauded posthumously in a biography by a white colleague as a "sanctified genius."[59]

During the American Revolution, the Patriot navy recruited free and enslaved African Americans from the start, "partly out of desperation for seamen of any color, and partly because many blacks were already experienced sailors, having served in British and state navies, as well as on merchant vessels in the North and the South."[60] Black sailors Cato Carlisle, Scipio Africanus, and Paul Jones served valiantly under the American Revolution's most famous commander: the founder of the American navy, John Paul Jones.[61] The memoirs of U.S. Navy Commodore James Barron, who served as a captain in the Virginia navy during the war, applauded the patriotism of several black seamen, including "the noble Africans pilot" Mark Starlins.[62] Starlins was an enslaved man with such knowledge of the James River that he was commonly referred to as "Captain." Starlins, along with two other skilled black pilots, Caesar Tarrant and Cuffee (killed in action), as well as sailors David Baker, Jack Knight, and Pluto, captured a British supply ship in 1779; they have been described as "among the heroes of the American Revolution."[63] Barron's memoir lauded the service of three additional enslaved sailors—Harry, Cupid, and Aberdeen—as "courageous patriots":

> Harry . . . distinguished for his zeal and daring; Cupid . . . on all occasions . . . the champion of liberty. . . . many of the African race were zealous and faithful soldiers in the cause of freedom . . . in particular . . . Aberdeen who distinguished himself so much as to attract the notice of many . . . including Patrick Henry, who befriended him as long as he lived.[64]

In Virginia, the service of enslaved Patriots in the American Revolution prompted a manumission act specifically acknowledging that Aberdeen and

A painting by John-Baptiste Le Paon commemorates the siege of Yorktown and depicts the Marquis de Lafayette and, possibly, James Armistead. Armistead's intelligence gathered from British troops aided the Patriots' victory in this final contest that resulted in American independence. Armistead, a literate slave who was among the first double-agents in U.S. military history, was freed by the Virginia Commonwealth for his Patriot service. Armistead's service may have helped to inspire the Marquis de Lafayette's subsequent efforts to eradicate slavery in the French Caribbean and a series of royal decrees by Louis XVI to protect the rights of slaves.

other enlisted slaves "contributed toward the establishment of American liberty and independence."[65] Virginia's manumission acts of 1782 and 1783 supported a tide of private manumissions in the post-Revolutionary period. Prior to the acts, individual owners had to petition the assembly to legally free enslaved individuals, and the assembly would pass individual acts to do so. John Hope, "otherwise called Barber Caesar," was among several men and women freed by such an act in 1779; he later placed ads seeking his own fugitive slaves, one of whom had served as the freedman barber's apprentice. Another runaway notice listed a jockey who was eventually freed by an act of assembly.[66] Virginia's acts concerning slavery, as well as runaway advertisements in the wake of the American Revolution, reveal a current of enslaved individuals creating their own freedom through flight or being granted freedom by the state. (One act declared slaves not born in Virginia to be freed after a year). This is not to say that late eighteenth-century officials or planters generally acknowledged the rights of Virginia slaves—a 1786 act immunized masters who murdered or maimed slaves "during correction"; the act was repealed two years later, but the practice was not necessarily forsaken.

James Armistead's wartime service directly abetted the Patriot victory. Born a slave in Virginia, he got the consent of his owner to volunteer to join the army and served as a spy under the command of the Marquis de Lafayette. Posing as a runaway slave, Armistead infiltrated the camps of Benedict Arnold and Lord Cornwallis. Operating as a double agent, Armistead collected information from the British and fed false information to them.[67] The intelligence Armistead provided to the Continental Army was instrumental to the Patriot victory at Yorktown and thus to the surrender of the British and the establishment of the United States.[68] After the war, Virginia granted Armistead freedom based on a commendation from Lafayette noting that Armistead had risked his life in his service to the nation. Adopting the surname of the marquis, James Armistead Lafayette eventually purchased forty acres of land and raised a family.

Armistead may have inspired some of Lafayette's efforts to mitigate Atlantic slavery. "Influenced in part by his encounter with black soldiers during the American Revolution, the marquis de Lafayette suggested to George

Washington that [they pursue an experiment towards] the elimination of slavery."[69] In the 1780s, Lafayette created two plantations in Guyana that paid salaries and provided education to enslaved workers. "Lafayette's influence in part might well have encouraged a series of [French] royal decrees for the improvement of slave conditions. . . . [which] helped set the stage

John Trumbull painted this portrait of George Washington and William Lee from memory around 1780, roughly five years after Trumbull had served as an aide-de-camp. William Lee was a mixed-race equestrian and valet who accompanied and assisted Washington throughout the American Revolutionary War; he ultimately received his freedom as well as a portion of Washington's estate. Another of Washington's slaves, Harry Washington, gained his freedom by fighting for the British. Another, Ona Judge, gained her freedom through flight; she made her exit from the then capital, Philadelphia, with the aid of the black community. Although the Washingtons sought her return (George Washington had signed the Fugitive Slave Law in 1793), she remained free with the assistance of her white and black neighbors in New Hampshire. The Washingtons' celebrated chef, Hercules, also succeeded in liberating himself from slavery through flight.

for later rumors that the king had freed the slaves—rumors that animated many of the revolts [in the French Caribbean] in the 1790s."[70] Like Will, the rebellious slave from St. John whose actions reverberated in the Danish and British colonies, Armistead's support of the American rebellion may have helped to cultivate resistance to slavery in the French colonies.

While Armistead is remembered as the first African American double agent, people of African descent regularly provided valuable intelligence and often acted as spies, officially and unofficially, during conflicts throughout New World history. In the case of the American Revolution, "[m]any blacks carried messages . . . on both sides."[71] A dramatic counterpoint to Armistead's service was the experience of Benjamin Whitecuff, a free black man from New York, "who reportedly saved 2,000 troops under [the British] General Clinton in New Jersey. Whitecuff also acted as a spy and was captured by the Americans and hanged, but an English cavalry unit [cut him down and] saved his life three minutes later."[72]

While many thousands of black Americans served the Patriot cause during the American Revolution, they were far fewer than the tens of thousands who chose to fight for freedom and against slavery by joining the Loyalists. Masses of enslaved women and men risked their lives to flee southern plantations and ally with the British, prompting the historian Gary Nash to call the American Revolution the largest slave rebellion in U.S. history.[73] In 1775, Virginia's royalist governor, Lord Dunmore, issued a proclamation offering to make "all indentured Servants, Negroes, or others . . . free that are able and willing to bear arms."[74]

As with subsequent mass emancipations during the Haitian Revolution, the Latin American independence wars, and the American Civil War, Dunmore's official proclamation was prompted by the presence of Afro-Americans already in his service, many of whom had liberated themselves and volunteered. Throughout American history, people of African descent recognized and capitalized on the opportunities for freedom that inhered in political instability. Dunmore capitalized on African Americans' desire for freedom, doubled the size of his army in a few weeks, and established the Ethiopian Regiment.

Among those who sought freedom through Dunmore's promise was

Harry Washington, a corporal who led a black Loyalist regiment known as the Black Pioneers. Born near the Gambia River, the man who came to be known as Harry had been purchased by George Washington in 1763. The future U.S. president initially put Harry to work in the Great Dismal Swamp (the maroon sanctuary on Virginia's border described above) and later at Mount Vernon in a move that separated Harry from his domestic partner (slaves could not legally marry). With the outbreak of war between Britain and the colonies, Harry and three European indentured servants liberated themselves from Mount Vernon—as would an additional eighteen slaves.[75] During the war, Harry Washington "rose quickly through the ranks, and soon Corporal Washington was nearly as famous among the blacks who carried the Union Jack as General Washington was among the white soldiers who carried the stars and stripes."[76]

George Washington sought the return of Harry Washington during negotiations at the conclusion of American Revolution but to no avail. As did many of the black Loyalists who sought freedom with the British, Harry Washington settled after his service in Birchtown, Nova Scotia. Ultimately, Washington and many of his cohorts settled in Sierra Leone. Thousands of self-liberated slaves and Loyalist veterans sought to protect their right to freedom by settling in Canada, West Africa, East Florida, the Bahamas, Jamaica, and London after the war. As Douglas Egerton has pointed out, the black Loyalist diaspora changed the British Atlantic empire: "In the same way black Patriots who returned to New England after fighting in the [Revolutionary] war were determined to impose abolition on their communities, black Loyalists . . . were not about to accept second class citizenship within the empire."[77]

Hundreds of soldiers of African descent, many of whom were self-liberated slaves, served among the Hessian armies that fought alongside the British during the American Revolution. Most listed South Carolina as their birthplace, but at least three were recorded as being from the Caribbean, five from West Africa, and one from Lisbon.[78] About seventy of the black American soldiers who joined the Hessian troops during the American Revolution settled in Germany after the war, transforming themselves "from slaves to subjects."[79]

Vincent Ogé relentlessly pursued the promise of The Declaration of the Rights of Man *in France and Haiti during the Age of Revolution. Ogé was among Saint Domingue's "gens de colour," a population of free people of African descent (roughly equal in size to the colony's white population), many of whom, like Ogé and his collaborator Julien Raimond were planters (and slave owners) themselves. Ogé and Raimond addressed France's National Assembly in 1790 pressing for political rights. While Raimond remained in France to continue to work for reform within the French government, Ogé returned to Haiti in 1790 (after meeting with the abolitionist Thomas Clarkson in London and a brief stop in Charleston) where he collaborated with Jean-Baptiste Chavannes (who like Raimond, was an Afro-Haitian veteran of the American Revolution) to champion citizenship rights through a carefully orchestrated insurgency that left Ogé and Chavannes martyrs for freedom and primed the emergence of the revolutionary war for Haitian independence in 1791.*

During the American Revolutionary War, black soldiers also fought for the Spanish Crown. The Spanish governor of Louisiana enlisted many Afro-American soldiers among his recruits from Louisiana, Cuba, and Mexico to drive the British from the Mississippi River valley and the Gulf Coast. Governor Galvez's successful campaigns were a crucial, if under-recognized, turning tide for Washington's beleaguered Continental Army; Afro-Americans, including black officers, were an integral part of that success and may have comprised as much as half of these Spanish forces.[80] In an official report, Galvez described these "companies of blacks and free mulattos" as conducting themselves with "valor and generosity."[81]

Six black officers were cited for bravery and received medals of valor awarded by the king of Spain. Afro-Cuban militiamen fought the British in the Florida campaigns as well as in the Bahamas. "Cuba's black troops fought for the Spanish monarch, but as they helped liberate British colonials, they gained some acquaintance with the rhetoric of independence."[82] Just as Afro-Cuban soldiers were becoming engaged in the Age of Revolution, so too were Afro-Haitians, with world-historical consequences.

The Haitian Revolution

Saint Domingue, France's most prosperous colony, was a linchpin of the Age of Revolution. In the eighteenth century, Saint Domingue was the most successful colony in the world. It produced almost a third of the world's sugar, over half of the world's coffee, and "stood at the center of world trading networks."[83] New England's trade with Saint Domingue was so extensive that it was the U.S.'s most important trading partner after Great Britain and was often regarded as the foundation of New England's prosperity. Saint Domingue was even more essential to the prosperity of France.

France's allegiance to the rebellious American colonies, vital to the success of the Patriots, stemmed in part from the desire to protect Saint Domingue from the British. It was the profits gleaned from the efforts of vast numbers of enslaved Haitians that allowed France to provide the enormous materiel support that undergirded the American war. Between 500 and 750 Afro-Haitian soldiers served with French forces during the American Revolution.[84] The *Chasseurs Volontaires de Saint-Domingue* was a volunteer unit of 549 Afro-Haitians who fought alongside the American Patriots at the six-week Siege of Savannah (commemorated in 2007 with the installation of a Haitian Monument in Savannah's Franklin Square).

By the mid 1700s, Saint Domingue's free black population, *gens de couleur*, roughly equaled its white planter population. Mixed-race children were sometimes sent to be educated in France, and many returned to Saint Domingue advocating full citizenship rights. One did not have to travel to Europe, however, to become acquainted with natural rights philosophies because the island of Saint Domingue itself was steeped in Enlightenment

Joseph Bologne, Le Chevalier de Saint-Georges, was a renowned Afro-French composer, violinist, and conductor, as well as a champion fencer and a colonel during the French Revolution. The son of a French planter and an enslaved woman of African descent in the colony of Guadeloupe, Bologne spent his childhood in the French Caribbean before his father brought the family to France. Bologne participated in the life of the French court, briefly shared a flat with Mozart, and was invited to head the Paris opera before he joined the National Guard after the outbreak of the French Revolution. In 1791 a delegation of free men of color led by Haiti's Julien Raimond pressed the National Assembly to create a black corps to fight for the egalitarian ideals of the French Revolution. Bologne was appointed its colonel and chose his friend Alexandre Dumas as lieutenant. Like Bologne, Dumas was the son of a French aristocrat and an enslaved woman of African descent; Dumas's son celebrated his father's feats in The Three Musketeers *and* The Count of Monte Cristo.

thought. Well before many North American cities, eighteenth-century Haitian urban centers had theaters, where *gens de couleur* and their servants observed Voltaire's latest works. "Haiti's scientific clubs 'certainly rivaled, if they did not eclipse' those of Philadelphia and Boston."[85]

At the start of the French Revolution in 1789, Afro-Haitian planter Julien Raimond headed the Society of Colored Citizens, an organization formed by Afro-Americans in France to advance republican rights. They sent an address to the French National Assembly as "free citizens of color," petitioning for the recognition of their "inalienable rights based on nature and the social contract."[86] (Afro-Frenchman Louis Guizot, a delegate at the National Assembly, authored the *cahier de doléances*—report of grievances—for his

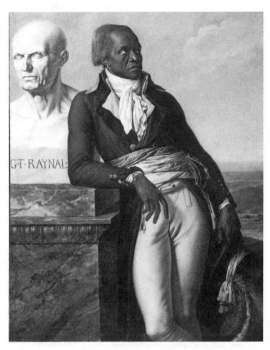

Jean-Baptiste Belley was born in Senegal, purchased his own freedom in Saint Domingue (Haiti), fought alongside the patriots in the American Revolution, led troops in the Haitian Revolution, and served as an active member and outspoken abolitionist in the National Convention and Council of Five Hundred in France. After his election to France's National Assembly, he instigated a successful vote to end slavery in the French colonies in 1794. Numerous free people of color from the Caribbean (including women like Jeanne Odo) advocated in Paris for the rights of republican citizenship during the French Revolution. This portrait hangs in the chapel of the Palace of Versailles.

French town at the outset of the revolution that provided a model to other towns. The reports, originally ordered by the king, ultimately helped to foment the French Revolution. Guizot served as a captain general of two revolutionary companies.[87]) In 1792, Raimond persuaded France's National Assembly to authorize a legion of Afro-Americans in France to defend the revolution, the Legion of the Americas. The Chevalier de Saint-Georges, formerly known as Joseph Bologne, was appointed its commander.

Born in Guadeloupe in 1745, Bologne became in France a champion fencer whose skill prompted King Louis XV to appoint the 25-year-old to the royal cavalry and make him a *chevalier*, or knight. As the Chevalier de Saint-Georges, Bologne went on to amaze French society as a violin virtuoso, the conductor of Paris' principal orchestra, a prolific, accomplished composer, and the music instructor of Queen Marie Antoinette. However, Saint-Georges was an avid supporter of France's revolutionary republican ideals. As commander of the all-black Legion of the Americas, Saint-Georges appointed his friend Alexandre Dumas—father of the author of *The Three Musketeers*—to serve as a general. Dumas, like Saint-Georges, had been born in the French Caribbean to an enslaved African woman and a French nobleman.[88]

In 1793, Saint-Georges's Legion of the Americas, in league with the Society of Colored Citizens headed by Raimond, sent an address to the National Assembly calling for the end of slavery. Jeanne Odo, an Afro-Haitian woman, led a delegation of *gens de couleur* at the Paris Convention. Jean-Baptiste Belley, a former slave turned Haitian planter (and American Revolutionary War veteran) was elected to the French National Convention where he spoke persuasively before the First French Republic voted to abolish slavery in 1794. Slavery had already been abolished by decree in Saint Domingue a few months prior, but Belley's contributions helped to extend formal citizenship to every enslaved individual in every French colony.[89]

While many free people of color pledged allegiance to the French revolutionary republic, enslaved Afro-Caribbean men and women were shaping a movement for revolutionary emancipation in the Americas. In 1789 slaves instigated an insurgency in Martinique, as they would in 1793 in Guadeloupe where enslaved insurgents "voiced their claims in terms of Republican rights."[90] In Saint Domingue, maroonage dramatically increased, slaves took up arms to support various factions, and in 1791 hundreds of enslaved leaders and organizers orchestrated the collaboration of a vast network of slaves, maroons, and free people of color into a highly organized military and civil government. Saint Domingue's black elite fomented Haiti's revolution, but it was the initiatives of Haiti's slave majority—and former slaves like Toussaint L'Ouverture—that made it a success.

When independent Haiti universalized citizenship in 1805, it also declared that all citizens were universally black. The nation's founding document defined blackness as a "generic designation," thus placing Haiti at the forefront of recognizing racial categories as political rather than biological manifestations. While acknowledging that "all distinctions of color will by necessity disappear," Haiti's Imperial Constitution of 1805 specified that the nation's black citizenry included "white women who have been naturalized . . . their present [and] future children" as well as naturalized "Germans and Poles."[91] Full citizenship was granted to the Polish and Germans soldiers who had defected from French troops, the widows of white planters, and a few French men.[92]

During the Haitian Revolution, about 500 Polish soldiers, dispatched to aid French forces, defected to the revolutionary freedom struggle and permanently settled as citizens in Haiti's nascent republic. The Afro-Polish General Wladyslaw Jablonowski did not choose Haitian citizenship; he died during his service to the French forces.[93] Jabolonowski was the adopted son of a Polish nobleman whose English wife had borne a child with an African father. Jablonowski served his native Poland alongside the great patriot Kosciouszko against Russia and was made a general in 1799. In 1802, perhaps feeling an affinity for Napoleon, his old schoolmate from military academy, Jablonowski requested to lead Polish troops in Haiti alongside French forces.

The Afro-Haitian Alexandre Pétion also had experience in France before serving as an officer during the Haitian Revolution; as Haiti's president, he "played a role of first importance in the history of the New World."[94] A founder of pan-Americanism, Pétion was a "steadfast republican and generous soul, who had made it known throughout the Caribbean that in his country all freedom seekers were welcome."[95] In 1815, he was instrumental to "the emancipation of the Spanish colonists of this hemisphere," when he provided sanctuary as well as financial and military support to the founding father of several independent nations in South America, Simón Bolívar.[96] Haitians not only helped to abolish slavery in South America but also established freedom in the Dominican Republic which it relieved twice from European control and abolished slavery.

REVOLUTIONARY UPRISINGS OF 1795

In the wake of the revolutionary events occurring in France and Saint Domingue and amidst the political tensions of imperialism, Afro-Americans participated in countless insurgencies throughout the Caribbean at the close of the century. These resistance movements of enslaved Afro-Americans, maroons, and free people of color were "insurrections that brought profound challenges and changes to the meanings of rights in the 1790s."[97] In a single year, 1795, events took place in Grenada, St. Vincent, St. Lucia, Venezuela, Curaçao, Cuba, Louisiana, Dominica, Guyana, and Jamaica.

Grenada and St. Vincent

Among the most significant of the 1795 events was an armed insurgency for republican rights in Grenada that lasted for over a year. Julien Fédon, an Afro-French planter born in Martinique, organized some 6,000 slaves, 500 free people of color, and 150 whites starting in May 1795.[98] "Fédon's actions were . . . clearly linked with the French revolutionary cause," and the conflicts that ensued highlighted the inherent weaknesses of race-based slavery in multiracial societies.[99] In 1794, a year before Fédon's uprising, perhaps 40 percent of Grenada's militia was composed of free men of color; additionally, a "major effect of the rebellion was that as a result of the . . . situation, whites made much greater use of slaves in the military."[100] As had been the case since the Spanish armed slaves to support the American conquest campaigns of the sixteenth century, military service often conferred an expectation of certain rights and allowances; during the Age of Revolution, these rights were articulated with particularly republican values. Throughout all of these epochs, the goal of increased autonomy remained constant.

"The watchwords of the French Revolution may well have meant different things to participating whites, free coloreds, and slaves, as indeed to different groups of free coloreds," observed Edward Cox. "The important thing is that like the Haitian Revolution, Fedon's Rebellion seemed to promise something to all of its participants."[101] Afro-Americans of various status—free and enslaved—capitalized on the language of republicanism to advance their claims to rights.

In the same month that Fédon initiated revolt, the Black Carib leader Joseph Chatoyer spearheaded a revolution in St. Vincent against the British; this uprising united the historically free Black Caribs with French radicals. The Black Caribs, now known as the Garifuna, were an independent

Afro-Amerindian maroon community founded in 1675 by shipwrecked slaves who intermarried with the Native population of St. Vincent. Like the former slaves who allied with French republicans to defend their freedom in nearby St. Lucia, Chatoyer's forces initially repelled the British. While the British would not regain control of St. Lucia until 1803, they relocated the Garifuna to Honduras in 1797.[102]

Venezuela and Curaçao

In May 1795, in the Coro region of Venezuela, some 400 enslaved and free persons of color, captained by José Chirino and José Gonzales, both free men of color, initiated a three-day uprising for abolition that was inspired by events in Haiti and then itself inspired subsequent anticolonial movements in Venezuela and a massive uprising in Curaçao. Venezuela had long offered sanctuary to slaves from Dutch Curaçao (as Spanish Florida had to slaves from British Florida); by the close of the eighteenth century, Venezuela's tens of thousands of maroons may have reached parity with the enslaved community. One of the leaders of the Coro revolt, José Gonzales, was himself an African-born refugee of the Dutch colony who in Venezuela "helped other Afro-Curaçaoans flee to freedom. . . . [and] worked to defend the lands of free blacks (including some Curaçaoans) . . . even travelling to Spain to testify on their behalf."[103]

The slave revolt that took place in Curaçao in 1795 continues to be "commemorated as a seminal event in the island's history, a courageous . . . rejection of slavery and colonial rule."[104] While the month-long uprising enacted by some 2,000 slaves was ultimately quelled by the militia, many of whom were of African descent, the event is celebrated annually as "the day of the struggle for freedom."[105] Tula Riguad, one of the enslaved men who led the revolt, has been officially recognized since 2009 as a national hero and martyr. While the 1795 revolt is perhaps the most widely recognized, it was preceded by smaller insurgencies for freedom in Curaçao in 1716, 1750, and 1774 and followed by a coup d'etat involving free people of color in 1796 and a series of upheavals 1799–1800.

Cuba and Louisiana

The spring and summer of 1795 saw a slave revolt in Cuba as well as a highly organized conspiracy in Louisiana; both were influenced by the revolutionary events occurring in Haiti and elsewhere. Cuba's uprising was instigated outside of Puerto Príncipe by two enslaved men, Romualdo, a former resident of Cuba's black settlement of Cobre (see Chapter Three) and Haitian-born Juan el Francés. While the event was short-lived and small-scale, Romualdo is documented as having asserted at its outset that "all men are free and equal."[106] Three years later, an official report on Cuban slavery lamented four additional "attempts at, or signs of, insurrection."[107]

Like Cuba, Louisiana was governed by Spain during this period, and as in Cuba, Spanish authorities were concerned about the "revolutionary contagion coming from France and Haiti."[108] The revolutionary antislavery plot of Point Coupée that united enslaved Louisianans, free people of color, and whites justified their concern. Furthermore, as historian Gwendolyn Hall has shown, the slaves of Point Coupée "were well informed about revolutionary developments in France, in Haiti, and throughout the world."[109]

Dominica and Guyana

The last decades of the eighteenth century saw powerful and protracted maroon wars in Dominica and a series of uprisings in the Dutch colonies that would eventually become Guyana and Suriname. With a long history of resistance, "the almost ungovernable island of Dominica" experienced maroon wars, led by Pharcell and others, from 1785 to 1790 followed by slave revolts in 1791 and 1795.[110] (Dominica experienced additional maroon wars from 1809 to 1814.) In 1794, the British offered Pharcell and his followers amnesty and land in return for their service as soldiers (joining the existing ranks of Black Rangers) in seeking out fugitive slaves. In 1795, Pharcell's maroon troops were put to the test when Dominica experienced the Colihaut rebellion, where, like Fédon's revolt in Grenada, revolutionary slaves and republican planters joined forces. Dominica's Eighth West India Regiment, which was "essential for the defense and control of the island" was composed almost entirely of enslaved soldiers starting in 1795—and initiated a revolt in 1802.[111] While at times the English called upon maroons to help suppress resistant slaves in Dominica (as they did in Jamaica), it was often the other way around. Throughout the Americas, black troops and colonial militias composed of black men, enslaved and free, were enlisted by the English, Dutch, French, and Spanish to quell maroon revolts as they did in St. John. The Afro-American soldiers who remained loyal to colonial powers were insisting on their citizenship in a substantially different but recognizable manner.

In 1795 the Dutch still laid to claim a series of neighboring plantation colonies between present day Venezuela and Brazil that now encompass the modern nations of Guyana and Suriname. In the eighteenth century, the colony known as Suriname had some of the largest maroon populations in the hemisphere, and the Dutch turned to troops of Black Rangers, composed of enslaved and free men of color, "considered far and away the most effective of all the anti-maroon forces."[112] Yet, unable to be subdued, two maroon communities in Suriname made treaties with the Dutch in 1760s, and in the 1770s, enslaved people were pouring out of plantations and forming and defending new maroon communities. In the nearby colony of Dutch Berbice, a massive slave revolt took place in 1763, following smaller revolts in 1733, 1749, 1752, and 1762. In another proximate settlement, known as Demerara, an uprising erupted in 1795 that was very difficult to dispel. Much like their counterparts in the American Revolution who capitalized on imperial conflicts to advance their agenda of greater autonomy, in Dutch Demerara "the slaves rebelled in 1795, taking advantage of the conflict between pro- and anti-French factions in the ruling class, and fighting against both."[113] Led by a mixed-race woman named Nancy Wood, rebellious slaves in Demerara collaborated with maroons to take advantage of the political instability generated by tensions between pro-British and French republican divisions.[114] As noted in the following chapter, enslaved individuals in British-controlled Demerara orchestrated one of the largest slave uprisings in the Americas in 1823.

Jamaica

In 1795 Jamaica's Trelawny maroon community (the largest of Jamaica's five officially recognized maroon communities) engaged British forces approximately five times their number, including a Jamaican militia that was about a third free Afro-Jamaicans. The British government had granted the Trelawny maroons legal status in a 1738 treaty ending the First Maroon War, which accorded them land and a quasi-autonomous state in exchange for their aid in tracking and returning fugitive slaves. In the wake of the Haitian Revolution, members of the Jamaican elite, and the governor in particular, feared that émigrés and ideas arriving from St. Domingue would incite revolution.

A French royalist confirmed their fears when he asserted—though he later recanted—that French Jacobin Commissioner Victor Hughes had sent Afro-Caribbean infiltrators to Jamaica. (Hughes did collaborate with armies of former slaves and free people of color in Guadeloupe and several of the colonies that rose up in 1795.) This climate of fear helped to inflame responses to an unsanctioned arrest and public flogging of two Trelawny maroon individuals that escalated into a nine-month guerilla war. The Second Maroon War ended when maroon captain Leonard Parkinson and British Major-General George Walpole agreed to a peace treaty, the terms of which were violated when Jamaica's governor deported 600 maroons to Nova Scotia. Outraged by the breach of trust, Walpole resigned his post in Jamaica and rejected his disbursement from the Jamaican Assembly. Eventually, the expatriated maroons were transported to Sierra Leone where they were pressed into service to resist black Loyalists like Harry Washington (described above) who protested the inequities of the British-run colony.

THE LATE EIGHTEENTH-CENTURY INSURGENCIES of enslaved and self-liberated Afro-Americans had wide-ranging consequences; they were politically destabilizing and required substantial military responses over the course of months or years. Furthermore, the European colonial powers repeatedly turned to black men, enslaved and free, to defend the colonies against the revolutionary insurrections of slaves, maroons, and free people of color fighting for their rights. The act in itself of arming black soldiers in the service of the state carried implications about eligibility for rights. In addition to the material strain and mortal sacrifice they placed on the colonial powers, these uprisings were ideologically provocative as they called attention to the

In 1789 Olaudah Equiano published one of the most influential pieces of anti-slavery literature in history. The first image, a portrait that hangs in the Royal Albert Memorial Museum, Exeter, is often associated with him; however, some scholars identify the date of the painting, based on the subject's clothes, as preceding the period of Equiano's adulthood. (Which would then beg the question: who was this man?) The second image was included in the frontispiece of Equiano's internationally renowned book, The Interesting Narrative of the Life of Olaudah Equiano. *His life was interesting indeed; enslaved in his youth, Equiano was a sailor in the Seven Years' War and made exploratory missions from the Arctic to Central America. After purchasing his freedom, Equiano's writings and efforts made him a key pioneer of the abolitionist movement and the outlawing of the slave trade. He served as England's first black civil servant when he was appointed to help start the colony of Sierra Leone.*

ways in which the discourse of rights and citizenship was fundamentally at odds with the realities of slavery.

ATLANTIC MOBILITY

The writing and political work of Olaudah Equiano focused international attention on the many ways in which the ideals of the Age of Revolution were fundamentally inconsistent with American slavery. Equiano was also a great example of how much mobility—geographic and social—black people could experience in the western world. Harry Washington's trajectory, from West Africa to Virginia to Canada and ultimately back to West Africa, was another case in point. Many Afro-Americans traversed geographies on both sides of the Atlantic, and several blazed trails and established or enhanced communities as they went.

Olaudah Equiano's public campaign against slavery had a wide-ranging impact; it helped to establish the world's first abolitionist movement. As a youth Equiano was purchased by a lieutenant in the Royal Navy in the Virginia colony and took part in the Seven Years' War. He later earned enough as a merchant in the West Indies to purchase his freedom from another master. Equiano was a pioneer of the nascent abolitionist movement in England, lecturing and writing about the horrors of the slave trade, working with Granville Sharp and Thomas Clarkson, and petitioning the English king in 1788. His book, *The Interesting Narrative of the Life of Olaudah Equiano or Gustavus Vassa, the African*, was one of the most influential pieces of abolitionist literature in history; it was widely read by international audiences and helped to instigate the 1792 British legislation that ended the slave trade in 1807.

First published in 1789, the book profoundly affected audiences on both sides of the Atlantic. "Equiano's autobiography was a best seller in its day, being published in eight English editions and one American in his own lifetime as well as translations into Dutch (1790), German (1792), and Russian (1794)."[115] Some scholars have questioned the veracity of Equiano's autobiographical description of his earliest years in West Africa, and some sources suggest he was born in South Carolina. Regardless of the author's nativity, his work was highly effective in fomenting abolitionism and advancing the legal termination of slavery. Some scholars have noted how astute Equiano was in navigating the political channels of publishing in London; perhaps he was as canny in crafting effective political literature.[116]

Equiano was among a small elite of well-known, formerly enslaved ladies and gentlemen of African descent in late eighteenth-century London. Dido Elizabeth Belle, the daughter of a British naval captain (and knight) and an enslaved African woman in the West Indies, was raised in England by her father's uncle, the Earl of Mansfield. Her great-uncle, the Chief Justice Lord Mansfield, rendered the decision in the Somerset case that essentially abolished slavery in England in 1772. Sources suggest that Belle assisted the chief justice with his correspondence and may have influenced some of her great-uncle's legal decisions championing freedom.

Equiano's antislavery colleagues included Ottobah Cugoano and Ignatius Sancho. Cugoano, after being kidnapped from Ghana and enslaved on a Granada sugar plantation, ultimately settled in England as a free man. His *Thoughts and Sentiments on the Evil and Wicked Traffic of the Slavery and Commerce of the Human Species,* first published in 1787, went through several printings and was translated into French. Born into slavery and migrating from Colombia to England in the 1730s, Sancho was a writer, actor, composer, and shopkeeper whose talents attracted patrons, creative colleagues, and abolitionists. In 1768, the British painter Thomas Gainsboro made a well-known portrait of Sancho in Bath, England. In 1782, two years after Sancho's death, his many letters were published as a collection and widely read. Like Cugoano and Sancho, Cesar Picton had been kidnapped from West Africa; in England, Picton became a successful coal merchant in the 1790s.

The internationally renowned boxer Bill Richmond was another Afro-American who gained fame after settling in England. When the British held New York during the American Revolution, Richmond, an enslaved teenager from Staten Island, came into the service of the British General Earl Percy (the future Duke of Northumberland). In 1777, Richmond returned to England with Percy. Though he apprenticed as a carpenter, Richmond became known for his talent for boxing, a sport then gaining significance in England. After a successful semi-professional career that made him the first black boxer to gain international recognition, Richmond opened and operated a London pub, the Horse and Dolphin, and a boxing academy where he trained Tom Molineaux, an African American from Virginia who would also gain fame as a professional boxer in England in the early 1800s.[117]

In the late eighteenth century, the accomplishments of yet another African American impacted Britain. The work of scientist, mathematician, and astronomer Benjamin Banneker influenced several of England's prominent abolitionists and was discussed in the House of Commons. The extraordinary mathematical ability of the African-born Thomas Fuller, who died in 1790 after a lifetime of enslavement in Virginia, was also publicized and familiar to abolitionists.

In 1791, Banneker was appointed to join the team surveying and planning the United States capital, Washington, DC. Thomas Jefferson, then the U.S. Secretary of State, wrote to the French mathematician, the Marquis de Condorcet, describing Banneker as "a very respectable mathematician. . . . I procured him to be employed under one of our chief directors in laying the new Federal City on the Potomac."[118] Banneker and Jefferson corresponded regarding the themes of universal equality and slavery; their letters were printed as a pamphlet and widely read. Banneker urged Jefferson to live up to the Enlightenment ideal of "the equal and impartial distribution of . . . rights" and to desist "in detaining by fraud and by violence so numerous of my brethren."[119]

While Banneker helped to site Washington in the 1790s, numerous enslaved and free black sawyers, quarrymen, masons, carpenters, and laborers built the White House. Enslaved Americans assisted the White House's occupants. Among them, Paul Jennings, who was born into slavery at Montpellier in 1799 (and whose father was white), served in the White House during James Madison's presidency. Jennings wrote the first White House memoir in American history.[120] His three sons went on to defend the nation as soldiers in the American Civil War.

Afro-Americans were active in the founding of Los Angeles. In 1785, Frances Reyes, a retired soldier described as "mulatto," was granted land and established a ranch with his family; in 1793, he became the mayor of what is today Los Angeles. In 1781, when the original Spanish settlement of Los Angeles was established, over half of its founders were of African descent. Among those first pioneers was Luis Quintero, a tailor who was the son of an enslaved African. Quintero's grandchild born in 1791, Maria Rita Valdez Villa, "grew up to become the 'owner' of Beverly Hills," where she established and operated a 4,500-acre ranch.[121] Afro-Americans continued to play pioneering roles in cities like Los Angeles and San Francisco in the following century.[122]

In the 1780s, Afro-Haitian Jean Baptiste Pointe du Sable became the first permanent settler in what would become known as Chicago. Du Sable was born free in Saint Domingue to an enslaved African mother and a free French mariner. He traveled to France with his father where he studied and mastered several languages and maritime arts. Du Sable then went from France to New Orleans and made his way north along the Mississippi River. He married a Native American woman, Catherine; they had two children, and one of their grandchildren may have been the first child born in Chicago in 1796. In the late 1700s, Du Sable settled with his family near Lake Michigan, built the first permanent residence in the region, and established a successful trading business.[123]

In 1783, black Loyalist veterans of the American Revolution founded Birchtown, Nova Scotia. It became the largest settlement of free people of color in eighteenth-century North America. As noted earlier, Harry Washington initially evacuated to Nova Scotia after the war, along with another 3,000 black Americans, and 600 maroons were forced to resettle there after Jamaica's Second Maroon War. Despite the profound hardships that these black settlers faced with few provisions and a largely unwelcoming climate (literally and figuratively), the existence of Birchtown and additional settlements in Nova Scotia and New Brunswick were in themselves a testament to Afro-Americans' sacrifices and persistence in the pursuit of liberty. For many self-liberated slaves and free people of color from the United States, Canada became an important region where African Americans could pursue sanctuary and opportunities in the following decades.[124]

Many Latin American cities offered social mobility to skilled Afro-Americans and their families. Despite guild restrictions, occupational opportunities were common enough that by the middle of the eighteenth century, nonwhite craftsmen comprised the majority of the urban artisan work force in Latin America.[125] Afro-Latin men joined the ranks of master craftsmen and artisans, often forming majorities in trades like masonry, carpentry, metalworking, tailoring, shoemaking and arts like silversmithing, sculpture, and painting. In Latin America, Afro-American professionals could be found as pharmacists, notaries, civil servants, lawyers, doctors, engineers, and professors. In the more racially restricted United States, fewer Afro-descended individuals could access these careers and often had to seek their professional training abroad. Even so, artisanal and other skills allowed some enslaved and free people of color degrees of autonomy in the American South, as evidenced in cities like Charleston, Richmond, Petersburg, and Baltimore; however, demographics and other restrictions prevented African Americans from dominating skilled sectors and entering professional classes in numbers comparable to Iberian America. By the end of the eighteenth century, free people of color outnumbered enslaved persons in Spanish America; skilled Afro-Latin workers outnumbered unskilled laborers; and at least a quarter of the population of the Latin Americas was recognized as mixed-race.

In Latin America, where free people of color developed several avenues for social mobility, enslaved individuals had solidified legal procedures to protect their rights and effect mobility by 1800. The legal custom of purchasing one's liberty in the Spanish colonies was introduced in the 1500s, but by the 1760s Afro-Spanish slaves had firmly established the practice. The custom of *coartacion*, whereby an individual could petition an official to set a fixed price so that one could make payments toward his or her own self-purchase, was a legal tactic that Afro-Latin slaves ultimately transformed into a right. What made *coartacion* truly an individual right is that it did not necessarily require the consent of one's master. While only small numbers of slaves exercised it in the 1700s, "the impact of *coartacion* was much more significant than the number of cases before Spanish tribunals suggests."[126] In Louisiana, during the 1762–1802 period of Spanish rule, some 1,000 individuals purchased their own freedom.

In Spanish Louisiana, slaves' awareness of the legal right to self-purchase "contributed to a huge increase in the number of 'voluntary' free purchase agreements."[127] Throughout the Americas "people of African descent were knowledgeable about and took advantage of legal avenues to freedom."[128] Starting in 1769, enslaved litigants in Spanish colonies were granted the right to petition for a different master in cases of mistreatment. Spain also created the office of *síndico procurador* (receiving attorney) as a means for enslaved persons to negotiate with their owners. "A municipal institution transplanted to the colonies in 1766, the síndicos were to provide legal representation for the slaves and to mediate in their conflicts with masters."[129] In Cuba, these officials were elected by town councils and were perhaps themselves owners of slaves. Still, "the very existence of the institution created clearly delineated institutional channels for enterprising slaves to claim rights."[130]

LATE EIGHTEENTH-CENTURY AMERICAN PATRIOTS

In the United States, slaves and freemen sought and established various means to claim their rights. In the wake of the American Revolution, many African Americans redoubled their efforts to secure a free republic in the United States, often by forming organizations and advancing initiatives to champion citizenship rights and civic participation. Many black organizations with democratic agendas, such as schools, newspapers, and clubs, were formalized in the late eighteenth and early nineteenth centuries.

Among the many veterans of the American Revolution who continued to fight vigorously for freedom long after the war, Prince Hall advocated republican ideals throughout the late eighteenth century. Hall was granted his freedom before enlisting in the Continental Army and likely served in the Battle of Bunker Hill. Just as many white intellectuals and revolutionaries like Benjamin Franklin and George Washington were Freemasons (among many others, including John Locke and Voltaire), so too was Prince Hall deeply aligned with the Enlightenment philosophies associated with Freemasonry.

In 1775 Prince Hall and fourteen other free black men were initiated into a Freemason lodge of British soldiers stationed in Boston. When the British soldiers departed the following year, Hall and the other black Masons were granted a dispensation authorizing the continued meeting of African Lodge Number 1. Despite obstacles posed by some white Masons in Massachusetts, Hall petitioned for and ultimately received a full charter from England in 1787 (via John Hancock's brother-in-law) to initiate new members. In 1791, Hall was appointed by the Prince of Wales to serve as the Provincial Grand Master of the African Grand Lodge of North America, which upon Hall's death became known as the Prince Hall Grand Lodge.[131]

Hall's organization was not only the world's first lodge of black Freemasons, it was also "the first society in American history devoted to social, political, and economic improvement."[132] Hall and his fellow Masons authored numerous petitions and speeches advocating abolition, African American education, and citizenship rights. They twice endeavored to pass legislation in the Massachusetts state senate. In a petition to eradicate slavery submitted to the Massachusetts legislature in 1777, Hall and others argued for "the Natural Right of all Men" and against "the inconsistency of [people] acting themselves the part which they condemn and oppose in others . . ."[133] Hall championed equal rights at every opportunity, including establishing a school for African American children in his home with teachers from Harvard.[134] Black Freemasons almost immediately organized additional lodges in Providence and New York and three in Philadelphia; they ultimately established thousands of lodges throughout the United States, Canada, the Caribbean, and Liberia.

Engaging in Enlightenment discourse, the black Freemasons of the late eighteenth century both accompanied and presaged a spate of black organizations dedicated to putting liberty and justice ideals into practice. The African Union Societies of Boston, New York, Philadelphia, and Newport overlapped with the Masons' membership rosters and aims in the 1780s. Black men and women used oratory as well as print to promote democratic agendas. Under the pen name Vox Africanorum, one such activist declared in the *Maryland Gazette* in 1783, "[W]e have an indubitable right to liberty. . . . Disparity in color . . . can never constitute a disparity in rights."[135]

John Marrant served as a chaplain to the Freemasons' Grand Hall Lodge in Boston. Marrant was born a free man in New York City in 1755, lived with his family in St. Augustine and Charleston as a child, excelled in writing and music, and was converted by an encounter with George Whitfield at age fourteen. According to his 1785 autobiography, Marrant lived among a Cherokee community for two years before being impressed by the Royal Navy as a musician for six years during the American Revolution. He was

Reverend Richard Allen grew up in slavery and purchased his own freedom at age twenty. Together with Reverend Absalom Jones, a fellow priest and former slave, Allen broke away from the Philadelphia church that insisted on segregating congregants; each formed their own congregations, Allen as a Methodist and Jones as an Episcopalian. While the priests formed distinctive parishes, they continually collaborated in their service to American society and civic engagement. In 1793, for example, Allen and Jones organized a black corps to help care for white Philadelphians suffering from a Yellow Fever epidemic.

ordained as a Methodist minister in 1785 and traveled to Nova Scotia for about four years, at the invitation of his brother, to minister to the African American Loyalists in Birchtown. Working with the Masons to end slavery, Marrant delivered a powerful discourse on equality at a Boston lodge in 1789 that was widely published.

In 1787, one month after the U.S. constitution was adopted by the Philadelphia convention, black Masons in Boston petitioned the Massachusetts legislature for equal school facilities. Only a few weeks later, New York City's African Free School was founded. Schools for African Americans predated the establishment of the United States. In 1704 a French colonist was granted permission by the English Crown to open a school for enslaved African Americans in New York City, and schools were established for black students in Philadelphia in 1758 and in Newport in 1763.

In 1799, Revolutionary War veteran John Chavis became the first African American college graduate in the United States, having attended both the

College of New Jersey (now Princeton) and Liberty Hall Academy (now Washington and Lee). Chavis opened an integrated private school in Raleigh, North Carolina in 1808 that specialized in the classics. The high caliber of the school prompted North Carolina's white elite to send their children there, including Governor Charles Manly. However, Chavis's increasingly outspoken abolitionist views and a changing political climate ultimately brought his pedagogical career to a close.

Richard Allen, a native of Philadelphia, purchased his freedom in 1783 and in the following years established what would become a global religious organization. In 1791, Allen bought a parcel of land to site a church, and in 1794 he founded Bethel, the first church of the first independent African American denomination, the African Methodist Episcopal Church. In 1799 Allen was ordained as a Methodist deacon and, ultimately, a bishop. His work was both religious and civic. He founded a school, opened his home to the Underground Railroad, and was a founder of the black convention movement, all of which were organizational ties that became associated with AME members in other states as well. Described as a Revolutionary Era "apostle of freedom," Allen's widely read sermons and community leadership urged the acknowledgment of African Americans as founding American citizens. Allen's prolific work as a spiritual and political leader was undergirded by the conviction that "black freedom was the true barometer of the success . . . of American democracy."[136]

Like Richard Allen, Absalom Jones was a former slave who turned to Methodism and ultimately became a champion of democracy. Jones became the first black American ordained as a priest by the Episcopal Church and established the African Episcopal Church in 1794. Despite their development of denominational differences, Richard Allen and Absalom Jones continually collaborated in civic leadership. In 1787, they established the Free African Society, a mutual aid society for people of color in Philadelphia. During Philadelphia's Yellow Fever epidemic of 1793, they rallied black residents to care for the city's afflicted. In 1797, Allen and Jones co-organized Philadelphia's African Masonic Lodge under the auspices of Prince Hall. Jones's descendants (Jones had purchased his wife's freedom before purchasing his own to ensure that their children would be free) made significant

In July 1776, James Forten was among the Americans who heard the first public reading of the Declaration of Independence. A Philadelphia native and American Revolution veteran, Forten dedicated his life to realizing the ideals put forth in the Declaration and advocating full citizenship rights for all Americans. An astute, highly-regarded, and very successful entrepreneur,  *Forten spent roughly half of his considerable fortune on promoting civil rights, including purchasing the freedom of others, funding anti-slavery journalism, authoring petitions and pamphlets, advocating women's suffrage, and founding a school. A civic leader as well as a businessman, Forten rallied black military support during the War of 1812 and was a seminal figure in the establishment and work of the American Anti-Slavery Society. His children and grandchildren were active in the political struggle to eradicate slavery; his wife and daughters helped to found the nation's first biracial abolitionist society for women.*

contributions themselves in the twentieth century.[137]

James Forten was a remarkable political activist dedicated to the ideals of the American Revolution long after the war ended. During the Revolution, he enlisted on a privateer and was captured along with the ship's crew and held on a British prison ship before being released in a prisoner exchange. Forten, who was born to free black parents in Philadelphia, was the great-grandson of an African slave who had arrived in the Delaware Valley in 1680, two years before William Penn had established a colony. Forten's grandfather was among the first slaves in Philadelphia to "obtain his own freedom."[138]

After the Revolutionary War, Forten became a successful entrepreneur. He developed the largest sail-making company in Philadelphia—with both white and black employees. A well-known and well-respected figure, Forten was a very outspoken opponent of slavery, champion of civil rights, and active in burgeoning abolitionist circles, hosting colleagues like William Lloyd Garrison and the Grimke sisters. He used his considerable wealth to free enslaved individuals, fund abolitionist media, and establish anti-slavery organizations. Forten's children and grandchildren were activists for freedom and citizenship rights as well.[139]

James Forten, Absalom Jones, and Richard Allen collaborated as civic leaders during the Age of Revolution. In 1799 Forten and Jones were among seventy African Americans who petitioned Congress to protest the federal fugitive slave law of 1793 and to advocate black citizenship. During the War of 1812, Forten, Jones, and Allen again showed their patriotism; they and the 2,500 black Philadelphians they rallied to protect the city, demonstrated their commitment to defend all American citizens.[140]

THROUGHOUT THE EIGHTEENTH CENTURY and the beginning of the nineteenth century, Afro-Americans fundamentally shaped the Age of Revolution. Black men and women challenged slavery on battlefields as soldiers, officers, maroons, and rebels, as well as in courtrooms, petitions, and print. Whether as Patriots during the American, French, and Haitian Revolutions or as Loyalists, people of African descent participated widely, as they did in all of the military contests that preceded and succeeded these revolutionary wars. In addition to their direct participation in the colonial wars of independence, Afro-Americans shaped the Age of Revolution when they continually took up arms throughout the hemisphere in slave revolts and maroon wars that challenged the colonial state. The French and Haitian revolutions fomented a spate of revolutionary activity throughout the Caribbean and coastal regions; armed black soldiers and military leaders on both sides of the contests staked claims in citizenship. In the wake of the American Revolution, African Americans in the United States developed religious, educational, and civic organizations to advance democratic ideals. During the course of the nineteenth century, Afro-Americans throughout the Americas again created and capitalized on circumstances to champion freedom. The actions of these black men and women eradicated slavery throughout the hemisphere.

NOTES FOR CHAPTER 4

1   Herbert S. Klein and Ben Vinson III, *African Slavery in Latin America and the Caribbean* (New York: Oxford University Press, 2007 [1986]), 17.

2   Vincent Brown, *The Reaper's Garden: Death and Power in the World of Atlantic Slavery* (Cambridge: Harvard University Press, 2008), 178, 188.

3   Peter M. Voelz, *Slave and Soldier: The Military Impact of Blacks in the Colonial Americas* (New York: Garland Publishing, 1993), 379.

4   Jane Landers, *Atlantic Creoles in the Age of Revolution* (Cambridge: Harvard University Press, 2010), 1–3.

5   Winthrop Jordan, *White Over Black: American Attitudes Toward the Negro, 1550–1812* (Chapel Hill: University of North Carolina Press, 1968), 171–172. North and South Carolina became distinct colonies in 1712.

6   John Hope Franklin, *The Free Negro in North Carolina, 1790–1860* (Chapel Hill: UNC Press, 1943), 10.

7   Mark Michael Smith, ed. *Stono: Documenting and Interpreting a Southern Slave Revolt* (Columbia: University of South Carolina Press, 2005), 16.

8   Catherine Clinton, *The Black Soldier: 1492 to the Present* (New York: Houghton Mifflin, 2000), 7.

9   Smith, *Stono*, 28; 12; xii. South Carolina enacted its first slave codes in 1712, modeled on those of the English colony of Barbados. (A century before, when the British established Barbados, most of the first laborers were indentured servants, many of whom had been kidnapped from the British Isles. To "Barbados" someone became a verb in the 1600s when tens of thousands of Irish dissidents and English indigents were routinely rounded up for involuntary plantation labor.) The codes stressed that enslaved people should not leave plantations nor carry arms without their master's permission. The year after Stono, 1740, South Carolina enacted its most restrictive slave codes, prohibiting assembly, literacy instruction, and earning wages, and authorized owners to murder rebellious slaves.

10 Jonathan Brooks, "From Freedom to Bondage: The Jamaican Maroons, 1655–1770," *Explorations* V (2010): 29.

11 Sylviane A. Diouf, *Slavery's Exiles: The History of the American Maroons* (New York: New York University Press, 2014), 26.

12 Frank Procter, III, "Slave Rebellion and Liberty in Colonial Mexico," in *Black Mexico: Race and Society From Colonial to Modern Times*, eds., Vinson and Restall (Albuquerque: University of New Mexico Press, 2009), 33.

13 Franklin Knight, ed. *General History of the Caribbean, Volume III* (London: UNESCO Publishing/Macmillan Education, 1977), 186.

14 Craton, quoting Edward Long in *Testing the Chains: Resistance to Slavery in the British West Indies* (Ithaca, NY: Cornell University Press, 2009 [1982]), 127.

15 Craton, *Testing the Chains*, 127.

16 Ibid.

17 Thomas Robert Day, "Jamaican Revolts in British Press and Politics, 1760–1865," (Masters Thesis, Virginia Commonwealth University, 2016), 13.

18   Trevor Burnard, *Mastery, Tyranny, and Desire: Thomas Thistlewood and His Slaves in the Anglo-Jamaican World* (Chapel Hill: University of North Carolina Press, 2004), 19.

19   For a gripping fictionalized but researched account of the St. John revolt see John Anderson, *Night of the Silent Drums* (New York: Scribner, 1975).

20   In 1815, the free black military mutinied in St. Croix. The following year, 331 signatories representing the free colored population in the Danish West Indies sent a petition to the king requesting rights, setting in motion a series of legislative changes. In 1848 an island-wide strike by slaves in St. Croix prompted the immediate abolition of slavery throughout the Danish West Indies by gubernatorial fiat. N. A. T. Hall, "The 1816 Freedman Petition in the Danish West Indies: Its Background and Consequences, *Boletín de Estudios Latinoamericanos y del Caribe*, 29 (December 1980), 64-66.

21   David Knight, *Mary's Point Hike*, St. John Historical Society VI, no. 5 (January 2007).

22   Jon F. Sensbach, *Rebecca's Revival: Creating Black Christianity in the Atlantic World* (Cambridge: Harvard University Press, 2005), 26.

23   Timothy James Lockley, ed. *Maroon Communities in South Carolina: A Documentary Record* (Columbia: University of South Carolina, 2009); Daniel O. Sayers, *A Desolate Place for a Defiant People* (Gainesville: University Press of Florida, 2014); Sylviane A. Diouf, *Slavery's Exiles: The Story of the American Maroons* (New York: New York University Press, 2014).

24   Brent Morris, "'Running Servants and All Others:' The Diverse and Elusive Maroons of the Great Dismal Swamp," *Voices from within the Veil*, eds., Alexander et al (Newcastle, UK: Cambridge Scholars Publishing, 2008), 85, quoting from Edmund Jackson, "The Maroons," *The Liberty Bell* (January 1, 1852): 12.

25   "Black Seminoles, Maroons, and Freedom Seekers in Florida," University of South Florida and The Africana Heritage Project. 2004.

26   Porter, Kenneth, *The Black Seminoles: History of a Freedom-Seeking People* (Gainesville: University of Florida Press, 1996): 6.

27   John Hope Franklin, *From Slavery to Freedom: A History of African Americans* (New York: Knopf, 2000 [1947]), 81.

28   Douglas R. Egerton, *Death or Liberty: African Americans and Revolutionary America* (New York: Oxford University Press, 2009), 55.

29   George Washington Williams, *History of the Negro Race in America, 1619–1880, Negroes as Slaves, Soldiers, and Citizens* (New York: Putnam, 1883), 364.

30   Gene Allen Smith, *The Slaves' Gamble: Choosing Sides in the War of 1812* (New York: Palgrave Macmillan, 2013), 11.

31   George Van Cleeve, "Somerset's Case and Its Antecedents in Imperial Perspective," *Law and History Review* 24, no. 3 (Fall 2006): 636.

32   In 1690, Katherine Auker requested to be discharged from her Barbadian master in absentia; the court granted her freedom until her master should return to England. Enslaved individuals "who had been brought to Paris by their masters demanded—and often won—their freedom. . . . The Admiralty Court of Paris freed nearly a hundred slaves in the eighteenth century." Laurent Dubois, *A Colony of Citizens: Revolution and Slave Emancipation in the French Caribbean, 1787–1804* (Chapel Hill: University of North Carolina Press, 2004), 64. Sue Peabody, *There Are No Slaves in France: The*

Political Culture of Race and Slavery in the Ancien Regime (Oxford: Oxford University Press, 1996).

33 Chernoh M. Sesay, Jr., "The Revolutionary Black Roots of Slavery's Abolition in Massachusetts,"*New England Quarterly* 87, no. 1 (March 2014); 108-109.

34 Egerton, *Death or Liberty*, 54.

35 Alfred Blumrosen, "The Profound Influence in America of Lord Mansfield's Decision in Somerset V. Stuart," *Texas Wesleyan Law Review* 13, no. 2 (2007): 645–658; Alfred and Ruth Blumrosen, *Slave Nation: How Slavery United the Colonies and Sparked the American Revolution* (Naperville, IL: Sourcebooks, 2005). Gerald Horne, *The Counter Revolution of 1776: Slave Resistance and the Origins of the United States of America* (New York: New York University Press, 2014).

36 Some judges interpreted Mansfield's ruling as the abolition of slavery in England and automatically granted freedom to enslaved litigants in British courts. Others saw Mansfield's decision as a finer legal point, that an enslaved individual could not be removed from the country involuntarily without judicial review. Regardless of Mansfield's intent, the decision prioritized the natural rights of an enslaved person over the property rights of a slave owner and thus defied the legitimacy of slavery. See William Wiecek, "Somerset: Lord Mansfield and the Legitimacy of Slavery in the Anglo-American World," *University of Chicago Law Review* 42, no. 1 (Autumn 1974): 86–146; National Humanities Center, Virginia Runaway Slave Advertisements, 1745–1775, 5; Blumrosen and Blumrosen, *Slave Nation*, 24–25.

37 Vincent Carretta, *Phillis Wheatley: Biography of a Genius in Bondage* (Athens: University of Georgia Press, 2011), 199. Clarkson was reading from his dissertation that took first place at the University of Cambridge in 1785.

38 Gary Nash, *The Unknown American Revolution* (New York: Penguin, 2005), 127.

39 Henry Louis Gates, *The Trials of Phillis Wheatley: America's First Black Poet and Her Trials with the Founding Fathers* (New York: Basic Civitas Books, 2010) back cover.

40 Gates, *Trial of Phillis Wheatley*, 17-38.

41 See "Eighteenth-Century Thought and the Crystallization of the Ideology of Race" in Audrey Smedley and Brian Smedley, *Race in North America: Origin and Evolution of a Worldview* (Boulder, CO: Westview Press, 2012).

42 Craig Steven Wilder, *In the Company of Black Men: The African Influence on African American Culture in New York City* (New York: New York University Press, 2001), 67; 53.

43 Egerton, *Death or Liberty*, 17. Afro-American men served in all of the eighteenth century military conflicts in North America, just as they did in the seventeenth. As noted in the previous chapter, African Americans fought in King Philip's War in 1676, King Williams's War in 1689, and Queen Anne's War in the early 1700s.

44 Smith, *Slaves' Gamble*, 10; Sidney Kaplan and Emma Nogrady Kaplan, *The Black Presence in the Era of the American Revolution* (Amherst: University of Massachusetts Press, 1989), 22, 47, 19.

45 Nash, *Unknown American Revolution*, 223.

46 The Gilder Lehrman Collection holds the certificate of Cuffee Wells's purchase of

freedom from April 30, 1781. Wells's son, after graduating from Dartmouth College and a career in teaching, served as Attorney-General in Haiti. Robert Ewell Greene, *Black Defenders of America, 1775-1973* (Chicago: Johnson Publishing Company, 1974), 22. James Durham of Philadelphia was another enslaved American who served as a physician's assistant during the American Revolution—to a Loyalist and a British army surgeon. In 1781, after Spanish and Afro-Spanish Patriot forces defeated the British at Pensacola, Florida, Durham was transported to New Orleans where he acquired his freedom and became a well-respected physician. When Durham returned to Philadelphia in 1788, he established a long professional relationship and correspondence with Dr. Benjamin Rush of founding father fame. Rush's esteem for Durham's work was evidenced when he included one of Durham's papers at a session of The College of Physicians and Surgeons of Philadelphia. Betty L. Plummer, "Letters of James Durham to Benjamin Rush," *Journal of Negro History* 65, no. 3 (Summer 1980): 261-269.

47 Rosemary Brana-Shute and Randy Sparks, eds., *Paths to Freedom: Manumission in the Atlantic World* (Columbia: University of South Carolina Press, 2009), 282.

48 Glenn A. Knoblock, *African American Historic Burial Grounds and Gravesites in New England* (Jefferson, NC: McFarland Publishers, 2016), 240.

49 Sharon M. Harris, "Lucy Terry: A Life of Radical Resistance, in *African American Culture and Legal Discourse*, eds., Lovalerie King and Richard Schur (New York: Palgrave Macmillan, 2009), 98; Gretchen Holbrook Gerzina, *Mr. and Mrs. Prince: How an Extraordinary Eighteenth-Century Family Moved Out of Slavery and into Legend* (New York: Harper Collins, 2008), 3–4, 206; Catherine Adams and Elizabeth H. Pleck, *Love of Freedom: Black Women in Colonial and Revolutionary New England* (New York: Oxford University Press, 2010), 70.

50 Gerzina, *Mr. and Mrs. Prince*, 6.

51 Venture Smith, *A Narrative of the Life and Adventures of Venture, A Native of Africa: But resident above sixty years in the United States of America* (New London: Holt, 1798).

52 Gary Nash, "Agrippa Hull: Revolutionary Patriot," BlackPast.org; Gary Nash and Graham Hodges, *Friends of Liberty: Thomas Jefferson, Thaddeus Kosciuszko, and Agrippa Hull: A Tale of Three Patriots, Two Revolutions, and a Tragic Betrayal of Freedom in the New Nation* (New York: Basic Books, 2008).

53 Adams and Pleck, *Love of Freedom*, 139.

54 Nash, *Unknown American Revolution*, 408. Nash observes that the American Revolution was the largest slave rebellion in U.S. history on the cover of his book and notes in his first chapter that the African American historian William C. Nell of Boston was the first to publicly document the sacrifices of black American Patriots in the 1850s. Historians tend to agree that at least 5000 black men saw active duty as Patriot soldiers and sailors, and that several thousand additional African American men and women supported the Patriot efforts as laborers, spies, and in other non-combat capacities.

55 Smith, *Slaves' Gamble*, 11.

56 Lanning, *African-American Soldier*, 9.

57 Nancy I. Sanders, *America's Black Founders: Revolutionary Heroes and Early Leaders* (Chicago: Chicago Review Press, 2010), 58–63.

58 Kaplan and Kaplan, *Black Presence*, 120.

59   Free men of color from the South also served in the Patriot army. William Flora of Virginia was widely recognized as the hero of the Battle of Great Bridge near Norfolk in 1775. According to his captain, during this battle "Flora, a colored man, was the last sentinel that came into the breast work. . . he did not leave his post until he had fired several times. Billy had to cross a plank to get to the breast work, and had fairly passed over it when he was seen to turn back, and deliberately take up the plank after him, amidst a shower of musket balls. He. . fired eight times." Flora ultimately became a successful businessman and purchased the freedom of his wife and children. Kaplan and Kaplan, *Black Presence*, 24; 119–130.

60   Africans in America: Black Revolutionary Seamen http://www.pbs.org/wgbh/aia/part2/2p51.html (accessed 4/9/14)

61   Sanders, *America's Black Founders*, 58.

62   Darlene Clark Hine and Earnestine Jenkins, eds. *A Question of Manhood: A Reader in U.S. Black Man's History and Masculinity*, Volume 1 (Bloomington: Indiana University Press, 1999), 182.

63   Luther P. Jackson, "Virginia Negro Soldiers and Seaman in the American Revolution," *Journal of Negro History* XXVII, no. 3 (July 1942), 265.

64   Kaplan and Kaplan, *Black Presence*, 48.

65   William Hening, *The Statutes at Large: Being a Collection of All the Laws of Virginia* (New York: Barlow, 1823), 308. This act specifically freed Aberdeen as well as any enslaved person who had been enlisted in the army as a substitute for their master. The act was intended to override masters who were "attempting again to force them into a state of servitude, contrary to the principles of justice." In the case of James Armistead below, additional legislation was required, while others, like Mark Starlins, remained in bondage.

66   To glance at the Official Records of Virginia Laws from 1751–1800 from the Digital Center of the University of Virginia, one can see how much officials wrestled with trying to manage servants and slaves, to draw a distinct line between the two overlapping groups (several laws address white servants and their offspring as well as mixed-race individuals), and to restrict, reduce, and in some cases manumit enslaved individuals. http://www2.vcdh.virginia.edu/gos/laws1751–1800.html (5/15/17). See Chapter Five for a discussion of the prevalence of black barbers and jockeys.

67   Scholars have not proved that Le Paon was depicting Armistead; however, the collaboration of the two men during the American Revolution is well documented. Laura Auriccio, "Lafayette at Yorktown (1782): Transformations and Interpretations," in the Grolier Club exhibition catalogue for *A True Friend of the Cause: Lafayette and the Antislavery Movement* (Easton, PA: Lafayette College, 2016). A definitive portrait of Armistead is in the collection of the Valentine Museum in Richmond, Virginia.

68   Kaplan and Kaplan, *The Black Presence*, 39.

69   Dubois, *Colony of Citizens*, 69–70.

70   Ibid.

71   Voelz, *Slave and Soldier*, 54–55, fn 36.

72   Ibid.

73   Estimates of how many black Americans sought freedom with the British during the

American Revolution range from 60,000 to 100,000. Benjamin Quarles, *The Negro in the American Revolution* (Chapel Hill: University of North Carolina Press, 1996 [1961]); Sylvia R. Frey, *Water from the Rock: Black Resistance in a Revolutionary Age* (Princeton: NJ, Princeton University Press, 1991); Gary Nash, *The Forgotten Fifth: African Americans in the Age of Revolution* (Cambridge: Harvard University Press, 2006).

74   John K. Thornton, *A Cultural History of the Atlantic World 1250–1820* (New York: Cambridge University Press, 2012), 481.

75   Washington owned several people named Harry. The Harry who worked in the Dismal Swamp and the Loyalist corporal may have been two different individuals. Henry Louis Gates, Jr. and Donald Yacavone, eds. *The African Americans: Many Rivers to Cross* (Carlsbad, CA: Smiley Books, 2013), 53.

76   Egerton, *Death or Liberty*, 195.

77   Egerton, *Death or Liberty*, 197.

78   George Fenwick Jones, "The Black Hessians: Negroes Recruited by the Hessians in South Carolina and Other Colonies," *South Carolina Historical Magazine* 83, no. 4 (Oct. 1982): 291–292.

79   Maria I. Diedrick, "From American Slaves to Hessian Subjects," in *Germany and the Black Diaspora*, eds., Mischa Honeck, et al (New York: Berghahn Books, 2013), 107.

80   Michael Lee Lanning, *African Americans in the Revolutionary War* (New York: Citadel Press, 2000), 14.

81   Lanning, *African-American Soldier*, 86.

82   Landers, *Atlantic Creoles*, 142.

83   Phillipe R. Girard, *The Slaves Who Defeated Napoleon: Toussaint Louverture and the Haitian War of Independence, 1801-1804* (Tuscaloosa: University of Alabama Press, 2011), 4.

84   John Garrigus, *Before Haiti: Race and Citizenship in French Saint-Domingue* (New York: Palgrave MacMillan, 2006), 19.

85   Ted Widmer quoting James E. McClellan in "How Haiti Saved America," *The Boston Globe*, March 21, 2010.

86   Garrigus, *Before Haiti*, 237.

87   Roger Little, "A Black Mayor in 1790 France," *The Enterprise of Enlightenment*, eds., Terry Pratt and David McCallam (Bern, Switzerland: Peter Lang Publishing, 2004), 168–169.

88   Gabriel Banat, *The Chevalier de Saint-Georges: Virtuoso of the Sword and Bow* (Hillsdale, NY: Pedragon Press, 2006), 442.

89   Dubois, *A Colony of Citizens*, 66. Belley, like Toussaint L'Ouverture, the former slave whose exceptional military leadership and political acumen were crucial to the success of the Haitian Revolution, was ultimately imprisoned by the French and died.

90   Dubois, *A Colony of Citizens*, 6.

91   Sibylle Fisher, "Appendix A, Imperial Constitution of Haiti, 1805," *Modernity Disavowed: Haiti and the Cultures of Slavery in the Age of Revolution* (Durham, NC: Duke University Press, 2003), 276.

92   Girard, *The Slaves Who Defeated Napoleon*, 325.

93 Girard, *The Slaves Who Defeated Napoleon*, 324–325; 205.

94 Dantes Bellegarde, "President Alexandre Pétion: Founder of Agrarian Democracy and Pioneer of Pan-Americanism," *Phylon*, 2, no. 3 (3rd Quarter 1941): 205.

95 Marie Arana, *Bolivar: American Liberator* (New York: Simon & Schuster, 2013), 178.

96 Bellegarde, "President Alexandre Pétion," 210.

97 Dubois, *A Colony of Citizens*, 31.

98 Kit Candlin, *The Last Caribbean Frontier, 1795–1815* (New York: Palgrave Macmillian, 2012), 8.

99 Edward L. Cox, "Fedon's Rebellion 1795–96: Causes and Consequences," *Journal of Negro History* 67, no. 1 (Spring 1982): 7.

100 Cox, "Fedon's Rebellion," 13–15.

101 Cox, "Fedon's Rebellion," 15.

102 Today the Garifuna and their descendants, numbering in the hundreds of thousands, reside in Central America and the U.S. Chris Taylor, *The Black Carib Wars: Freedom, Survival, and the Making of the Garifuna* (Jackson: University Press of Mississippi, 2012).

103 Linda M. Rupert, "Marronage, Manumission and Maritime Trade in the Early Modern Caribbean," *Slavery and Abolition* 30, no. 30 (September 2009): 367.

104 Wim Klooster and Geert Oostindie, *Curaçao in the Age of Revolutions, 1795-1800* (Leiden, Netherlands: 2011), 1.

105 Klooser and Oositindie, *Curaçao in the Age of Revolutions*, 2.

106 David Geggus, "Slave Resistance in the Spanish Caribbean in the Mid-1790s," in *A Turbulent Time: The French Revolution and the Greater Caribbean*, eds., Gaspar and Geggus (Bloomington: Indiana University Press, 1997), 134.

107 Ada Ferrer, "Speaking of Haiti: Slavery, Revolution, and Freedom in Cuban Slave Testimony," in *The World of the Haitian Revolution*, 228.

108 Hall, Gwendolyn Midlo, "The 1795 Slave Conspiracy in Pointe Coupée: Impact of the French Revolution," *Proceedings of the Meeting of the French Colonial Historical Society* 15 (1992): 130.

109 Hall, "1795 Slave Conspiracy," 131.

110 Craton, *Testing the Chains*, 224.

111 Craton, *Testing the Chains*, 228.

112 Richard Price, ed., *Maroon Societies: Rebel Slave Communities in the Americas* (Baltimore, John Hopkins University Press, 1996 [1979]), 9.

113 Klooser and Oositindie, *Curaçao in the Age of Revolutions*, 30.

114 Craton, *Testing the Chains*, 272.

115 Paul Edwards and David Dabydeen, eds., *Black Writers in Britain, 1760–1890: An Anthology* (Edinburg: Edinburg University Press, 1995), 54.

116 Vincent Carretta and Philip Gould, eds., *Genius in Bondage: Literature of the Early Black Atlantic* (Lexington: University Press of Kentucky, 2001).

117 Pierce Egan, *Boxiana: Or Sketches of Ancient and Modern Pugilism From the Days of the Renowned Broughton and Slack to the Championship of Cribb, Volume 1* (Elbiron Classics,

2006 [1830]). Egan, one of the first professional sports commentators, described Richmond as among the "first-rate heroes of the milling art" (454) and Molineaux as ranking "high as a scientific pugilist," (369).

118 Silvio A. Bendini, "Benjamin Banneker and the Survey of the District of Columbia, 1791," *Records of the Colombia Historical Society* 47 (1970): 12.

119 Benjamin Banneker, "Copy of a Letter from Benjamin Banneker to the Secretary of State With His Answer," University of Virginia, Electronic Text Center.

120 Clarence Lusane, *The Black History of the White House*, City Lights (San Francisco: City Lights, 2011), 103-130; Elizabeth Dowling Taylor, *A Slave in the White House: Paul Jennings and the Madisons* (New York: St: Martin's Press, 2012), 207.

121 Jean Kinney Williams, *Bridget "Biddy" Mason: From Slave to Businesswoman* (Minneapolis, MN: Compass Point Books, 2006), 14; Robert Lee Johnson, *Notable Southern Californians in Black History* (Charleston: The History Press, 2017), 10-18.

122 In the 1840s, William Liedesdorff, a gentleman of color from St. Croix, played a formative role in the founding of San Francisco. An accomplished businessman, Liedesdorff opened San Francisco's first hotel, launched the first steamboat in San Francisco Bay, served on City Council, developed the school system, and hosted the city's most important visitors. Mary Ellen Pleasant's contributions to San Francisco history and Bridget "Biddy" Mason's development of Los Angeles are discussed in Chapter Five. W. Sherman Savage, "The Influence of William Alexander Liedesdorff on the History of California," *Journal of Negro History* 38 (July 1958): 322-332; Delilah Beasley, *The Negro Trailblazers of California* (Lexington: KY, [1919] 2014), 107.

123 Carole Boyce Davies, *Encyclopedia of the African Diaspora* (Santa Barbara, CA: ABC-CLIO, 2008), 403.

124 Mary Ann Shadd, for example, was a U.S.-born journalist, teacher, lawyer, and democracy activist who became the first female publisher in Canada in the mid-nineteenth century. She was the granddaughter of a native Hessian soldier, Hans Schad, a German who served the British in the Seven Years' War and Elizabeth Jackson, a free African American woman, who had married in Pennsylvania in 1756. Shirley J. Yee, *Black Women Activists: A Study in Activism, 1828-1860* (Knoxville: University of Tennessee, 1992), 161. Jane Rhodes, *Mary Ann Shadd Cary: The Black Press and Protest in the Nineteenth Century* (Bloomington: Indiana University Press, 1998), 2.

125 Lyman Johnson "Artisans," *Cities and Societies in Colonial Latin America*, eds., Hoberman and Socolow (Albuquerque: University of New Mexico Press, 1986), 238.

126 Kenneth Aslakson, *Making Race in the Courtroom: The Legal Construction of Three Races in Early New Orleans* (New York: New York University Press, 2014), 59.

127 Aslakson, *Making Race in the Courtroom*, 59.

128 Ibid.

129 Alejandro de la Fuente, "Slaves and the Creation of Legal Rights in Cuba: Coartacion y Papel," *Hispanic American Historical Review* 87, no. 4 (2007): 659–692.

130 Ibid.

131 A. Keith Jones, *A View to Masonic Education: The Blue House Lodge* (Bloomington, IN: Authorhouse, 2010), 22.

132 Jones, *View to Masonic Education*, 18.

133 Sidney Kaplan, *The Black Presence in the Era of the American Revolution* (Amherst: University of Massachusetts Press, 1989), 204.

134 Sanders, *America's Black Founders*, 108.

135 Lanning, *African Americans and the Revolutionary War*, 172.

136 Richard S. Newman, *Freedom's Prophet: Bishop Richard Allen, the AME Church, and the Black Founding Fathers* (New York: New York University Press, 2008).

137 Absalom Jones's black descendants include Robert Abele, a doctor and co-founder of Philadelphia's Mercy Hospital in 1907 and his brother, Julian Abele, an award-winning architect who designed hundreds of historic American structures, such as those on the campuses of Duke University and Harvard, Philadelphia's Museum of Fine Art and the Free Library, as well as mansions for the magnates of Woolworths, Dodge, and the American Tobacco Company.

138 Julie Winch, *A Gentleman of Color: The Life of James Forten* (New York: Oxford University Press, 2002), 11.

139 James Forten's daughter Harriet lectured widely on civil rights and suffrage; she married Robert Purvis, an influential abolitionist who helped to found the American Anti-Slavery Society. James Forten's granddaughter, Charlotte Forten, was an activist, author, educator, and the first black teacher hired in Massachusetts to teach white students and among the first to serve as a teacher and a nurse during the Civil War. She married Francis Grimke, the nephew of the well-known activists Sarah and Angelina Grimke. Brenda Stevenson, ed., *The Journals of Charlotte Forten Grimke* (New York: Oxford University Press, 1988).

140 In 1800, James Forten wrote a letter connected with the 1799 petition initiated by Absalom Jones to the Massachusetts congressman who had presented the petition to the House of Representatives. The 1799 petition was preceded by one authored by ex-slaves from North Carolina in 1797. Winch, *Free Gentleman of Color*, 175; Dickson D. Bruce, Jr., *The Origins of African American Literature, 1680-1865* (Charlottesville: University of Virginia Press, 2001), 72.

∾ TIMELINE ∾

1800   Gabriel Prosser organizes wide network of freedom fighters in Virginia

1801   Toussaint L'Ouverture enacts Haitian constitution banning slavery

1804   York accompanies Lewis and Clark on the first U.S. expedition to the western part of the continent

1807   Britain (influenced by Equiano) outlaws slave trade, U.S. follows suit in 1808

1807   African American sailors catalyze War of 1812 in *Chesapeake Leopard* Affair

1808   −26 Afro-American soldiers and officers serve heavily in South America's independence wars

1810   −21 Afro-American soldiers serve in Mexico's independence wars

1811   Charles Deslondes leads 500 in fight for freedom in Louisiana

1812   Black sailors, soldiers, and officers (including Haitians) serve U.S. in War of 1812

1812   Afro-Cubans initiate series of uprisings for freedom known as the Aponte Rebellion

1813   Juana Ramírez commands an all-female military unit in Venezuela

1816   Haiti president Pétion aids Bolívar in exchange for abolition in Gran Colombia

1816   British Caribbean Emancipation Wars begin with Barbados rebellion

1816   U.S. army attack on maroons at Negro Fort initiates the First Seminole War

1821   Denmark Vesey organizes thousands to seize freedom in South Carolina

1821   Lott Carey sails for Liberia, leading way for U.S. and Caribbean emigrants

1823   Demerara Rebellion in Guyana unites 10,000 for freedom

1823   Padilla defeats Spain at Maracaibo, initiating Venezuela's independence

1825   Bernardino Rivadavia becomes first president of Argentina

1829   Vicente Guerrero becomes second president of Mexico, abolishes slavery

1831   Christmas Revolt in Jamaica prompts 1838 British outlawing of slavery

1831   Nat Turner leads violent protest for freedom in Virginia

1835   Fugitive slaves and Black Seminoles defeat U.S. army in Second Seminole War

1841   Underground freedom movement *La Escalera* threatens colonial slavery in Cuba

1848   Joseph Roberts becomes world's first African American president (Liberia)

1849   Buenaventura Báez elected president in Dominican Republic

1865   Jamaica's Paul Bogle leads Marant Bay protest for civil rights that ultimately prompts government overhaul

5

Nineteenth-Century Afro-American
Patriots and Liberators

At the dawn of the nineteenth century, the establishment of Haiti as the first free republic in the Americas heralded the decisive role of Afro-Americans in the rise of democracy. Throughout the 1800s, Americans of African descent brought slavery to a close throughout the Western Hemisphere and advocated universal citizenship in multiple ways. The military contributions of slaves in the Caribbean, Latin America, and the United States were essential to the outcomes of the Haitian Revolution, the Latin American Wars of Independence, and the American Civil War. Enslaved Americans played crucial roles in the process of liberation not only during wartime, but also as rebels whose actions helped to pave the way for these wars of abolition and independence.

Haiti's political and economic transition from plantation colony to republic was far from ideal; nonetheless, the triumph of the revolution itself fundamentally altered Western history and inspired proponents of freedom from Virginia to Venezuela, Canada to Cuba. As Louis Boisrond-Tonnere, the author of Haiti's declaration of independence, wrote in 1804, "mankind by its nature carries freedom in its heart and the keys to freedom in its hands."[1]

The Haitian Revolution was arguably "the single most important international event of the early modern era."[2] The political and military actions of Afro-Caribbean slaves and free persons of color universalized the Enlightenment principles that shaped the Age of Revolution. By 1794 Afro-Haitians had prompted France to enact abolition and grant citizenship throughout its colonies. By 1804 Afro-Haitian revolutionaries had defeated the armies of France, England, and Spain and established national independence. By 1806 Afro-Haitians had established the second republic in the Americas and had made theirs the first New World nation to abolish Atlantic slavery. While independent Haiti's executive regimes might later undermine the ideals for which so many had fought, revolutionary Haitians had irrevocably reshaped the meaning of liberty and citizenship.[3]

Just as Afro-Americans in the French Caribbean helped to create new ideas about and opportunities for citizenship, so too did Afro-Americans in Latin America. In the early 1800s Spain's vulnerability to Napoleon helped inspire campaigns for independence in the Spanish colonies, and the support and participation of Afro-Latins were crucial to their success. It was during South America's Wars of Independence, from 1808 to 1821, that republican ideals like democracy and nationhood were first explicitly described in terms of transcending race. Throughout Spanish America, Afro-Americans "not only constituted the corps of the Patriot army but also participated actively in the construction of the new political systems."[4] These Afro-Latin Americans shaped emerging discourses of citizenship when they posited racial equality as the foundation of nationalism. As soldiers and commanders in the armies of Guerrero in Mexico, Bolívar and San Martín in South America, and Maceo in Cuba, and as citizens, professionals, and officials in the new sovereign states they championed, Afro-Latins staked claims in the nation building that followed.

Despite the American Revolution's promise of liberty and equality, between 1800 and 1860 about 40 percent of Americans living in the U.S. South were enslaved.[5] The rhetoric of freedom and the republican ideology of rights that fueled American independence failed to yield a democracy and left slavery constitutionally protected. However, in the wake of the American war for independence, slavery was abolished in many northern states and free black populations expanded in many southern cities.

News of the Haitian Revolution spread through the press as well as by word of mouth; by 1800 over 12,000 Afro-Haitians had already entered the United States.[6] The Haitian Revolution instilled hope in the hearts of many and fear in the hearts of others—hopes and fears that shaped nineteenth-century struggles for independence and liberation across the hemisphere. Broadly speaking, many Afro-Americans in the United States, Cuba, Jamaica, Venezuela, Colombia, Guadeloupe, Brazil and other regions took inspiration while authorities took precautions. In the early nineteenth century, laws curtailing the rights of free people of color and the enslaved proliferated in many parts of the Americas; therefore, so did black activism. Regardless of whether one was aligned with or alarmed by the success of Haiti's revolution, it was "a crucial moment in the history of democracy . . . that laid the foundation for the continuing struggles for human rights" throughout the Americas.[7]

KEY EVENTS IN THE EARLY U.S.

The Louisiana Purchase

The great American scholar W. E. B. Du Bois (who was of Haitian descent) observed in his 1896 Harvard doctoral thesis that it was Napoleon's defeat by the Haitian army, the majority of whom were former slaves, that prompted him to sell the Louisiana territory. Thus, when Haitian forces terminated France's authority over its most lucrative American colony, they also defeated Napoleon's dream of a North American empire. The District of Louisiana spanned from the Mississippi River to the Rocky Mountains and had become French territory in 1699. In 1762 it was ceded back to Spain, its original European claimant, then was recovered by Napoleon in 1800. Exceeding 800,000 square miles, the Louisiana Purchase was the largest land acquisition in American history; it doubled the size of the United States and set it "on course to become a continent-wide nation."[8] Today the region that France gave up in the transfer includes fifteen U.S. states as well as two Canadian provinces.

Under the influence of Spanish and French colonization, slavery and race relations in the District of Louisiana and its capital New Orleans (from 1723) had more in common with colonial Saint Domingue—with its large and highly mobile free population of color, often descended from white elites—than with the American South, where Anglo planters often kept relations of color in bondage. French and Spanish stewardship had enmeshed the Louisiana colony in a fluid network of people, goods, and ideas traveling to and from Saint Domingue, Cuba, and France. During the decades surrounding the Haitian Revolution, Louisiana and Cuba were hubs where emigrant Haitians concentrated. In fact, in eastern Cuba and New Orleans, Haitian refugees "doubled the size of local populations and permanently altered the character of local life."[10] Thousands of Afro-Haitians arrived in Louisiana during this period, many of whom profoundly shaped its history.[11]

In 1811 one of these former Saint Domingue residents, Charles

President Thomas Jefferson commissioned the Lewis and Clark expedition to explore and map the vast lands acquired in the Louisiana Purchase. York was an enslaved African American explorer who accompanied the expedition to the Pacific (1804–1806) and "contributed significantly to [its] success"; the York Islands in the Missouri River were named in his honor. In 2001 York was posthumously granted the rank of honorary sergeant in the U.S. Army. He is depicted in at least five paintings by C. M. Russell, the prolific "cowboy artist" of the late nineteenth and early twentieth century, as well as in works by J. K. Ralston and Edgar Paxton. Here in Russell's Lewis and Clark on the Lower Columbia, *York is depicted seated in the foreground boat right below Sacajawea (standing).*

Deslondes, led some five hundred armed enslaved individuals in one of the largest insurrections for freedom in North America. Deslondes, a mixed-race Afro-Haitian slave driver on a sugar plantation outside of New Orleans, was, like many of Louisiana's black residents, attuned to the political and intellectual currents radiating from the French and Haitian revolutions. The insurgents advanced in military-style formations led by Deslondes and additional enslaved leaders, including African-born revolutionaries Quamana and Kook, as well as Harry Kenner, an enslaved carpenter from Virginia. This "slave army" was "ethnically diverse, politically astute, and highly organized."[12] The U.S. army and local militia ultimately suppressed the insurrection; in the aftermath, roughly one hundred of its participants were executed. Authorities also suppressed the uprising in the written record, which silenced the event for two centuries. Recent research has shown that "the revolutionaries of 1811 were heroes who deserve a place in our national memory. Their actions are a testament to the strength of the ideals of freedom and equality."[13]

The War of 1812

While the freedom fighters in the 1811 slave revolt faced off against the U.S. military, Afro-Americans in Louisiana—and Afro-Haitians in particular—played significant roles supporting the United States military in the War of 1812. The United States' first official war, a rematch with Britain, has been viewed as a carryover from the American Revolution, in which some five thousand black Patriot soldiers served. Yet the new nation had restricted the ability of people of color to serve in the armed forces in the wake of the Revolution. Despite these restrictions and the further elaboration of a white supremacist social structure, countless Afro-Americans risked their lives to serve their country during the War of 1812.

While many American schoolchildren may have memorized that the Chesapeake-Leopard Affair was an inciting event of the War of 1812, few have been exposed to the details. The *U.S.S. Chesapeake* was one of the six warships that had been ordered by President George Washington in 1794 to found a navy that was needed in part to defend against Barbary pirates who had been attacking U.S. merchant ships and selling whites to North

African slave markets for decades. Between 1625 and 1812 several hundreds—perhaps thousands—of North American colonists were held as slaves in North Africa, which "forced the government to pay humiliating tributes in cash and arms to African rulers" (these were a fraction of the hundreds of thousands—perhaps a million—Europeans enslaved by North Africans and Turks for two centuries).[14]

However, in the wake of U.S. independence and embroiled in the Napoleonic Wars, Great Britain was desperate for naval labor. Thousands of British seamen had become Americans as of the 1783 Paris Treaty that ended the American Revolution. Subsequently, British naval captains had made a practice of boarding American vessels to seize and force back into British service seamen who had, in the view of English authorities, deserted from the royal navy.

In 1807, off the coast of Norfolk, Virginia, the captain of the British ship *Leopard* demanded that the U.S.S. *Chesapeake* surrender four of its crewmen deemed British deserters. Three—William Ware, Daniel Martin, and John Strachin—were African American sailors who had indeed deserted the H.M.S. *Melampus* at Hampton Roads and enlisted in the U.S. navy.[15] President Thomas Jefferson compared the event to the Battle of Lexington in terms of galvanizing a public cry for war, and his Embargo of 1807 only temporarily forestalled military conflict.

When the War of 1812 broke out, African Americans again stepped up to serve their nation. Black Patriot veterans like James Forten rallied 2,500 African American men to guard Philadelphia. A total of 247 men of color enlisted in the Twenty-sixth U.S. Infantry in Philadelphia.[16] The New York African Society brought together thousands of black New Yorkers. Michigan's governor issued commissions to black Americans like Lieutenant Ezra Burgess and Ensign Bossett as well as Captain Peter Denison, who had previously mustered an all-black company in Detroit.[17]

African Americans participated in every major naval battle of the War of 1812. When Charles Ball, a self-liberated former slave, enlisted in the U.S. navy, black Americans comprised about 20 percent of its sailors.[18] Commander Thomas McDonough "credited much of his success against the British on Lake Champlain to the accuracy of his gunners—mostly black volunteers." Nathaniel Shafer described his black crewmen as "exceptionally brave."[19] Commodore Oliver Hazard Perry, who famously declared, "We have met the enemy and they are ours," praised the bravery of his crew, a quarter of whom were African American, three of whom he cited individually: Cyrus Tiffany, Jessie Walle, and Abraham Chase.[20] Another black sailor who gained public attention was Richard Crafus; known as "King Dick," Crafus was the charismatic leader of the thousand black seamen held as American prisoners of war in the British admiralty's Dartmoor Prison. After the war, Crafus became the subject of many media accounts.[21]

John Bathan Vashon was a free black sailor who fought for the U.S. during the War of 1812 and was taken prisoner by the British. Released after two years, Vashon eventually married and moved to Pittsburgh, Pennsylvania, where he became a successful businessman and barber and opened the town's first bathhouse—which was said to cater to white clients by day and fugitive slaves braving the Underground Railroad by night. A Virginia native, Vashon was the son of an enslaved woman and her owner. He organized and hosted the first meeting of the Pittsburgh Anti-slavery Society in his home in 1833 and engaged in numerous efforts for civic advancement, like founding the Pittsburgh African Education Society and an independent school as well as participating in political conventions. Vashon used his considerable wealth to support democratic endeavors and abolitionist media, as well as to purchase the freedom of one of his barber apprentices and to highly educate his own children, who became active abolitionists in their own right. His daughter, Mary Frances, was a journalist, and his son, George, was a lawyer and educator. John Vashon died of heart failure in 1853 while traveling as a delegate to the National Convention of Veterans of the War of 1812, "in the last act of service to his brethren, and in obedience to the summons of his country, in the person of one of her delegated warriors."[22]

Soon after Louisiana became a state, the First and Second Battalions of Free Men of Color were mustered to defend it in the War of 1812. The region's black military tradition began in the early 1700s with the free colored Spanish and French militia units of colonial Louisiana who defended the territory in 1729, 1736, 1746, and 1762 as well as fought against the British during the American Revolution. In 1803 two companies of free men of color participated in the parade celebrating the transfer of Louisiana from France to the United States.[23] When Great Britain threatened to invade New Orleans in 1814, General Andrew Jackson mustered some 600 black soldiers into the U.S. army. Jackson addressed these men as "sons of freedom" and "Americans" in his public appeal.[24]

Roughly 350 of Jackson's 600 black recruits were native-born veterans of the Spanish militia. Among them, Noel Carriére had served with Galvez during the American Revolution.[25] The First Battalion of Free Men of Color consisted of 353 men, most of whom had long histories of military service in Louisiana; six companies served with black officers such as Second Lieutenant Isodore Honoré and Major Vincent Populus.[26] In addition to the veterans of the Spanish militia, many of the black veterans of the Haitian Revolution who had settled in Louisiana were mustered as well.

An Afro-Haitian battalion of 256 recruits was decisive for the American victory at the Battle of New Orleans. The Second Battalion of Free Men of Color was organized and commanded by Joseph Savary, a free black officer from Saint Domingue who had served in the French army. Savary, a devotee of republican ideals, "was given the rank of Second Major" making him "the highest ranking black man in the United States army at the time."[27] Black women contributed to the war effort by volunteering in local hospitals while seventy nine free black volunteers served in the home guard.[28] Savary's battalion was praised by Andrew Jackson but ejected from New Orleans by anxious planters after their service. Savary and several of the other Haitian veterans joined up with pirate Pierre Lafitte in Spanish Texas and joined Mexican revolutionaries—with support from Haitian president Alexandre Pétion—in their fight for national independence from Spain.[29]

General Jackson and others wrote favorably of the valor and skill of the black fighters, and the victory they achieved during the Battle of New Orleans helped to foster the national popularity that would get Andrew Jackson elected president in 1828. The national glory symbolized by the victory at New Orleans was celebrated in numerous artworks, at least two of which depict black soldiers. One is a woodblock engraving by John Andrew from the mid nineteenth century. Another is a painting by Julien Hudson, *Battle of New Orleans*. Hudson was a mixed-race free person in antebellum

New Orleans who pursued classical painting in Europe as well as at home. Hudson's depiction of himself in his 1839 painting is the earliest known self-portrait by an African American artist.[30]

Despite Jackson's praise, many of the Afro-American soldiers who risked their lives for the United States were rewarded with a summary dismissal from armed service because of their race. Enslaved persons who supported the U.S. during the war in civilian and military capacities were required by law to return to slavery:

> Slave and free, African-Americans served, fought, suffered, and died for their country before, during, and after the War of 1812. The vast majority did so willingly in what can only be described as a noble display of patriotism. Their sacrifice was particularly compelling because African-Americans were fighting to preserve the fundamental rights of the United States of America; rights they themselves were not privileged to enjoy.[31]

Many Africans Americans therefore sought freedom through British military service during the War of 1812. Just as Dunmore's proclamation offered freedom to Loyalists during the American Revolution, England's Vice-Admiral Cochrane issued a proclamation in 1814 that made official the efforts of thousands of African American slaves to free themselves through military service and resettlement. The black sailors and soldiers who fought for the British served alongside the First and Fifth West India Regiments. These British regiments included approximately a thousand black soldiers from Jamaica, Barbados, and the Bahamas. The roots of the West India Regiments stretch back to the American Revolution when enslaved African Americans enlisted in 1779 to serve alongside the British in a "Carolina Corps" that was relocated to Jamaica after the war. The black West India Regiments served Britain in a series of Caribbean contests with France—which also had a highly trained free black militia.[32]

As they had during the American Revolution, thousands of African American families sought liberty by pursuing the promise of freedom and resettlement offered by the British during the War of 1812. Some four thousand African Americans achieved their liberty by serving in the British forces, making it the largest mass emancipation in the U.S. between the American Revolution and the Civil War. Roughly two thousand African Americans joined black American Loyalists in Nova Scotia and five hundred settled in New Brunswick. Others joined Loyalist communities in Bermuda. Seven hundred of the African American freedom fighters who served in the Corps of Colonial Marines (two Marine units composed of self-liberated American slaves) settled in Trinidad in 1816; the descendants of these ex-Marines, known as the Merikens, continue to celebrate them today.[33] Some fugitive slaves continued to serve the British navy. Still others allied with the Black Seminoles and maroon communities in Florida.

The Seminole Wars

Many African Americans fled to freedom in Spanish Florida during and after the War of 1812. Several of their predecessors had secured freedom and property in exchange for military service for the Spanish in Florida as far back as 1687. In 1811, on the eve of the War of 1812, the United States dispatched General George Matthews to annex Spanish Florida. Spain countered by bringing up black troops from Havana to join the St. Augustine garrison that consisted of four hundred whites and five hundred black soldiers.[34] Soon enslaved individuals in Georgia and the Carolinas began to make their way in large numbers to join the Spanish garrison or their Seminole supporters. "Black-instigated resistance" defeated the U.S. forces and restored peace to East Florida for another five years.[35]

In 1814, during the War of 1812, the British established a garrison in Spanish Florida for the British Royal Marines, including the African American freedmen who composed the Corps of Colonial Marines referenced above. Known as the Negro Fort, the garrison continued to be occupied by some three hundred self-liberated American slaves and Seminole allies after the war ended in 1815. Led by an African American named Garson and an Amerindian ally, the soldiers of the fort launched raids across the border into Georgia as well as protected a growing colony of fugitive slave settlers in Florida. Some eight hundred additional fugitive slaves from the United States settled in areas surrounding the fort. Located on Prospect Bluff along Florida's Apalachicola River, the region had long served as sanctuary for maroons.

In 1818, Andrew Jackson initiated the First Seminole War and the conquest of Florida when he ordered the U.S. navy to attack the Negro Fort. The Negro Fort's soldiers took the initial advantage, but a fortuitous shot by American forces detonated the garrison's powder magazine. The explosion killed most of the garrison's occupants but spared its leaders and about forty maroons. Jackson's subsequent invasion of Spanish Florida, which concluded the First Seminole War, destroyed the homes and property of hundreds of Native and black Americans. Many of the surviving maroons resettled further south. Jackson wrote that he regarded "Negros and Indians" as desiring war with the U.S.[36] As a contemporary observer put it, "the main drift of the Americans is to destroy the black population of Suwany."[37]

As a borderland and buffer between Spanish and English domains, Florida provided opportunities to communities initiated by freedom-seeking fugitive slaves starting in the 1600s. By the early 1800s Florida was home to several independent maroon settlements of successful agriculturalists. Among them, a maroon settlement near present-day Sarasota known as Angola had perhaps as many as 900 black homesteaders. As noted above, the region around the Negro Fort was the site of multiple independent black settlements. As described in Chapter 4, large numbers of former slaves from Georgia and the Carolinas joined with and adapted to the Creek Indian culture that came to be called Seminole, some of whom formed distinct Black Seminole communities.

Florida's robust maroon population exemplified an extraordinary devotion to the principles of independence and individual rights. "The maroons of Gulf Coast Florida, in the Age of Revolution with its massive upheavals, had impressive leaders who knew the transnational discourses of freedom and liberty."[38] Many of the Afro-descended members of these maroon communities came to be known as Black Seminoles, thousands of whom defended their freedom as combatants in the Seminole Wars. In 1821, when the Spanish ceded Florida to the United States, hundreds of Black Seminoles migrated to the Bahamas' Andros Island, where their descendants retain ties to the Gullah culture of Georgia ancestors.[39]

In Andros, at the time part of the British Bahamas, "the former slaves were immediately recognized as British subjects [and] allowed to participate in the island's government."[40] Over the next two decades, additional maroons from Florida settled on Andros Island and established Nicholls Town, named in honor of the British officer who had initiated Florida's Negro Fort.[41] "As had been the case at Prospect Bluff, the former slaves owned property and became successful farmers and businessmen who formed an important part of the Andros Island's economy."[42] Other Black Seminoles found freedom in the American West and in Mexico.

One of the primary goals of Andrew Jackson's presidency was the removal of Native Americans from the eastern United States and free blacks from Florida specifically. A year into his first term, Jackson signed the Indian Removal Act of 1830. While the First Seminole War (which Jackson called a "Savage and Negro War") had gained Florida from the Spanish, U.S. forces were unable to fully defeat the alliance of Seminoles, Black Seminoles, and self-liberated slaves from Georgia and Alabama in the Second Seminole War (1835–1842) and found themselves again at war in 1855–1858 for the Third Seminole War.[43]

The Second Seminole War was among the most effective slave revolts in United States history.[44] When the U.S. army went up against the Black Seminoles, the fighters defending their freedom were composed not only of Florida's longstanding maroons but also of a new wave of fugitives who liberated themselves from southern plantations during the conflict. Between 1835 and 1838, a black force of approximately one thousand free and self-liberated African Americans, under the guidance of the Black Seminole John Horse (also known as Juan Cavallo), became "the first black rebels to *defeat* American slavery."[45] At the height of the revolt, "at least 385 slaves fought alongside the black and Indian Seminole allies, helping them destroy more than twenty-one sugar plantations in central Florida."[46] U.S. officials believed that these slave rebels, whose numbers may have been as high as 465, had been conspiring with Florida's maroons for a significant period of time, planning a mass uprising with the intention of seeking refuge in Cuba.

In 1838, after the U.S. army was unable to defeat these black freedom fighters in three years of combat, the U.S. government offered them freedom in the West in exchange for surrender. Approximately 500 of these individuals accompanied their Native allies in resettlement. Among the black

Private John Jefferson served in the United States Army during World War I. The grandson of Black Seminole leader and statesman, John Horse, Jefferson was a Negro Seminole Scout and Buffalo Soldier, as were many of the Black Seminoles who fought for freedom in Florida and resettled in the West. Because of their African ancestry, they were often attached to the black regiments established after the Civil War that came to be known as the Buffalo Soldiers. Active from 1866 to 1951, Buffalo Soldiers played vital roles in U.S. nation-building in the American West at the end of the nineteenth century. Many saw wartime service in Cuba, the Philippines, and Mexico as well as WWI and WWII.

rebels who migrated was a small contingent of recent fugitive slaves, but most were returned to their plantations. John Horse was among the many Black Seminoles who resettled in Oklahoma and ultimately joined the U.S. army—as did their descendants. From 1870 to 1917, black Seminole scouts served alongside the Buffalo Soldiers who defended the western territories and were among U.S. forces who fought in Cuba, the Philippines, Mexico, and in World War I in the late nineteenth and early twentieth centuries.

Latin American Revolutions

Mexican Independence

While Afro-Americans were fighting for independence in Louisiana and Florida, Afro-Mexicans were participants and leaders in the Mexican war for independence (1810–1821). Afro-Mexicans contributed militarily as well as to the intellectual arguments that shaped the founding of the Mexican nation.[47] José Maria Morelos, a Catholic priest of African and Amerindian heritage, wrote elegant tracts against slavery and served as one of the nation's founding revolutionaries and key generals. When the revolution's founder, Father Miguel Hidalgo, was executed in 1810, Morelos took up the lead. Morelos expertly led military campaigns, often with armies that were entirely black or mixed-race. In 1813, Morelos organized a congress of leaders in rebel-controlled areas and drafted *The Sentiments of the Nations* which declared independence from Spain and outlined a government based on republican principles. He was captured by the Spanish and executed in 1815. Morelos is honored as a founding father with his likeness on Mexican currency and with a stadium, port, train station, museum, city, and state bearing his name.

After Morelos's execution, his lieutenant, Vicente Guerrero, also of African and Amerindian descent, took control of the national army. Guerrero, known as the "consummator of independence," continued the revolution despite Spain's retributions, negotiated terms with Spain based on civil rights, and ultimately served as Mexico's second president.[48] As the historian J. A. Rogers observed, Guerrero was both the George Washington and Abraham Lincoln of Mexico, having led the military struggle for independence and then as president, enacting the formal abolition of slavery.[49] Like Morelos, Guerrero was among the four revolutionary heroes to have Mexican states named for them.

South American Independence

Between 1808 and 1826, Venezuela, Colombia, Ecuador, Bolivia, Peru, Panama, Uruguay, Chile, and Argentina fought for independence from Spain, and enslaved Afro-Latins were essential to these struggles. "In taking up arms to fight for their freedom, slaves not only won independence for the societies in which they lived but also helped launch the first great wave of social and political reform in Latin American history."[50] Throughout South America, slaves served in military companies "in numbers that far exceeded their numbers in the population," and in many instances they "determined the difference between success and failure."[51] Without the contributions and

José María Morelos and Vicente Guerrero, both of known African ancestry, are two of Mexico's most important founding fathers and national heroes. Morelos led the Mexican War of Independence from 1811 until his capture and execution by Spanish colonial authorities in 1815. Guerrero (depicted in the adjacent portrait) served alongside Morelos as a general and became president of the new nation in 1829. As president, Guerrero abolished slavery, prompting some to dub him "the Washington and Lincoln of Mexico." Considering that Africans outnumbered Europeans in Mexico until about 1810, it should not be surprising that the nation's founding fathers would be of mixed Amerindian, African, and European descent. Afro-Americans played major roles in the wars of independence throughout Latin America.

sacrifices of enslaved Afro-Latins, "the patriot cause . . . would have been greatly weakened."[52]

Observed Simón Bolívar, the "Patriot Liberator" of Venezuela, Colombia, Panama, Ecuador, Bolivia, and Peru, "we are more a mixture of Africa and America than we are children of Europe."[53] Bolívar (himself a slave owner who may not have been of exclusive European ancestry) recognized the demographic strength of Afro-descended South Americans and the realities of racial mixing and *mestizaje* throughout the colonies. In initiating revolution in his native Venezuela, Bolívar soon realized his appeals to white liberals were useless without gaining the support of the *llaneros*, the large population of black cowboys who resented the *criollo* (American-born) elite and initially "utterly defeated the patriots."[54] Bolivar recognized that, "As long as the *llaneros* opposed them, the patriots would never win in Venezuela."[55] Bolivar used appeals of nativism and liberalism to court Venezuela's Afro-American cowboys; when they switched sides, "momentum moved to the patriot cause."[56]

Bolívar and the Spanish American struggles for independence also greatly benefited from the support of Haitians. Haiti's President Alexandre Pétion provided supplies and soldiers, including Afro-Haitian officers, to serve in South America. "The refuge and assistance President Pétion provided to Simón Bolívar in 1816 made a vital contribution to the winning of national independence in northern South America."[57] Moreover, "the payment Pétion stipulated was slavery's abolition in the liberated regions."[58] Bolívar offered to honor Pétion by proclaiming his benefactor the patron of South American independence and declaring the Afro-Haitian "the author of American liberty."[59] For Pétion the glory was in the liberation itself—"No, don't mention my name; my only desire is to see that those who tremble under slavery's yoke are free: Liberate my brothers, and that will be payment enough."[60] Bolívar promised to abolish slavery in South America if he should be victorious.[61]

In Ecuador, one-third of Bólivar's recruits were legally slaves, and in Colombia some five thousand enslaved Afro-Latins joined patriot forces between 1819 and 1821. Cartagena, in particular, "was a crucial theater of the independence struggles, in which people of African descent—a demographic majority—played a key political and military role."[62] In Cartagena "the loyalty—or lack thereof—of people of African descent was key to the success or failure of the patriot army; and like Venezuela, Caribbean Colombia contributed some of the most important black officers and heroes of the independence era."[63]

Pedro Romero, a Cuban-born blacksmith and militia member, led Cartagena's "Colored Patriots" against Spain, initiating Colombia's movement for independence. Lieutenant Pedro Camejo, Colonel Juan José Rondón, and Colonel Leonardo Infante were among the black officers who sacrificed their lives for the liberation of Gran Colombia (comprising present-day Venezuela, Colombia, Ecuador, and Panama).

Throughout the Americas, many enslaved Afro-Latins gained their

Alexandre Pétion was a founding father and president of the republic of Haiti (1806–1818). An originator of Pan-Americanism, he advanced republican ideals throughout the hemisphere as a supporter of Mexican sovereignty and as an ally of Simón Bolívar in South America, to whom he gave military and political aid and from whom he extracted the promise to abolish slavery in Venezuela, setting in motion the end of South American slavery. Correspondence shows that Pétion declined Bolívar's offer to publicly recognize the Haitian president as the liberator of Venezuela and New Granada.

freedom in exchange for their military service, but all of the Latin American colonies had long-standing free black populations as well. "[I]n country after country, free blacks and mulattos formed the backbone of liberal rebellions, guerilla movements, and armies."[64] After helping to achieve national independence, Afro-Latins were active in electoral and party politics and the establishment of the new republics. Black elected officials like Colombia's magistrate Valentín Arcía and senator Remigio Márquez championed the ideals of justice and equality, even in the face of political rivals who endeavored to undermine them.

Among the most politically influential black officers was Admiral José Padilla, the greatest naval hero of the independence wars of Gran Colombia and the founder of the Colombian navy. In his youth, Padilla served in the Spanish Royal Navy, first as a cabin boy and later as a boatswain. During the Napoleonic Wars, he was taken prisoner by the British during the Battle of Trafalgar in 1805 and returned to Cartagena in 1808. "By this time his travels had no doubt made him familiar with stories about the French Revolution, the Haitian Revolution, and English abolitionism."[65]

Padilla was made a patriot general in Bolívar's war against Spain and led several victorious battles—most famously in Maracaibo in 1824—which made him a national hero. Tragically, when Padilla's support, and that of his constituency, for Colombia's liberal constitution came into conflict with Bolívar's desire for conservative reform and fear of black political dominance ("pardocracy"), the latter had the former executed for sedition, making Padillo an American martyr for freedom. Padilla was not the first black officer Bolívar had executed. Manuel Piar, a black patriot hero who had fought for his nation's sovereignty, was executed in 1817.[66]

South of Gran Colombia, independence struggles in Argentina, Chile, and Peru were also disproportionately fought by Afro-Americans. In Argentina, even before the struggles led by José San Martín, black people served in and led militias to defeat the occupying British. Some estimate that, within free colored units and slave battalions, fully one-third of Argentina's black population served the cause of national liberation. Black troops from Buenos Aires fought the Spanish in Uruguay, northwestern Argentina, Bolivia, Chile, Peru, and Ecuador.[67] As many as five thousand Afro-Argentine slaves joined revolutionary forces between 1819 and 1821.[68]

According to a contemporary observer in Peru in 1822, San Martín's "'entire army' was composed of slaves."[69] The observation underscored that "slaves were a strikingly visible part of the patriot armies fighting on the west coast of South America, just as they were elsewhere on the continent."[70] When San Martín invaded Chile in 1817, half or more of his soldiers were former slaves. The 8th Regiment of the Andean Liberation Army was comprised entirely of formerly enslaved individuals. Thousands of Afro-Argentines risked and often gave their lives for the liberation of Chile. "Of the 2000 to 3000 Argentine [freedmen] who crossed the Andes into Chile with San Martín, fewer than 150 returned."[71] Large numbers of Afro-Argentines gave their lives a few decades later in the Paraguayan War from 1865–1870.[72]

While many Afro-Latin men gave their lives for the cause, Afro-Latin women were active participants in South American independence as well. Venezuela's Juana Ramírez, who had been born into slavery in 1790, commanded an all-female artillery unit in 1813. Dubbed *La Avanzadora*, Ramírez led troops that "were instrumental in resisting Spanish soldiers' attempts to reconquer the newly independent Venezuela and return it to colonial rule."[73]

Presaging the impact of African American women in the American Civil War, many enslaved women assisted the patriot armies of Latin America as spies, nurses, cooks, and camp aides as well as combatants. Noncombatants, including enslaved women, capitalized on the opportunities that inhered in these political upheavals, especially the republican ideology that accompanied them. Angela Batallas, for example, an enslaved Ecuadoran woman, sought her freedom directly from Simon Bólivar in 1823, arguing "I do not believe that meritorious members of a republic that . . . have given all necessary proofs of liberalism . . . would want to pledge to keep me in servitude."[74] Some female slaves negotiated benefits based on their husband's service to purchase their own freedom. Numerous enslaved persons sought freedom through various forms of resistance during and after the independence wars.

In South America slave soldiers won freedom for their countries, for themselves, and for their children. Afro-Latin slaves "played a crucially important role in winning independence for Spanish South America," and their national service "triggered the programs of gradual emancipation."[75] In the 1810s and early 1820s, Argentina, Peru, Colombia, Venezuela, Ecuador, and Uruguay enacted "free womb" laws that emancipated the children of enslaved women. Republican forces in Chile declared any slave who would bear arms "free from that instant" and summarily ended slavery in 1823.[76] Throughout South America, "manumission, freedom through military service, high rates of mortality (both in the wars and in daily life), [along with] the absence of any further slave births," combined to significantly reduce the population of Afro-Latins in perpetual slavery.[77] Enslaved soldiers fought not only for their own freedom but also to ensure the liberty of others. They did so on the battlefield, in their everyday lives, and through legal channels.

By 1824, at the close of the independence wars, "the constitutions of all the nations in Spanish America granted legal racial equality to their free populations of African descent."[78] For many elites, including Bólivar, the potential for Afro-Latin dominance was troubling, and the fear of a "race war" became a rationale to check black political power. Despite the perseverance of racism, new nations like Colombia "enshrined for the first time the principle of racial equality as a fundamental value for modern democracies," however, "it also set limits on its full implementation."[79]

Several Afro-Latins were promoted to high military rank as a result of their patriot services.[80] These black officers contributed to the national formation and republican development of Latin America's newly independent states. The distinguished military service of Afro-Americans like Sergeant Major José Romero in Chile, Colonel Lorenzo Barcala in Argentina, Colonel Feliciano Gonzales in Uruguay, General Antonio Maceo in Cuba, and General José Domingo Espinar in Panama made them national heroes. In the nineteenth century, seven Americans of African descent served as Latin American presidents: Bernadino Rivadavia in Argentina (1825–1827), Vicente Guerrero in Mexico (1829), Vicente Roca in Ecuador (1845–1849), Juan José Nieto Gil in Colombia (1861), Juaquín Crespo in Venezuela (1884–1886, 1892–1897), and Buenaventura Báez (1849–1853) and Ulises Heureaux (1882–1899) in the Dominican Republic.[81]

While Afro-Latin officers and officials influenced national politics as individuals, black populations shaped popular politics as influential constituencies. In the nineteenth century, Afro-Latins initiated a powerful populist political tradition, and "black support contributed materially to liberalism's eventual triumph throughout Spanish America."[82] However, Afro-Latins did not share a uniform political consciousness; moreover, party politics was in many circumstances overshadowed by patronage networks.

EARLY NINETEENTH-CENTURY REBELLIONS FOR FREEDOM

While slaves capitalized on the South American independence wars to become "agents of their own freedom," Afro-Americans in the United States and the Caribbean organized their own liberation movements in the first half of the nineteenth century.[83] Like the New Orleans slave revolt of 1811, revolutionary organizers in Virginia, South Carolina, and Cuba looked to Haiti for inspiration as they endeavored to establish independence. The British Caribbean experienced some two dozen rebellions for freedom in the first decades of the nineteenth century, prompting England to abolish slavery throughout her American territories in the 1830s.

Prosser's Rebellion

In 1800 Gabriel Prosser, an enslaved blacksmith from Richmond, Virginia, endeavored to coordinate a large-scale movement to end slavery and realize a republican vision of freedom in the United States. Deeply influenced by the Haitian Revolution that was continuing to unfold as well as by the republican ideology of the artisan contemporaries in his midst, Gabriel lived in a time and place, according to historian Douglas Egerton, where skills and ambitions were fostered and revolutionaries might have "realistic dreams of freedom."[84]

At the turn of the nineteenth century, Richmond, like many commercial centers at the time, was home to a large skilled black population, enslaved and free. Gabriel lived on Thomas Prosser's tobacco plantation outside of town, but he was often hired out in Richmond where he spent several nights a month on his own. Gabriel devised a plan to end slavery that included a three-pronged insurgency to capture the state capital (and Governor James Monroe), the prison, and the arsenal in an attack that would be coordinated with rebels in various cities throughout the state.

Gabriel and his collaborators in Richmond, Petersburg, Norfolk, Suffolk and four surrounding counties made this a particularly wide-ranging effort to overturn U.S. slavery. Gabriel and his followers initially recruited black artisans "whose talents and skills had made them self-sufficient and nearly free in their unique urban world."[85] They joined ranks with additional urban slaves and free people of color, rural slaves, a few working-class white men, and two Frenchmen.

By August 1800, Gabriel's army and its munitions were in place. The coordinated uprising for freedom was ultimately derailed by a thunderstorm on the appointed date and by enslaved informants who alerted authorities. In a bitter irony, while Gabriel and his collaborators had endeavored to achieve freedom for all African Americans, only three ultimately gained their liberty: the two enslaved informants as well as a third enslaved person who testified against the conspirators at trial.[86]

In 1802, a surviving enslaved accomplice named Sancho attempted another rebellion, the Easter Plot, without success. That same year "the *Richmond Recorder* announced that American editors had been fomenting restlessness among Virginia slaves by reprinting the St. Domingo constitution."[87] The failed insurgencies had a continuing impact on the Virginia Assembly, who for the next five years debated a policy of gradual emancipation and colonization.

Vesey's Rebellion

In 1821, Denmark Vesey, a free black carpenter who admired the accomplishments of the Haitian Revolution, organized a conspiracy for freedom involving perhaps nine thousand enslaved Americans in South Carolina. Born on St. Thomas, Vesey spent time in Haiti and at sea before moving to Charleston where he purchased his freedom. In 1817, he founded a branch of the African Methodist Episcopal Church; the strength of its congregation and its revolutionary potential worried local authorities.[88]

Charleston was the United States' fifth largest city in the early nineteenth century, and Vesey orchestrated a campaign to seize its arsenal and the ships in its preeminent port. Months in advance, Vesey "prepared six infantry and cavalry companies of armed slaves" and "corresponded with the president of the new black republic of Haiti in hope of obtaining that nation's military aid."[89]

Authorities were ultimately tipped off by an informant, arrested some one hundred and thirty individuals and executed thirty-six, including Vesey, after a long and secretive trial. Militias were called on to suppress demonstrations during the executions. While Charleston's black population had been forbidden to wear mourning clothes, many did so.

Forty years later African Americans would fight a war to end slavery that took 800,000 lives. At the start of the Civil War, Frederick Douglass invoked the memory of Denmark Vesey in his recruitment of black troops. At the close of the Civil War, Vesey's son celebrated the nation's triumph when the U.S. flag "was raised for the first time since the beginning of the war over the rubble that was now Fort Sumter in Charleston Harbor."[90] According to accounts, "a crowd of more than 4,000 people, most of them ex-slaves from surrounding plantations, began to sing 'The Star-Spangled Banner.' Among them was Denmark Vesey's son."[91]

Turner's Rebellion

In 1831 another revolt "fired the imagination of American abolition-ists, helping lead the [United States] down the long road of civil war."[92] In Southampton, Virginia, Nat Turner—an American who had been inherited as the legal property of a nine-year old boy—organized seventy freedom fighters including freemen of color, Billy Artis and Berry Newsome, as well as Turner's wife. The subsequent slayings of sixty white men, women, and children were intended to be in the service of a larger revolution for freedom.

Turner's revolt and its aftermath highlight the complexity of social rela-tions that shaped antebellum American life.[93] Some of the rebels collaborat-ing with Turner chose to protect particular white people from harm. Some slaves who did not conspire with Turner also protected particular white individuals. In the revolt's aftermath, a white slaveholder named Nathaniel Francis publicly "embraced his slave Easter, who had saved Mrs. Francis [during the uprising], whereupon a mob 'almost killed' him 'for defending a negro woman,' and then murdered her. Francis later claimed to have killed between ten and fifteen blacks."[94] Several white Virginians expressed alarm not only for the violence of the Turner revolt, but also for the widespread, indiscriminate violence in retaliation.

Aponte's Rebellion

While the early nineteenth century did not offer Cubans of color the opportunity to pursue citizenship through wartime service (which would happen at the end of the century), free and enslaved Afro-Cubans nonetheless challenged slavery throughout the century. In January 1812, enslaved Cubans and free people of color launched a series of five uprisings across the island. The militia, army, and vigilantes suppressed the revolts, executed fourteen rebels, and sent sixty-three prisoners to St. Augustine. However, hundreds of rebels fled and another insurrection erupted shortly thereafter. Alarmed authorities made extensive investigations, hundreds were imprisoned, and thirty-two rebels were put to death. Among the executed was José Antonio Aponte, whom colonial authorities condemned as the organizer.

Like Denmark Vesey, Aponte was a free black carpenter. He was a captain in Cuba's black militia and a veteran of the American Revolution.

Aponte had served with distinction under the governor of Spanish Louisiana, Bernardo de Galvez, who organized Afro-Americans from Louisiana, Mexico, and Cuba to aid the American Patriots.[95] For Cuban officials, the most compelling evidence of Aponte's guilt was a book of drawings he had made that included portraits of Haitian revolutionaries and maps of Havana's fortifications.

Aponte was not the first Afro-Cuban to look to the Haitian Revolution for inspiration. In 1795, an enslaved Cuban named Romualdo led a small revolt in Puerto Principe, Cuba, and the free mulatto Nicolas Morales led an aborted uprising in Bayamo, Cuba. "Participants in both alluded to the uprising of slaves in Saint Domingue."[96] According to Antonio José, an enslaved informant, Aponte's rebels had planned to take over Cuba's military arsenals—just as Prosser's rebels in Virginia had twelve years prior. The Aponte Rebellion became the official designation of the series of protests that brought together Afro-Cubans, enslaved and free, rural and urban, African- and Cuban-born, to challenge slavery in 1812.

Some scholars believe that Aponte may have been a scapegoat for an anxious planter elite; still, the Haitian Revolution shaped Cuba's multiple slave uprisings in 1812 in several ways. With the success of Afro-Haitians in overturning slavery, Haiti ceased to be a predominant supplier of the world market for sugar and coffee. Early nineteenth-century Cuba and Brazil responded by importing large numbers of involuntary African laborers—despite the ban on the slave trade—and expanding their plantation economies.

As in other New World plantation societies, Cuba's growing slave populations led to greater restrictions for both enslaved and free people of color. And, as in the rest of the Atlantic world, people of African descent fought against the repression. Afro-Cubans were bolstered not only by the example of Haiti but also by the organizational networks they had in place as members of black civic organizations like *cabildos* and colonial militias.[97] During the Great African Slave Revolt of 1825, recently arrived involuntary immigrants organized to alter their condition and initiated a wave of uprisings that continued for two decades.[98] Cuban slaves, and their free black and white collaborators, organized additional bids for freedom in 1826, 1830, 1837, and 1840.[99]

La Escalera

From 1841 to 1844, an underground rebel freedom movement connecting urban and rural participants prompted another series of insurgencies that challenged Cuban slavery. Cuban authorities deemed it *La Escalera* or "the Conspiracy of the Ladder" and subsequently tortured, imprisoned, and executed hundreds of enslaved and free Afro-Cubans in 1844. The advocates for freedom associated with La Escalera were seen as a grave and imminent threat to colonialism and slavery.[100] One of the sites where enslaved Cubans rose up, the Triunvirato sugar plantation in Matanzas, was declared a national monument in 1978. In 1991 La Escalera was again publicly recognized as a national step toward Cuban freedom with a monument depicting three of the freedom fighters, including Carlota Lucumí, an Afro-Cuban woman and principal leader of the movement who was killed in battle. Another Afro-Cuban woman, Fermina, became a martyred revolutionary leader when she was executed in the wake of the uprising.[101]

Emancipation Wars in the British Caribbean

In the first decades of the nineteenth century, the British Caribbean was rocked by two dozen or more insurgencies. As Matt Childs put it, "the British Caribbean experienced a cycle of slave insurrections that hammered the final nails into slavery's coffin."[102] Some of these coordinated resistance efforts have been dubbed "the Emancipation Wars," starting with the 1816 Barbados rebellion led by African slave driver Bussa and several collaborators.[103]

One of the largest of the Emancipation Wars occurred in 1823 in Demerara (now Guyana, a nation that borders Venezuela, Brazil, and Suriname) when approximately ten thousand enslaved individuals challenged slavery, armed and in unison. As noted in Chapter 4, an earlier uprising for freedom took place in there in 1795. The British, having recently taken over the colony from the Dutch, declared martial law and condemned numerous rebels to death, including an English missionary sympathetic to the cause. One of the largest uprisings in the history of the Americas, the Demerara Rebellion—which began on the family plantation of Britain's future liberal prime minister William Gladstone—weighed heavily on elite deliberations over abolition in the British Empire.[104]

Eight years after the Demerara Rebellion, Afro-Jamaican preacher Samuel Sharpe helped to instigate a general strike to protest slavery. The 1831 Jamaican uprising became known as the Christmas Rebellion, the largest slave revolt in the British Caribbean, and the capstone of the Emancipation Wars. While the rebellion of approximately 30,000 individuals (some estimates double this number) was ultimately put down by British forces, days after Sharpe's execution Parliament appointed a committee to dismantle slavery. Pushed to the brink by the large and small insurgencies initiated by enslaved and free people of color, slavery in the British Empire came to a close with the passage of legislation in 1833 that resulted in complete abolition in 1838.

WHILE SLAVES THROUGHOUT SOUTH America liberated themselves as soldiers in the first half of the nineteenth century, slave rebels in the United States and the Caribbean took matters into their own hands. Thousands of Afro-Cubans rose up for freedom during the Aponte Rebellion and the Escalera insurgency and in several uprisings in between. In the United States Afro-Americans organized armed rebellions for freedom in Louisiana, Florida, Virginia, and South Carolina. The South Carolina conspiracy for freedom of 1822 may have enlisted upwards of 9,000 enslaved individuals. The following year, an uprising in British Demerara engaged 10,000 armed, enslaved freedom-seekers. Eight years later, 30,000 Jamaicans violently protested slavery. Two years after that, England abolished slavery throughout the British Caribbean.

SIERRA LEONE AND LIBERIA

In the early 1800s, many Americans, black and white, viewed the expatriation of African Americans as a solution to the problem of black freedom in a racist society. In the aftermath of Gabriel Prosser's collaboration and Haiti's struggles for sovereignty, Governor James Monroe wrote to President Thomas Jefferson urgently requesting a plan for colonization to remove Virginia's free black population. Jefferson replied to Monroe in November 1801, "Could we procure lands beyond the limits of the U.S. to form a receptacle for these people?"[105] The American Colonization Society was formed in 1817 to resettle black Americans outside the United States.

As African Americans and Afro-Cubans went to war for freedom in the 1860s, the Baptist Deacon Paul Bogle, who was among the few Afro-Jamaicans wealthy enough to meet the colony's voting requirements, led a protest for universal male suffrage and civic equality in the British colony in 1865. (Seven months prior, Afro-Jamaicans had petitioned Queen Victoria to assess policies which stymied economic development.)

While the movement that Bogle shepherded—which became known as the Morant Bay Rebellion—was brutally suppressed (outraging many in England including John Stuart Mill and Charles Darwin), it resulted in some favorable policy changes. Bogle was officially declared a national hero in 1969 and honored on two forms of Jamaican currency. Bogle shares the status of publicly recognized national hero with his predecessor, Samuel Sharpe, who in 1831 organized a labor strike on Christmas day to protest slavery. Sharpe is commemorated with a teachers' college and public square named in his honor, and the Jamaican fifty-dollar note bears his image. Queen Nanny, the adroit maroon leader, is featured on the five hundred dollar bill. Born in Ghana, she governed a Jamaican maroon community designated as Nanny Town in the early 1700s. Considered a gifted military leader by friend and foe, she repeatedly defended her community against colonial militias and organized raids that liberated approximately one thousand Afro-Jamaicans.

While some proponents of and arguments for colonization were steeped in an ideology that disdained black people and celebrated their elimination, others saw colonization as the most realistic and realizable means to achieve full civil rights and political equality for people of African descent. Many African Americans from Virginia to New England saw colonization as a means to ameliorate the inequities and disadvantages engendered by racism. In England, proponents of colonization mobilized Britain's establishment of the Sierra Leone colony in 1787. The U.S. followed suit with the establishment of Liberia in 1821.

Sierra Leone

The British colony in Sierra Leone was originally conceived as a solution to London's surging population of indigent Afro-descended men, many of whom were former U.S. slaves and Loyalist veterans. British officials settled the Anglo-African "Province of Freedom" in Sierra Leone with "a batch estimated at 459 persons, including 112 white women prostitutes, drugged and bundled onto the ship as partners to the black men."[106] This endeavor to relocate poor black men and poor white women can be viewed as part of a larger history of official British efforts to remove members of the underclass, whether they be English peasants displaced by the Enclosure Acts, Irish insurgents, or British convicts, by transferring them voluntarily and involuntarily to the far reaches of the empire as servants, settlers, or impressed seamen.

In many ways the Sierra Leone colony failed to live up to its promise of freedom for the formerly enslaved—to the disappointment of proponents like Olaudah Equiano (see Chapter 4), who had been appointed commissary to the Sierra Leone expedition by the British government. After the outlawing of the slave trade by the British in 1807, Sierra Leone was also meant to serve as a refuge for kidnapped Africans intercepted by British ships.

Despite conflicts between officials, colonists, and native residents in Sierra Leone, black abolitionists—many of whom were former U.S. slaves—developed a community committed to anti-slavery and democracy that had far-reaching effects.[107] Many African Americans who sought liberty by serving in the British forces during the American Revolution and the

War of 1812 ultimately settled in Sierra Leone. Thomas Peters, a former enslaved millwright from North Carolina (kidnapped from Nigeria), who was twice wounded during the American Revolution, organized a petition among black Americans in Nova Scotia to be resettled in Sierra Leone. After the American Revolution and again after the War of 1812, thousands of black Loyalist veterans and their families were initially settled in Nova Scotia. These new Canadians, many of whom had liberated themselves from plantations in the American South, faced severe weather as well as British provisional neglect and inhospitable neighbors.

By the early nineteenth century some 1,200 of these black Americans living in Canada had sought refuge in Sierra Leone. Among them was Harry Washington (see Chapter 4), formerly of Mount Vernon. Another was David George, who liberated himself from a Virginia plantation, became a minister in Georgia, and established the first black church in the United States in 1775 as well as churches in Canada and Sierra Leone. As Lamin Sanneh has documented, African Americans brought with them a commitment to a democratic vision of Christianity that helped to establish "a new and revolutionary conception of society" in western Africa that not only dealt the slave trade a "body blow" but also established abolitionism as "a universal movement for human rights."[108]

Liberia

While many African Americans helped to settle Britain's Sierra Leone colony in West Africa, many more African Americans helped to found, develop, and govern the American colony of Liberia. Lott Carey, for example, a self-liberated former slave from the outskirts of Richmond, Virginia, was one of the key founders of Liberia, originally sponsored by the American Colonization Society. Self-educated with an interest in political economy, Carey used his wages from hiring out as a shipping clerk in a tobacco factory to purchase his and his children's freedom. Carey became a Baptist minister in 1813 and founded the African Missionary Society in 1815. In 1821, he sailed to West Africa where he established several churches and schools. Carey was among thousands of black Americans, predominantly from Virginia, who helped to create Liberia, Africa's first independent republic. Some

Joseph Jenkins Roberts became the first African American president in the world when he became the first head of state in Liberia in 1848. Roberts, the son of a formerly enslaved woman and their former owner, grew up with his mother and step-father, a successful free black entrepreneur, in Petersburg, Virginia. Building on his career as a successful businessman and international merchant, Roberts was a tireless diplomat and education advocate (he served as the president of Liberia's university and was re-elected as Liberia's seventh president as well). His brothers, a physician and a bishop, also played prominent roles in Liberia's founding.

16,000 African Americans sought freedom and independence in Liberia, especially during the mid-eighteenth century.[109]

In 1848, Joseph Jenkins Roberts became the world's first African American president when he was elected to govern the newly independent nation of Liberia. Roberts, the son of a former slave and her owner, had been raised by free black parents in Virginia and grew up among the flourishing free black populations of Norfolk and Petersburg. He inherited property from his stepfather (a free black waterman who managed a lucrative business on Virginia's James River), developed a successful international trading business with a free black barber named William Colson, and emigrated to Monrovia in 1823 under the auspices of the American Colonization Society. Roberts became sheriff and then governor of the colony of Liberia. He served as the independent republic's first president (1847–1856) as well as its seventh (1872–1876).

Roberts traveled widely on diplomatic missions to gain recognition for the new country, advocate for the end of slavery, and fund educational development. He served for a decade as the president of the University of

Liberia, which he helped to found in 1862. As a founding father of the free black republic, Roberts likened the establishment of Liberia to the founding of Jamestown.[110] One of his brothers served as the region's first black bishop while another served as a physician. Upon his death, Roberts left his estate to Liberia's educational system.

Roberts's mother, Amelia, married his stepfather after she and her seven children were freed from slavery by their biological father, a white planter presumably named Jenkins. The Roberts family lived among a thriving free black community in Petersburg, Virginia. While nearby Richmond and Norfolk also had robust and highly skilled free colored communities, Petersburg had, proportionally, the largest free black population—African American residents outnumbered white Americans until 1860—in the antebellum South.

Roberts trained in business under his stepfather, but he found another free black mentor in William Colson after his stepfather's death. Together, Roberts and Colson established a thriving business that traded goods between Virginia and Liberia. Colson was a barber and minister with an extraordinary personal library.[111]

The Colsons were part of a substantial and long-standing community of successful free black families in Virginia. Among their neighbors in Petersburg were Richard Jarrett who owned a business carrying cargo between Petersburg and Norfolk, the descendants of the black physician Dr. Thomas Stewart, and the Afro-Haitian shop-owner and real estate investor, Madame Betsy. Godfrey Mabry, Henry Mason, Thomas Garnes, Christopher Stevens, and Charles Tinsley were among the large numbers of skilled black workers who made their livings as artisans. "When opportunity and financial situation permitted, Petersburg blacks purchased the freedom of friends and relatives. In fact, after 1806 one-third of the slaves emancipated in Petersburg were set free by blacks."[112]

In the antebellum South, the economic success of free black Americans was in itself a critique of the brutal system of slavery and the dangerous racial mythologies designed to justify it. Take for example the family of the craftsman Thomas Day, a sought-after furniture designer and successful businessman whose work is preserved in museums. Day was born to free black parents in southeastern Virginia in 1801. Day's mother, Mourning Stewart, was the daughter of Thomas Stewart, a successful free mulatto doctor who owned 874 acres—and several slaves—adjacent to Petersburg.[113] Day's father, John Day Sr., was the grandson of a white plantation mistress in South Carolina and her enslaved coachman.[114]

Thomas Day and his brother, John Jr., were apprenticed until they were 21 (as required by Virginia law) and by 1823 had opened their own cabinet and furniture business in Milton, North Carolina. John soon left the business and eventual fame to his brother and pursued religious studies, later joining the large migration of black Americans from Virginia who sought full citizenship in Liberia. A founder of the colony, John Day served in Liberia as a teacher, missionary, and Chief Justice of the Supreme Court. His accomplishments abroad were part of a deliberate, collective campaign to reject the failures of American democracy and create a free republic for Americans of African descent.

In North Carolina, Thomas Day established one of the largest furniture producing companies in the state. His fine work became renowned, and Day was commissioned to produce furniture and architectural woodwork for governors and universities. His business relied on a labor force of white, black, and mixed-race individuals, including apprentices, journeymen, wage laborers, and slaves.[115] He became a large property-holder as well as a shareholder in a North Carolina bank. His family sat in the front pew—of his design—in their predominantly white church. Thomas Day's local socioeconomic success and his community standing as "a good and valuable citizen" publicly challenged an oppressive antebellum status quo in the American South.[116]

THE DIFFERENT FATES OF the Day brothers point to different trajectories that free Afro-Americans from the South charted in American history. The Day brothers established their own autonomy and success, one in the American South and the other as a Liberian national. As noted above, patriots like York, John Vashon, Joseph Savary, and Juana Ramírez bravely served their countries, and revolutionaries like Charles Deslondes, John Horse, Gabriel Prosser, Carlota Lucumí, and Samuel Sharpe led armed rebellions for freedom. National heroes such as Mexico's President Vicente Guerrero and Colombia's Admiral José Padilla did both, as did the hundreds of thousands of African Americans and Afro-Cubans who joined armies in the second half of the nineteenth century, risking and giving their lives for their countries and the promise of liberty and citizenship for all.

NOTES FOR CHAPTER FIVE

1. David Geggus, ed. *The Impact of the Haitian Revolution in the Atlantic World* (Columbia: University of South Carolina Press, 2001), x.

2. David Geggus, "The Sounds and Echoes of Freedom: The Impact of the Haitian Revolution on Latin America," *Beyond Slavery: The Multilayered Legacy of Africans in Latin America and the Caribbean*, ed. Darien J. Davis (Lanham, MD: Rowman & Littlefield, 2007), 19.

3. "The war-torn former colony, with a capsized economy, no foreign friends and lingering communal antagonism, offered a difficult space for realizing its own lofty ambitions. But . . . it gave tangible examples of what was needed and broke once and for all with the endless procrastination of the European legislators and philanthropists for whom slavery had to be dismantled at an excruciatingly slow pace. . . ." Robin Blackburn, *The American Crucible: Slavery, Emancipation, and Human Rights* (New York: Verso, 2011), 197. Laurent Dubois, *Avengers of the New World: The Story of the Haitian Revolution* (Cambridge: Belknap Press of Harvard University Press, 2004); *A Colony of Citizens: Revolution and Emancipation in the French Caribbean, 1787–1804* (Chapel Hill: University of North Carolina Press, 2004).

4. Marixa Lasso, *Myths of Harmony: Race and Republicanism during the Age of Revolution, Colombia, 1795–1831* (Pittsburgh: University of Pittsburg Press, 2007), 5.

5. Thomas Piketty, *Capital in the Twenty-First Century* (Cambridge: Belknap Press of Harvard University Press, 2014), 159. In 1860, close to half of the populations of Alabama, Florida, Georgia, and Louisiana were of African descent, and black Americans were majorities in South Carolina and Mississippi. While Virginia's enslaved population had declined from 40 percent in 1810 to 30 percent in 1860, Virginia had the most enslaved Americans in absolute terms in 1860, and in several cities and thirty-nine counties black Americans were at least half of the population if not a majority. *Map Showing the Distribution of the Population of the Slave Population in the Southern States Compiled from the Census of 1860* (Washington DC, Census Office, Department of the Interior, 1861.) https://www.census.gov/history/pdf/1860_slave_distribution.pdf; *Historical Statistics of the United States* http://faculty.weber.edu/kmackay/statistics_on_slavery.htm; *Virginia Humanities Encyclopedia* https://www.encyclopediavirginia.org/media_player?mets_filename=evm00002821mets.xml

6. Douglass Egerton, "The Scenes Which Are Enacted in St. Domingo: The Legacy of Revolutionary Violence in Early National Virginia," in *Antislavery Violence: Sectional, Racial, and Cultural Conflict in Antebellum America*, eds., McKivigan and Harold (Knoxville: University of Tennessee Press, 1999), 43.

7. Dubois, *Avengers of the New World*, 7.

8. Thomas Bender, "The Age of Revolution: Founding Fathers Dreamed of Uprisings, Except in Haiti," *The New York Times*, July 1, 2001.

9. Rhoda Blumberg, *York's Adventures with Lewis and Clark: An African-American's Part in the Great Expedition* (New York: Harper Collins, 2004), back cover. Robert B. Betts, *In Search of York: The Slave Who Went to the Pacific With Lewis and Clark* (Boulder: University Press of Colorado, 2002).

10. Sara E. Johnson, *Fear of French Negroes: Transcolonial Collaboration in the Revolutionary Americas* (Berkeley: University of California Press, 2012), xix.

11. One Afro-Frenchman from Louisiana profoundly shaped history in a specific way. In the early nineteenth century, as sugar production increased in Brazil, Cuba, Florida, and Louisiana, an African American engineer from Louisiana invented a technology that made sugar refining safer and more efficient. In 1834, Norbert Rillieux, inventor, engineer, and instructor of applied mechanics at Paris' Ecole Central, revolutionized the sugar industry with his multiple effect vaccum evaporator. The son of a French planter (a relation of Edward Degas) and a free woman of color, his innovation in chemical engineering became the basis for all modern industrial evaporation. Christopher Benfey, *Degas in New Orleans* (Berkeley: University of California Press, 1997), 127–131; Louis Haber, *Black Pioneers of Science and Invention* (New York: Harcourt, 1970), 20–29.

12. Daniel Rasmussen, *American Uprising: The Untold Story of America's Largest Slave Revolt* (New York: Harper Perennial, 2012), 1.

13. Daniel Rasmussen, "America's Forgotten Slave Revolt," *The Daily Beast*, January 9, 2011.

14. Paul Baepler, *White Slaves, African Masters: An Anthology of American Barbary Captivity Narratives* (Chicago: University of Chicago Press, 1999), 2; Robert C. Davis, *Christian Slaves, Muslim Masters: White Slavery in the Mediterranean, the Barbary Coast, and Italy*, 1500–1800 (New York: Palgrave McMillian, 2004).

15. Gerard T. Altoff and Roby Opthoff Lilik, *Among My Best Men: African-Americans and the War of 1812* (Put-in-Bay, OH: The Perry Group, 1996), 4–5.

16. Robert Ewell Greene, *Black Defenders of America, 1775–1973: A Reference and Pictorial History* (Chicago: Johnson Publishing Company, 1974), 29.

17. In 1792 a U.S. federal militia act stipulated that "free able-bodied white male citizens" serve in the militia, but only Connecticut, Massachusetts, and South Carolina explicitly exempted African Americans. North Carolina and Virginia permitted African Americans to muster and the remaining states took no position. Smith, *The Slaves' Gamble*, 15, 38.

18. Charles Ball, *Slavery in the United States: A Narrative of the Life and Adventures of Charles Ball, a Black Man, Who Lived Forty Years in Maryland, South Carolina and Georgia, as a Slave Under Various Masters, and was One Year in the Navy with Commodore Barney, During the Late War* (New York: John S. Taylor, 1837).

19. Michael Lee Lanning, *The African American Soldier* (New York: Citadel Press, 1997), 22.

20. Lanning, *African American Soldier*, 23.

21. W. Jeffrey Bolster, *Black Jacks: African American Seamen in the Age of Sail* (Cambridge: Harvard University Press, 1997), 102.

22. William Cooper Nell, *The Colored Patriots of the American Revolution, With Sketches of Several Distinguished Colored Persons* (Boston: Robert F. Wallcut, 1855), 188.

23. Greene, *Black Defenders of America*, 344.

24. Caryn Cossé Bell, *Revolution, Romanticism, and Afro-Creole Protest Tradition in Louisiana, 1718–1868* (Baton Rouge: Louisiana State University Press, 1997), 53.

25. Smith, *Slaves' Gamble*, 162.

26. Prior to the war Vincent Populus ran a very successful shoemaking business with his brother who purchased "an enslaved skilled cobbler" in 1818 to assist them. Emily Clark, *The Strange History of the American Quadroon: Free Women of Color in the Revolutionary Atlantic World* (Chapel Hill: University of North Carolina Press, 2013), 91.

27. Harold Youmans, "War Leader Profile: Joseph Savary," *Journal of the War of 1812* 12, no. 1 (Spring 2009): 6.

28. Smith, *Slaves' Gamble*, 163.

29. Catherine Reef, *African Americans in the Military* (New York: Facts on File, 2010), 204.

30. African-descended artists were active throughout the Americas starting with Brazil's celebrated Aleijadinho and his Baroque church facades and sculptures from the 1700s which made him a national icon. Freed in 1782, Joshua Johnson worked throughout Maryland and Virginia as a successful portrait artist in the late eighteenth and early nineteenth century. In the mid 1800s Robert S. Duncanson was acclaimed as the greatest landscape painter in the American West. In the late nineteenth century, the paintings of Henry Ossawa Tanner gained international acclaim. Tanner moved to Paris in 1891 where he collaborated with other prominent African American painters like Palmer Hayden and Laura Wheeler Waring in the early 1900s. The American sculptor Edmonia Lewis exhibited in the U.S. in the 1860s and '70s, but she studied and settled in Rome. Meta Fuller, another African American sculptress and painter, was the first to be commissioned by the U.S. government in 1907 after winning acclaim from her mentor, Auguste Rodin in Paris. Cuba's most celebrated early twentieth-century painter, Wilfredo Lam was an Afro-Cuban artist of Chinese descent and a colleague of and collaborator with Pablo Picasso, Henri Matisse, and André Breton.

31. Altoff and Lilik, *Among My Best Men*, 166.

32. Major A. B. Ellis, *The History of the First West India Regiment* (Crystal Palace Press, 1885).

33. John McNish Weiss, *The Merikens: Free Black American Settlers in Trinidad, 1815–1816* (Austin: University of Texas, 2002).

34. Kenneth Porter, *The Black Seminoles: History of a Freedom-Seeking People* (Gainesville: University of Florida Press, 1996). 8.

35. Porter, *Black Seminoles*, 12.

36. In 1814 Andrew Jackson led a series of raids in Georgia and Alabama that displaced Creek peoples from twenty million acres of land. Andrew Jackson, *The Papers of Andrew Jackson, Volume IV, 1816–1820*, eds., Harold Moser et al (Knoxville: University of Tennessee Press, 1994), 198–199.

37. The author, a white trader, penned this line in a letter to his son before being executed by Jackson; he was referring to the Suwannee River of northern Florida and

southern Georgia. Jane Landers, "Maroon Women in Colonial Spanish America," *Beyond Bondage: Free Women of Color in the Americas*, eds., David Gaspar and Darlene Clark Hine (Chicago: University of Illinois Press, 2004), 14.

38. Uzi Baram, "A New Chapter in African Diaspora History in Southwest Florida: The Evidence for a Maroon Community on the Manatee River," (paper presented at the Southeastern Archeological Conference, Tampa, Florida, November 8, 2013).

39. Rosalyn Howard, *Black Seminoles in the Bahamas* (Gainesville: Florida University Press, 2002).

40. Nathaniel Millett, *The Maroons of Prospect Bluff and Their Quest for Freedom in the Atlantic World* (Gainesville: University Press of Florida, 2013), 252.

41. Kevin Mulroy, *Seminole Freedmen: A History* (Norman, OK: University of Oklahoma Press, 2007), 20.

42. Millett, *Maroons of Prospect Bluff*, 252.

43. Andrew Jackson, *The Papers of Andrew Jackson, Volume IV*, 199.

44. Anthony Dixon, "Black Seminole Involvement and Leadership during the Second Seminole War, 1835–1842," (PhD diss. Indiana University, ProQuest, 2007).

45. University of Texas professor of history J. B. Bird's website "Rebellion: John Horse and The Black Seminoles, the First Black Rebels to Beat American Slavery," documents the accomplishments of "maroon warriors, descendants of free blacks and fugitive slaves in the American South, [who] led the largest slave revolt in American history, influenced Abraham Lincoln and the emancipation movement, and were the most successful black freedom fighters in the U.S. prior to the Civil War." http://www.johnhorse.com/index.html (copyright 2005, accessed 7/10/2016).

46. Ibid.

47. Ted Vincent, "The Blacks Who Freed Mexico," *The Journal of Negro History* 79, no. 3 (Summer 1994): 257–276.

48. Theodore G. Vincent, *The Legacy of Vicente Guerrero: Mexico's First Black Indian President*, Gainesville: University Press of Florida, 2001), 117.

49. J. A. Rogers, *World's Great Men of Color* (New York: Macmillon Publishing, 1972 [1946]), 182.

50. George Reid Andrews, *Afro-Latin America* (New York: Oxford University Press, 2004), 55.

51. Peter Blanchard, *Under the Flags of Freedom: Slave Soldiers and the Wars of Independence in Spanish South America* (Pittsburgh, PA: University of Pittsburgh Press, 2008), 2–3.

52. Ibid.

53. Marie Arana, *Bolivar: American Liberator* (New York: Simon and Schuster, 2013), 223.

54. Leslie B. Rout Jr., *The African Experience in Spanish America* (New York: Cambridge University Press, 1976), 173.

55. John Chasteen, *Born in Blood and Fire: A Concise History of Latin America* (New York: W. W. Norton, 2001), 101.

56. Ibid.

57. David Geggus, ed. *The Impact of the Haitian Revolution in the Atlantic World* (Columbia, SC: University of South Carolina Press, 2001), xv.

58. Ibid.

59. Dantes Bellegarde, "President Alexandre Pétion: Founder of Agrarian Democracy and Pioneer of Pan-Americanism," *Phylon* 2, no. 3 (1941): 212.

60. Arana, *Bolivar*, 179.

61. Rout, *African Experience*, 177.

62. Marixa Lasso, "Race War and Nation in Caribbean Gran Colombia, Cartagena, 1810–1832," *The American Historical Review* 111, no. 2 (April 2006): 341.

63. Ibid.

64. Andrews, *Afro-Latin America*, 93.

65. Marixa Lasso, "Haiti as an Image of Popular Republicanism in Caribbean Columbia," in Geggus, *Impact of the Haitian Revolution*, 184.

66. Aline Helg, "Simón Bolívar and the Spectre of *Pardocracia*: José Padilla in Post-Independence Colombia," *Journal of Latin American Studies* 35, no. 3 (August 2003): 447–471; Aline Helg, *Liberty and Equality in Caribbean Colombia* (Chapel Hill, NC: University of North Carolina Press, 2004).

67. George Reid Andrews, "The Afro-Argentine Officers of Buenos Aires Province, 1800–1860," *Journal of Negro History* 64, no. 2 (Spring 1979), 85.

68. Andrews, *Afro-Latin America*, 62.

69. Blanchard, *Under the Flags of Freedom*, 86.

70. Ibid.

71. Andrews, *Afro-Latin America*, 62.

72. Rout, *African Experience*, 166–171.

73. Ramírez's contributions as a revolutionary heroine were lauded in an official ceremony when her remains were joined with those of Simón Bolívar in the National Pantheon of Venezuela in 2015. Rachel Boothroyd Rojas, "First Black Woman Independence Fighter is Honoured in Venezuela's National Mausoleum," venezuelanalysis.com, October 26, 2015. (http://venezuelanalysis.com/news/11617 January 31, 2015); Elvia Duque Castillo, *Aportes del Pueblo Afrodescendiente: La Historia Occulta de América Latina* (Bloomington, IN: iUniverse, 2013), 320–321.

74. Peter Blanchard, "The Language of Liberation: Slave Voices in the Wars of Independence," *Hispanic American Historical Review* 82, no. 3 (August 2002): 519; Andrews, "Afro-Argentine Officers," 85.

75. Andrews, *Afro-Latin America*, 64.

76. Rout, *African Experience*, 168.

77. Andrews, *Afro-Latin America*, 64.

78. Lasso, "Race War and Nation in Caribbean Gran Colombia," 336.

79. Lasso, *Myths of Harmony*, 154.

80. Andrews, "Afro-Argentine Officers," 85.

81. Conservative president Buenaventura Báez served five terms in the Dominican Republic's executive office starting in 1859. President Báez's mother, Teresa de Jesus Mendez,

was a former slave. According to the Dominican Institute of Genealogy, Mendez, via her son, was the principal ancestor of a vast proportion of the nation's oligarchy throughout the twentieth century. In addition to the seven Afro-Latin presidents who served in the nineteenth century, additional American presidents with known African ancestry include Nilo Peçanha in Brazil (1909), Carlos Mendoza in Panama (1910), Fulgencio Batista in Cuba (1940–1944, 1952–1959), Hugo Rafael Chávez Frías in Venezuela (1999–2013), and Barack Obama in the United States (2008–2016).

82. Andrews, *Afro-Latin America*, 99–100.

83. Carlos Aguirre, *Agentes de su Propia Libertad: Los Escalvos de Lima y la Desintegración de la Esclavitud: 1821–1824*, (Lima: Pontificia Universidad Católica del Perú, Fondo Editorial, 1993).

84. Douglas Egerton, *Gabriel's Rebellion: The Virginia Slave Conspiracies of 1800 and 1802* (Chapel Hill: University of North Carolina Press, 1993), 192.

85. Egerton, *Gabriel's Rebellion*, 199.

86. James Sidbury, *Ploughshares into Swords: Race, Rebellion, and Identity in Gabriel's Virginia, 1730–1810* (New York: Cambridge University Press, 1997), 95.

87. Winthrop Jordan, *White Over Black: American Attitudes Toward the Negro, 1550–1812* (Chapel Hill: University of North Carolina Press, 1968), 384.

88. This is the South Carolina church where nine congregants were massacred by an avowed white supremacist in 2015.

89. David M. Richardson, *Denmark Vesey: The Buried Story of America's Largest Slave Rebellion and the Man Who Led It* (New York: Vintage Books, 2009), 4–5; Douglas R. Egerton, *He Shall Go Out Free: The Lives of Denmark Vesey* (Lanham, MD: Rowman & Littlefield, 2004).

90. Richardson, *Denmark Vesey*, 4.

91. Ibid.

92. Bird, *Rebellion*, http://www.johnhorse.com/highlights/essays/largest.htm

93. Patrick K. Breen, *The Land Shall Be Deluged in Blood: A New History of the Nat Turner Revolt* (New York: Oxford University Press, 2015).

94. Kenneth S. Greenburg, ed., *Nat Tuner: A Slave Rebellion in American History and Memory* (New York: Oxford, 2003), 69.

95. Jane Landers, *Atlantic Creoles in the Age of Revolutions* (Cambridge, MA: Harvard University Press, 2010), 148.

96. Landers, *Atlantic Creoles,* 150.

97. Matt D. Childs, *The 1812 Aponte Rebellion and the Struggle Against Atlantic Slavery* (Chapel Hill: University of North Carolina Press, 2006).

98. Manuel Barcia, *The Great African Slave Revolt of 1825: Cuba and the Fight for Freedom in Mantanzas* (Baton Rouge: Louisiana State University Press, 2012).

99. Mark A. Sanders, ed., *A Black Soldier's Story: The Narrative of Ricardo Batrell and the Cuban War of Independence* (Minneapolis: University of Minnesota Press, 2010 [1912]), xv.

100. Robert L. Paquette, *Sugar Is Made with Blood: The Conspiracy of La Escalera and*

the Conflict between Empires over Slavery in Cuba (Middletown, CT: Wesleyan University Press, 1988).

101. Ana Lucia Araujo, *Shadows of the Slave Past: Memory, Heritage, and Slavery* (New York: Routledge, 2014), 198; Aisha k. Finch, *Rethinking Slave Rebellion in Cuba: La Escalera and the Insurgencies of 1841–1844* (Chapel Hill: University or North Carolina Press, 2015).

102. Childs, *The 1812 Aponte Rebellion*, 182.

103. Hilary Beckles, "The Slave-Drivers' War: Bussa and the 1816 Barbados Slave Rebellion," *Boletín de Estudios Latinoamericanos y del Caribe* 39 (December, 1985): 85–110; Michael Craton, *Testing the Chains: Resistance to Slavery in the British West Indies* (Ithaca, NY: Cornell University Press, 2009 [1982]), 260–266; Jerome Handler, "The Barbados Slave Insurrection of 1816: Can It Properly Be Called 'Bussa's Rebellion?'" *Sunday Advocate*, March 26, 2000.

104. Emilia Viotti da Costa, *Crowns of Glory, Tears of Blood: The Demerara Slave Rebellion of 1823* (New York: Oxford University Press, 1994).

105. Nathanial T. Bacon, "Some Insular Questions," *The Yale Review* 10 (New Haven, CT: Tuttle, Morehouse, and Taylor Co., May 1901-Feb. 1902): 163.

106. Lamin Sanneh, *Abolitionists Abroad: American Blacks and the Making of Modern West Africa* (Cambridge, MA: Harvard University Press, 2000), 41.

107. Lamin Sanneh, *Abolitionists Abroad: American Blacks and the Making of Modern West Africa* (Cambridge, MA: Harvard University Press, 2000).

108. Sanneh, *Abolitionists Abroad*, 6; 246.

109. James Ciment and John Radzilowski, *American Immigration: An Encyclopedia of Political, Social, and Cultural Change* (New York: Routledge, 2015), 649.

110. Marie Tyler-McGraw, "Virginia Emigrants to Liberia," Virginia Center for Digital History, University of Virginia.

111. William Colson's father, James Colson, was emancipated from slavery in Williamsburg around 1791 and lived in Petersburg by 1794, where he became a barber and purchased property. William Colson's son, James Colson, married Fannie Meade Bolling in 1852, a free woman of color known for her poetry as well as for founding a private school in Petersburg after the Civil War. One of James and Fannie's sons, James Major Colson III ultimately graduated from Dartmouth College in 1883 after which he returned to live and teach in Petersburg. Luther P. Jackson, "Free Negroes of Petersburg," *Journal of Negro History* 12, no. 3 (July 1927): 377–378.

112. L. Diane Barnes, *Artisan Workers in the Upper South: Petersburg, Virginia 1820–1865* (Baton Rouge: Louisiana University Press, 2008), 130; 132.

113. Patricia Philips Marshall and Jo Ramsay Leimenstoll, *Thomas Day: Master Craftsman and Free Man of Color* (Chapel Hill: University of North Carolina Press, 2010), 10.

114. Marie Tyler-McGraw, *An African Republic: Black and White Virginians in the Making of Liberia* (Chapel Hill: University of North Carolina Press, 2008) 68.

115. Marshall and Leimenstoll, *Thomas Day*, 41–42.

116. Marshall and Leimenstoll, *Thomas Day*, 40.

～ TIMELINE ～

1815   Paul Cuffe sponsors colonization and economic development in Sierra Leone

1817   Jacob Oson gives address "A Search for Truth" in New Haven and New York

1827   John Russwurm and Samuel Cornish found U.S. newspaper *Freedom's Journal*

1828   Sojourner Truth successfully sues planter for custody of her enslaved son

1829   David Walker's *Appeal* reverberates throughout U.S. East Coast

1829   Charlotte Dupuy sues Henry Clay for her and her children's freedom

1831   Maria Stewart publishes essay in *The Liberator*, lectures publicly on politics

1835   David Ruggles founds interracial Vigilance Committee that frees 300 slaves

1836   José Manuel Valdes becomes the chief medical officer of Peru

1836   Inventor, entrepreneur Robert Lewis authors history text *Light and Truth*

1840   Samuel Ringgold Ward, Henry Highland Garnet, Henry Bibb found Liberty Party

1841   U.S. Supreme Court rules defendants in *Amistad* revolt legally free

1843   George and Rebecca Latimer prompt Massachusetts protection of fugitive slaves

1848   Lewis Temple revolutionizes whaling industry with new harpoon

1848   Robert Morris argues against segregated schools in *Roberts v. Boston*

1849   James Pennington speaks at World Peace Conference in Paris

1849   Haitian-American Charles Reason is first black professor at a white U.S. college

1853   Sarah Remond wins suit after forcible removal from Boston opera

1854   Mary Ann Shadd Cary publishes newspaper *The Provincial Freeman*

1855   Elizabeth Jennings case results in desegregation of all New York City transit

1863   Harriet Tubman is first woman to lead a U.S. army military raid

1864   Dr. Rebecca Crumpler awarded medical degree from Boston University

1865   Paul Jennings (former slave of Madison) publishes first White House memoir

1866   Mary Ellen Pleasant challenges segregation in public transport in California

1868   Enslaved Afro-Cubans take up arms for abolition and national independence

1875   Bass Reeves (original Lone Ranger) appointed U.S. Marshal in Oklahoma

1891   Dr. Daniel Williams performs successful open-heart surgery

1892   Homer Plessy protests Jim Crow in U.S. courts

1895   Ida Wells-Barnett publishes first exposé of U.S. lynching epidemic

1896   Regional clubs merge into the National Association of Colored Women

1898   Buffalo Soldiers help Cuban patriots (largely Afro-Cuban) gain independence

6

Nineteenth-Century
Afro-American Nationals

A frican Americans established democracy in the United States when they helped save the Union and brought U.S. slavery to an end during the American Civil War. While the bravery of the hundreds of thousands of black Americans who risked their lives to flee plantations and then risked them again on the battlefield made emancipation a *fait accompli*, they were preceded by countless black men and women who had been fighting for democracy in courtrooms, in print, and in various organizations and professions. While Afro-Latins secured their own freedom in independence wars from Mexico to Chile and nations in between, in Cuba and Brazil—which along with the U.S. were the last nations in the hemisphere to maintain slavery—democracy activists looked to civic and professional engagement to challenge inequality.

In addition to those who fought for freedom as rebels and soldiers, enslaved and free people of color shaped the nineteenth century as activists who used courts of law as well as print, oratory, and professional engagement to champion the rights and responsibilities of citizenship. The biographical details of many of these Afro-American advocates reveal ancestral and ideological connections that spanned the Atlantic world. Internationally, nineteenth-century Afro-Americans established a "wide variety of strategic alliances . . . in their quests for freedom, equality, and profit."[1]

NINETEENTH-CENTURY NORTH AMERICAN ACTIVISTS

When Frederick Douglass liberated himself from slavery in Maryland in 1838, he disguised himself as a sailor "because free black seamen were then so common as to draw few second looks."[2] Upon reaching New York

City, Douglass was received in the safe house of David Ruggles. A former seaman himself, Ruggles was an influential journalist, editor, activist, and author and publisher who established a bookstore and his own imprint. He advocated for individual rights and against slavery both in the many periodicals he contributed to (he edited the magazine *Mirror of Liberty*) and the pamphlets he produced.

Ruggles led and publicized the New York Committee of Vigilance, a biracial organization that informed workers of their rights, assisted fugitive slaves, and formed the nucleus of the Underground Railroad. Ruggles and his colleagues used the press, the courts, and direct action to resist the regular practice of kidnapping black New Yorkers for sale further south. By recording and publicizing threats to Afro-Americans (including publishing the names of individual slave catchers), alerting authorities to crimes (human trafficking in particular), and physically intervening in attempts to capture individuals (for which many members suffered retribution), the Committee of Vigilance "tackled the daily task of protecting liberty and fighting slavery in New York."[3] Ruggles repeatedly risked his life—and saved others—as a key founder and linchpin in the Underground Railroad. In addition to Frederick Douglass, Ruggles abetted the self-liberation of hundreds of Americans.[4]

Throughout the first half of the nineteenth century, African Americans in the North used courts and professional endeavors as well as print and oratory to assert citizenship rights and challenge slavery. Early nineteenth-century African Americans formed newspapers, civic societies, and political organizations to defend and demand democracy. Others, like the entrepreneur Paul Cuffe, sought to advance democracy through their investments. Cuffe, sea captain, entrepreneur, and philanthropist, was a native of Massachusetts. The son of an African-born, formerly enslaved father and a Native American mother, in his teens Cuffe worked as a whaler, managed his late father's one hundred and sixteen-acre farm, and was held prisoner by the British for three months during the American Revolution. Around age 20, having built a boat with his brother, Cuffe delivered cargo to nearby ports (repeatedly fending off pirates), an endeavor that eventually expanded into a lucrative fleet of ships.

In 1780, Cuffe, along with his brother, John, and five additional black men, submitted a petition to the Massachusetts legislature arguing that their ineligibility to vote was unjust in light of their payment of taxes and military service. They highlighted the irony that black men who fought in an American Revolution to end taxation without representation were tax-payers who were still denied the franchise.[5] The courts ultimately ruled in 1783 that African American men who paid taxes in Massachusetts could vote.[6]

Around 1810, Cuffe began to correspond with other philanthropists as well as British and U.S. officials about developing Sierra Leone's economic potential for Africans and Afro-Americans. Cuffe's goal, as outlined in a petition to the British Parliament, was to cultivate a trade in West African agricultural and marine products that would eclipse the trade in people.[7] In 1811 Cuffe made the first of three visits to Sierra Leone and established a cooperative trading organization with other black entrepreneurs dedicated to commercial development. However, colonial authorities in Sierra Leone saw Cuffe's plan as an "unacceptable encroachment on their economic interests and blocked it."[8] Undeterred, Cuffe financed an expedition that brought thirty-eight African American passengers and a cargo of industrial materials to the colony in 1815. In the United States, Cuffe, an ardent supporter of education, used his own resources to establish an integrated school in Westport, Massachusetts.

Sea captain, businessman, and activist Absalom Boston also expanded educational opportunities for Americans. Boston's uncle, Prince Boston, had won his freedom in court after refusing to turn over his pay from a whaling expedition in the 1770s, helping to dismantle slavery on Nantucket. In the 1820s, Absalom Boston commanded an all-black crew on the whaling ship *Industry*. Other black whaling captains included Paul Cuffe's son, William, and son-in-law, Pardon Cook, as well as Samuel Harris, Alvin Phelps, Petter Green, and Edward J. Pompey.[9]

Black New Englanders played significant roles in advancing education and civil rights. In 1840, Eunice Ross passed the exam for admission to a Nantucket high school but was denied admission because of her race. Ross wrote a letter arguing for her intellectual fitness and filed a petition with the Massachusetts State house. Her case galvanized the community, and in 1842 hundreds of Nantucket residents insisted to the school board that equal access to public schools was a constitutional right. In 1844 black and white families collaborated in protesting educational segregation by keeping their children home from their respective schools. In 1845, Edward J. Pompey, himself a successful businessman and civil rights activist, and some one hundred others petitioned the Massachusetts State House demanding that all children have "their equal right to the schools." Later, 252 white residents of Nantucket joined in support of Pompey's petition.

Massachusetts passed the first civil rights bill in the United States in 1848, guaranteeing equal educational access to all students and permitting parents to sue their towns for damages if their children were excluded. In 1846, when Absalom Boston's daughter, Phebe Ann, was denied admission to the same Nantucket school that had excluded Eunice Ross, Boston ably used the 1845 legislation to make his case in court on behalf of both students. The case, and Absalom Boston's community leadership, helped to spur the election of a new school board. As a result of Boston's actions—which built on those of Ross, Pompey, and others—integration was implemented throughout Nantucket schools in 1847.[10]

African Americans contributed to the whaling industry not only as captains and sailors, but also as innovators. John Mashow, a former slave from South Carolina and son of a white planter, became a master shipbuilder and an admired naval architect in Massachusetts. He established his own shipyard and designed some one hundred vessels. His obituary observed that Mashow had produced "some of the finest and stanchest of the vessels which comprise the whaling fleet."[11]

In 1848 in New Bedford, Connecticut, Lewis Temple, a blacksmith, inventor, shop owner, and self-liberated slave from Richmond, fashioned a new type of harpoon that came to be known as the Temple toggle and "the most important invention in the history of whaling."[12] Temple's design revolutionized the American whaling industry— vital to the U.S. economy in the nineteenth century—and became the industry standard through the 1920s. Temple was an outspoken advocate of freedom who was active in the Massachusetts Anti-Slavery Society as well as New Bedford's Union Society.

Black Yankee mariners contributed significantly to the American economy as well as to American society when they publicly advocated for equal pay,

Born in Jamaica to an enslaved mother and white merchant father in 1799, John Russwurm moved to Quebec and then Maine where he attended Bowdoin College and studied the Haitian Revolution. After graduation, Russwurm moved to New York City where he and Samuel Cornish established and edited the anti-slavery newspaper Freedom's Journal *in 1827. The paper had a national and international readership with agents in Canada, England, and Haiti. Russwurm ultimately relocated to Liberia where he was a journalist and a governor.*

equal access to schools, and voting rights. They were among thousands of African American activists who sought meaningful citizenship during this period. Like Paul Cuffe, Stephen Smith and William Whipper were successful black businessmen who used their resources to champion equal rights and abolition. Smith and Whipper (both born to black women in Pennsylvania and fathered by their white owners/employers) independently established successful businesses before partnering in lumber and coal ventures that grossed millions annually in today's valuation. Smith and Whipper used their means and community roles to assist fugitive slaves, host anti-slavery organizations, lead political conventions, and establish religious organizations.[13]

Afro-Jamaican Bowdoin College graduate John Russwurm and the Reverend Samuel Cornish established the nation's first abolitionist newspaper, *Freedom's Journal*, in New York in 1827. African Americans had been using pamphlets, broadsides, articles, and sermons since the eighteenth century, but *Freedom's Journal* heralded the rise of a national black press in the early nineteenth century. *Freedom's Journal*, though it only ran for two years, had a powerful long-term effect; it published debates on civic life and citizenship that "shaped the activism of both African American and white leaders and reformers for generations to come."[14]

Freedom's Journal was a major catalyst of the abolition movement, as was its frequent contributor David Walker, the son of an enslaved man and free black woman in North Carolina, who became a business owner in Massachusetts and antislavery collaborator. In 1829 he published his *Appeal, in Four Articles, Together with a Preamble, to the Colored Citizens of the World, but in Particular, and very Expressly to Those of the United States of America.* Walker's *Appeal* was a founding document of abolitionism that presaged and primed the political divisions that led to the American Civil War.[15]

Walker's *Appeal* challenged the assumptions of the American Colonization Society by insisting that African Americans were not only valid and valuable American citizens but also American founders. "Let no man budge us one step," he wrote, "and let slave-holders come to beat us from our country. America is our country, we have enriched it with our blood and tears."[16] Walker's *Appeal* challenged slavery on theological, moral, and political grounds. He invoked "natural rights" to underscore revolution as the right of the oppressed: "See your Declaration [of Independence] Americans! Do you understand your own language?"[17] He reminded readers of their inalienable rights, inherent equality, and political duty to reject despotism.

Just as Thomas Paine's pamphlet *Commonsense* helped to foment the American Revolution, Walker's *Appeal* helped to galvanize the political bifurcation that led to the American Civil War. The *Appeal* was reprinted several times and widely circulated in the North (including in the inaugural issue of William Lloyd Garrison's newspaper, *The Liberator*), making it a touchstone of the growing abolitionist movement for both black and white Americans. The *Appeal* was also distributed via the South's port cities, often by white agents or black seamen or discovered sewn into the clothing that Walker vended. The *Appeal's* circulation prompted Georgia, South Carolina, North Carolina, and Louisiana to make black literacy and antislavery literature illegal and partially inspired the quarantine of black sailors who docked in Charleston, South Carolina. While Walker's *Appeal* for equal rights and the revolutionary overthrow of slavery inspired many Americans and alarmed others, his son, Edwin Walker, a prominent lawyer and activist, was elected to the Massachusetts State Legislature in 1866.

Walker's *Appeal* built on the sentiments of black intellectuals like Richard

Allen and inspired others like Maria Stewart, who published and lectured forcefully on women's rights, abolitionism, civic equality, and social justice in the 1830s. Maria Stewart is thought to be the first American woman to publicly address an audience of both men and women, audiences that included both black as well as white Americans, starting in 1832. Her late husband was a War of 1812 veteran who served under the iconic naval captain Stephen Decatur and survived being held prisoner of war before establishing himself as a successful businessman in the whaling industry.

The Stewarts were married by the Reverend Thomas Paul in the African Baptist Church of Boston in 1826. Mrs. Stewart later lectured in the African Meeting House that contained the church, which, like many nineteenth-century black churches, established an independent black school as well as served as an intellectual and political focal point for the community.[18] In the 1830s, the building hosted the first meetings of the New England Abolitionist Society. Reverend Paul and John T. Hilton, a prominent black barber and businessman, collaborated with Walker to support *Freedom's Journal* from Massachusetts. Starting in the 1820s, Hilton also served as Grand Master of the Prince Hall Masonic Lodge, another organization that fostered political engagement.[19]

Hilton and other black freemasons, including Walker, founded the Massachusetts General Colored Society in 1826. The organization advocated civil rights and merged with the New England Abolitionist Society in 1833. Hilton's wife, Lavinia, was a prominent activist and organizer and a close friend of Thomas Paul's daughter, Susan, who pursued her own anti-colonization, anti-slavery, pro-civil rights agenda as a teacher and book publisher.[20]

In 1836 Robert Lewis, inventor, entrepreneur, sailor, and War of 1812 veteran, published *Light and Truth*, a history of African Americans and Native Americans. Lewis, a free man from Maine descended from an African slave, Native Americans, and with possible French ancestry, was awarded three patents in the early nineteenth century for industrial inventions in ship building and dry cleaning as well as for a commercially successful hair product. His book was reprinted in 1844, 1848, and 1851. Its assertions of the common origins of humankind challenged the white supremacist conventions of contemporary ethnography, and Lewis's cultural observations made clear how widespread was the practice of racial mixing. Lewis was among nineteenth-century black scholars whose historiography was "linked to the quest for freedom and citizenship . . . in an avowed effort to force the nation to live up to the promises of its founding documents."[21]

In the 1830s and through the 1850s, public discourse was further cultivated in political meetings and organizations that came to be known as the Negro Convention Movement. As noted in Chapter 4, the first of these national, state, and local conventions took place in Philadelphia in 1830, presided over by AME Church founder Richard Allen. The African American attendees of the meetings were concerned with abolition as well as education, health, labor issues, and, perhaps most centrally, voting rights. In 1840 black activists, including Samuel Ringgold Ward, Henry Highland Garnet, and Henry Bibb, helped to establish and promote the Liberty Party, "the first political party in the United States organized to oppose slavery."[22] While short-lived, the Liberty Party helped to move abolition to the center of national politics and "offered a vehicle of protest against slavery for those committed to electoral politics."[23]

Liberty Party spokesman Henry Bibb was a "professional fugitive."[24] Like his colleagues Frederick Douglass and William Wells Brown, Bibb was born to a slave mother, fathered by a slave owner, freed himself, and then advocated for the freedom of others. Born in Kentucky in 1815, Bibb made his way to Detroit, Michigan, and settled in its politically active black community by 1842. In his 1849 autobiography and his writings in newspapers (including his own, *Voice of a Fugitive*), Bibb often called on his personal experience to make political arguments for democracy. He insisted on going to the polls in Michigan despite his ineligibility to vote.

Throughout the nineteenth century, enslaved Americans continued to free themselves through daring escapes; in the 1830s and '40s their actions, and those of their free black conspirators, shaped state and national policy. When Thornton and Ruthie Blackburn, fugitive slaves from Kentucky, were arrested in Michigan and jailed on the charges of slave catchers, Detroit erupted in the Blackburn Riots of 1833. The couple made it to safety in Canada with the help of collaborators, including a brave Caroline French who in an elaborate ruse took Mrs. Blackburn's place in the jail cell as a decoy.[25] In Canada, the Blackburns established Toronto's first cab company and became activists in support of abolition and fugitive slaves. The Blackburns' Canadian sanctuary created a diplomatic crisis between Michigan's Territorial Governor and the British colonial government over extradition, resulting in "British North America's first articulated legal rationale for harboring fugitive slaves."[26] Thus the Blackburn case "formally established Canada as the main terminus of the Underground Railroad."[27]

In 1836 African Americans again championed every American's inherent right to freedom when they led the daring recovery of Eliza Small and Polly Ann Bates from a Massachusetts State Supreme Court. In what became known as the Boston Slave Rescue, Small and Bates were tried in a Boston court against the claims of a Baltimore slave catcher. After the chief justice ruled that the women should be released, the agent for the Baltimore slave owner requested additional arrests; black and white observers formed a crowd and absconded with the purported slaves from the courtroom.[28]

African Americans in Northern states repeatedly interceded with attempted recaptures of fugitive slaves—quietly through the Underground Railroad and more dramatically by encouraging contests in courts, raising funds, assisting in representation, signing petitions, and, sometimes, physically removing fugitives from danger. The rescue of the Blackburns in 1833 and the Boston Slave Rescue of 1836 were "part of an emerging pattern of action" in the antebellum United States. "At least three dozen times between the 1830s and the 1850s, crowds headed by black men and women took similar action, rescuing slaves or those at risk of enslavement."[29]

In 1843 the self-liberation of George and Rebecca Latimer prompted the Massachusetts legislature to pass the "Latimer Act" to protect personal liberty. The Latimers fled from slavery in Virginia to Massachusetts in 1842. George Latimer, the son of an enslaved woman and the brother of one of his masters, passed for white during their escape, while Rebecca, who was pregnant at the time, passed as her husband's slave. When slave catchers prompted their arrest in Boston, the case spurred widespread political organization and a petition that garnered sixty-five thousand signatures.[30]

Throughout the first half of the nineteenth century, tens of thousands of black American fugitives, vigilantes, litigants, lawyers, and participants in the Underground Railroad initiated legal and extra-legal challenges to the fugitive slave provision of 1793. Historian Eric Foner chronicles the efforts surrounding the Underground Railroad as examples of "genuine patriotism" embedded in a courageous "struggle to create a better country that might truly live up to its professed ideals."[31] The self-liberated slaves and the Americans who abetted them deepened sectional divisions. Their efforts encouraged the sympathy of many Northern whites for abolitionism, and the oppositional measures they prompted caused many to worry about political overreach from elite Southern interests. These collective efforts were so successful that slaveholders called for more restrictive legislation as part of the Compromise of 1850 between Southern slaveholders and Northern Free Soilers.[32] A result was the 1850 Fugitive Slave Act, which seemed on its face antithetical to the aims of black activists, but was nonetheless a testament to their efficacy as well as a powerful catalyst of the coming war that would end slavery. The 1850 act prohibited accused fugitives from testifying on their own behalf and barred them from trial by jury. Penalties were imposed on federal marshals who failed to hand over fugitives.

Nonetheless, slaves continued to liberate themselves in large numbers. The 1851 case of Shadrach Minkins, a Virginia-born self-liberated waiter in Boston, who was arrested and rescued from the courtroom, prompted the U.S. president to deploy federal troops. Minkins ultimately settled with a community of fugitive slaves in Montreal, Canada, where he ran a restaurant and a barbershop, married an Irish woman, and established a family. Those who had assisted in Minkins's escape, like the self-liberated businessman and leading abolitionist Lewis Hayden and Minkins's black attorney, Robert Morris, were tried and acquitted by Boston juries.[33]

Nineteenth-century black Americans turned to the courts to protect fugitive slaves' right to liberty as well to enforce the civil rights of free people of color. In 1842, predating *Plessy* by half a century, Charles Remond protested segregated railway cars by invoking the sanctity of democracy and describing Boston as the "Athens of America" in testimony to the Massachusetts House of Representatives. His public demonstrations against segregation were not isolated. "Massachusetts newspapers in 1838 reported frequent incidents of Negroes refusing to sit in Jim Crow sections and being forcibly removed from the train."[34] In response, legislators proposed an act to halt discrimination, but it failed to pass. However, because of their continued pressure, by 1843 rail companies in Massachusetts had voluntarily abandoned segregation.

Remond was also a lifelong advocate of universal rights for women. He gained acclaim in the U.S. and Britain by lecturing, sometimes alongside William Lloyd Garrison or Susan B. Anthony, for abolition and suffrage (Frederick Douglass named a son Charles Remond Douglass). Remond's father was a native of Curaçao, and his maternal grandfather was a black Patriot veteran of the American Revolution. Remond's parents were successful entrepreneurs in early nineteenth-century Salem, Massachusetts, and were active abolitionists, hosting figures like William Lloyd Garrison, Wendell Phillips, and a young Charlotte Forten.

In 1853, Remond's sister, Sarah, won $500 in damages when she sued the city of Boston after being forcibly removed from her seat at the opera. In 1856, she began lecturing internationally for the American Anti-Slavery Society before pursuing medical degrees in Europe and, ultimately, practicing as a physician in Florence, Italy. Sarah Remond became a collaborator with the republican revolutionary Giuseppe Mazzini and his successful campaign to establish a unified Italy. [35]

In 1855 Elizabeth Jennings Graham successfully sued New York's segregated streetcars, setting in motion the desegregation of all New York City public transit. A kindergarten teacher, she was running late to play music at her church when she insisted on riding the streetcar. Future U.S. president Chester Arthur was her attorney. Her father, Thomas Jennings, was a prominent activist and businessman—and the first African American awarded a U.S. patent (in 1821). Jennings collaborated with other civil rights advocates like J. W. Pennington and Dr. James McCune Smith to advance American democracy.

In 1866, Mary Ellen Pleasant, who also had been forcibly removed from a streetcar, desegregated San Francisco's public transportation by bringing two lawsuits and setting precedent in the California State Supreme Court. Pleasant arrived in San Francisco in 1852, following decades of work with the Underground Railroad and antislavery activists in Nantucket, New Bedford, and Boston. A savvy businesswoman who used her substantial resources to help John Brown before the Civil War, Pleasant's "business strategies ran the gamut from operating boardinghouses . . . to investing in mines and real estate. . . . She financed enterprises that shaped the western economy in the second half of the nineteenth century."[36] Her efforts as a litigant shaped a western civil rights movement, and "she formed part of San Francisco's black elite . . . who organized California's black convention movement, the press, churches, and schools."[37]

While free people of color were bringing civil rights violations to court in the nineteenth century, enslaved black men and women pressed for their own freedom and that of their loved ones through direct legal challenges as well. Freedom suits were brought in every century during New World slavery; however, they peaked across the hemisphere in the nineteenth century.

In St. Louis, Missouri, alone, African Americans filed 301 legal petitions for freedom between 1814 and 1860.[38] Among them was the petition of Dred Scott (and his wife Harriet) which prevailed in the lower courts but was overturned by the U.S. Supreme Court in 1857. Others, like Missouri's Polly Berry, who filed in 1839, permanently established her right to freedom in court. Berry's daughter, Lucy Delany, a future author, was freed in a second suit filed by her mother in 1842.

In 1829, Charlotte Dupuy sued U.S. Secretary of State Henry Clay for her and her children's freedom. Clay was a Kentucky planter, lawyer, and politician who served as the U.S. Speaker of the House for three terms, was a key supporter of the American Colonization Society, and was an architect of the Compromise of 1850.[39] During the eighteen months that the case was being decided, Dupuy earned wages working for future president Martin Van Buren in Washington while Clay returned to Kentucky with Dupuy's enslaved children and spouse. The court ultimately denied her petition, and Dupuy was jailed before being transported to Kentucky.[40]

Clay freed Dupuy and her daughter ten years later. Dupuy's son and husband were eventually granted their freedom as well. In 1846, one of Clay's former slaves, Lewis Richardson, publicly accused Clay of cruelty. In 1847, Lewis Hayden, a former slave turned Boston businessman and activist, published an article stating that Clay had sold Hayden's first wife and their child to a Southern slave market.[41]

Around 1827, future abolitionist and suffragist Sojourner Truth, nee Isabella Baumfree, sued an Alabama slave owner for custody of her son. Truth had been born into slavery and sold away from her children several times in New York State. In 1827 she was able to secure her freedom and that of her infant daughter before winning her case for her son. In 1851, when a white female orator at the Ohio Women's Rights convention was left speechless by a heckler, Truth offered an impromptu discourse that captivated the audience and became a clarion call for universal rights. The analytic power of Truth's "Ain't I a Woman" speech gained renewed attention in the late twentieth century as a critique of racial and gender bias. In 1862, Truth publicly supported the Union with a dramatic visit to an Indiana courtroom while wearing Patriot colors and performing "The Star-Spangled Banner"; she was taunted by mobs and arrested but ultimately released.[42] In 1865 Truth worked to desegregate the public horse carriages of Washington, D.C.

In 1856, nurse, philanthropist, and entrepreneur Bridget Mason won her freedom in a Los Angeles courthouse. Born into slavery in Georgia, Mason accompanied her owner from Mississippi to California where she ultimately sued him for her freedom and that of thirteen other women and children. With her savings accrued from midwifery, Mason made significant returns on wise investments in real estate and used her substantial wealth to support the Los Angeles community and develop its central business district. She gave generously to philanthropic organizations and individuals in need, financed the building of church on land she donated, and founded a school. A Los Angeles park bears her name.[43]

Some African Americans legally freed their loved ones by purchasing them. In the early 1800s, President Thomas Jefferson arranged for Edith Fossett, the daughter of slaves on his Virginia plantation, to train in French cooking techniques at the White House. After Jefferson's presidency, Fossett became the head of Monticello's kitchen and was responsible for the elaborate meals enjoyed by Jefferson's guests. In his will, Jefferson ultimately freed her husband, Joseph Fossett, but Edith and their ten children remained enslaved. In 1837, Fossett purchased his wife, four of their children, and five of their grandchildren from Jefferson's heirs. Fossett's transaction bestowing freedom to ten Americans is recorded in the Albemarle County Deed Book with the preamble: "Know all men by these presents that I Joseph Fossett of the County of Albemarle and state of Virginia have manumitted, emancipated and set free, and by these presents do manumit, emancipate and set free the following negro slaves . . ."[44]

NINETEENTH-CENTURY IBERO-AMERICAN FREEDOM SEEKERS

Enslaved people in Spanish America had been arguing for their freedom in court since the late sixteenth century, and in the eighteenth they advanced the legal custom of *coartacion*—purchasing oneself. In the nineteenth century Afro-Cubans made this legal tactic a right. A surge of Cuban court cases involving slavery resulted in the 1842 *Reglamento de Esclavos* (Slave Regulation) that codified both the right to purchase oneself at an officially designated price and the right to seek out another master in the case of mistreatment (*pedir papel*). Neither process required the consent of one's master. Afro-Americans helped to establish these legal customs and transform them into basic rights in the nineteenth century.

The influx of cases brought by Afro-Cubans in the 1840s–1850s prompted the rulings that reified these legal customs and, in effect, permitted slaves to quit their master at will. Owners complained that these rights "had relaxed slavery completely" and "impaired the subordination" on which slavery was based.[45] In the decades when sugar production peaked in Cuba, slaves challenged the system not only through armed protest, but also by altering the legal framework and discourse of rights. Their actions, and those of the Afro-Americans across the hemisphere who insisted on rights, continually chipped away at the legal and cultural foundations of slavery in the Americas.

In the first half of the nineteenth century, between a third and a half of Brazil's population was enslaved. Brazil was the largest destination for slaves throughout New World history; it became home to the largest numbers of transatlantic Africans in the Americas. Like Cuba, Brazil helped to fill the void in sugar and coffee production after the Haitian Revolution. Also like Cuba, Brazil introduced multitudes of African-born individuals into its population throughout the 1800s. In the nineteenth century Africans were "increasingly visible as contributors to [Brazil's] wealthiest and most influential regions."[46] Though Cuba in 1886 and Brazil in 1888 were the last nations in the Western Hemisphere to abolish slavery, by mid-century the freedom-seeking actions of Afro-Brazilians as rebels and soldiers, professionals and activists, helped to erode slavery.

Enslaved Brazilians in Bahia organized some twenty-five uprisings after 1807; the 1835 Malé rebellion may have been the largest urban slave revolt in the Americas.[47] While it did not result in freedom for the rebels, the Bahia movement had national repercussions, including prompting the Brazilian Parliament to debate the abolition of slavery and the slave trade.[48] The uprising for freedom was initiated by hundreds of city-dwelling, African-born Malé (Muslim) slaves, most of whom were ultimately tortured or killed. These martyred freedom fighters signaled the unsustainability of Brazilian slavery and fostered a growing mainstream abolitionist movement.

One of the key organizers of the Malé revolt, the African-born activist Luisa Mahin, was captured by authorities; her son Luís Gama, however, advanced the Brazilian struggle for freedom and democracy as a writer and lawyer in the following decades. Gama, also a former slave, was an outspoken and influential advocate of abolition and civil rights as a prolific poet, journalist, and organizer as well as an attorney. Gama freed more than one thousand Afro-Brazilian individuals to whom he provided legal representation and for whom he raised funds.[49] After helping to found the Brazilian Republican Party in 1873, Gama and his black and white collaborators established the Luís Gama Emancipation Fund to purchase the freedom of enslaved Brazilians in 1881 and the Abolitionist Center of Sao Paulo in 1882.[50]

Like the African Americans who protested the failures of U.S. democracy by seeking their civil rights in Liberia and Sierra Leone, many nineteenth-century Brazilian freedpersons repatriated to western Africa in search of more meaningful citizenship. While the bulk of these repatriations took place in the 1840s and 1850s, they continued throughout the century. In 1879, for example, Amaro Marinho, "having previously purchased his freedom and that of this wife, obtained a passport in Bahia, and sailed with his wife and three children for Lagos, Nigeria."[51] In the 1880s another former slave from Brazil, Marcos Cardozo, a skilled mechanic and community leader, organized

Andre Rebouças helped found the Brazilian Anti-Slavery Society. As a lieutenant in the engineering corps during the Paraguayan War in 1864, he invented the torpedo. After the war, Rebouças taught at Rio's Polytechnical School and published articles that advanced abolitionism and addressed Brazil's social and economic issues. His father, Antonio Rebouças, the son of a slave, was a lawyer who served in the Brazilian Parliament and was an advisor to Portugal's King Pedro II.

the building of Nigerian churches and schools with funding from "ex slaves who had returned to Lagos from Brazil, Cuba, and the West Indies."[52]

Afro-Brazilians developed and supported numerous anti-slavery organizations and publications in the second half of the 1800s. José Carlos do Patrocínio, the son of a former slave and a vicar/politician, became deeply engaged in abolitionist writing after he completed his studies of pharmacology and medicine. He, José Ferreira de Menezes, and Andre Rebouças were among the founders of Brazil's Anti-Slavery Society in 1880. That same year, Menezes, a lawyer, poet, and editor, founded an influential abolitionist newspaper. In 1881 Patrocínio took over the newspaper to which Rebouças contributed a regular column.

Like Patrocínio, Rebouças was well known for purchasing enslaved Brazilians and manumitting them. A gifted engineer, dedicated teacher, and prolific journalist, Rebouças served as a military strategist during the Paraguayan War; he invented the torpedo during the conflict.[53] The Paraguayan War, which embroiled Argentina, Uruguay, and Brazil against Paraguay from 1864 to 1870, relied heavily on the service of enslaved and free Afro-Brazilian soldiers and officers. In addition to the work of black activists and journalists, the significant contributions of Afro-Brazilians to the nation during wartime critically shaped emerging discourses of black citizenship.

NINETEENTH-CENTURY PROFESSIONALS

Throughout the nineteenth century black professionals like Andre Rebouças challenged the limits of racial discrimination and advocated equal rights as they made significant contributions in their respective fields. The professional accomplishments in themselves undermined the social and cultural conventions of racial hierarchy across the hemisphere, especially in the countries that maintained slavery well into the century—Cuba, Brazil, and the United States.

In 1835, Afro-Cuban poet Juan Francisco Manzano began writing what may be the first slave autobiography in Spanish America. Having published two books of poetry (*Poesias Liricas* in 1821 and *Flores Pasageres* in 1830), Manzano went on to publish a play in 1842. Set in sixteenth-century Mauritania, *Zafria* makes metaphoric commentary on colonialism, slavery, and the Haitian Revolution. Through his work, "Marzano was engaging in aesthetic—and political—dialogue with Enlightenment values and ideas of nation."[54] Manzano's own freedom was purchased through a collaboration of several of his literary colleagues. He died shortly after being imprisoned on false charges surrounding the 1844 La Escalera insurgency.

While swaths of the Afro-Cuban elite were decimated during the La Escalera uprisings, "the black middle and upper class soon rebuilt itself."[55] Mid-nineteenth-century colonial Cuba experienced its most dramatic social regulations of people of color as authorities and planters worried over the stability of the island's regime. Afro-Cubans resisted the imposed limitations by continuing to advance economically and educationally. In 1854, the governor of Havana complained of the relentless ambition of free Afro-Cubans and "'the propensity of this race to excel the white' in economic and professional achievement."[56]

Free Afro-Brazilians similarly advanced their professional and educational careers as plantation slavery peaked in the nineteenth century. As Afro-Latins fought in independence wars and other struggles for republican representation in South America, Afro-Brazilians initiated their own uprisings in the 1820s and '30s and established a politically oriented black press that called for increased access to higher ranks of government. Nineteenth-century Afro-Brazilians pursued law and medical degrees as well as advanced education that gave them entrée to journalism, the arts, and teaching. While some professional Afro-Brazilians publicly protested discrimination and the persistence of slavery, others were fully incorporated into the colonial state as members of the government, the legislature, the clergy, and the army. Two of Brazil's most prominent conservative politicians were of African descent.[57] Many foreign observers as well as Brazilians propagated a notion of "racial democracy" as a key feature of Brazilian national culture. While such rhetoric spoke to the demographic significance of Afro-Brazilians and the assimilation of mixed-race Brazilians, it could also function to suppress attention to racial disparities in the political economy.

In Peru, the black physician José Manuel Valdéz was incorporated into the nation's highest ranks and established a broad platform to encourage social change. In 1835 the Afro-Peruvian surgeon was appointed to the highest medical rank in Peru (*el Protomédico de la República*), a position of "scientific and political prominence in nineteenth-century Spanish America."[58] With a distinguished career that began in the 1780s, Valdéz was among a small but significant group of black doctors in late colonial and early republican Peru. Black physicians like José Manuel Dávalos and José Pastor de Larringa "actively joined the reform efforts of influential figures of the Peruvian Enlightenment . . . and became part of the scientific revolution that overtook the medical profession in Peru in the second half of the eighteenth century."[59] As José Jouve Martín demonstrates, these individuals and their scientific accomplishments established a degree of authority that allowed them to publicly address contemporary social and political issues in Latin America. Their medical discourse and practice, for instance, of initiating public vaccination campaigns "was part of a modernization effort that would necessarily lead to the economic and social progress of [Peru]."[60]

In Latin America and in the United States as well, black professionals could become public intellectuals who shaped political and scientific discourse. James McCune Smith was an American physician, activist, and scholar born in 1813 in New York City to a "self-emancipated" mother and a merchant. (Smith later suggested he was the descendant of both Southern slaves and slave-owners.) He was an exceptional student at the African Free School and received his M.D. from the University of Glasgow in 1837. (Smith was not the first Afro-American to earn his medical degree from a university in Scotland; in 1814, the Edinburgh University awarded the Doctorate of Medicine to an Afro-Jamaican named William Fergusson and to John Baptist Philip, an Afro-Trinidadian, in 1815.) After some clinical training in Paris, Smith returned to New York City in 1837 where he established a private medical and surgical practice as well as taught evening classes out of his home and volunteered as the physician to the Colored Orphan Asylum until it was destroyed in the Draft Riot of 1863. Dr. Smith advanced the science of statistics through his writings in profes-

James McCune Smith

sional medical journals. He advanced the discourse of democracy through his writings on social and political matters including advocating abolition and women's voting rights. Smith, a visionary intellectual and scientist, was elected to the prestigious American Geographical Society in 1854.

Until recently, Edward Bouchet, class of 1874, was thought to be Yale College's first black graduate. Bouchet's 1876 Ph.D. from Yale put him among the first Americans in U.S. history to be awarded doctorates in physics. However, in 2014 an archivist found a cache of letters revealing that Richard Henry Green was an 1857 Yale graduate.[61] Green went on to study medicine at Dartmouth and served in the navy during the American Civil War as an assistant surgeon. Green was in fact among a cohort of "five colored men . . . [who] graduated from the different schools of Yale . . ."[62]

Among them, Cortlandt Van Rensselaer Creed graduated from the Yale School of Medicine in 1857. Like Green, Dr. Creed served the Union during

MARY ANN SHADD CARY *was an educator, journalist, publisher, lawyer, and civil rights activist. Born in Delaware and educated in Philadelphia, Shadd established the first abolitionist newspaper in Canada in 1853. She was appointed a recruiting officer during the American Civil War and resumed teaching and lecturing in the U.S. in its wake. She earned a degree in law in 1883, five years after Charlotte Ray. Mary Ann Shadd's brother, Abraham W. Shadd, a former Union captain was also an attorney (his son became a physician). Their sister Emaline Shadd was appointed to the faculty at Howard University, and their brother I. D. Shadd served in the Mississippi Legislature in the 1870s.*

Starting in 1857, GEORGE DOWNING *lobbied for the desegregation of schools in Newport, Rhode Island, until it was achieved in 1865. Downing, along with his four siblings, attended New York's African Free School. In Newport, he became a successful restaurateur in the 1840s, as well as a developer and philanthropist. From 1865 to 1877, George Downing managed the House of Representatives dining room in Washington, D.C., which put him in contact with the political elite. Throughout his life, Downing was a civil rights activist, abolitionist, and labor organizer, and in 2003 he was inducted into the Rhode Island Heritage Hall of Fame. His nephew, Henry Francis Downing, was a U.S. Navy veteran, world traveler, U.S. consul, author, and playwright who helped to organize the First Pan-African Congress in London in 1900.*

JOHN MERCER LANGSTON *(left) graduated from Oberlin College, passed the Ohio bar exam, and in 1855 was elected a town clerk. Langston founded the National Equal Rights League, established the nation's first black law school, and helped draft the Civil Rights Act of 1875. One U.S. president appointed Langston to the District of Columbia's Board of Health and another appointed him to serve as a U.S. diplomat in Haiti for eight years. He also was the first president of Virginia State University. In 1888, he became the first black congressman elected from Virginia. His nephew, Langston Hughes, helped to found the Harlem Renaissance in the 1920s and profoundly influenced intellectual and political currents on both sides of the Atlantic.*

Abolitionist attorney ROBERT MORRIS *(right) challenged segregated schools in 1848. (Black Bostonians had petitioned the legislature for equal educational facilities for African Americans as early as 1787.) Morris regularly represented individuals seeking their freedom in courts as well as raised funds for their passage to citizenship. In 1851, he represented Shadrach Minkins in a case testing the Fugitive Slave Act of 1850. Morris and collaborators whisked Minkins to safety in Canada in a prearranged intervention for justice. After being acquitted of charges for abetting Minkins's freedom, Morris continued to represent numerous African Americans and Irish Americans in court and was ultimately appointed a magistrate by the governor of Massachusetts.*

the American Civil War. Creed's paternal grandfather was a Revolutionary War veteran, Prince Duplex, who had been granted freedom for his Patriot service. His descendants would eventually serve in WWII and the civil rights movement. By the time Creed died in 1900, nine more African Americans had earned medical degrees from Yale.[63]

At Harvard, Martin Delany, already trained as a physician's assistant, was admitted to the School of Medicine in 1850. However, a group of white students argued that the admission of black people was "highly detrimental to the interests and welfare, of the Institution of which we are members, calculated alike to lower its reputation," and Delany and two other black students were dismissed.[64] Harvard Medical School ultimately accepted Robert Tanner Freeman, the son of former slaves, in 1867.[65]

While Delany's subsequent political activism often encouraged African American emigration, his commitment to democracy in the United States was evidenced by his service as a recruiter of black troops during the American Civil War, and he became the first African American U.S. Army field grade officer. Delany, the son of an enslaved father and free black mother, also shaped American history as a prolific writer and journalist (he founded a newspaper in 1843 that he published until he became co-editor of Frederick Douglass's *North Star*) and as a political figure (he narrowly lost an election for lieutenant governor of South Carolina in 1874).[66]

Dr. David Jones Peck, another medical pioneer and a friend of Delany, collaborated with his colleague's evolving views on emigration. Peck was born in 1826 to a politically active African American family who founded a school in Pittsburgh (along with John Vashon, described above). In 1847 Peck earned a medical degree in Chicago and opened a practice in Philadelphia. In 1852, after many discussions with Delany and a venture to California, Peck moved his medical practice to Nicaragua where he became the mayor of a town comprised of African Americans who had relocated to Central America in search of full citizenship rights. In 1854 Peck served in Nicaragua's Civil War and was killed in battle in the service of republican ideals; he was laid to rest as a hero in the town square of Granada, Nicaragua.[67]

Dr. Rebecca Crumpler earned her medical degree from the New England Female Medical College in 1864. (In 1860, of the 54,543 physicians in the

The Afro-Jamaican nurse Mary Seacole, the daughter of a free colored Jamaican "doctress" and a Scottish soldier, treated patients in the Caribbean and Central America before setting off for England to offer her services during the Crimean War. In 1855, she established an organization in the Crimean Peninsula to care for soldiers and was known to treat the wounded on the battlefield, even under fire. Despite an uneasy relationship  *with Florence Nightingale, the two were honored together in London for their wartime service. In 1857, Seacole published her autobiography in Britain,* **Wonderful Adventures of Mrs. Seacole in Many Lands.**

United States with medical degrees, only 300 were women.)[68] A free black native of Delaware, Crumpler practiced as a physician in Boston until after the Civil War when she joined the Freedman's Bureau in Richmond, Virginia, to help care for former slaves. She ultimately returned to her practice in Boston, and in 1883 she published a medical text titled *Book of Medical Discourses*. Rebecca Cole received her medical degree from the Women's College of Pennsylvania in 1867. (She was an alumna of Philadelphia's Institute for Colored Youth described below.) Dr. Cole practiced medicine for half a century and advanced public health as a lecturer and author.[69]

Dr. Daniel Hale Williams's father had been a member of the Equal Rights League in Pennsylvania; however, after his father's early death, Daniel was mentored by a free black barber in Wisconsin. In 1883, Williams graduated from the Chicago Medical College. After gaining the experience and reputation of an outstanding surgeon, he returned as an instructor; eventual Mayo Clinic founder Charlie Mayo was among his students. Williams was appointed to the Illinois State Board of Health in 1889. Unable to find a permanent hospital appointment despite his success and renown, Williams founded the first interracial hospital in the U.S. in 1891. It was there, in Chicago's Provident Hospital, where Dr. Williams performed one of the world's first successful open-heart surgeries.[70]

Henry Highland Garnet was among the many notable nineteenth-century alumni of New York's African Free School. The son of parents who had obtained their freedom via the Underground Railroad, Garnet took an international stage as an activist, minister, educator, and the first president of Avery College. He founded the Garrison Literary and Benevolent Association to bring young black New Yorkers together politically, and, at an 1843 National Negro Convention in Buffalo, he called on enslaved Americans to liberate themselves through rebellion. He brought his antislavery activism to Cuba, England, Scotland, and Jamaica and died in Liberia where he had been appointed to a post.

Daniel Coker, a former slave and educator who established a school in Baltimore in 1807, also sailed for Liberia but ended up in Freetown, Sierra Leone, where he established a church. One of Coker's pupils, William Watkins, a civil rights activist and Underground Railroad supporter, established his own school in Baltimore in 1820, the Watkins Academy. Watkins's niece, Frances Harper, attended the school and went on to become a prominent civil rights activist, writer, and orator starting in the 1850s. Harper's literary work was influential, particularly her novel *Iola Leroy*. An active member of the American Anti-Slavery Society and Underground Railroad network in the mid-nineteenth century, Harper was a founding member and vice president of the National Association of Colored Women in 1894.

In 1849 the Haitian-American mathematician, linguist, educator, and poet Charles Reason became the first black professor in a predominantly white college in the U.S. when he joined the faculty of New York Central College as a professor of classical languages and mathematics. Reason's parents were from Saint Domingue and Guadeloupe and had immigrated to the United States during the Haitian Revolution in 1793. Charles, a math prodigy, began teaching at New York's African Free School—at age 14—where his brothers also studied. His brother Patrick Reason was an exceptional engraver and lithographer from an early age whose work, such as the frontispiece for Henry Bibb's 1848 autobiography, promoted anti-slavery politics. Patrick's son was a physician in Cleveland. Charles Reason, after serving as principal of the Institute for Colored Youth in Philadelphia from 1852 to 1856, returned to New York where he became an educational administrator, activist, and a key advocate for the passage of the 1873 statute to desegregate New York City's public schools.

In 1850, Charles Reason was joined by two additional black professors at New York Central College, William Allen and George Vashon. William Allen, a professor of classics, was a mixed-race Virginian who had been adopted and raised by well-to-do free black parents. Allen's engagement to his longtime white sweetheart triggered enormous controversy; their marriage and Allen's writings inspired a story by Louisa May Alcott titled *M.L.* published in 1863.

Vashon, in 1844 the first of Oberlin College's many nineteenth-century black graduates, was a scholar, poet, and attorney. After passing the New York bar exam in 1848, he moved to Haiti to teach classics. He returned to practice law in New York, where he authored an epic poem to honor Vincent Ogé, the free colored planter who prefigured the massive 1791 slave revolution in Haiti. Vashon was later appointed the second president of Avery College, became Howard University's first black professor, and ultimately taught mathematics and classical and modern languages at Alcorn University in Mississippi.

In 1869, Ebenezer D. Bassett was appointed U.S. ambassador to Haiti, making him the first African American diplomat. A Yale-educated scholar, educator, and civil rights activist, Bassett headed Philadelphia's prestigious Institute for Colored Youth. Founded in 1837, the ICY, now known as Cheney University, is the nation's oldest institution of higher learning designated for African Americans. During the Civil War Bassett used the ICY as a recruitment site.

Bassett's work in Haiti was of great importance. Although Haiti had established independence in 1804, the U.S. refused to recognize its sovereignty until 1862. When Bassett and his family arrived for their eight years of Foreign Service, coups d'état and civil war created an extremely dangerous

Afro-Cuban violinist and composer José Silvestre White won first prize for violin at the Paris Conservatory in 1856. He performed with the New York Philharmonic in 1875–1876, as well as in Boston, Philadelphia, and Washington. However, his biggest impact on music may have been during his tenure in Paris. White was director of the Imperial Conservatory in Rio de Janeiro, Brazil from 1877 to 1899. He lived his last years in Paris and died in 1918.

and delicate context, which Bassett navigated with skill and success. As Christopher Teal has put it, "Bassett's work . . . forever altered U.S. foreign policy" and "helped change the way the world saw the United States."[71]

As headmaster of the ICY, Bassett had taken on a young "Renaissance man," Octavius Catto, as an instructor and assistant to the principal. Catto, the son of prominent free black parents from South Carolina, had been educated at the ICY (he was valedictorian in 1858) and in Washington, D.C. Catto tirelessly promoted academia, sports, politics, and the Enlightenment ideals of scientific reason and political equality. Catto founded the Banneker Literary Institute, was inducted into the Franklin Institute (an international scientific organization), and was the founder and captain of the Pythian Baseball Club. An avid republican, Catto was active in the ICY's recruitment efforts during the Civil War, was instrumental in desegregating Philadelphia's public transportation, and was a founding member of the National Equal Rights League. A well-known advocate of voting rights, Catto was martyred on Election Day, October 10, 1871.[72]

Actress Mary Webb and her husband, writer Frank J. Webb, were well received in England. Mary Webb was a free-born woman from the North, the daughter of a fugitive slave from Virginia and a "Spanish gentleman." She was famous for her public readings of Shakespeare, Longfellow, and a version of *Uncle Tom's Cabin* that Harriett Beecher Stowe adapted especially

New York native Ira Frederick Aldridge gained international acclaim as an actor and interpreter of Shakespeare in the first half of the nineteenth century. As a young man, Aldridge attended the African Free School and Shakespeare productions at the African Grove Theater in Greenwich Village. In Europe, he was honored with Prussia's Gold Medal in Arts and Sciences, Russia's Golden Cross of Leopold, Switzerland's Maltese Cross, and a memorial plaque at Stratford-upon-Avon's Royal Shakespeare Theater.

for her. In addition to Longfellow and Stowe, her fans included Charlotte Forten, William Lloyd Garrison, William Cooper Nell, and John Greenleaf Whittier.

In England, Frank Webb, a native of Philadelphia, became in 1857 the second African American to publish a novel.[73] Webb's *The Garies and Their Friends* was a political and social critique, which he dedicated to his friend Lady Byron (the wife of the poet Lord Byron). The Webbs later moved to Jamaica, but as a widower Frank ultimately returned to the U.S. where he was an educator, activist, and continued to publish his writing in periodicals, including an 1897 article about the Cuban war hero, Antonio Maceo.

Among at least a hundred African Americans who traveled to Great Britain during this period to bring attention to the failures of U.S. democracy were the Remonds, Frederick Douglass, James McCune Smith, Henry Highland Garnet, Samuel Ringgold Ward, Josiah Henson, James Watkins, Moses Roper, William Powell, Zilpha Elaw, Henry "Box" Brown, William Allen, Robert Douglas, and J. W. Pennington. Ira Aldridge permanently took up residence in England to raise a family and nurture his career in theater. After having helped to found the African Grove Theater in New York's Greenwich Village along with the Afro-Caribbean playwright William Henry Brown in the 1820s, "Aldridge travelled farther, was seen by more people in more nations, and won a greater number of prestigious honors, decorations, and awards than any other actor in the nineteenth century."[74]

THE *Amistad* AND *Creole* REVOLTS

In the 1839 *Amistad* mutiny, abducted West Africans liberated themselves from captivity and afterwards pursued their legal freedom in the U.S. Supreme Court. The events brought international attention to the issue of universal civil rights, solidified the abolitionist movement, led to the founding of schools in the U.S. and Africa, and further intensified the tensions over slavery that would lead to the American Civil War.

Fifty-three West Africans were being transported by Spanish traders near Cuba aboard the sailing ship, the *Amistad*, when the captives, led by Sengbe Pieh (whom the Spanish called Joseph Cinque), escaped their shackles and overpowered the crew. The ship's cook and captain were killed. The cabin boy, a black teenager named Antonio, and two surrendering crew members were spared. After two months of sailing in the Atlantic, the *Amistad* arrived at New London, Connecticut.

Spain, the two *Amistad* crewmen, and the commander of a U.S. Coast Guard vessel that had towed the *Amistad* into port, made competing legal claims on its contents, including the West Africans. U.S. President Martin Van Buren was anxious to comply with Spain's demands in part to avoid exposing illegal slave trading in Cuba and inviting British intervention. With the 1840 presidential election on the horizon, Van Buren was also eager to maintain support from pro-slavery Southern democrats and protect his tenuous North-South alliance by avoiding a public controversy over slavery. Some believe he was negotiating privately with Spanish authorities.

A Yale philologist determined that the asylum seekers were Mende-speakers from southern Sierra Leone. He located a translator by walking the waterfronts of New York and New Haven, counting aloud in Mende. The Mende words ultimately caught the ear of two Sierra Leone-native seamen on the British navy warship, the *Buzzard*.[75]

Two of the *Amistad*'s Cuban crewmen claimed the cabin boy, Antonio, as their property. Because Antonio had been born in Havana, his status was not affected by the 1817 treaty between Spain and England that prohibited the transport of slaves from Africa to Spanish colonies. The U.S. court ordered his return to Spanish officials. However, Antonio escaped to freedom in Canada in another instance of African Americans organizing to intercede in the reclamation of fugitive slaves.

During the civil trial over the *Amistad*, attorneys for the West Africans presented evidence for their legal standing as free persons on the grounds that they had not been born into legal slavery in Cuba but were kidnapped illegally from Sierra Leone. In 1841, the case came before the U.S. Supreme Court (five of the nine justices were current or former slaveholders). Former president and sitting congressman John Quincy Adams defended the captives by arguing that the principles of natural rights underlying the Declaration of Independence gave the West Africans an inherent right to freedom.

On March 9, 1841, the Supreme Court issued a landmark ruling based on the universal right of all people to resist extreme oppression. The verdict declaring that the *Amistad* individuals were free persons was an ideological victory for the principles of human liberty and justice but did not mitigate the political conflict surrounding the case. Pro-slavery senator John Calhoun authored resolutions calling for the return of the Mende captives to the Spanish. President John Tyler, who had succeeded Van Buren, refused to provide a ship for the West Africans' return.

An *Amistad* Committee had formed around the case, and it helped charter a ship to carry the thirty-four surviving Mende back to Sierra Leone; they were accompanied by five American missionaries, including two African Americans, Mr. and Mrs. Henry Wilson. In 1846, several members of the Amistad Committee formed the American Missionary Association, which subsequently established the Mendi Mission School in Sierra Leone.[76]

THE AMERICAN MISSIONARY ASSOCIATION that evolved from the *Amistad* Committee was an interracial organization that actively promoted civil rights before and after the American Civil War. Among its founders, James W. C. Pennington was an influential author, abolitionist, and civil rights

James W. C. Pennington

activist from the 1830s to the 1880s. After liberating himself from slavery in Maryland, Pennington became the first African American to attend Yale College. To raise funds for the defendants in the *Amistad* case, he founded the Union Missionary Society in 1841, which joined with other organizations to become the American Missionary Association, the largest abolitionist organization in U.S. history. The AMA established hundreds of educational organizations, including universities and educational programs that influenced the leaders of the American civil rights movement in the twentieth century and continue today. In 1841, Pennington published one of the earliest histories of African Americans, *The Origin and History of the Colored People.* His autobiography, *The Fugitive Blacksmith*, appeared in 1849, the same year he was awarded an honorary doctorate from the University of Heidelberg (resulting from an association that began when his talk at the 1849 World Peace Conference in Paris deeply impressed the German vice president; other attendees included William Wells Brown and the French writer Victor Hugo).[77]

In addition to the Mendi Mission and other schools in West Africa, the AMA established hundreds of antislavery-oriented churches in the U.S. as well as schools for former slaves in Canada and for Chinese immigrants in California. During and after the Civil War, the AMA founded hundreds of schools for freed people, including eight colleges and universities that still operate as of 2018.

In 1841, Madison Washington, among others, led a mutiny on a ship sailing with one hundred and thirty-five slaves from Richmond to New Orleans. Washington, who had liberated himself from slavery once before only to be recaptured when he went back for his wife, allied with nineteen other enslaved individuals to overpower the crew of the *Creole*. The rebels intended to seek freedom in Liberia, but the ship's limited provisions forced them to divert to the British Bahamas, a free territory because the British had passed the Slavery Abolition Act in 1833. However, British officials offered citizenship to all on board except the nineteen mutineers. Like the *Amistad* case, the *Creole* case stirred tensions between abolitionists and slavery supporters in the U.S. and between the U.S. and another nation, in this case Great Britain. In 1842 the *Creole* rebels were officially liberated in a British court.[78]

Slave revolts on land and at sea pulled at the threads of unraveling Atlantic slavery. As noted in Chapter 2, roughly one in ten slave voyages experienced some shipboard revolt—perhaps 500 insurgencies over the course of the Middle Passage. But those of the *Amistad* and *Creole* represented their culmination and the eventual triumph of human rights. The actions of the mutineers, those of the Mende and their supporters in particular, popularized in contemporary newspapers, appearances, exhibits, and plays—forced observers to grapple with the ethical, political, and legal dimensions of nineteenth-century slavery. Revolts on land, as demonstrated by the operations of the Underground Railroad, constantly eroded human bondage as an institution. The success of self-liberated slaves and free people of color, in every field, undermined the rationale of slavery, while their activism in print and courtrooms directly challenged the legal framework of humans as property, impacted state and federal policies, and generated the political tensions that propelled the nation to civil war.

THE AMERICAN CIVIL WAR

The American Civil War was, in effect, a massive slave revolt in which half a million black Americans liberated themselves and hundreds of thousands fought for others' liberty. The result was the demise of slavery and the establishment of democracy in the United States. As they had throughout the history of the Americas, enslaved men and women capitalized on the opportunities offered during wartime to pursue freedom. Fleeing their owners, entering Union lines, and offering their assistance as soldiers, laborers, guides, nurses, and spies, enslaved Americans forced recognition of their importance to the Union's success. "The slaves' resolute determination to secure their liberty converted many white Americans to the view that the security of the Union depended on the destruction of slavery."[79]

This shift constituted a direct rebuttal to the South's justifications for the "War Between the States." South Carolina's 1860 *Declaration of the Immediate Causes Which Induce and Justify the Secession* had stated that the provisions for the return of fugitive slaves were "so material to the compact [of the United States Constitution] that without it that compact would have not have been made."[80] In other words, the continuous self-liberation of enslaved Americans had been a significant threat to the institution of slavery since the founding of the nation. The declaration of secession went on to state that the North's lack of cooperation in returning fugitive slaves evidenced a larger disregard for the "right of property" and an overarching "hostility to slavery." Thus, the "states' right" for which the South fought was the right to own another individual as property.

Harriet Tubman, for example, certainly exhibited "an overarching hostility to slavery." In 1863, she became the first American woman to command a military raid for the United States army. During the Civil War, Tubman, a former slave who had liberated herself and many others through the Underground Railroad, served as a spy, courier, scout, and nurse. When she organized and guided Colonel James Montgomery and the 2nd South Carolina Volunteers, an African American unit, in the Combahee Ferry Raid liberating some eight hundred slaves in Beaufort, South Carolina—many of whom went on to join the Union army—Tubman was highly praised by various newspapers and emulated by subsequent Union tacticians. An extraordinary advocate of abolition, women's suffrage, and human rights, Tubman was given a full military funeral upon her death in 1913.[81]

Like Tubman, Mary Elizabeth Bowser was a former slave who risked her life as a Union spy during the Civil War. Bowser was freed in the mid 1800s in Richmond, Virginia, was educated in Philadelphia, and lived briefly in Liberia. When the war broke out, her former owner helped to organize a ring of spies. Posing as a slave, Bowser procured full-time employment in Jefferson Davis's home in Richmond, the capital of the Confederacy. She feigned a dim wit, but in fact her literacy and photographic memory allowed her to obtain and pass along crucial wartime intelligence.[82]

At the start of the Civil War it was illegal for free black men, much less enslaved persons, to serve in the military. While some states banned black men from militias and the Federal Militia Act of 1792 officially prohibited their armed service, slave and free African Americans nonetheless fought in every U.S. military engagement from King Williams's War in 1683 through the War of 1812. During times of crisis unit commanders might accept black volunteers despite official policy, and authorities often lifted bans, if only for the duration of the conflict. During the Civil War, the massive influx of black volunteers prompted both; their perseverance resulted in a shift in federal policy that legally transformed slaves into citizens.

During the first years of the conflict, combat status for African Americans was intensely debated by politicians, military commanders, abolitionists, and the general public, black and white. The politics of black enlistment and emancipation were inseparable, and deeply rooted ideologies of white supremacy clashed with measures that implied racial equality. President Lincoln's concern for maintaining the loyalty of slave-holding Border States initially prevented him from initiating policy to permit black men to serve in the Union army. Lincoln had repeatedly declared his repugnance to slavery; however, he was not an abolitionist, nor a proponent of racial equality prior to the war. He believed that slavery was morally wrong but did not believe he had the authority to offer a unilateral political solution to override its constitutional protection. While he considered gradual abolition where owners were compensated and former slaves were colonized in Liberia and Haiti as a potential solution, Lincoln's "primary object" at the start of the Civil War was not to end slavery but rather "to preserve the Union."[83]

Days after the Confederate attack on Fort Sumter, free black men in the North began offering their services to the Union. Jacob Dodson, a government employee who had participated in three of John C. Frémont's expeditions to the West in the 1840s, immediately petitioned the Secretary of War to offer his services along with those of three hundred free black men from Washington, D.C., whom he had recruited. His and similar efforts of African Americans in Boston and Providence who organized black regiments were initially rejected.[84]

Within weeks of the outbreak of war, fugitive slaves reached Union camps and volunteered for the war effort. By the end of 1862, between 500,000 to 700,000 fugitive slaves had risked their lives to reach safety behind federal lines.[85] While the public debate over black enlistment continued, individual Union generals were forced to make practical decisions about handling the huge numbers of enslaved men and women and to consider their military use despite legal restrictions.[86] Some Union generals engaged the volunteers and pursued the recruitment of black men without congressional authority. Black women often served unofficially, providing medical and maintenance support in the camps. When African Americans arrived at Fort Monroe in May 1861, General Butler put the men to work, with compensation, in his quartermaster department, and Lincoln let Butler's policy stand. Four months later, Congress passed the First Confiscation Act, which nullified the claims of slave owners to slaves who had aided the Confederate war effort.

Both Union commanders and enslaved individuals quickly took advantage of the legislation. In August 1861, the head of the Department of the West, General John C. Frémont, issued an edict freeing the slaves of Missouri rebels. But Lincoln overruled Frémont's unauthorized proclamation lest the policy alienate slave-holders in the Border States. Still, enslaved men and women continued to free themselves by crossing behind federal lines.

In Secretary of War Simon Cameron's annual report in December 1861, he removed, at Lincoln's prompting, passages advocating emancipation and the engagement of self-emancipated slaves in the Union army.[87] In March 1862, Congress enacted an additional article of war that further undermined the fugitive slave laws. Lincoln began to urge the Border States to enact gradual, compensated abolition and advocated the colonization of former slaves outside of the U.S. A step ahead of federal policy, Union General David Hunter, Commander of the Department of the South, began arming self-liberated slaves at Port Royal, South Carolina, in April 1862; the following month, he declared all slaves in South Carolina, Alabama, and Florida to be free.

Lincoln issued a proclamation to nullify Hunter's edict, and the War Department initially refused to pay or equip his black soldiers. Still, the 1st South Carolina Volunteers, composed entirely of formerly enslaved individuals, served the Union army. A few months later, Kansas senator James H. Lane began to recruit former slaves from Missouri and Arkansas for the 1st Kansas Colored Volunteer Infantry, later known as the 79th Infantry Regiment. At the insistence of American ex-slaves determined to fight for the freedom of others, the tide of federal policy was turned.

In July 1862, Congress passed two measures that directly linked African American enlistment to emancipation. The Second Confiscation Act freed slaves owned by rebels and permitted the seizure of the latter's property; prohibited military personnel from surrendering fugitives or deciding on the validity of an escaped slave's claim to freedom; and authorized the president to employ "persons of African descent" in any capacity to suppress the rebellion. The Militia Act provided for the employment of African Americans in "any military or naval service for which they may be found competent" and granted freedom to slaves so employed and to their families if their owners were rebels.

On September 22, 1862, Lincoln issued the preliminary Emancipation Proclamation. The final Emancipation Proclamation of January 1, 1863, authorized that emancipated slaves "will be received into the armed service of the United States to garrison forts, positions, stations, and other places, and to man vessels of all sorts in said service." While the proclamation only liberated slaves in Confederate territory not under Union control, and left slavery in the Border States intact, it established emancipation as an official objective of the war. It also instigated the active recruitment of African American soldiers. In May 1863, the federal government established the Bureau for Colored Troops to systematize African American recruitment and enlistment.

The hundreds of thousands of slaves who freed themselves and fled to Union lines made black military service and emancipation inevitable, and Lincoln, motivated by military exigency, issued the Emancipation Proclamation to officially liberate these fugitive slaves and permit their armed service on the largest possible scale. However, Lincoln's policy did not address whether African Americans who served the Union would receive the same treatment as their white counterparts.

Throughout the Civil War black men and women risked their lives to support the federals, but deeply rooted racial prejudice often meant that the work of these Americans went unrecognized and uncompensated. The Union army discriminated against black soldiers with substandard supplies, equipment, rations, training, medical care, and pay. Many black soldiers, as well as their white commanders, strongly protested salary discrepancies. The 54th Massachusetts Regiment chose to serve a year without pay rather than accept substandard wages. The fact that Confederate forces showed black prisoners of war no quarter underscores the extraordinary valor of African American servicemen.

Approximately 180,000 African American soldiers enlisted in the Union army, constituting ten percent of all Union troops that served in the war. Approximately three-quarters of these soldiers were former slaves who had liberated themselves. Unknown thousands of self-liberated slaves worked for the Union army in unofficial non-combat capacities such as teamsters, cattle drivers, stevedores, laborers, and camp aides. Another 20,000 black men served as sailors during the Civil War (in 1813 almost a quarter of the U. S. Navy was of African descent). The Union army commissioned between eighty and one hundred African American officers: eight black men served as federal army surgeons, including Lieutenant Colonel Alexander T. Augusta, the highest-ranking black soldier in the Civil War. An unknowable number of men with unrecognized African ancestry fought with white regiments.[88]

The greatest number of United States Colored Troops served in the Virginia theater as part of General Grant's Petersburg-Richmond campaigns. Fourteen black soldiers received the Medal of Honor for their bravery and leadership during the Battle of New Market Heights outside of Richmond in 1864. At the start of 1865, the 3rd U.S. Colored Cavalry liberated a thousand slaves in Mississippi. In April 1865, the 5th Massachusetts Colored Cavalry was among the first units to enter Richmond upon its capture. Black troops were among the Union forces at the Appomattox Court House when General Robert E. Lee surrendered.[89]

AFRICAN AMERICAN MEN HAD long served on American naval vessels, and black sailors faced much less official discrimination than did African American soldiers during the Civil War. Black sailors served in integrated crews and received the same pay, benefits, legal recourse, and living standards as white sailors. At the war's outbreak, numerous escaped slaves sought refuge on navy vessels; many provided intelligence on Confederate movements and fortifications.

As early as July 1861, U.S. Secretary of the Navy Gideon Wells had established a policy to recruit black sailors. Within months, thousands of men of African descent, from the U.S. and abroad, transformed the composition of the Union navy and served in every major naval battle and campaign. After Admiral "Damn the torpedoes" Farragut was victorious in the Battle of Mobile Bay in 1864—arguably the most important naval contest of the war—four black sailors from his crew were awarded the Medal of Honor;[90] four other African American sailors also won the Medal of Honor during the Civil War. Gideon Wells would later recall that, "'the rebellion rapidly increased the anti-slavery sentiment everywhere, and politicians shaped their course accordingly.'"[91]

Several who served in the Union navy had liberated themselves in daring escapes from slavery. On May 23, 1862, Robert Smalls, enslaved in Charleston, South Carolina, commandeered the Confederate ship *Planter*. An expert pilot, Smalls boarded his family members and those of his enslaved crewmen, donned the Confederate captain's hat and jacket, and sailed past several Confederate lookouts. He delivered the ship and its contents

Robert Smalls

*Union veteran William B. Gould, seated, with his sons. In 1862, Gould
and seven colleagues from Wilmington, North Carolina, liberated
themselves from plantations and boarded a Union gunboat. Gould then
served in the U.S. navy for the next three years. All six of Gould's sons
followed their father into military service; five defended democracy in
World War I, and one served in the Spanish-American War.*

to the U.S. navy and garnered freedom for himself, seven crewmen, and
their families. Smalls went to Washington to encourage President Lincoln
to emancipate and enlist the ex-slaves who were pouring into Union lines
with their families by the hundreds of thousands. He was instrumental in
obtaining the order that permitted the enlistment of the 1st and 2nd South
Carolina Volunteers (some of whom fought alongside Harriet Tubman in
the Combahee raids). He hand-delivered the order from the Secretary of
War to officially muster the first black U.S. army battalion. Smalls became
the first African American captain of a U.S. Navy vessel.

After his wartime service, Smalls returned to South Carolina. There he
purchased his former master's home but permitted his ailing former mistress

Sergeant Major Christian Fleetwood, right, received the Medal of Honor for his Civil War service. Countless numbers of black men and women served unofficially, without pay or recognition, like volunteer nurse, teacher, and camp aide Susie King Taylor, left above. These African American men and women made abolition inevitable and helped to establish democracy in the United States.

to reside there and cared for her until her death. Smalls was instrumental in establishing the Republican Party in South Carolina, was elected to the U.S. Congress five times, and authored legislation to establish the state's (and the nation's) first free and compulsory public school system.[92]

Another African American who "seized his freedom" to serve the U.S. navy during the Civil War, William B. Gould, chronicled in a diary his escape from slavery in North Carolina and his naval experiences in the U.S. and Europe, including his observations of the events and issues surrounding the war and American politics.[93] Gould was the son of an enslaved woman and a white father. He worked as a plasterer before he made his daring escape with seven enslaved colleagues along the Cape Fear River and into

This image was the frontsipiece from Elizabeth Keckley's 1868 memoir. Keckley's mother was an enslaved Afro-Virginian woman; her father, a colonel in the War of 1812, was their owner. After purchasing her own and her son's freedom, Keckley set up a business in 1860 designing dresses for elite women in Washington, D.C. Her clients included the wives of Jefferson Davis, Robert E. Lee, and Abraham Lincoln. She worked in the White House as the personal modiste and confidant of First Lady Mary Todd Lincoln. During the American Civil War, Keckley collaborated with hotelier James Wormley to operate the Contraband Relief Association to assist formerly enslaved Americans.

the Atlantic Ocean. Gould saw the Union forces as "defending the holiest of causes, Liberty and Union" as well as "Right and Equality."[94]

ALTHOUGH LINCOLN WAS INITIALLY opposed to arming black Americans, in 1864 he acknowledged that emancipation and the arming of slaves were crucial to the Union's victory.[95] In addition to the officially mustered African American units, numerous black men and women aided Union forces in unofficial capacities, supplying labor, resources, and information. Between 40,000 and 60,000 enlisted African Americans lost their lives in the Civil War. Twenty-three black soldiers and sailors received the Medal of Honor for their Civil War service. After the war, several black regiments assisted the Army of Occupation and Reconstruction efforts until 1867.

RECONSTRUCTION

James Wormley was a freeborn man of color. His sons served the United States as sailors and soldiers during the Civil War; his hotel served as a hub of national politics during Reconstruction. An internationally renowned establishment situated near the White House, "Wormley's Hotel was the most luxurious in the city in an era during which hotels played a significant role in politics and government."[96]

Wormley's father, Lynch Wormley, had engaged attorney Francis Scott Key to aid with his procuring his own free papers. Perhaps best known for writing the lyrics of the national anthem, Key was a lawyer who represented several enslaved individuals in freedom suits as well as vehemently protected the property of slave-owners. Key himself owned slaves as well as manumitted them. He favored colonization and was a staunch opponent of abolition.[97]

Like the contradictions embodied in the person of Francis Scott Key, the Wormley Hotel was the site of one of the most tragic contradictions of United States history. It was there that Rutherford B. Hayes and Samuel Tilden held the secret meetings that yielded the Compromise of 1877.[98] The Compromise led to the collapse of Reconstruction and the removal of federal protections for the civil and political rights of freed slaves and all American citizens of African descent, thus paving the way for the violent retributions of Jim Crow segregation.

Like Wormley's, the sons of Frederick Douglass served with the Union forces. Lewis Henry Douglass, a sergeant major in the Union army, survived being wounded at Fort Wagner, went on to integrate the printer's union (despite intimidation), edit a newspaper, and serve on the capital's legislative council where he introduced a law in 1872 to make segregation in public accommodations illegal. Charles Remond Douglass worked in the Treasury Department after his wartime service as an officer. He and his wife Laura founded one of the nation's earliest black resort towns, Highland Beach, where prominent black political figures like John Mercer Langston, Mary and Robert Terrell, P. B. S. Pinchback, and James Wormley invested.

Buffalo Soldiers and Black Horsemen

At the end of the American Civil War, Congress authorized six black regiments to serve in the regular U.S. army. While African Americans had served in every military engagement in American history, this was the first time black soldiers were permitted to serve during peacetime. The Buffalo

Soldiers, as these soldiers and cavalrymen were dubbed, were crucial to "how the West was won," the American expansion in the late nineteenth century. Isaiah Dorman served the U.S. army as an interpreter during Custer's Last Stand in 1876. Corporal George Jordan was awarded the Congressional Medal of Honor for his valor and skill in defending an American town during an Apache raid in New Mexico in 1880.[99] Self-emancipated Cathay Williams (who enlisted as Williams Cathay) served in a Buffalo Soldier regiment and was later revealed to be a woman.[100] These black soldiers and cavalry helped to establish the western United States by defending it, mapping it, and connecting it to the rest of the county with roads and telegraph wires. Twenty-four were awarded the Congressional Medal of Honor for their bravery during the western campaigns. These Buffalo Soldiers who "performed a crucial role in protecting settlers [and] paving the way for peace"[101] were part of a much larger community of African descent in the West.

African Americans also shaped the settlement of the American West as cowboys. Across the hemisphere, Afro-Americans were often predominant in cattle ranching, and they were instrumental in establishing and innovating its practices. The origins of the lasso go back to West African herders who roped animals from the ground; in the New World, Afro-Americans in early colonial Mexico were the first to adapt the technique while on horseback.[102]

Latin American cowboys, the majority non-white, roamed the range for three centuries before the small historic window for U.S. cowboys was closed with the advent of barbed wire, railroads, and refrigeration.[103] Afro-Americans were among the original Spanish settlers and defenders of towns like San Antonio, Laredo, and El Paso. While the origins of the American cowboy lie in New Spain—until 1848 most of the American Southwest was part of Mexico—many of the cowboys in the American West in the nineteenth century were former U.S. slaves who had migrated from the east.

Between about 1866 and 1895 at least one quarter of Texas cowboys were black.[104] Women like Johanna July were among them. July, "a Black Seminole . . . had her own method of taming horses in the Rio Grande for the soldiers at Fort Duncan."[105] Nat Love was a former slave from Tennessee who found work as a cowboy in Texas in the 1870s. His wrangling and rodeo skills earned him the nickname, Deadwood Dick. His autobiography described his accomplishments and adventures, including drinking with Billy the Kid and surviving being wounded and captured by a band of Native Americans.[106]

The most successful black ranchers in antebellum Texas may have been the Ashworth brothers. Born in South Carolina, the four brothers, William, Aaron, Abner, and Moses, settled in Texas in the 1830s. Two of the Ashworths, like other wealthy ranchers, sent surrogates to comply with mandatory military service during the Texas revolution. "Eventually the brothers acquired nearly two thousand acres in southeast Texas, and Aaron Ashworth owned twenty-five hundred head of

Bass Reeves, maybe the original "Lone Ranger"?

cattle, the largest herd in Jefferson County."[107] In fact, in 1850, "Aaron Ashworth was the only resident of the county wealthy enough to afford a tutor for his children."[108]

Bass Reeves, a former slave who had made his way from Texas to "Indian Territory," may have been the historical inspiration for the Lone Ranger. During the Civil War, Reeves broke with his owner, a Texas state legislator who recognized Reeves's exceptional marksmanship and horsemanship. Reeves moved to Oklahoma where he lived with Seminoles, Creeks, and Cherokees, and, after the passage of the Thirteenth Amendment, became a homesteading farmer in Arkansas. In 1875 Reeves was appointed a U.S. marshal, initiating an illustrious 32-year career in Oklahoma, Arkansas, and Texas. When Oklahoma became a state in 1907, Reeves was made an officer of the Muskogee police department. With a command of several Native American languages and ambidextrous marksmanship, Reeves gained fame for his detective skills and remarkable record of apprehending a claimed 3,000 felons. Reeves was said to have a Native American sidekick, use disguises,

George McJunkin was an American cowboy, homesteader, and former slave from Texas with a strong interest in science and fluency in Spanish. His discovery of fossils in Folsom, New Mexico, in 1908 revolutionized archeology. McJunkin called attention to the potential significance of ancient bison remains that contained a human-made weapon, which, when confirmed by scientists in 1922, indicated that humans inhabited North America 7,000 years earlier than had been thought. Many of the cowboys in Texas and the American West, as well as those who preceded them throughout the Americas, were of African descent. Afro-Mexican cowboys were among the first to refine the technique of the lasso, a skill first demonstrated in Madrid in the 1640s by an American-born slave.

never get wounded—qualities leading to the observation, "Bass Reeves is the closest real person to resemble the Lone Ranger on the American frontier in the nineteenth century."[109]

In addition to being experienced horsemen on frontiers and ranches, black equestrians dominated the United States' first national sport: horseracing. Southern planters often engaged enslaved African Americas to train and care for their horses, including training and jockeying race horses. "When President Andrew Jackson moved into the White House in 1829, he brought along his best Thoroughbreds and his [enslaved] black jockeys."[110] Starting in the eighteenth century, horse racing offered some a route to freedom, fame, and fortune. The Kentucky Derby was established in 1875, and "former slaves and their sons starred at Churchill Downs."[111] Thirteen of the fifteen riders of the first Derby were black, and black jockeys won fifteen of the first twenty-eight Derbys. Oscar Lewis, a nineteen-year-old African American rider from Kentucky, was the first jockey to win the Derby, riding a horse trained by a former slave and renowned horseman named Ansel Williamson. Isaac Murphy, the son of a former slave, won his third consecutive Derby in 1891 (44 percent of his Derby mounts) and ranks among the greatest jockeys in history.[112]

Cuban Independence

During the Spanish-American War of 1898, many of the Buffalo Soldiers who had defended U.S. sovereignty in the West assisted in the

"Some of our brave colored Boys [sic] who helped to free Cuba," during the Spanish-American War. These are some of the soldiers of the 10th Cavalry, who fought with extraordinary bravery among Roosevelt's Rough Riders in the Battle of San Juan. The 10th Cavalry was but one of several "colored" regiments that fought with distinction to liberate Cuba. For their bravery during the Spanish-American War, five African American soldiers and two sailors were awarded the Medal of Honor. Among these men was Sergeant Major Edward Baker who rescued a drowning soldier under heavy fire and was later promoted to the rank of Captain. Baker's grandson, Dexter Gordon, became an internationally renowned jazz saxophonist and founding figure of bebop in the twentieth century. (Gordon's father, Baker's son-in-law, was a prominent black physician who counted Duke Ellington and Lionel Hampton among his patients.)

liberation of Cuba. It is well known that the entry of the U.S. into the Spanish-American War was spurred by the sinking of U.S.S. *Maine*—the U.S. navy's first commissioned battleship. It is less well known that among the American servicemen on board during the attack were thirty-three black sailors—twenty-two of whom were killed.[113]

While numerous black Americans risked their lives for the U.S. forces in Cuba, Cuba's patriot armies were principally people of African descent. Cuban nationalist uprisings against Spanish rule preceded the Spanish-American War and U.S. intervention in 1898. On October 10, 1868, Carlos Manuel de Céspedes, poet, lawyer, and sugar planter, made a speech declaring freedom for his slaves and inviting them to join in a war for Cuban independence. This speech, which mobilized several dozen like-minded planters and their slaves, became known as the "*Grito de Yara*" (Cry of Yara) and the opening salvo of Cuba's first war for independence, or the Ten Years' War. The Cuban Liberation Army and the revolutionary republican government that followed was composed of eastern planters (many of whom were unable to compete economically with the mechanized, large-scale sugar plantations of western Cuba), slaves (some of whom self-liberated while others were freed by their owners or insurgent forces), and free Cubans of color (a significant part of the island's eastern population). Estimates suggest that over the course of Cuba's liberation struggles, Afro-Cubans composed 60 to 80 percent of the patriot army, though Cubans of African descent were roughly only 40 percent of the general population at the time.[114]

Antonio Maceo, son of an Afro-Venezuelan father and Afro-Cuban mother, quickly ascended the ranks of the Cuban Liberation Army during the Ten Years' War and was an exceptional military leader and an "exemplary patriot" in all three of Cuba's wars for independence.[115] Maceo's powerful leadership and extensive ranks of supporters, including Cuban national-ist José Martí (who declared, "Maceo has as much strength in his mind as in his arm"), and the multiracial character of the insurgent army at all levels prompted Spanish authorities to play on the racial anxieties of some white Cubans and their fears of a race war and "another Haiti." In 1878, the provincial leaders of the Cuban Liberation Army in Camagüey signed a peace treaty with Spain, the Pact of Zanjón. Because the treaty stopped

short of independence and full abolition (it offered freedom only to slaves who had served in
combat, on either side), Maceo denounced
the armistice at a meeting with Spanish
authorities in Baraguá and in a circular,
"The Protest of Baraguá." Maceo and his
corps of some one thousand men, the
majority of whom were Cubans of color,
continued to resist Spanish forces in the
eastern province of Oriente. Despite the
surrender of the Cuban Liberation Army
in the following months, the Ten Years'
War was the commencement of a thirty-year
struggle for Cuban independence.

Antonio Maceo

The Ten Years' War was an anticolonial,
democratic revolution that failed militarily
but had a powerful and enduring ideological impact.[116] Antiracist rhetoric
and the multiracial character of the insurgency undermined early support
from some white revolutionaries. However, the intertwining of independence
and abolition as the primary aims of revolution, first signaled by Céspedes's
"Grito de Yara" and reinforced by Maceo's "Protest of Baraguá," transformed
the meaning of Cuban nationalism as it linked the end of colonialism with
the end of slavery and established a rhetoric of social equality, justice, and
national identity that transcended race. The political mobilization and
extensive participation of Cubans of color in the Ten Years' War hastened
full abolition in 1886, engendered a racially inclusive conception of Cuban
citizenship, and laid the groundwork for the *Guerra Chiquita* (Little War)
of 1879–1880 and the 1895 War of Independence (that culminated in the
Spanish American War in 1898).

Rather than passive recipients of freedom, Afro-Cubans were political
agents who pressed for national sovereignty and democratic conceptions of
citizenship. Black activists initiated and intertwined Cuban sovereignty and
abolitionism as a national agenda. The Afro-Cuban progenitors of Cuban
independence had "a sophisticated nationalism that in time broadened to

make them an advance guard of Third World anti-imperialism."[117] Afro-Americans had made emancipation and citizenship an essential achievement of the Haitian Revolution, the Latin American wars of independence, and the American Civil War; they did so in Cuba as well.

Maceo's revolutionary work in the service of justice, liberty, and Enlightenment ideals had its origins in the work of his mother, Mariana Grajales. The daughter of Haitian émigrés, Grajales was among the significant Afro-Cuban women who actively advanced the anticolonial and abolitionist struggle. In addition to raising and supporting a family of patriots who served, led, and sacrificed themselves during the wars for Cuban sovereignty, Grajales operated settlements and hospitals that put her on the front lines; she carried wounded soldiers from the battlefield. Rosa Castellanos, also known as La Bayamesa, became a free woman at the start of the Ten Years' War. She served in battle, established a hospital for the wounded, and was awarded military honors. Maria Hidalgo Santana, an Afro-Cuban woman from Mantanzas, served among the infantry during Cuba's Wars of Independence.[118]

In 1864, at just twenty-one years old, Antonio Maceo joined the Masonic Lodge of his hometown, Santiago de Cuba, where, like his Freemason counterparts in the U.S., he encountered like-minded Afro-Americans dedicated to democratic ideals. After his service in the Ten Years' War (Maceo survived numerous wounds, but his father and two brothers were killed in the line of duty), Maceo corresponded and collaborated with other republican revolutionaries during his stays in Jamaica, Haiti, Honduras, Costa Rica, New York, and Key West. He traveled to New Orleans several times, where he briefly took up residence with his family in 1884. His work attracted the attention of African American intellectuals and writers. In New Orleans, he joined an established community of revolutionary Cuban émigrés. Their political commitment to freedom and civic equality resonated with the region's population of color, many of whom had Afro-French roots that connected them to the republican ideals of the French and Haitian revolutions.

PROTECTING FREEDOM

At least one of Homer Plessy's collaborators in challenging Louisiana's Separate Car Act of 1890, Pierre Carmouche, was a declared Maceo supporter.

In 1892, Plessy (whose paternal grandfather was a French-born, Haitian émigré) purchased a ticket on the East Louisiana Railroad and refused to be removed from the whites-only car, prompting the landmark 1896 Supreme Court case that unsuccessfully challenged segregation and thus enshrined "separate but equal" as U.S. policy for a half century.

While Plessy is well known, few are familiar with his many predecessors and contemporaries in Louisiana who endeavored to safeguard equal rights through civic and political organizations. From the Civil War veteran and state policymaker Edouard Tinchant to the lawyer, physician, and newspaper founder Louis Martinet, Louisiana's champions of citizenship were within a larger pan-American struggle for justice and democracy inextricable from that of their Caribbean antecedents and counterparts.[119]

Not long after Homer Plessy boarded the train in Louisiana (four decades after Elizabeth Jennings Graham won her 1855 case contesting New York's segregated streetcars), Ida B. Wells purchased a first-class train ticket and was forcibly removed from the whites-only accommodation in Memphis, Tennessee. While the initial litigation over her attempt to defend equality was successful, the courts ultimately ruled against her. The child of enslaved parents and born into slavery herself, Wells gained international acclaim as a journalist, activist, and businesswoman. She became known as Ida Wells-Barnett after she married attorney F. L. Barnett, who edited a black newspaper in Chicago.

When three of her friends—successful local business owners and community leaders—were lynched in 1892, Wells-Barnett challenged the escalating culture of racial terrorism by staging an effective economic boycott and publishing her investigations of a series of recent murders. After vandals destroyed her newspaper and imperiled her life, she took a job at a New York newspaper and became one of the first to document the epidemic of lynching in book form, garnering an international audience. In the early twentieth century, Wells-Barnett would join forces with numerous African American activists to found the NAACP as well as organizations for women's rights. According to Duke University scholar Lee D. Baker, "she stands as one of our nation's most uncompromising leaders and most ardent defenders of democracy."[120]

Throughout the nineteenth century black men and women fought to realize freedom, justice, and equality, not just as rebels, soldiers, and leaders, but also as lawyers, plaintiffs, politicians, journalists, scholars, medical professionals, and public figures. Attorneys like Robert Morris, Luís Gama, and Charlotte Ray, publishers like David Ruggles, Mary Ann Shadd Cary, and Ferreira de Menezes, doctors like James McCune Smith, José Manuel Valdéz, Rebecca Crumpler, and David Jones Peck championed democracy throughout their lives and through their work. Wartime heroes such as Harriet Tubman, Mary Bowser, Robert Smalls, and Antonio Maceo risked their lives for the rights of others. Just as Afro-Americans were central to the independence struggles and abolition in Latin America and the Caribbean, multitudes of African Americans played paramount roles in the U.S.'s "second war for independence"—the American Civil War—as well as in the events that preceded it.

By the close of the nineteenth century, slavery had been outlawed throughout the Americas, with the U.S., Cuba, and Brazil the last three nations to do so. In these regions in particular, racial discrimination and, in many cases, racial terrorism replaced the social controls that legal slavery had afforded. In the United States, as Homer Plessy and Ida B. Wells broadcast to the world, Americans of African descent faced a systematic denial of access to public space and institutions as well as chronic threats and manifestations of violence. While Afro-Americans had been instrumental in the political and military campaigns for liberty and national sovereignty throughout the hemisphere in the nineteenth century, many would find themselves fighting for freedom and equality in the twentieth.

NOTES FOR CHAPTER 6

1. Sarah E. Johnson, *The Fear of French Negroes: Transcolonial Collaboration in the Revolutionary Atlantic* (Los Angeles, UCLA Press, 2012), back cover.

2. W. Jeffrey Bolster, *Black Jacks: African American Seamen in the Age of Sail* (Cambridge: Harvard University Press, 1997), 2.

3. Graham Russell Gao Hodges, *David Ruggles: A Radical Black Abolitionist and the Underground Railroad in New York City* (Chapel Hill: UNC Press, 2010), 106.

4. Hodges, *David Ruggles*, 17–21.

5. The petition read, "Having no vote or Influence in the Election of those that Tax us yet many of our Colour (as is well known) have Cherfully [sic] Entered the field of Battle

in the defense of the Common Cause and that (as we conceive) against a similar Exertion of Power (in Regard to taxation) too well known to need a Recital in this place." Lamin Sanneh, *Abolitionists Abroad: American Blacks and the Making of Modern West Africa* (Cambridge: Harvard University Press, 1999), 90. In South Carolina in 1791, three African Americans (a bricklayer and two butchers) submitted a formal memorial to the senate on behalf of the state's free black population to protest their not being permitted to serve on a jury despite paying taxes. Sidney Kaplan and Emma Nogrady Kaplan, *The Black Presence in the Era of the American Revolution* (Amherst: University of Massachusetts Press, 1989), 268.

6. Darlene Clark Hine, et al, *The African-American Odyssey* (Upper Saddle River, NJ: Prentice Hall, 2011), 115.

7. Lamont D. Thomas, *Paul Cuffe: Black Entrepreneur and Pan-Africanist* (Urbana: University of Illinois Press, 1986), 54.

8. Sanneh, *Abolitionists Abroad*, 92.

9. Jim Murphy, *Gone A-Whaling: The Lure of the Sea and the Hunt for the Great Whale* (New York: Clarion Books, 1998), 58–60; Martha Putney, *Black Sailors: Afro-American Merchant Seamen and Whalemen Prior to the Civil War* (Westport, CT: Greenwood Press, 1987), 60; Frances Karttunen, *Law and Disorder on Old Nantucket* (Nantucket, MA: Nantucket Press, 2007), 125; Robert Johnson, "Black-White Relations on Nantucket," *Historic Nantucket* 51, no. 2 (Spring 2002).

10. Barbara White, "The Integration of Nantucket Public Schools," *Historic Nantucket*, 40, no. 3 (Fall 1992), 59–62. Frances Karttunen, *The Other Islanders: People Who Pulled Nantucket's Oars* (New Bedford, MA: Spinner Publications, 2005), 85.

11. Sydney Kaplan, *American Studies in Black and White, Selected Essays, 1949–1989* (Amherst: University of Massachusetts Press, 1991), 300–302.

12. Clifford Ashley, *The Yankee Whaler* (Mineola: NY: Dover Publications, 1991 [1926]), 86.

13. Hine, *African-American Odyssey*, 182.

14. Jacqueline Bacon, *Freedom's Journal: The First African-American Newspaper* (Lanham, MD: Lexington Books, 2007), 2.

15. Sean Wilentz, "Introduction," in *David Walker's Appeal*, xx-xxi.

16. David Walker, *David Walker's Appeal* (New York: Hill and Wang 1995), 68.

17. Walker, *David Walker's Appeal*, 75.

18. Marilyn Richardson, ed., *Maria W. Stewart: America's First Black Woman Political Writer* (Bloomington: Indiana University Press, 1987), 3.

19. Stephen Kantrowitz, *More Than Freedom: Fighting for Black Citizenship in a White Republic, 1829–1889* (New York: Penguin, 2012), 23.

20. Jean Feagan Yellin and John C. Van Horne, *The Abolitionist Sisterhood: Women's Political Culture in Antebellum America* (Ithaca, NY: Cornell University Press, 1994), 129.

21. Claire Parfait et al eds., *Writing History from the Margins: African Americans and the Quest for Freedom* (New York: Routledge, 2016), 11.

22. Jacqueline L. Tobin with Hettie Jones, *From Midnight to Dawn: The Last Tracks of the Underground Railroad* (New York: Anchor Books, 2008), 82.

23. John T. Cumbler, Review of Johnson, Reinhard O., *The Liberty Party, 1840–1848: Antislavery Third-Party Politics in the United States*, H-CivWar, H-Net Reviews (February 2010).

24. Tobin, *From Midnight to Dawn*, 81.

25. Karolyn Smardz Frost, *I've Got a Home in Glory Land: A Lost Tale of the Underground Railroad* (New York: Farrar, Straus, and Giroux, 2007), 174.

26. Frost, *I've Got a Home*, xii.

27. Ibid.

28. Leonard W. Levy, "The 'Abolition Riot': Boston's First Slave Rescue," *New England Quarterly* 25, no. 1 (March 1952): 88.

29. Kantrowitz, *More Than Freedom*, 66.

30. Kantrowitz, *More Than Freedom*, 73. While Mr. and Mrs. Latimer became renowned for their antislavery work, their youngest son, Lewis Latimer, became a pioneering inventor, engineer, and a key collaborator with Thomas Edison toward the end of the century. See Chapter 7.

31. Ryan Dearinger, "Interracial Roads to American Freedom," *Common-Place: The Journal of Early American Life* 16, no. 1 (Fall 2015) http://common-place.org/book/interracial-roads-to-american-freedom/; Eric Foner, *Gateway to Freedom: The Hidden History of the Underground Rail Road* (New York: W. W. Norton, 2015).

32. The 1793 Fugitive Slave law sanctioned the seizure and return of runaway slaves who had entered another state or federal territory and judges could unilaterally determine an individual's slave or free status. The law was based on Constitution Article IV Section II: "a person charged in any state with treason, felony, or a crime, who shall flee justice and be found in another state, shall on demand of the executive authority of the state from which he fled, be delivered, and removed to the state having jurisdiction of the crime. No person held to service or labor in one state, under the laws of thereof, escaping into another, shall in consequence or any law or regulation therein, be discharged from such service of labor, but shall be delivered up on claim of the party to whom such service or labor may be due."

33. Gary Lee Collison, *Shadrach Minkins: From Fugitive Slave to Citizen* (Cambridge: Harvard University Press, 1998), 195; John D. Gordon, *The Fugitive Slave Rescue Trial of Robert Morris* (Clark, New Jersey: Talbot Publishing, 2013).

34. Susan Salvatore, et al, "Civil Rights in America: Racial Desegregation of Public Accommodations: A National Historic Landmarks Theme Study," National Parks Service, US Department of the Interior, 2009 [2004], 8.

35. Sirpa Salenius, *An Abolitionist Abroad: Sarah Parker Remond in Cosmopolitan Europe* (Amherst: University of Massachusetts Press, 2016), 2.

36. Lynn Hudson, *The Making of Mammy Pleasant: Black Entrepreneur in Nineteenth Century San Francisco* (Urbana: University of Illinois Press, 2003), 1–2.

37. Hudson, *Making of Mammy Pleasant*, 7.

38. St. Louis Circuit Court Historical Records Project

39. The African American poet Langston Hughes claimed kinship with Henry Clay through his paternal grandfather.

40. The combined result of the ban on international slave trade with the continued federal support for the lucrative sugar and cotton plantation economy in the lower South was that the U.S. saw an enormous increase in the domestic slave trade in the first half of 1800s. As part of the removal of individuals from the mid-Atlantic states to the Deep South, enslaved people spent, on average, 117 days in prison. Calvin Schermerhorn, "Commodity Chains and Chained Commodities: Following the Money of American Slavery in the 1830s," presentation for the Virginia Foundation for the Humanities November 12, 2013.

41. Kantrowitz, *More Than Freedom,* 117–118.

42. Nell Irvin Painter, *Sojourner Truth: A Life, A Symbol* (New York: W. W. Norton, 1997), 180.

43. Jean Kinney Williams, *Bridget "Biddy" Mason: From Slave to Businesswoman* (Minneapolis, MN: Compass Point Books, 2006).

44. The Monticello Classroom, Thomas Jefferson Foundation 2007.

45. Alejandro de la Fuente, "Slaves and the Creation of Legal Rights in Cuba: Coartacion y Papel," *Hispanic American Historical Review* 87, No 4 (2007): 659–692; Ariele Gross and Alejandro de las Fuente, "Slaves, Free Blacks, and Race in the Legal Regimes of Cuba, Louisiana, and Virginia: A comparison." UNC School of Law North Carolina Law Review, al No5 (2013): 1700–1756.

46. Paulina L. Alberto, *Terms of Inclusion: Black Intellectuals in Twentieth-Century Brazil* (Chapel Hill: University of North Carolina Press, 2011), 7.

47. Dale Torston Graden, *From Slavery to Freedom in Brazil: Bahia 1835–1900* (Albuquerque: University of New Mexico Press, 2006), xx-xxi.

48. Joao José Reis, *Slave Rebellion in Brazil: The Muslim Uprising of 1835 in Bahia* (Baltimore, MD: The Johns Hopkins University Press, 1993), xiii.

49. Robert Edgar Conrad, *The Destruction of Brazilian Slavery, 1850–1888* (Berkeley: University of California Press, 1972), 155.

50. James H. Kennedy, "Luiz Gama: Pioneer of Abolition in Brazil," *Journal of Negro History* 59, no. 3 (July 1974): 264.

51. Lorenzo D. Turner, "Some Contacts of Brazilian Ex-Slaves with Nigeria, West Africa," *Journal of Negro History* 27, no. 1 (1942): 60.

52. Tuner, "Some Contacts of Brazilian Ex-Slaves," 61.

53. Carl W. Hall, *A Biographical Dictionary of People in Engineering*, West Lafayette (IN: Purdue University Press, 2008): 181.

54. Margaret M. Olsen, "Marzano's *Zafira* and the Performance of Cuban Nationhood," *Hispanic Review* 75, no. 2 (Spring 2007), 135.

55. George Reid Andrews, *Afro-Latin America: 1800–2000*, (New York: Oxford University Press), 109.

56. Ibid.

57. Francisco de Sales Torres Homem, Viscount of Inhomerim, and João Maurício Wanderly, Baron of Cotegipe. Andrews, *Afro-Latin America*, 110.

58. José R. Jouve Martín, *The Black Doctors of Colonial Lima: Science, Race, and Writing*

in Colonial and Early Republican Peru (Montreal: McGill-Queen's University Press, 2014), xvi.

59. Martín, *Black Doctors*, xvii.

60. Ibid.

61. Carole Bass and Mark Alden Branch, "Yale College's First Black Grad: It's Not Who You Think," *Yale Alumni Magazine*, February 28, 2014.

62. Ariel Kaminer, "Discovery Leads Yale to Revise a Chapter of Its Black History," *New York Times*, February 28, 2014.

63. Ronald E. Mickens, *Edward Bouchet: The First African American Doctorate* (World Scientific Publishing Company: 2002), 15.

64. Robert S. Levine, *Martin R. Delany: A Documentary Reader* (Chapter Hill: University of North Carolina Press, 2003), 184.

65. Heather Denny, "Shared History: Harvard School of Dental Medicine Celebrates 150 Years," *Harvard Medicine Magazine* (Boston: Harvard Medical School, Winter, 2007). http://magazine.hms.harvard.edu/connections/shared-history. Freeman's grandson, Robert C. Weaver, served in the cabinet of President Lyndon Johnson.

66. Levine, *Martin R. Delany*, 1–2.

67. David M. Harris, "David Jones Peck, M.D.: A Dream Denied," *Journal of the National Medical Association* 102, no. 10 (October 2010): 954–955.

68. Henry Louis Gates Jr. and Evelyn Higginbotham, eds., *African American Lives* (New York: Oxford University Press, 2004), 200.

69. Gates, *African American Lives*, 182.

70. Louis Haber, *Black Pioneers of Science and Invention* (New York: Harcourt Inc., 1970).

71. Christopher Teal, *Hero of Hispaniola: America's First Black Diplomat* (Westport, CT: Praeger Publishing, 2008), 4–5.

72. Daniel R. Biddle and Murray Dubin, *Tasting Freedom: Octavius Catto and the Battle for Equality in Civil War America* (Philadelphia: Temple University Press, 2010).

73. William Wells Brown had published *Clotel, Or the President's Daughter* in 1852.

74. R. J. M. Blackett, *Building an Antislavery Wall: Black Americans in the Atlantic Abolitionist Movement, 1830–1860* (Baton Rouge: Louisiana State University Press, 1983). Bernth Lindfors, ed. *Ira Aldridge: The African Roscius* (Rochester, NY: University of Rochester Press, 2007), p. 1. Roscius was a famous actor who had been born into slavery and was widely celebrated for his talent in ancient Rome.

75. James Covey, a seaman, and Charles Pratt, a cook, were natives of Sierra Leone and served on the *Buzzard*; both translated for the *Amistad* detainees. Sailors of African descent had long served in the British navy, which was perhaps one-quarter black in the late nineteenth century.

76. The Mendi Mission School produced generations of educators and patriots. One of the *Amistad* captives, Sarah Margru, graduated from the school, then came to the U.S. to study at Oberlin College before returning to Sierra Leone to teach in the Mendi Mission. Barnabas Root and Thomas Tucker were Mission graduates who pursued advanced

degrees in the U.S.; after the Civil War, Root ministered to ex-slaves in Alabama, and Tucker became president of what would become Florida A&M University.

77. Mischa Honeck, et. al. eds., *Germany and the Black Diaspora* (New York: Berghahn Books, 2013), 157–158.

78. George Hendrick and Willene Hendrick, *The Creole Mutiny: A Tale of Revolt Aboard a Slave Ship* (Chicago: Ivan R. Dee, 2003).

79. Ira Berlin, "Who Freed the Slaves? Emancipation and Its Meaning in American Life." *Quaderno 5*, 1993, 30.

80. *Declaration of the Immediate Causes Which Induce and Justify the Secession of South Carolina; and the Ordinance of Secession*, (Charleston, SC: Evans and Cogswell, 1860), 7–10. If the Confederacy declared war on the United States over states' rights, the contemporary documents show that the right for which they killed some 620,000 Americans was the right to own another individual as property.

81. Donald E. Markle, *Spies and Spymasters of the Civil War*, (New York: Hippocrene Books, 2004), 59.

82. In 1995, Bowser was inducted into the U.S. Army Military Intelligence Hall of Fame, as "one of the highest-placed and most productive espionage agents of the Civil War." Catherine Reef, *African Americans in the Military* (New York: Facts on File, 2010) 31.

83. Eric Foner, *The Fiery Trial: Abraham Lincoln and American Slavery* (New York: W. W. Norton, 2010). 186.

84. David Williams, *I Freed Myself: African American Self-Emancipation in the Civil War Era* (New York: Cambridge University Press, 2014), 68.

85. John David Smith, ed., *Black Soldiers in Blue: African American Troops in the Civil War Era* (Chapel Hill: University of North Carolina Press, 2002), 23.

86. Berlin et. al. show how the persistence of African Americans transformed the Civil War into a fight for liberty in an analysis based on documents in the National Archives. See Ira Berlin, Joseph Reidy, and Leslie S. Rowland, *Freedom's Soldiers: The Black Military Experience in the Civil War* (New York: Cambridge University Press, 1998).

87. Foner, *The Fiery Trial*, 188.

88. Lucia Stanton documented four descendants of slaves of Thomas Jefferson who served in white Union units in *"Those Who Labor for My Happiness": Slavery at Thomas Jefferson's Monticello* (Charlottesville: University of Virginia, 2012). Hundreds of thousands of white Southerners served in the Union army.

89. Less than a week before Lee surrendered, Confederate President Jefferson Davis signed a bill authorizing the enlistment of slaves and their emancipation.

90. Steven J. Ramold, *Slaves, Sailors, Citizens: African Americans in the Union Navy* (De Kalb: Northern Illinois University Press, 2001), 130.

91. Foner, *The Fiery Trial*, 190.

92. Andrew Billingsly, *Yearning to Breathe Free: Robert Smalls of South Carolina and His Families* (Columbia, SC: University of South Carolina Press, 2007); Phillip Dray, *Capitol Men: The Epic Story of Reconstruction Through the Lives of the First Black Congressmen* (New York: Mariner, 2010).

93. Published by his great-grandson, a law professor at Stanford. William B. Gould IV, ed., *Diary of a Contraband: The Civil War Passage of a Black Sailor*, Stanford, CA: Stanford University Press, 2002.

94. Four of his sons served as officers in World War I, and one, William Jr. served the U.S. army in the Spanish-American War. Gould, *Diary of a Contraband*, 186, 47.

95. In 1862 Lincoln wrote "What I do about slavery and the colored race, I do because I believe it helps to save the Union." He wrote in 1863, "The colored population is the great available . . . force for restoring the Union" and later that year, "black men . . . with silent tongue, and clenched teeth, and steady eye, and well-poised bayonet, they have helped mankind on to this great consummation." In 1864 he wrote, "Any different policy in regard to the colored man, deprives us of his help. . . . Keep it and you can save the Union. Throw it away, and the Union goes with it." Roy B. Basler, ed., *The Collected Works of Abraham Lincoln*, Vols. 5 (p. 389) 6 (p. 150, 407) & 8 (p. 2), Brunswick, NJ: Rutgers University Press, 1953.

96. This hotel dated to about 1871, but Wormley had previously owned smaller hotels and a catering business that was patronized by the Washington elite. He was highly regarded by many, including Anthony Trollope, Daniel Webster, Abraham Lincoln, Frederick Douglass, and John Mercer Langston. In addition to the politicians, diplomats, and military officers who conducted business at Wormley's, his patrons included Thomas Edison, Henry James, and John Jacob Astor. Charles Sumner gifted his personal copy of the Thirteenth Amendment with original signatures to his friend, Mr. Wormley. Carol Gelderman, *A Free Man of Color and His Hotel: Race, Reconstruction, and the Role of the Federal Government* (Dulles, VA: Potomac Books, 2012), 1. See also Graves Donet, Wormley Hotel, The White House Historical Association, whitehousehistory.org.

97. Jefferson Morley, *Snow-Storm in August: The Struggle for American Freedom and Washington's Race Riot of 1835* (New York: Anchor Books, 2013), 41, 154, 217–218.

98. Gelderman, *Free Man of Color*, 99.

99. Catherine Clinton, *The Black Soldier: 1492 to the Present* (Boston: Houghton Mifflin, 2000), 35–38.

100. DeAnne Blanton, "Cathay Williams: Black Woman Soldier (1866–1868)," in *African American History in New Mexico: Portraits from Five Hundred Years*, ed., Bruce A. Glasrud (Albuquerque: University of New Mexico Press, 2013).

101. Bruce A. Glasrud and Michael N. Searles, eds., *Buffalo Soldiers in the West: A Black Soldiers Anthology* (College Station: Texas A&M University Press, 2007), 6.

102. Andrew Sluyter, *Black Ranching Frontiers: African Cattle Herders of the Atlantic World, 1500–1800* (New Haven, CT: Yale University Press, 2012), 51–54.

103. Richard W. Slatta, *Comparing Cowboys and Frontiers: New Perspectives on the History of the Americas* (Norman: University of Oklahoma Press, 1997), 177–179.

104. Sarah R. Massey, ed., *Black Cowboys of Texas* (College Station: Texas A&M University Press, 2000), xv.

105. Massey, *Black Cowboys of Texas*, xvii.

106. Nat Love, *The Life and Adventures of Nat Love, Better Known in the Cattle Country as "Deadwood Dick," by Himself; a True History of Slavery Days, Life on the Great Cattle*

Ranges and on the Plains of the "Wild and Wooly" West, Based on Facts, and Personal Experiences of the Author (Los Angeles, CA: 1907).

107. Quintard Taylor, *In Search of the Racial Frontier: African Americans in the American West, 1528–1990* (New York: Norton, 1998), 38.

108. Ibid.

109. Art T. Burton, *Black Gun, Silver Star: The Life and Legend of Frontier Marshall Bass Reeves* (Lincoln: University of Nebraska Press, 2006), 14.

110. Lisa K. Winkler, "The Kentucky Derby's Forgotten Jockeys," *Smithsonian Magazine*, April, 2009.

111. Christopher Klein, "The Kentucky Derby's Forgotten Jockeys," History.com, 2013.

112. Edward Hotaling, *The Great Black Jockeys: The Lives and Times of the Men who Dominated America's First National Sport* (Roseville, CA: Prima Lifestyles, 1999); Pellom McDaniels III, *The Prince of Jockeys: The Life of Isaac Burns Murphy* (Lexington: University Press of Kentucky, 2013).

113. Clinton, *Black Soldier*, 41.

114. Mark A. Sanders, ed. *A Black Soldier's Story: The Narrative of Ricardo Batrell* (Minneapolis: University of Minnesota Press, 2010), xiii, xxxvi.

115. "Exemplary patriot" comes from the inscription on the monument to Antonio Maceo in the Havana park named in his honor. "[Maceo] is honored as an unwavering fighter for independence, an anti-imperialist, and a consistent spokesman for the equality of all Cubans, black and white." Philip S. Foner, *Antonio Maceo: The "Bronze Titan" of Cuba's Struggle for Independence* (New York: Monthly Review Press, 1977), 1–2.

116. Ada Ferrer, *Insurgent Cuba: Race, Nation, and Revolution, 1868–1898*, Chapel Hill: University of North Carolina Press, 1999.

117. James D. Henderson, "Mariana Grajales: Black Progenitress of Cuban Independence," *Journal of Negro History* 63:2 (April 1978): 135.

118. Ana Garcia Chichester, "Activistas y Madres: La Mujer Afro-Cubana en las Guerras de Independencia de Cuba," unpublished paper; Henderson, "Mariana Grajales," 135–148.

119. Rebecca Scott, "The Atlantic World and the Road to Plessy v. Ferguson," *Journal of American History* 94 (December 2007): 726–733.

120. Lee D. Baker, "Ida B. Barnett-Wells and Her Passion for Justice" (April 1996), http://people.duke.edu/~ldbaker/classes/aaih/caaih/ibwells/ibwbkgrd.html.

~∾ TIMELINE ∾~

1900	In London, first Pan-African Conference unites black intellectuals and activists
1904	Afro-British doctor Allan Minns elected mayor of Norfolk, England
1905	Niagara Movement founded by leading African American intellectuals in U. S.
1907	Alain Locke awarded Rhodes Scholarship
1908	George McJunkin makes archaelogical find from 9000 BCE in New Mexico
1908	Joaquim Machado de Assis is president of Brazilian Academy of Letters
1908	Cubans Estenoz, Ivonnet, others found first black political party in Americas
1909	W. E. B. Du Bois, Mary Terrell, Ida Wells-Barnett, others establish NAACP
1909	Nilo Peçanha becomes seventh president of Brazil, implements reforms
1910	Carlos Mendoza becomes president of Panama
1914	Jamaica's Marcus Garvey establishes UNIA, international civil rights group
1916	Charles Young becomes U.S. Army's first African American colonel
1918	"Harlem Hellfighters" in combat longer than any other American military unit during WWI, then must fight for democracy at home
1918	Oscar Micheaux directs, produces *The Homesteader*, first of his many films
1918	Afro-Brazilian scholar Manuel Querino publishes watershed history article
1920	Nurse, activist Mary Eliza Mahoney is among first U.S. women registered voters
1927	U.S. Public Health Service adopts William Hinton's test for syphilis
1930	WWI veteran Pedro Albizu Campos heads Puerto Rico's Liberation Party
1930	Dr. Ernest Just is first American researcher at Keiser Wilhelm Institute
1931	Brazil's first black political party, Frente Negra Brasileira, is formed
1935	Sadie Mossell & Raymond Alexander draft Pennsylvania antidiscrimination law
1935	Historian, activist Luther Jackson founds Petersburg League of Negro Voters
1935	Frederick Jones develops portable refrigeration for food & medicine transport
1938	Afro-Trinidadian intellectual, activist CLR James publishes *The Black Jacobins*
1940	Surgeon Charles Drew invents blood bank, heads American Red Cross
1941	Protests lead FDR to ban racial discrimination in the U.S. defense industry
1942	Dorie Miller becomes first American hero of WWII for actions at Pearl Harbor
1948	After protests by Charlotta Bass and others, U.S. Supreme Court overturns restrictive residential deed covenants
1950	Mary Terrell's sit-in leads to the desegregation of restaurants in the U.S. capital

7

Twentieth-Century Afro-American
Freedom Fighters

As the Afro-Brazilian scholar Abdias do Nascimento observed in 1949, racism is "incompatible with democracy."[1] In the United States, the twentieth-century civil rights movement was a powerful and perilous mobilization for democracy, within which black and white Americans organized multifaceted initiatives for equal access and equal protection under the law. The movement reverberated internationally and provided a global model to challenge inequities based on gender, caste, class, religion, and sexual orientation. While many of the most widely recognized achievements of the movement took place in the second half of the nineteenth century, this chapter examines a small sample of the many champions of American democracy who operated during the first half of the 1900s.

Just as the aims of the United States' civil rights movement can be regarded in a broader temporal scope, the geographic sweep and international interconnections among Afro-American activists throughout the Americas in the first half of the twentieth century were extensive. Afro-Americans (including people from the United States) were influential in the early twentieth-century revolutions in Mexico and Cuba, in particular, as well as in liberation movements on both sides of the Atlantic. Some might think of the American, African, and European axes of the "Atlantic world" as belonging to the epoch of New World colonialism and slavery; yet, many of the twentieth century's Afro-American architects of democracy operated in an international arena.

The early twentieth-century innovators described below should be seen as part of the much larger tradition of democracy advocates described in previous chapters. Their accomplishments were all the more significant coming as they did amid anti-black discrimination and violence that swelled in the wake of Reconstruction at the end of the nineteenth century. In the first half of the twentieth century, racial terrorism replaced slavery as the social mechanism to maintain white supremacy in the United States. Public and private spaces and organizations explicitly excluded African Americans while vigilante violence regularly threatened and routinely took the lives of black veterans, business owners, voters—in essence, Americans of color were frequently targeted by those who perceived them to be encroaching on the prerogatives of whiteness. African Americans organized in various ways to combat the systematic denial of equal rights and equal protection in the decades leading up to civil rights movement. They often collaborated with the growing ranks of Caribbean activists and intellectuals whose work was shaping democratic movements on both sides of the Atlantic.

In the twentieth century, Afro-Latin Americans continued the work they had done between 1800 and 1900 that "transformed the terms of their participation in national life and . . . helped build nineteenth-century nations and societies."[2] In the twentieth century, black and brown people continued to shape Latin American politics and culture as journalists, politicians, lawyers, educators, artists, and activists. Just as many white Americans in the United States resisted and ultimately restricted black political power after the American Civil War and Reconstruction, so too were Afro-Latin Americans often disempowered. In the late nineteenth and early twentieth centuries new "sciences" sprang up to support white hegemony, yet notions of racial identity and social stratification varied throughout the Americas. Conventions of race and conceptions of freedom had local, regional, and temporal dimensions. Broadly speaking, many Latin American communities retained a corporate social structure, even after national independence, where patronage networks and class could potentially be more dominant than racial categories.

In Latin America as in the U.S., whiteness was associated with power and purity and blackness with inferiority, but in Latin America whiteness was enormously fluid. Latin Americans with African ancestry could be "whitened" through intermarriage, accomplishment, comportment, class, and, for a brief period (about 1750–1810), legal fiat. Throughout Latin American history, full siblings could be granted different racial designations—by the priests who made racial determinations in baptismal records as well as by cultural conventions that often recognized race in terms of gradation rather than bifurcation. The tremendous complexity, diversity, and fragmentation among Latins of African descent in terms of class, culture, and region was sometimes a detriment to political mobilization, particularly in the wake of independence when nationalist rhetoric in many parts of Latin America claimed to supersede race—rendering dissent inherently unpatriotic. Yet despite the array of obstacles that black activists faced in Latin America, countless fought for freedom in the twentieth century.

Early Twentieth Century Political Organizing

Pan-African Congress

In 1900, black intellectuals from around the globe met in London's Westminster Town Hall and inaugurated a transnational pro-democracy, anti-imperialist movement that came to be known as pan-Africanism. These Afro-American activists and professionals were concerned with the suppression of freedom in colonial and post-colonial states in the Americas. They were also responding to Europe's invasion and occupation of Africa. The 1884 Berlin Conference had been a turning point for European policies that once recognized the sovereignty of African states but had devolved into "carving up" the continent for colonization and expropriation—in 1870 Europe controlled 10 percent of Africa; by 1914, 90 percent.

The resulting Pan-African Conference was the first of six that brought together democracy advocates from around the world to address international development and human rights. Subsequent conferences were held in 1919 (Paris), 1921 (London, Brussels, Paris), 1923 (London and Lisbon), 1927 (New York), and 1945 (Manchester). While the initial conference focused on the citizenship rights of colonial subjects in Africa and the Americas, successive objectives came to include the rights of the many thousands of black veterans who served in two World Wars as well as the issues of labor rights, women's rights, and civil liberties.

The initiator of the 1900 London conference was Henry Sylvester-Williams, a Trinidadian teacher who became a lawyer, writer, and activist in England after having lived in New York and Nova Scotia. In 1897, he established the African Association, a London-based organization that used correspondence and the international press to endorse the rights of British subjects of African descent in Africa and the West Indies. By 1900 the organization had been renamed the Pan-African Conference Committee and included men and women from the United Kingdom, Africa, the Caribbean, India, and the United States. Sylvester-Williams went on to become the South Africa colony's first black barrister in 1903 and one of Britain's first black elected officials in 1906.[3]

John Richard Archer, another attendee of the first Pan-African Conference, was also elected to public office in England in 1906. Seven years later, Archer, English-born of Barbadian descent and a former seaman, was elected a mayor in London in 1913. As the head of the council for the London borough of Battersea, Archer was Britain's second mayor of African ancestry; Dr. Allan Glaisyer Minns, an Afro-British physician and politician, had been elected mayor of Thetford, Norfolk, in 1904. Minns's grandmother, Rosette, was a slave in the Bahamas before she married his paternal grandfather, John, an English émigré.

Anténor Firmin, the pioneering Haitian anthropologist, was an organizer of the conference and a founding figure of Pan-Africanism. In Haiti, Firmin studied classics, history, and law and held various political offices before taking a diplomatic post in Paris where he was admitted to the Society of Anthropology. Firmin's 1885 publication *Of the Equality of the Human Races* was a foundational text of an emerging discipline of anthropology based on empiricism; his work was an explicitly scientific refutation of the flawed racial pseudoscience proposed by Arthur de Gobineau and others.

Henry Francis Downing, an American, attended in 1900. Also a former seaman, Downing was a descendant of free black entrepreneurs from New York. His grandfather, Thomas Downing, a native of Virginia born to enslaved parents in 1791, became Manhattan's first eminent purveyor of oysters (whose clientele included Queen Victoria and Charles Dickens). Henry's uncle, George Thomas Downing, was a prominent civil rights activist and businessman in Rhode Island. A United States navy veteran, well-traveled, and politically active, Henry Francis Downing was appointed U.S. consul to Angola by president Grover Cleveland in 1887; however, Downing spent most of his life as a playwright and novelist in London.

The internationally acclaimed composer-conductor-professor Samuel Coleridge-Taylor performed at the first Pan-African Conference. Eventually dubbed in New York as "the African Mahler," the young composer was the British-born son of a doctor from Sierra Leone: Daniel Taylor, who received his medical training in England and was appointed Imperial Coroner in British West Africa, descended from African American slaves who had sided with the British during the American Revolution.

Dr. John Alcindor, who would be awarded a Red Cross medal for his services in World War I, was also in attendance in 1900. A Trinidadian who trained in medicine in Scotland, established his own practice, and became the senior medical officer of London's Paddington district, Alcindor presided over subsequent Pan-African conferences in 1919 and 1921. W. E. B. Du Bois attended the first conference and was instrumental in the organization of subsequent meetings of the Pan-African Congress.[4]

Prominent American scholar, educator, and activist Anna Julia Cooper delivered a paper at the 1900 conference. Born into slavery in Raleigh, North Carolina (fathered by her

Anna Julia Cooper is the only woman quoted in the current U.S. passport: "The cause of freedom is not the cause of a race or a sect, a party or a class—it is the cause of humankind, the very birthright of humanity."

owner), the gifted Cooper earned a master's degree in mathematics from
Oberlin College in 1887 and in 1892 published *A Voice from the South*,
which encapsulated much of her oratory advocating civil rights and gender
equality. Cooper spoke widely, including at the 1893 Chicago World's Fair's
"World's Congress of Representative Women" alongside Susan B. Anthony,
Jane Addams, and fellow Oberlin alumna Lucy Stone. Cooper became the
fourth African American woman to earn a Ph.D. when she received her
doctorate in history from the Sorbonne in 1924. She is commemorated on
a U.S. postage stamp and shares a designated Episcopalian feast day with
fellow educator and humanitarian Elizabeth Evelyn Wright, the daughter
of former African American and Native American slaves, who founded
Voorhees College in 1902.

The Niagara Movement

In 1905 W. E. B. Du Bois and William Monroe Trotter organized
a three-day meeting in Buffalo, New York, that established the Niagara
Movement, forerunner of the National Association for the Advancement
of Colored People, the United States' most enduring civil rights organization. While short-lived compared to the NAACP, the Niagara Movement
aimed to ameliorate the failures of American democracy—specifically the
discrimination and violence of the Jim Crow era—and to realize the nation's founding principles. Its goals included equal access to educational
and economic opportunities and equal protection under the law, as well as
the fulfillment of civic duties such as voting, education, work, and respect
for the rights of others.

William Monroe Trotter was a descendant on his mother's side of
Monticello's Edith Fossett, Jefferson's enslaved chef (see previous chapter).
His father, James Trotter, was a distinguished African American Civil War
lieutenant (see Introduction). Like Du Bois, William Trotter was an alumnus
of Harvard, where he earned a Phi Beta Kappa key, graduated magna cum
laude in 1895, and earned a master's degree in 1896. Trotter founded the
Boston Guardian in 1901 as well as the Boston Historical and Literary Association and was instrumental in the founding of the Niagara Movement.

W. E. B. Du Bois was the principal author of the Niagara Movement's

Ida Gibbs Hunt was the daughter of Mifflin Wistar Gibbs, a nineteenth-century entrepreneur, philanthropist, and diplomat. She received bachelor's and master's degrees from Oberlin where she matriculated with Mary Church Terrell and Anna Julia Cooper (all three taught at the Dunbar school in Washington, D.C., and Gibbs later taught at Florida A&M College). In 1897 she met William Hunt, former slave, jockey, and Williams  *student, who initially worked with and then succeeded her father as U.S. consul. After they married, she accompanied Hunt on assignments to Madagascar, France, Portugal, Guadeloupe, and Liberia and published and spoke internationally about human rights, women's suffrage, and foreign policy. Ida Gibbs Hunt was active in various organizations, including the Femmes de France, the Bethel Literary Society, the NACW, the NAACP, the Washington Welfare Association, the Women's International League for Peace and Freedom, and the Red Cross. She participated in the Second Pan-African Congress in Paris in 1919 and delivered a paper, "The Coloured Races and the League of Nations," in 1923 at the Third Pan-African Congress in Paris where she co-chaired the Conference's Executive Committee with W. E. B. Du Bois.*

1905 *Declaration of Principles,* which affirmed the founding principles of the Declaration of Independence and called out the negligence of many Americans to live up to them:

> We note with alarm the evident retrogression in this land of sound public opinion on the subject of . . . rights, republican government, and human brotherhood, and we pray God that this nation will not degenerate into a mob of boasters and oppressors, but rather will return to the

faith of the fathers, that all men were created free and equal, with certain unalienable rights.[5]

The Niagara Movement established chapters in twenty-one states, several of which lobbied effectively for specific civil rights issues. In the wake of the mass violence unleashed during riots against Americans of African descent in Springfield, Illinois, in 1908 (which displaced some 2,000 black residents), several members of the Niagara Movement founded the NAACP in 1909 as a biracial national organization dedicated "to ensure the political, educational, social, and economic rights of all persons."[6]

Alonzo Herndon was among the original twenty-nine African American entrepreneurs, educators, and clergy who attended the founding Niagara Movement meeting. Herndon was born into slavery in Georgia to an enslaved mother and her white owner (who fathered at least four additional children with enslaved women in his household.) After emancipation, Herndon began as a sharecropper, but he amassed great wealth, first by investing in a barbershop with a black barber in Atlanta and ultimately by founding the Atlanta Life Insurance Company. He would go on to invest his significant resources in civic and educational organizations, including Atlanta University.[7]

Garveyism

While African Americans endeavored to support civil rights as individuals as well as in organizations like the NAACP, Marcus Garvey's vision of equality and justice lodged in economic strength initiated a global mass movement. In 1914, after years of travel and study in Costa Rica, Panama, and England, Marcus Garvey returned to his native Jamaica. There he founded the United Negro Improvement Association with his future wife, Amy Ashwood. In 1917, they established a UNIA headquarters in New York City and soon after founded an international newspaper and a shipping line. After five years of working together, Ashwood and Garvey were briefly married in 1919. A prolific political activist in her own right, the Jamaican-born Amy Ashwood grew up in Panama and, in addition to New York, continued her work in London, West Africa, and the Caribbean. Along with her leadership in the UNIA, Amy Ashwood Garvey promoted democracy and women's rights internationally through the multiple organizations she established.

With a membership that tallied in the millions, the UNIA was among the largest political movements in history. By 1920 there were 700 UNIA branches in 38 U.S. states. The spread of Garveyism was fostered not only by the grassroots organizing promoted by Marcus and his second wife—coincidentally also a Jamaican-born activist named Amy; Amy Jacques Garvey's writings, speeches, and management were critical to the success of the UNIA—but also by a well-established network of black intellectuals on both sides of the Atlantic during the First World War. The Garveys' brand of Pan-Africanism was transmitted globally by labor activists in Central America and the Caribbean, by community organizers throughout the United States, and by religious networks throughout Africa. While some African American intellectuals, and the NAACP in particular, were initially critical of the militant black nationalism associated with the Garveys, the UNIA's principles inspired a vast transnational audience and continued to provide an ideological touchstone for subsequent religious and political movements from the Nation of Islam to Rastafarianism. Despite earlier philosophical disagreements, W. E. B. Du Bois ultimately collaborated with Amy Jacques Garvey, whose widely read 1944 Memorandum to the United Nations pressed for human rights and the decolonization of Africa. Amy Jacques Garvey worked with Du Bois to organize the Fifth Pan-African Congress in Manchester in 1945—where Amy Ashwood Garvey, at the invitation of Du Bois, chaired the opening day and spoke out for gender equality.[8]

The NACW and Civic Leadership

African American women championed democracy by participating in women's clubs, civic groups, and political organizations with roots stretching back into the nineteenth century. The establishment of the National Association of Colored Women in 1896 had unified some one hundred organizations promoting universal citizenship rights and philanthropy created during the African American women's club movement, including the National Federation of African American Women, the National League of Colored Women, and the Women's Era Club of Boston. "By 1914, the

Above, Josephine St. Pierre Ruffin; right, Josephine Silone Yates

NACW represented fifty thousand middle-class, educated black women in twenty-eight federations and over one thousand clubs."[9] In addition to Josephine Ruffin, Josephine Silone, and Mary Terrell, key founders of the NACW included Harriet Tubman, Frances Harper, Charlotte Ray, and Ida Wells-Barnett.[10] Several of the founders of the NACW went on to play key roles in the founding and development of the NAACP in the early twentieth century.

The unification of women's clubs in 1896 was initiated by Josephine St. Pierre Ruffin. She organized, directed, and integrated several clubs to advance women's rights, published a newspaper, and was among the founding members of the NAACP. St. Pierre was born in Boston; her father was from Martinique and her mother was from England. She married George Lewis Ruffin, who was born to free black parents in Richmond, Virginia, in 1834. He initially worked in Boston as a barber, graduated Harvard Law School in 1869, and served in the Massachusetts legislature, on Boston's city council, and as a municipal judge. In 1869, Josephine St. Pierre Ruffin collaborated with Lucy Stone and Julia Ward Howe to form the American Women's Suffrage Association. She published the *Women's Era* newspaper from 1890 to 1897. In 1895, she collaborated with Maria Baldwin to convene the first national convention of the Women's Era Club, which eventually became the National Association of Colored Women. Among its objectives was to promote the enforcement of civil and political rights for all citizens.

A correspondent for the *Women's Era,* Josephine Silone Yates was elected president of the National Association of Colored Women in 1901. She also founded the Women's League of Kansas City, an organization that established schools and housing. A brilliant scholar of chemistry, history, and literature and the granddaughter of a former slave, Josephine Silone was the first American woman granted a full professorship and the first to chair a college science department (at Lincoln University).[11] Amid her academic work, she was a frequent contributor to *Women's Era* as well as the *Boston Herald, Los Angeles Herald,* and other publications under the pseudonym R. K. Porter. Josephine Silone began her studies at Philadelphia's Institute for Colored Youth (now Cheyney University) where she was mentored by its celebrated principal, Fanny Jackson Coppin.

Like her protégé, Coppin wrote for newspapers and served as vice president of the NACW. Jackson also made significant contributions to American education. Coppin, who had been born into slavery in Washington, D.C., was an exceptional student and later a teacher at Oberlin College from 1860 to 1865. During her forty-year career at Philadelphia's prestigious Institute for Colored Youth (she replaced Ebenezer Bassett as principal when he became "America's first black diplomat" in 1869), she had a citywide impact.

In Philadelphia, Coppin implemented educational policies that were adopted by other schools and established programs that offered educational and social support to the wider community. (Fluent in Greek and Latin as well as advanced mathematics, she served as a French interpreter for Philadelphia's courts.) In 1902, she traveled with her husband, Levi Jenkins Coppin, a bishop and missionary in the African Methodist Episcopal Church, to Cape Town, South Africa, where they founded a school called the Bethel Institute.[12] In 1926, a teacher training school in Baltimore, Maryland was named the Fanny Jackson Coppin Normal School in honor

The fierce advocacy of California newspaper publisher Charlotta Bass often put her in the crosshairs of the KKK, the FBI, and other powerful forces. Yet Bass never backed down, not when the Klan sued her in court for libel (Bass won) nor when vigilantes stalked her.

of her contributions to American pedagogy; today the school, Coppin State University, is part of the University of Maryland system.

Maria Baldwin was a widely renowned civic leader, journalist, and, like Fanny Jackson Coppin, among the earliest female principals and public school masters in the United States. Baldwin studied, taught, and lectured widely as well as collaborated with Josephine St. Pierre Ruffin in the founding of the Women's Era Club, the forerunner of the NACW. As a student at Harvard, William Trotter was a member of the Cambridge literary society headed by Maria Baldwin. A former president of Harvard (where Baldwin had been herself a student) declared Baldwin "the best teacher in New England."[13] Her acolytes, including W. E. B. Du Bois, were legion. The poet E. E. Cummings, a one-time student of Miss Baldwin, wrote an encomium to his former teacher in *Six Nonlectures.* In 1950 a Harvard dormitory was named Maria Baldwin Hall.

In addition to the NACW, members of other organizations as well as thousands of individual women worked to advance democracy in civic life. Among them, journalist Charlotta Spear Bass advanced citizenship rights on local and national levels. In 1912, she became the publisher and editor of the *California Eagle* (founded 1879), which she transformed into a national beacon. Born in South Carolina, she settled in Los Angeles in 1910, purchased the paper at the request of its late founder, and hired veteran journalist and editor Joseph Bass, whom she wed in 1914. She protested the 1915 release of D. W. Griffith's *The Birth of a Nation,* the popular film about Reconstruction that glorified the Ku Klux Klan and demonized blacks and Northerners. Bass also exposed the widespread practice of police brutality and the racially exclusionary hiring practices of the Los Angeles County Hospital, the Southern California Telephone Company, the Los Angeles Fire Department, Railway, and, later, the Boulder Dam Project. Her activism ultimately placed her on a national and international stage and pitted her against the KKK and the FBI. Placing her commitment to public justice and the security of others above her own safety, she has been described as an early progenitor of the Black Power Movement. Bass's incisive journalism and effective community organizing prompted the California Supreme Court, and ultimately the United States Supreme Court in 1948, to strike down restrictive housing covenants. In 1952, Bass became the first African American women to run for national office as the Progressive Party's candidate for vice president.[14]

ARTS AND CULTURE

Joel Dinerstein's study of the emergence of jazz in the United States in the early twentieth century recognized the many ways in which African Americans were protagonists and mediators who helped the globe adapt to modernization and industrialization.[15] In the hundred years from the founding of the African Grove Theater in the 1820s to the emergence of the Harlem Renaissance of the 1920s, African Americans used performance arts to shape American culture and identity. Blackface minstrelsy, one of the nation's early forms of popular entertainment, encapsulates the intertwined histories and identities of black and white Americans. Starting in the 1830s, white minstrels—and later, black ones—performed caricatures of African Americans.[16] James Bland, a black New Yorker (whose father was among the cohort of black graduates of Oberlin College from the 1840s) came into contact with Southern culture during his studies at Howard University. A gifted composer, James Bland used the minstrel circuit to present his work. He wrote more than seven hundred compositions, toured the United States and Europe, and performed for England's Queen Victoria. Bland initially gained fame for "Carry Me Back To Old Virginny," which was published in 1878 and became the official state song of Virginia in 1940[17]. That Virginia's state song, which romanticized the slave-culture of the Old South, was composed by a black New Yorker is a revealing example of how fundamentally interconnected Americans are, black and white, North and South, slave and free, urban and rural.

Like James Bland, Bob Cole and J. Rosamond Johnson were prolific composers. They created numerous songs for white musicals as well as several African American productions in the late nineteenth and early twentieth century. In 1907, Cole and Johnson produced *The Shoo-Fly Regiment*, a musical that centered on black soldiers who fought in the American Civil War and featured the actor Sam Lucas. Born in 1850, Lucas, a free black American from Ohio (and a former barber) gained national popularity and financial success first on the minstrel circuit and later as a serious actor. Lucas played the titular role on stage in 1878 and in a film in 1914. In his first dramatic production, *Out of Bondage*, Lucas co-starred with Emma and Anna Hyers. Professionally trained opera singers, the Hyers Sisters toured nationally as well as helped to produce and perform in several plays, including *Out of Bondage* in 1876, which some critics regard as a pioneering work of American musical theater that broke with the minstrel tradition.[18]

The comedic artist Bert Williams embodied the ways in which vaudeville replaced minstrelsy in the early twentieth century as America's popular entertainment. A native of the Bahamas, Williams moved from the minstrel stage to international recognition as a star of the Ziegfeld Follies. Considered by some a precursor to Charlie Chaplin, Williams was admired by peers such as W. C. Fields and was billed as "The Greatest Comedian on the American Stage."[19] In 1915, the same year *The Birth of a Nation* was released, Biograph Films—D. W. Griffith's studio—invited Williams to produce, direct, and star in his own films, resulting in *Natural Born Gambler* in 1915 and *The Fish* in 1916.

While Williams's work as a filmmaker was overshadowed by his tremendous success on the stage, the author-director-producer Oscar Micheaux became the most prolific black filmmaker of the twentieth century.[20] Micheaux, the son of former slaves, began his career by turning three of his own novels into feature films, starting with *The Homesteader* in 1918, a commercial success. His body of work of some forty feature-length films repeatedly addressed complicated social themes while underscoring the importance of citizenship rights.

Playwright Mary P. Burrill also crafted dramas to address fundamental issues of American citizenship and justice.[21] Burrill's *Aftermath*, published in 1919 and produced in 1928, examined the experience of a black World War I veteran who returned from serving his country to find that his father had been lynched in South Carolina. The work thus incorporated the epidemic of lynching that gripped the nation for more than half a century, as well as the pronounced discrimination that black military veterans had faced for three centuries. A graduate of the Dunbar School in Washington, D.C., and Emerson College, Burrill returned as a teacher to the Dunbar School; among her students was Willis Richardson, an award-winning dramatist who in 1923 became the first black playwright to have dramatic work produced on Broadway.

The Afro-Peruvian playwright and composer Nicomedes Santa Cruz Aparicio lived briefly in New York in the early 1900s. His son, Nicomedes Santa Cruz, born in 1925, became a nationally renowned performance artist, public intellectual, and "the foremost Afro-Peruvian poet of the twentieth century and one of the most important representatives of the African legacy and its contribution to Peruvian national culture."[22] Santa Cruz became the central figure of Peru's engagement with the Afrocentric cultural and literary movements that radiated through the Atlantic world from the 1920s to

Quentin Bandera was another distinguished general and war hero of Cuba's Independence Wars. His protestations and mobilizations resulted in his execution by police in 1906.

the 1960s and focused on the African roots of American cultures. He was among the most influential Afro-Latin intellectuals of the twentieth century.

LATIN AMERICAN MOBILIZATIONS FOR DEMOCRACY

While African Americans engaged U.S. politics as cultural producers and civic activists in the early twentieth century, Afro-Latin Americans shaped national politics as artists, activists, journalists, educators, and statesmen. U.S. citizens effectively mobilized against overt discrimination and ubiquitous violence against black Americans in the wake of the Civil War and throughout the first half of the twentieth century; this mobilization culminated in the civil rights movement. But in Latin America, the rhetoric of racial democracy and *mestizaje* (cultural mixing) often meant that while mixed-race individuals could be fully assimilated, de facto racial barriers and discrimination were difficult to mobilize against. Despite obstacles, democratic activists in Cuba, Brazil, and Uruguay formed the first black political parties in the Western Hemisphere and established a robust black press. Individual Afro-Latin politicians had tremendous influence on national politics in countries like Puerto Rico, Venezuela, and Panama.

In the early twentieth century Afro-Cubans formed civic, literary, and political organizations throughout their newly sovereign nation. Cuba's black veterans of the independence wars were politically active, as evidenced in the

Juan Gualberto Gomez was a Cuban journalist, politician, and national hero during the decades surrounding 1900. The son of slaves, Gomez began his press career in France, but returned to the Americas where he organized efforts for Cuban independence and wrote articles and books advocating liberty and equality in Latin America. After a period of exile and imprisonment by the Spanish government, Gomez again returned to Cuba in the 1890s where he formed a directorate of a hundred Afro-Cuban organizations, began publishing the influential newspaper Equality, *and organized campaigns that prompted antidiscrimination laws. (Gomez sent his son, along with three other Afro-Cuban students, to study at Tuskegee in 1901.) After serving as a general in the War of Independence, Gomez served the new nation as a congressman in the 1910s and as a senator in the 1920s.*

mobilization of the Action Committee of Veterans and Societies of Color in 1902 just days after Cuba's first president took office. The committee was organized by the military hero Captain General Campos Marquetti and comprised two hundred veterans as well as the leaders of Cuba's many societies of color. Marquetti requested that the national government end the segregation and discrimination introduced during U.S. occupation. The Committee petitioned the Cuban president and Congress demanding that "equality and justice become facts."[23]

Around the time that W. E. B. Du Bois and Marcus Garvey were establishing black political organizations in the United States, Afro-Cubans established the first black political party in the Americas. In 1908, Evanisto Estenoz (of the 1902 Action Committee), Pedro Ivonett, and Gregorio

Consuelo A. Serra Heredia was a journalist, educator, and feminist in the early Cuban republic. Educated at Hunter College in New York City, she returned to Havana and founded a residential school for girls, taught in Havana's normal schools, and earned graduate degrees in pedagogy and philosophy. She wrote for Cuban newspapers and journals in the 1920s and '30s including Adelante, *a progressive publication with a pan-American perspective. Her father, Rafael*

Serra, was a prominent Afro-Cuban journalist, editor, and independence leader who collaborated with José Martí to establish New York's La Liga, an educational society for Afro-Caribbean immigrants.

Surín founded Cuba's Independent Party of Color (*Partido Independiente de Color*). Organized by veterans of Cuba's War of Independence, the party sought to unify Afro-Cubans in full political participation and to safeguard the rights of Cuba's black citizenry.

Although the majority of Cuba's triumphant revolutionary army was of African descent and Cuban nationalist discourse claimed to transcend race, in practice Afro-Cubans were often excluded from substantial political and economic opportunities in the new republic. The *Partido Independiente de Color* (PIC) aimed to harness their political power. Centered in the largely Afro-descended eastern half of the island, the PIC protested when the government effectively outlawed them in 1912. The Cuban government responded with a widespread, indiscriminate massacre of Afro-Cubans. While documentation of the massacre has been sparse, estimates of the number of victims ranges from three thousand to four times that figure.[24]

Though the Cuban government put a violent end to the hemisphere's first black political party in 1912, Afro-Cubans continued to pioneer numerous pro-democracy civic and literary organizations. Starting in the late nineteenth century, Afro-Cuban intellectuals used and created media to advocate for full implementation of their citizenship rights. Afro-Cuban men and women formed more than a hundred societies and periodicals that significantly "contributed to debates on citizenship and national identity formation."[25]

Among these Afro-Cuban democracy advocates, Úrsula Coimbra de Valverde wrote for *Minerva*, a periodical published between 1888 and 1915 that examined republican and civic concerns from the vantage point of women of color. *Minerva* become an important political medium for Afro-Cuban intellectuals like Juan Gualberto Gómez and Nicolás Guillén and had an international readership that included exiles in the U.S. and Caribbean. When the African American entrepreneurs John Merrick and Dr. Aaron Moore visited Havana in 1912, *Minerva* covered them. In 1904 Coimbra began writing for the newspaper founded by the republican activist and journalist Rafael Serra, *El Nuevo Criollo*; in Cuba (and large swaths of Latin America) *criollo* (creole) was used to signify American-born, hence one might aptly translate the title as *The New American*. Coimbra was among a community of female Afro-Cuban journalists who wrote about rights and citizenship in the early twentieth century, including Ana Hidalgo Vidal and Maria G. Sánchez.[26]

In the late nineteenth and early twentieth centuries, black newspapers were a common forum that Afro-Americans developed in tandem with political and civic organizations to advance democratic ideologies and concerns for political equality. These organizations were most prevalent in the United States (where they originated in the late 1700s), Cuba, and Brazil. In the early 1900s most Cuban provinces had their own black newspaper and in many cases a variety of media outlets for black political thought, a multiplicity reflected in the black civic clubs that were briefly united in the 1936 National Federation of Black Societies.[27]

While Cuba's black press was extensive, Brazil had by far the largest number of black newspapers in Latin America. Starting in 1903 Afro-Brazilian newspapers advocated civic engagement to transcend the "incomplete emancipation" that troubled the nation.[28] Afro-Brazilians established in 1931 the hemisphere's second national black political party, *Frente Negra Brasileira* (FNB), to advance citizenship rights and democratic participation. Preceding the establishment of the formal political party, "Afro-Brazilian newspapers were information vehicles of unions, clubs, and associations with objectives similar to the FNB."[29] The Afro-Brazilian literary journal *O Clarim (The Clarion)* was among the many Afro-Brazilian periodicals of the era; its journalists collaborated with the editor of the *Chicago Defender* and reprinted articles from Marcus Garvey's *Negro World*.[30] Contributors to *O Clarim* were also associated with *Centro Cívico Palmares,* the activist organization founded in 1926. Its name invoked the powerful seventeenth-century Palmares maroon federation, while the civic center itself advanced journalism to champion a progressive, international vision of democracy. Arlindo and Isoltino Veiga Dos Santos were members of the *Palmares* organization in the 1920s; they would become key leaders in the *Frente Negra* political party in the 1930s.[31]

On a per capita basis, Uruguay had the most active black press in all of Latin America between 1870 and 1950.[32] Montevideo's port was a hub in the South American slave trade until slavery was abolished in 1842. By 1800 about a quarter of Uruguay's population was African or Afro-descended. Afro-Uruguayans served as soldiers in the independence wars of the early 1800s and in the many civil wars thereafter; they formed numerous organizations from mutual aid to literary societies throughout the nineteenth and early twentieth centuries. A nation of highly educated citizens, Uruguay's relatively smaller black population resisted inequality with a vigorous press and formed the third independent black political party in the Americas in 1936, the *Partido Autóctono Negro.*

Physician, journalist, and statesman José Celso Barbosa was fundamental in Puerto Rico's politics in the early twentieth century. Born in Bayamón, Barbosa earned his M.D. from the University of Michigan, where he was valedictorian in 1880. He returned to Puerto Rico to practice medicine and pioneered an early form of health insurance. A fierce advocate of democracy, Barbosa established the Puerto Rican Republican Party to advocate autonomous, federalist statehood for the island in 1899. He founded the island's first bilingual newspaper in 1907. Considered the "father of Puerto Rican statehood," Barbosa served in Puerto Rico's executive cabinet from 1900 to 1917 and in the Senate from 1917 until his death in 1921.[33] The birthday of this Afro-Puerto Rican founding father is a national holiday.

Luis Beltrán Prieto Figueroa was awarded a Ph.D. in political and social science from the Central University of Venezuela in 1934. He helped found several political organizations, including Venezuela's National Democratic Party (*Partido Democrático Nacional*) in 1936 and Democratic Action (*Acción Democrática*) in 1941. He served in the Senate 1936–41 and 1959–69, including as Senate president for five years. In addition to his accomplishments as a professor, author, minister of education, and his overseas work with UNESCO, Prieto Figueroa was a popular contender for Venezuela's presidency in 1968. His contributions to Venezuela were manifold, particularly in education. Known as El Maestro Prieto, he developed organizations, programs, and laws that strengthened the nation's commitment to education.[34]

In Panama, Carlos Antonio Mendoza became president in 1910. The prominent Afro-Panamanian lawyer and civil war veteran crafted the country's Declaration of Independence. While Mendoza's commitment to safeguarding his nation's democracy made him a popular statesman in the new republic, the United States, which began building the Panama Canal (with Afro-Caribbean workers) in 1904, and expanding its control in the region, demanded Mendoza's resignation on racial grounds.[35]

MILITARY HEROES

Throughout Latin America, military service was one avenue of social mobility for Afro-American men, to a greater extent than in the United States. As the Niagara Movement's *Declaration of Principles* observed in 1905, "We regret that this nation has never seen fit adequately to reward the black soldiers who, in its five wars, have defended their country with their blood, and yet have systematically been denied the promotions that their abilities deserve."[36] The *Principles* went on to declare as unjust the general exclusion of African Americans from military training schools.[*EN]

Just as the Afro-Cuban veterans of Cuba's independence wars suffered discrimination as they endeavored to contribute to the nation they had fought to liberate, so too did the American Buffalo Soldiers, many of whom had fought for Cuba's independence as well. These black U.S. regiments initially consisted largely of African American servicemen who had defended their nation during the American Civil War (as well as Black Seminoles who had sought their own freedom) and were stationed in the American West in the late 1800s. The hegemonic ideology that justified American expansion and imperialism, along with the subjugation of Native Americans and Mexicans it entailed, also meant that African Americans were not spared the indignities of racism despite their role in the historic process of "Manifest Destiny." In the face of bigotry and discrimination, Buffalo Soldiers risked their lives on behalf of the United States in the expansion of the American West and in the Spanish-American War, the Philippine-American War, and the Mexican Revolution as well as in WWI (see John Jefferson).

The Mexican Revolution (1910–1920) has been called the first social and political revolution of the twentieth century, and like every other American revolution, African Americans participated in this historic event.[37] Among them was Charles Young, who was born into slavery in 1864 in Kentucky (the 1863 Emancipation Proclamation excluded the Border States) but was liberated when his father moved the family to Ohio so that he could serve in the federal army during and after the American Civil War. Charles Young graduated from West Point in 1889, and in 1901, Captain Young led his troops with distinction in the Philippine-American War. He became a national park superintendent in 1903, and he and his Buffalo Soldiers repelled poachers and ranchers, while building the first road into the Giant Forest of the Sequoia National Park.[38] In between his stints as the U.S.'s first black military attaché (in Haiti and Liberia), he returned to the Philippines.

Young became renowned for his distinguished service and leadership in Mexico and was promoted to the rank of colonel. He led the 10th Cavalry, composed of Buffalo Soldiers, against Pancho Villa and his forces, saving the lives of many U.S. soldiers who had been outflanked. Young had regularly surmounted incidents of racial discrimination at West Point and afterwards, but racism finally capped his advancement during World War I. Colonel Young's continued wartime service would have made him eligible for the

This U.S. Signal Corps photo is captioned, "Twenty-four of the first contingent of Negro nurses assigned to the European Theater of Operations." In 1944, sixty-three African American nurses joined the 168th Station Hospital in England; others served in Australia, Liberia, Burma, New Guinea, and the Philippines. During World War II, the National Association of Colored Graduate Nurses, under the leadership of Mabel Keaton Staupers, pressured the U.S. to permit black nurses to serve. The NACGN had been established in 1908 by Mary Eliza Mahoney, Adah Thoms, Martha Minerva Franklin, and others who sought equal opportunity to serve during WWI and the 1918 flu epidemic.

rank of brigadier general, but his biographer documents how his path to promotion was blocked by a spurious health assessment by the Army.[39]

While Young was excluded from service in World War I, some 370,000 African Americans did serve, even if in segregated military units. The African American and Afro-Puerto Rican 369th Regiment that came to be known as the Harlem Hellfighters was on the front lines longer than any other American unit. In 2015, Harlem Hellfighter Private Henry Johnson, who survived twenty-one combat injuries, was posthumously awarded a Medal of Honor for helping his unit repel a German attack and preventing the capture of a wounded comrade on the night May 15, 1918.[40]

The commander of the Harlem Hellfighters, Benjamin O. Davis, Sr., became the first black general in the United States army in 1941. A graduate of the Dunbar School, General Davis began his career as a volunteer in the Spanish American War under the command of Charles Young who became his mentor. Davis's son, Benjamin O. Davis, Jr., was the fourth African American to graduate from West Point and went on to command the Tuskegee Airmen during World War II, eventually becoming the nation's first black Air Force general. In addition to his distinguished military career, Davis, Jr. served the United States as head of the Federal Sky Marshal program as well as an Assistant Secretary of Transportation.

Because of racial tensions in the United States Army, the black troops of the 369th, 370th, 371st, and 372nd regiments were assigned to the French army; upwards of 171 African American servicemen were awarded the French Legion of Honor for their WWI service. Among them was Eugene Bullard, the world's first black fighter pilot and a descendant of enslaved Haitians and Creeks from Georgia.[41] The veteran fighter pilot opened a jazz club in Paris after the war, which put him in contact with luminaries like Langston Hughes, Louis Armstrong, and Josephine Baker. During World War II, both Bullard and Josephine Baker aided the French Resistance.[42] Both were named Chevaliers of the Legion of Honor by the French government.

Raphael Elizé served French forces in both world wars. Born in Martinique in 1891, a descendant of slaves and dedicated republican Freemasons, Elizé completed a degree in veterinary medicine in France before joining the army during World War I. His wartime service as a soldier and a veterinarian earned him a Croix de Guerre from the French government. In 1929, Elizé was elected mayor of Sablé sur Sarthe. (Elizé was not France's first black mayor—that distinction belongs to the Afro-French revolutionary Louis Guizot who was elected by a landslide in 1790.)[43] Like Bullard and Baker, Elizé was active in the French Resistance during World War II. He was deported to the Buchenwald concentration camp where he was killed in 1945.

During the Second World War, more than one million black Americans risked their lives for democracy abroad. Corporal Waverly Woodson of

Louis Latimer

Philadelphia saved numerous lives as a medic under fire at Normandy on D-Day, despite being wounded himself; he was awarded a Bronze Star and a Purple Heart. Vaughn Love was also among the two thousand African Americans who landed on D-Day. For his service at Normandy, Love earned a Purple Heart; the following year he was awarded another Purple Heart as well as a Bronze Star for his service at the Battle of the Bulge. Previously, Love had served with the American volunteers in the Spanish Civil War along with roughly one hundred fellow African Americans, including Harlem Hospital nurse Salaria Kee. Love's father, Walter J. Love, had served the U.S. army as a surgeon during WWI.[44]

Innovators

All Allied troops who saw combat in World War I benefited from the use of gas masks which some have traced to the design of an African American inventor named Garrett Morgan. A black Freemason, Morgan was the son of former slaves (his paternal grandfather—his father's owner—was a Confederate colonel) in Kentucky and moved to Ohio at 14. In 1907, he opened his first of many businesses, and in 1908 he helped to found the Cleveland Association of Colored Men, which later merged with the NAACP. He filed for a patent for his "safety hood" for firefighters to breathe in smoke-filled areas in 1912 and established the National Safety Device Company in 1914. His breathing mask gained national attention when he personally led the rescue of workers trapped in a tunnel under Lake Erie. After witnessing an accident at an intersection, Morgan also patented a traffic signal in 1922. Two U.S. schools, a water treatment plant, and a

Maryland street bear his name.

Lewis Howard Latimer was another hero of American technological development. Latimer's parents, Rebecca and George, were born into slavery in Norfolk, Virginia, but emancipated themselves by escaping to Massachusetts (see "Latimer Law"). At fifteen, young Lewis Latimer served in the U.S. navy during the American Civil War; as an adult, he was an influential innovator in the field of electrical engineering. An excellent draftsman and inventor who was awarded his first patent in 1874, Latimer was tapped by Alexander Graham Bell to draft Bell's original telephone blueprints for a patent in 1876. As a supervisor at the United States Electric Company, Latimer patented an electric lamp and improved the emerging technology of light bulbs with his 1881 patent for a new long-lasting carbon filament.

In 1884, Latimer joined Thomas Edison's team in New York where he helped Edison in the laboratory, to advance lighting technology, and in the courtroom, to protect his patents. Edison brought numerous suits against rivals, most of which were decided in his favor. After losing two patent suits to the prolific African American inventor Granville Woods, hailed in contemporary newspapers as "the Black Edison," Edison invited Woods to join the Edison Company; Woods, however, declined.[45] In 1890, Latimer published *Incandescent Electric Lighting: A Practical Description of the Edison System*. In 1918 Latimer was among the twenty-eight charter members of the prestigious Edison Pioneers. Around this time, Latimer, who was active in civic organizations, volunteered to teach recent immigrants mechanical engineering and English at New York's Henry Street Settlement House. In 2006 Latimer was inducted posthumously into the U.S.'s National Inventors Hall of Fame.

Bessie Blount Griffin, born in Virginia in 1914, was a physical therapist and forensic scientist as well as an inventor. She developed a close friendship with Thomas Edison's son (after having treated his mother-in-law), and it was in his home that she invented a disposable emesis basin, the receptacle used in medical and surgical wards to collect medical waste; her design was adopted widely in Belgium. During World War II, while helping to rehabilitate wounded U.S. soldiers, she developed what the director emeritus of the American College of Surgeons called "a most ingenious apparatus"

George Franklin Grant

that allowed those who had lost the use of their arms to feed themselves.[46] Griffin's electronic feeding device permitted individuals to bite down on a tube that delivered discrete morsels of food. While the American Veterans Association refused to recognize Griffin's innovation (as they did with the basin), she granted the French government the rights to her design, and her device was implemented throughout military hospitals. Griffin was active in the NAACP, wrote for two newspapers, and was an activist for Americans with disabilities. In the 1970s, after serving in three Virginia police departments as a forensic scientist, Griffin "became the first American woman ever accepted into advanced studies at the Document Division of Scotland Yard."[47] Griffin's work was expressly "for the benefit of humankind."[48]

Griffin's contributions to public health were preceded by those of Dr. Sophie Bethena Jones who published on the subject in 1913, the year before Griffin was born. Jones took her medical degree from the University of Michigan in 1885 and soon became the first black faculty member of Spelman College. "Jones not only practiced medicine for many years but also founded nurses training at Spelman College and was resident physician at Wilberforce University."[49] Jones, who was born into a politically active family in Canada in 1857, was descended from enslaved African Americans from North Carolina. Her grandfather, Allen Jones, had purchased his own freedom and that of his family, including his father, Charles, who had made the Middle Passage. As a free man, Allen Jones collaborated with other black families in North Carolina to build a school that was destroyed by arson three times, prompting Jones to relocate and send his five sons, including Sophie's father, to Oberlin College. James Monroe Jones moved to Canada in 1849 where he became an award-winning gunsmith, a magistrate, and a colleague of John Brown, as well as the father of Sophie and Anna Jones.[50]

Dr. Jones's sister, Anna H. Jones, was a career educator who served as Wilberforce University's "lady-principal" from 1885 to 1892. Anna Jones was also a women's rights activist and author who presented at the Pan-African Conference in London in 1900 and chaired the Department of Education for the National Association of Colored Women.[51]

Evelyn Boyd Granville's Smith College yearbook photo

Ida Gray Nelson Rollins studied medicine at the University of Michigan around the same time as Sophie Jones. Gray earned her degree in dentistry in 1890, married Spanish-American War veteran Sanford Nelson, and practiced in Chicago until she retired around 1930. She remarried after her first husband's death and was active in Chicago's professional women's clubs. Another pioneering dentist—and the son of former slaves—Dr. George Franklin Grant became Harvard's first black faculty member after graduating from Harvard's School of Medicine in 1870. As the Harvard Odontological Society (which Grant helped to found) observed in a memorial upon his death in 1910, Grant was a "pioneer" in his field, with "exceptional technical abilities" who had a tremendously beneficial impact on the practice of dentistry, including the invention of "numerous devices for the correction and treatment of cleft palate."[52] However, his most enduring invention may be the golf tee, which he patented in 1899.[53]

Starting in the 1940s, several African American women contributed to the science that paved the way for NASA's "giant step for mankind" and shaped the United States' participation in the space race. As the result of labor shortages during World War II, the National Advisory Committee for Aeronautics (the federal agency that became the National Aeronautics and Space Administration—NASA—in 1958) began recruiting African American women from math and science programs to serve as "human computers" who performed mathematical calculations to support engineering.[54] Among them, as Margot Lee Shetterly's *Hidden Figures* has brought to light, was Miriam Daniel Mann, a chemistry major with a minor in mathematics, who worked at NASA for two decades. Her colleague Katherine Johnson was specifically selected by John Glenn to verify the trajectory calculations for his 1962 mission to orbit the Earth. In the early 1960s, "Mann, Johnson, and the rest of NASA's black female computers were playing an instrumental yet hidden role in the space race."[55] Evelyn Granville, also contributed to the space program in the early 1960s. Granville attended Washington's Dunbar School, graduated summa cum laude from Smith College in 1945 and earned a Ph.D. in mathematics from Yale in 1949 (after completing a master's degree in mathematics and theoretical physics). Dr. Granville began developing computer programs at IBM in the 1950s and worked on NASA's projects Vanguard, Mercury, and Apollo before returning to IBM as a senior mathematician. She became a professor of mathematics at California State University and the University of Texas as well as a master mathematics educator who trained teachers and authored a textbook.[56]

Dr. Louis Tompkins Wright, a surgeon and physician as well as the chairman of the board of the NAACP, made enormous contributors to medicine and science. Born in Georgia in 1891, Wright's late father, Dr. Ceah Wright, had been a physician, valedictorian, and a former slave, and his stepfather, Dr. William Penn, graduated from Yale medical school in 1898. In 1915, the year he graduated cum laude from Harvard medical school, the young Louis Wright took time off to protest D. W. Griffith's *The Birth of a Nation*. In 1917, he entered the U.S. Army Medical Corps where he pioneered the intradermal smallpox vaccination that is still in use, rose to the rank of lieutenant colonel, and was awarded the Purple Heart. At Harlem Hospital he became a surgical specialist (advancing head and neck surgical techniques) and a pioneer in cancer and antibiotic research.

In addition to authoring eighty-nine scientific publications, Wright championed democracy at home and abroad. He led a group of physicians in founding the Manhattan Medical Society to challenge the creation of segregated hospitals in New York, which for Wright would have represented "a duality of citizenship in a democratic government that is wrong."[57]

He was also a sponsor of the Negro People's Committee in 1937, which fought against rising fascism in Spain. Eleanor Roosevelt was among the prominent Americans who honored and eulogized Dr. Wright upon his passing. Both of his daughters became physicians; Dr. Jane Wright Jones, became an associate dean of a medical college and in 1964 was appointed to a presidential commission on cancer after having directed the research foundation established by her father.

Lloyd Hall was also a man of science and research who served in World War I. A chemist who advanced the science of food preservation, Hall served during wartime with the U.S. Ordnance Corps as Chief Inspector of Power and Explosives. Hall was born in Illinois, where his grandmother had settled after freeing herself via the Underground Railroad. He earned his bachelor of science degree at Northwestern University and his master's degree at the University of Chicago. He was the chief chemist in several different companies and amassed some one hundred patents. In addition to his research, Hall volunteered much of his time for civic and scientific organizations such as the United Nation's Food and Agriculture Organization and the U.S. Food for Peace program. He was inducted into the National Inventors Hall of Fame in 2004.[58]

Like Louis Wright and Lloyd Hall, Frederick McKinley Jones was a veteran of World War I. In 1935, this Minnesotan revolutionized the transportation of food and medicine when he invented portable cooling units. While Jones's technological innovations—he was granted sixty U.S. patents—ranged from inventing a device to synchronize sound with motion pictures to portable x-ray machines, the impact of his portable refrigeration introduced the long-haul transportation of perishable goods to the world. Jones's refrigeration units were widely used to preserve blood, food, and medicine during WWII and initiated the frozen food industry. In the twentieth century Jones was posthumously awarded the National Medal of Technology by U.S. president George H. W. Bush.

Dr. Charles Drew's ingenuity helped provide blood to World War II soldiers. Drew was a distinguished physician, surgeon, and researcher who discovered that blood plasma could replace whole blood in transfusions, revolutionizing the storage and shipment of blood and creating the blood bank. In 1940 he helped save innumerable lives when he was called upon to spearhead the "Blood for Britain" campaign just as the Allies were facing their highest numbers of casualties. His success led to his being named the director of the blood bank for the American Red Cross.[59] A professor and chief surgeon, Drew became the first African American examiner for the American board of surgery.

Percy Lavon Julian, a brilliant chemist, also contributed to the survival of Allied forces. His fire-retardant compound derived from soybeans was used widely on ships throughout the war to combat grease and oil fires and saved the lives many sailors. Julian, the grandson of former slaves from Montgomery, Alabama, earned his master's degree from Harvard and his doctorate from the University of Vienna and became "one of the most important scientists of the twentieth century."[60] He developed a glaucoma medication in 1935 that would later be recognized as among the top contributions in the history of American chemistry.[61] He also pioneered the large-scale derivation of steroids and hormones from soybeans and yams, which led to the production of cortisone to treat arthritis and progesterone, which would be crucial for oral contraceptives as well as to prevent miscarriages. He left his executive research position at the Glidden Company in Chicago to start his own laboratory in 1954. The $2 million plus sale of Julian Laboratories in 1961 made this innovative American chemist one of the earliest African American millionaires. Julian also ran a nonprofit organization, the Julian Research Institute, and he supported the efforts of the NAACP, particularly its Legal Defense and Education Fund. He was awarded the NAACP's highest award in 1947 and was inducted into the National Academy of Science in 1973.[62]

Annie Malone—whose parents had escaped slavery and whose father was a Civil War veteran—had by 1914 created an international cosmetics company valued at well over a million dollars. A talented inventor, savvy businesswoman, and generous philanthropist, in 1920 she financed the construction of an orphanage in St. Louis, Missouri, that is known today as the Annie Malone Children and Family Services Center. One of her sales agents, Sarah Breedlove, developed her own company and became well known as the cosmetics magnate "Madame C. J. Walker." Walker used her

Mary Church Terrell

significant commercial success to support many charitable causes, orphanages, and the NAACP.[63]

After studying chemistry at Columbia and business at Northwestern, in 1913 Virginia-born Sarah Spencer Washington established in Atlantic City, New Jersey, what would become Apex, an extremely lucrative international empire of beauty products and schools. With a chain of Apex beauty colleges extending as far away as Johannesburg, South Africa, and a variety of establishments in Atlantic City, including an upscale hotel, golf course, and a farm to provision them, Madame Washington was recognized at the 1939 World's Fair in New York as "Most Distinguished Businesswomen." A member of the Atlantic City Board of Trade, Washington was also a prolific philanthropist. She regularly challenged segregation by establishing integrated alternatives like the Apex restaurant and pharmacy and an annual, public Easter parade. In 1945, when a whites-only Atlantic City restaurant refused her service, she rented the entire restaurant and dined there; the restaurant shortly thereafter renounced its "race ban."

CIVIL RIGHTS ADVOCACY

Businessman and philanthropist Robert Reed Church was the first black millionaire in the American South. Church, the son of an enslaved woman and their master, married Louisa Ayres, a former slave and successful businesswoman herself. In 1866 they survived a three-day siege during which white mobs attacked hundreds of African Americans in race riots in Memphis, Tennessee. Ignited by a confrontation between a white police officer and black Union soldiers, white assailants attacked Church's establishments. Despite being gravely wounded, Robert Church (himself a Union veteran) survived and rebuilt, ultimately establishing a bank and an auditorium that hosted a visit by President Theodore Roosevelt.[64]

The same year as the riots in Memphis, another anti-black massacre took place in New Orleans.[65] These 1866 race riots, amid other atrocities targeting black Civil War veterans, garnered national attention and motivated the U.S. Congress to extend voting rights to black men.[66] Race riots and mob violence targeting politically active and economically successful black Americans—and black veterans in particular—continued through the first half of the twentieth century. As noted earlier, twenty-five violent anti-black uprisings occurred in 1919 alone.[67] The Tulsa Race Riot of 1921, for example, besieged the successful black district of Greenwood, destroying two hospitals and more than a thousand residences, and looting another four hundred, totaling the equivalent of $17 million in damages and displacing thousands of residents. White mobs injured 800 black Americans and killed between an estimated 175 to 300 individuals.[68] While these events were called "race riots," they were not battles between racial groups but assaults by bands of white Americans on black communities.

Throughout the first half of the nineteenth century, Robert Church's daughter, Mary Church Terrell, was an educator, writer, and champion of democracy. After a friend was murdered by a lynch mob in

Sadie Tanner Mossell

Sadie Tanner Mossell Alexander had distinguished forebears: top, her Tanner family; bottom, her Mossell family. Her grandfather, Bishop Benjamin Tucker Tanner, was a minister, author, newspaper editor, and educational activist. His son, Henry Ossawa Tanner, gained international acclaim as a painter. His daughter, Dr. Halle Tanner Dillon Johnson, was an accomplished physician (and the first woman to pass the Alabama state medical examination)—who founded a school of nursing. Sadie's uncle, Dr. Nathan Mossell, was a surgeon who founded a hospital while another uncle, Lewis Baxter Moore, served as the dean of Howard University.

1892, Terrell became an outspoken civil rights activist and a collaborator with Frederick Douglass, with whom she visited President Benjamin Harrison at the White House to discuss the lynching epidemic. In 1892 alone, at least 230 Americans were murdered by mobs; the vast majority of the victims were black.[69] Between 1877 (the end of Reconstruction) and 1950, some 4,400 black Americans were murdered in lynchings.[70]

Before she helped to establish the NAACP in 1909, Terrell collaborated with Susan B. Anthony in the National American Woman Suffrage Association, co-founded the Federation of Afro-American Women, and served as the first president of the National Association of Colored Women. In 1895 Terrell was appointed to the Board of Education in Washington, D.C. Her husband, Robert Terrell, was a Virginia native and Harvard Law graduate who became the principal of D.C.'s Dunbar School (then known as the M Street School), and was appointed a municipal judge by Theodore Roosevelt in 1901.

In 1904, Mary Church Terrell received an ovation when she spoke—in German, French, and English—at the Berlin International Congress of Women. She published numerous articles and lectured widely, navigating the considerable obstacles of the segregated South, to advance equality and justice. In 1950, at age eighty-six, a decade before university students sat-in in Greensboro, North Carolina, she and three friends were denied service in a Washington restaurant; their subsequent lawsuit ended legal segregation in restaurants in the District of Columbia.

While Mary Church Terrell championed universal civil rights in her oratory and activism, John Merrick turned to corporate philanthropy. Merrick was born into slavery in North Carolina and worked his way up from a bootblack at a barbershop, to barbering, to owning barbershops, to founding the North Carolina Mutual Life Insurance Company in 1899. It became the largest black-owned corporation in the world.[71] Merrick, along with his business partner and philanthropic collaborator, the physician Dr. Aaron Moore, helped to found Durham's Lincoln Hospital as well as a library, church, and college, among other institutions.

One of Merrick's assistant actuaries in North Carolina Mutual Insurance was Sadie Tanner Mossell, who in 1921 had been awarded a Ph.D.

in economics. After her work with Merrick, Mossell returned to her alma mater, the University of Pennsylvania, for law school.[72] When Mossell joined Raymond Pace Alexander's firm and married him, they became one of the first husband and wife legal teams in the United States. Together they helped draft the 1935 Pennsylvania law that prohibited discrimination in public accommodations. Raymond Alexander, a graduate of Pennsylvania's Wharton School and Harvard Law School, was a successful civil rights attorney who went on to become Philadelphia's first black judge while Sadie Alexander started her own practice.

When President Truman selected Sadie Alexander as a member of his Committee on Civil Rights in 1946, she became the first African American woman appointed to a presidential commission. In 1948 the committee issued *To Secure These Rights*; "the report provided recommendations for increasing civil rights protections for all Americans, regardless of race, religion, or national origin [which] became the basis for future civil rights policies and legislation, including the desegregation of the armed forces."[73] Alexander championed citizenship rights and expanded democracy in a variety of ways throughout her long career, including legal work (often pro bono), scholarship, service, and leadership in various professional and civic organizations as well as her appointments in local and federal government.

James Weldon Johnson was a lawyer and activist as well as a journalist, poet, critic, novelist, diplomat, and professor. He joined the NAACP in 1917 and served as a chief officer throughout the 1920s. Though Johnson was born in Jacksonville, Florida, his maternal grandparents had lived in Cuba after the Haitian Revolution and before settling in the Bahamas, where his grandfather served in the House of Assembly for three decades. At the close of the nineteenth century, after graduating from Atlanta University in 1894, James Weldon Johnson concurrently served as a school principal, founded a newspaper, passed the Florida bar examination, and developed a law practice in Jacksonville. In 1900, before setting off for a career as a writer (originally for Tin Pan Alley) in New York with his brother, who had recently graduated from the New England Conservatory of Music, the brothers composed the music and lyrics to "Lift Every Voice and Sing" for a celebration at Johnson's school, scarcely aware it would become a national hymn.

James Weldon Johnson was appointed U.S. consul in Venezuela from 1906 to 1908 and in Nicaragua from 1909 to 1913. In 1912, when revolution broke out in Nicaragua, "Johnson's role in aiding U.S. marines in defeating the rebels drew high praise from Washington."[74] In 1920, Johnson traveled to Haiti to investigate its occupation by U.S. marines ; he encountered egregious civil rights violations, which he exposed in a four-part series in *The Nation*. The articles were unsparingly critical of the oppressive U.S. military intervention that began in 1915 and continued until 1934, and they galvanized Americans to petition the U.S. State Department as well as organizers in Haiti to provide documentary evidence of atrocities. "Though they did not bring about an immediate alteration to United States policy, [Johnson's articles] laid a foundation for it."[75]

A prolific writer and critic, Johnson was a literary leader in the Harlem Renaissance, producing original work, curating anthologies, and mentoring artists. Johnson's original compositions and edited compendiums were landmarks of American poetry. He also continued to produce even more overtly political work as a journalist and organizer of massive NAACP anti-lynching campaigns shaped both by his conviction and his legal training. Johnson unified his commitment to education, the arts, and American progress in his teaching that spanned from New York University—he was NYU's first black professor—to the segregated South when he taught at Fisk University in Tennessee in his later years.

The prominent activist and poet Langston Hughes's work between roughly 1920 and 1960 profoundly shaped liberation movements not only in the United States but around the world. A key figure of the Harlem Renaissance, Hughes had a noteworthy lineage. His paternal grandfather, whose parents were the children of enslaved black women and the white men who owned them, was said to be a relation to Henry Clay. His mother's line descended from an enslaved woman and her owner who traced his lineage to the seventeenth-century English poet Francis Quarles. Hughes's maternal grandmother was among the first black women to attend Oberlin College; her first husband gave his life in support of John Brown's raid of Harper's Ferry. Her second husband and Hughes's grandfather, Charles Henry Langston, helped lead Ohio's Antislavery Society, along with his brother, the influential lawyer and statesman John Mercer Langston (see previous chapter). Langston Hughes was named in honor of his great-uncle.

Hughes translated the work of the Haitian intellectual and politician Jacques Roumain into English. In 1930, he traveled to Cuba for the second time where he met Nicolás Guillén, the Afro-Cuban poet and activist with whom he would develop a long personal and professional relationship. Guillén, deeply impacted by Hughes (whose work had been translated into Spanish), would ultimately become known as Cuba's "national poet." Hughes translated Guillén's work into English. Hughes' father had at various points lived in Cuba and Mexico, and Langston's command of Spanish had been strengthened during the time he lived with his father.[76]

Hughes's work had a tremendous impact on the Afro-French intellectual movement founded by Léon Damas, Aimé Césaire, and Léopold Senghor. Damas, a poet, politician, and professor, was born in French Guyana and attended school in Martinique where he met Aimé Césare, a native of Martinique who would also become an influential poet, politician, and professor. As university students in Paris in the 1930s, Damas and Césare joined with Senghor (the Senegalese poet and intellectual who would serve as Senegal's first president for two decades starting in 1960) to found a literary journal as well as an intellectual movement for liberation. Damas went on to serve in the French Army during World War II, was elected to the French National Assembly, served as a senior advisor to UNESCO, lectured throughout the Atlantic world, and taught at Georgetown and Howard universities.

Hughes directly inspired another prominent advocate of democracy, the Afro-Brazilian writer, scholar, and politician, Abdias do Nascimento. After joining Brazil's army in his teens, Nascimento became politically active in the Frente Negra Brasileira in the 1930s. In 1944 Nascimento founded Brazil's *Teatro Nacional do Negro* to advocate democracy through education, literacy, theater, and poetry. The pro-democracy currents in the theater organization were further developed and disseminated through a newspaper called *Quilombo* (a Brazilian term for a maroon settlement), founded and edited by Nascimento starting in 1948.

Nascimento endeavored to "use to the principles and channels of democracy [and] civic participation" to establish equal rights and universal citizenship for all Brazilians.[77] Nascimento and the organizations he coalesced sponsored national conventions in 1938, 1945, and 1950. A "Manifesto to the Brazilian Nation" issued during the 1945 Black National Convention demanded that Brazil's Constitution enforce equal rights as a matter of law and that discrimination in both the public and private sectors should be regarded as a crime against the nation. In 1946 the manifesto was explicated by Nascimento in the mainstream press and "taken up by representatives of Brazil's populist and labor parties," signaling the broad reach of the democratic efforts initiated by Afro-Brazilians.[78] In the 1970s, after being forced into exile, Nascimento taught in universities from New York and New Haven to Nigeria while helping to found the Democratic Labor Party of Brazil from abroad. He ultimately returned to Brazil to serve as a congressman and senator.

The powerful U. S. civil rights organizer Ella Baker grew up in North Carolina in the early 1900s while listening to her grandmother, Josephine Elizabeth Ross, tell stories of life under slavery. "Bet" Ross was the child of her master; her mother, a light-skinned enslaved woman, was said to have been poisoned by his jealous wife on Christmas Day.[79] Baker, after graduating valedictorian of her class at Shaw University in 1927, went on to a long and very effective career as a democratic activist and organizer, starting as a journalist and later playing seminal roles in organizations like the NAACP, the Southern Christian Leadership Conference, and the Student Nonviolent Coordinating Committee.[80]

As a young organizer in the political and intellectual epicenter of Harlem in 1930s, Ella Baker became friends with civil rights activist, feminist poet, and future lawyer Anna Pauline Murray. Like Baker, Pauli Murray had grown up in North Carolina, and, like Baker, her grandparents had been enslaved. In 1938 Murray attempted to desegregate the University of North Carolina. Despite her initial backing from the NAACP, Murray's attempt failed, as did her attempt to enter Harvard Law School's master's program with a recommendation from President Franklin Roosevelt in 1944. Traditionally Harvard accepted Howard Law School's valedictorian, but Murray was rejected explicitly because of her gender. She earned her research doctorate in law at Yale, where her name was placed on a residential college in 2017.[81]

After having been jailed in 1940 for protesting segregation on a Virginia bus and several subsequent efforts to desegregate public spaces, Murray's 1951 publication of *States' Laws on Race and Color* was described by Thurgood Marshall as "the bible" for civil rights lawyers and as crucial to the preparation of the historic *Brown v. Board of Education* case.[82] Moreover, Marshall's colleague in litigating *Brown* was Murray's former law professor, Spottswood William Robinson III. To build their case, Robinson sought out and shared Murray's final law school paper where she had pioneered an argument that attacked the "separate" rather than the "equal" part of the doctrine. In 1964 Murray co-authored another watershed legal paper, "Jane Crow and the Law: Sex Discrimination and Title VII." A relatively little-known catalyst of American democracy, Pauli Murray should be recognized as a founder on multiple grounds:

> [S]he articulated the intellectual foundations for two of the most important social justice movements of the twentieth century, first when she made her argument for overturning *Plessy*, and later, when she co-wrote a law-review article subsequently used by a rising star at the A.C.L.U.— Ruth Bader Ginsburg—to convince the Supreme Court that the equal protection clause applies to women.[83]

A long-time friend of Eleanor Roosevelt and an appointee by President John F. Kennedy, Murray collaborated with Betty Freidan to establish the National Organization for Women in 1966 before becoming ordained as an Episcopal priest in 1977. A tireless activist and visionary for human rights across race, class, and gender, Murray, along with her Congress of Racial Equality (CORE) colleague, Bayard Rustin, with whom she collaborated on the 1941 March on Washington, may be among the most underexposed champions of democracy of the twentieth century.

Bayard Rustin was arguably the most important architect of the American civil rights movement. His democratic work, starting in the 1930s, was deeply influenced by the philosophy of Gandhi, which he studied in India in the late 1940s, before traveling to West Africa. Rustin helped A. Phillip Randolph to organize the proposed March on Washington of 1941, which was cancelled when President Franklin D. Roosevelt met activists' demands for equal opportunity in the defense industry.[84]

Rustin shaped much of the organization of the civil rights movement as well as its strategies. Rustin contributed significantly to Martin Luther King Jr.'s precepts of nonviolent activism and maneuvered to help propel King to the center of the movement. Rustin participated in the 1947 Journey of Reconciliation, a two-week pilgrimage in the segregated U.S. South that directly inspired the Freedom Rides of 1961. A founder of CORE, he also helped to organize the Southern Christian Leadership Conference (SCLC). Rustin was an adviser to King during the Montgomery Bus Boycott and was the principal organizer of the 1963 March on Washington for Jobs and Freedom. For his extraordinary international career of six decades to advance freedom and justice, Rustin should be universally recognized as a hero of modern democracy.[85]

THE FOREGOING ARE MERELY a few of the countless Afro-Americans who advanced freedom in the first half of the twentieth century. Their names and stories suggest the deeper and broader roots of the commitment to democracy associated with the modern civil rights movement. The origins of that commitment to freedom and sacrifice for justice stretch back centuries and transcend the borders of the United States. The emphasis here on activists whose lives and works predate 1950 is not meant to diminish the significance of the freedom fighters, black and white, who risked and gave their lives in the service of American democracy, justice, and equality in the second half of the century.[86] Rather, they are meant to show that Afro-American perseverance, ingenuity, and valor in the face of oppression, injustice, and exploitation is a much longer, richer, and broader history than is often imagined. Theirs is a history to which all Americans are connected and indebted. Americans of African descent have been the protagonists of democracy and nation-building throughout the hemisphere since their arrival with—and as—the first New World explorers and settlers in the sixteenth century.

NOTES FOR CHAPTER SEVEN

1. Paulina L. Alberto, *Terms of Inclusion: Black Intellectuals in Twentieth-Century Brazil* (Chapel Hill: University of North Carolina Press, 2011), 175.

2. George Reid Andrews, *Afro-Latin America 1800–2000* (New York: Oxford University Press, 2004), 117.

3. Marika Sherwood, *Origins of Pan-Africanism: Henry Sylvester Williams, Africa, and the African Diaspora* (New York: Routledge, 2011).

4. The University of Massachusetts has archived a series of letters between Dr. Du Bois and Dr. Alcindor as they collaborated in organizing the Pan-African Congress of 1923. In a letter dated October 13, 1923, Du Bois wrote to Alcindor that Sydney Olivier was hoping to attend and speak at the conference. Olivier was a British civil servant, Governor of Jamaica, Secretary of State of India, and a member of the Fabian Society that founded and shaped the British Labor Party as well as the London School of Economics in the service of advancing democracy and equality. Olivier's nephew was the renowned twentieth-century actor Laurence Olivier.

5. The 1908 Springfield riot was preceded by deadly anti-black riots in Wilmington, North Carolina (1898), New York City (1900), Evanston, Indiana (1903), Springfield, Ohio (1904, 1906), Greensburg, Indiana (1906), and Atlanta, Georgia (1906). Roberta Senechal de la Roche, *In Lincoln's Shadow: The 1908 Race Riot in Springfield, Illinois* (Carbondale: Southern Illinois University Press, 1990), 2; Cary D. Wintz, ed., *African American Political Thought, 1890–1930* (New York: Routledge, 2015), 104.

6. Paul Finkelman, ed. *Encyclopedia of American Civil Liberties* (New York: Routledge, 2006), 1063.

7. Alonzo Herndon's son and successor, Norris Bumstead Herndon (who at age seven attended the founding Niagara Movement meeting with his father), established the Herndon Foundation to support educational development and civil rights. Carole Merritt, *The Herndons: An Atlanta Family* (Athens: University of Georgia Press, 2002), 9.

8. Adam Ewing, *In the Age of Garvey: How a Jamaican Activist Created a Mass Movement and Changed Global Black Politics* (Princeton: Princeton University Press, 2014); Ula Yvette Taylor, *The Veiled Garvey: The Life & Times of Amy Jacques Garvey* (Chapel Hill: UNC Press, 2002), 154, 179, 184; Mark Matera, *Black London: The Imperial Metropolis and Decolonization in the Twentieth Century* (Oakland: University of California Press, 2015), 108, 126–138.

9. Joel Blau with Mimi Abramovitz, *The Dynamic of Social Welfare Policy* (New York: Oxford University Press, 2010), 223.

10. Another key founder was Margaret Murray Washington, an orator, activist, educator, and principal of Tuskegee University who became Booker T. Washington's third wife and was inducted into the Alabama Women's Hall of Fame in 1972.

11. Jeannette E. Brown, *African American Women Chemists* (New York: Oxford University Press, 2012), 15.

12. Linda M. Perkins, "Heed Life's Demands: The Educational Philosophy of Fanny Jackson Coppin," *Journal of Negro Education* 31, no. 3 (Summer 1982): 181–190; Fanny Jackson Coppin, *Reminiscences of School Life and Hints on Teaching* (Nabu Press, 2012 [Philadelphia, A.M.E. Book Concern, 1913]).

13. Kwame Anthony Appiah and Henry Louis Gates, Jr., eds., *Africana: The Encyclopedia of African & African-American Experience* 2nd Edition (New York: Oxford University Press, 2005), 346.

14. Roger Streitmatter, *Raising Her Voice: African-American Women Journalists Who Changed History* (Lexington: University Press of Kentucky, 1994).

15. Joel Dinerstein, *Swinging the Machine: Modernity, Technology, and African-American Culture Between the World Wars* (Amherst: University of Massachusetts Press, 2003). Ann Douglas examines how black and white Americans shaped modernism in *Terrible Honesty: Mongrel Manhattan in the 1920s* (New York: Farrar, Straus, and Giroux, 1995).

16. The disturbing and distinctly American phenomenon of minstrelsy has been ably analyzed by many scholars and artists—Eric Lott's *Love and Theft: Blackface Minstrelsy and the American Working Class* (New York: Oxford University Press, 1993) is among the best of them.

17. It was demoted in 1997 to "state song emeritus."

18. Kortiha Michell, *Living with Lynching: African American Lynching Plays, Performance, and Citizenship, 1890–1930* (Champaign: University of Illinois Press, 2011).

19. Camille F. Forbes, *Introducing Bert Williams: Burnt Cork, Broadway, and the Story of America's First Black Star* (New York: Basic Books, 2008), xi.

20. Pearl Bowser, Jane Gains, and Charles Musser, eds., *Oscar Micheaux and His Circle: African-American Filmmaking and Race Cinema of the Silent Era* (Bloomington: Indiana University Press, 2001), 70.

21. Prior to Lorraine Hansberry's nationally celebrated production of *A Raisin in the Sun* on Broadway in 1959, African American female playwrights had published some sixty plays. Kathy A. Perkins, *Black Female Playwrights: An Anthology of Plays Before 1950* (Bloomington: Indiana University Press, 1989), 2.

22. Martha Ojeda, "Nicomedes Santa Cruz and Black Cultural Traditions in Peru: Renovating and Decolonizing the National Imaginary," in Antonio D. Tillis, ed., *Critical Perspectives on Afro-Latin American Literature* (New York: Routledge, 2012), 120; Heidi Carolyn Feldman, *Black Rhythms of Peru: Reviving Musical Heritage in the Black Pacific* (Middletown, CT: Wesleyan University Press, 2006), 83–88.

23. Melina Pappademos, *Black Political Activism and the Cuban Republic* (Chapel Hill: University of North Carolina Press, 2011), 125.

24. Aline Helg's 1995 publication, *Our Rightful Share: The Afro-Cuban Struggle for Equality, 1886–1912* (Chapel Hill: UNC Press) brought this event to light for many U.S. readers and is likely the most thoroughly researched account thus far. The great Afro-Puerto Rican historian, activist, and writer Arturo Schomburg, memorialized by the New York Public Library's research center that bears his name, wrote about the PIC in the NAACP publication *The Crisis* in 1912.

25. Takkara Brunson, "Constructing Afro-Cuban Womanhood: Race, Gender, and Citizenship in Republican-Era Cuba, 1902–1958" (PhD diss. University of Texas, Austin, 2011), 67.

26. Brunson, "Constructing Afro-Cuban Womanhood," 79; Carmen Montejo Arrechea, "Minerva: A Magazine for Men and Women of Color," in *Between Race and Empire*, eds., Brock and Fuertes (Philadelphia: Temple University Press, 1998).

27. Pappademos, *Black Political Activism*, 221.

28. Alberto, *Terms of Inclusion*, 170.

29. Ollie Johnson III and Rosana Harringer, eds., *Race, Politics, and Education in Brazil* (New York: Palgrave Macmillan, 2015), 66.

30. Michael Gomez, *Reversing Sail: A History of the African Diaspora* (New York: Cambridge University Press, 2004), 182.

31. Alberto, *Terms of Inclusion*, 146; Kim Butler, *Freedoms Given, Freedoms Won: Afro-Brazilians in Post-Abolition Sao Paulo and Salvador* (New Brunswick, NJ: Rutgers University Press, 1998), 103.

32. George Reed Andrews, *Blackness in the White Nation: A History of Afro-Uruguay*, (Chapel Hill: UNC Press, 2010), 5.

33. Serafín Méndez-Méndes and Ronald Fernández, *Puerto Rico Past and Present: An Encyclopedia, Second Edition* (Santa Barbara, CA: Greenwood, 2015), 41–43.

34. Eliva Duque Castillo, *Aportes del Pueblo Afrodescendiente: La Historia Oculta de América Latina* (Bloomington, IN: iUniverse, 2013), 357–359; Michael Coppege, *Strong Parties and Lame Ducks: Presidential Patriarchy and Factionalism in Venezuela* (Stanford, CA: Stanford University Press, 1994), 55, 100.

35. Andrews, *Afro-Latin America*, 99.

36. Louis Post, ed., *The Public: A Journal of Democracy* 8, no. 382 (July 29, 1905): 266.

37. The first black graduates of the U.S. military academy West Point (the oldest continually operating army post dating from the American Revolution) were exceptions who overcame extraordinary obstacles to serve their country. West Point's first black graduate, Henry Flipper, was a former slave. Flipper was educated in schools founded by the American Missionary Association and at Atlanta University in the 1860s, after which he secured the support of his congressman to apply to the federal military academy. He was enrolled at West Point among four other black cadets; however, he was the only one able to navigate the extremely hostile environment long enough to graduate in 1877. A talented engineer, Flipper's service in the American West involved not only leading U.S. troops against Apache warriors, but also building a drainage system for Fort Sill in Oklahoma ("Flipper's Ditch" is a National Historic Landmark). The prejudice of a white superior led to a dishonorable discharge, an injustice that Flipper endeavored to overturn throughout the rest of his long career as an engineering consultant and bilingual expert in land and law. Among his professional undertakings, Flipper advised a U.S. senator and a secretary of the Interior as well as private American firms regarding projects in Mexico and Venezuela. A bill to reinstate him and restore his rank in the United States army was first introduced to Congress in 1898 so that he could serve in the Spanish-American War, but Flipper's honorable discharge and full pardon did not come until the end of the twentieth century. In 1888, John Alexander became the second African American graduate of West Point. Alexander's father was a successful barber and property owner in Arkansas who purchased his own freedom and sent three of his children to Oberlin College. At West Point, Alexander was known as a "splendid scholar" and skilled boxer, and upon graduation took command of a Buffalo Soldier regiment in Nebraska and later Wyoming. Months after his appointment as a professor of military science at Wilberforce University

in 1894, Alexander suffered a fatal aortic rupture. In 1918, the U.S. Department of War named a military installation in Newport News, Virginia, Camp Alexander in his honor.

38. Gerald Horne, *Black and Brown: African Americans and the Mexican Revolution, 1910–1920* (New York: New York University Press, 2005).

39. U.S. national parks originally were not segregated although several would be between 1920 and 1950. Susan Shumaker, "Untold Stories from America's National Parks: Segregation in the National Parks." (Boston: Public Broadcasting Service, n.d.)

40. Young's medical report of June 1917 described high blood pressure and nephritis, but in July his examining board of three senior officers and two physicians concluded that in light of Young's "history of both health and performance of arduous duty . . . and in view of the present war conditions . . . he be promoted to the next higher grade." Around the same time, President Woodrow Wilson wrote to the U.S. Secretary of War, Newton Baker, regarding a complaint from a Mississippi senator that a lieutenant assigned to the Tenth Cavalry "is a Southerner and not only finds it distasteful but practically impossible to serve under a colored commander." Baker, who pressed for Young's medical retirement, promptly replied that "the cause of the trouble" was removed. Brian G. Shellum, *Black Officer in a Buffalo Soldier Regiment: The Military Career of Charles Young* (Lincoln: University of Nebraska Press, 2010), 249-254.

41. Michael Shear, "Two World War I Soldiers Posthumously Receive Medal of Honor," *New York Times*, June 2, 2015. The other honoree, Sergeant William Shemin, a Jewish American, had not been officially recognized earlier because, like Private Johnson, the acknowledgement of his heroism and sacrifice for the United States had been eclipsed by prejudice.

42. Larry Greenly, *Eugene Bullard: World's First Black Fighter Pilot* (Montgomery, AL: NewSouth Books, 2013).

43. Baker carried messages about German troop movements written in invisible ink on her musical scores, and her tours offered the perfect cover for meetings with dignitaries. Baker returned to the United States for the 1963 March on Washington where she wore the Medal of the Resistance awarded to her by Charles De Gaulle and took the podium with Dr. Martin Luther King. Heather Roberson, "Black Venus and Her Rainbow Tribe," *California Magazine* (January-February 2008); Peggy Caravantes, *The Many Faces of Josephine Baker: Dancer, Singer, Activist, Spy*, (Chicago: Chicago Review Press, 2015), 87, 99, 138.

44. Roger Little, "A Black Mayor in 1790 France," in *The Enterprise of Enlightenment*, eds., Terry Pratt and David McCallam (Bern, Switzerland: Peter Lang Publishing, 2004), 69.

45. Linda Hervieux, *Forgotten: The Untold Story of D-Day's Black Heroes, At Home and at War* (New York: Harper Collins, 2015), 4–5. Woodson was recommended for a Congressional Medal of Honor; however, at the height of Jim Crow, black men were deemed ineligible for the U.S. Army's highest honor on the basis of their race. This restriction was not in place during the Civil War, when the award was initiated, through the Spanish-American War, a span of time when 52 African Americans were bestowed the Medal of Honor— including Robert Augustus Sweeney who in 1883 joined the ranks of the 13 servicemen who have received two Medals of Honor for two separate acts of valor. During WWI four African Americans were recommended for the Medal of Honor;

two were ultimately awarded many decades after the fact. In 1996, awards given to seven black WWII heroes were officially upgraded to Medals of Honor by the U.S. Congress. Charles Hanna, *African American Recipients of the Medal of Honor* (New York: McFarland, 2002),105,120,124. Gail Buckley, *American Patriots: The Story of Blacks in the Military from the Revolution to Desert Storm* (New York: Random House, 2002), xxiii, 249.

46. Granville T. Woods was an "electromechanical genius" who "revolutionized the railroad and electric railways industries" and vastly improved their safety (especially with his induction telegraph system that allowed dispatchers and conductors to communicate in real time); his 50 patents included telephones, telegraphs, transmitters, automatic safety cutouts for electrical circuits, air brakes, galvanic batteries, and what is known as the "third rail" in electronic railways. Michael C. Christopher, "Granville T. Woods: The Plight of a Black Inventor," *Journal of Black Studies* (March 1981), 274, 272. Rayvon Fouché, *Black Inventors in the Age of Segregation: Granville T. Woods, Lewis Latimer, and Shelby Davidson* (Baltimore, MD: Johns Hopkins University Press, 2005).

47. Sam Maggs, *Wonder Women: 25 Innovators, Inventors, and Trailblazers Who Changed History* (Philadelphia: Quirk Books, 2016), 150.

48. Maggs, *Wonder Women*, 151; Charles E. Shaw, *The Untold Stories of Excellence* (Bloomington, Indiana: Xlibris Publishing, 2011), 36.

49. Maggs, *Wonder Women*, 148.

50. Ruth Bordin, *Women at Michigan: The Dangerous Experiment, 1970s to the Present*, (Ann Arbor: University of Michigan Press, 2001), 38.

51. Gwen Robinson, "Grandfather Arrived Aboard Slave Ship," *Chatham Daily News*, February 25, 2017; Jacqueline L. Tobin with Hettie Jones, *From Midnight to Dawn: The Last Tracks of the Underground Railroad*, (New York: Doubleday, 2007), 50.

52. Sherwood, *Origins of Pan Africanism*, 239.

53. Edward C. Kirk, D.D.S., *The Dental Cosmos: Monthly Record of Dental Science* Volume 53, (Philadelphia: The S. S. White Dental Manufacturing Company, 1911), 125–126.

54. Dave Rogers, *Inventions and Their Inventors, 1750–1920*, (Middlesex, UK: Danercon, 2011), 151.

55. Margot Lee Shetterly, *Hidden Figures* (New York: William Morrow), 2016.

56. Tanya Sichynsky, "How World War II Opened the Door for One of the First Black Women at NASA," *Washington Post*, September 19, 2016.

57. Charlene Morrow and Teri Perl, eds, *Notable Women in Mathematics: A Biographical Dictionary* (Westport, CT: Greenwood Press, 1998), 69.

58. Louis Haber, *Black Pioneers of Science and Invention* (New York: Harcourt Inc., 1970), 212.

59. National Inventors Hall of Fame. http://invent.org/ (07/07/2016)

60. Dr. Drew (another Dunbar High graduate) resigned from his position at the American Red Cross in protest of their segregationist policies. For a biographical account of Drew along with the historical and cultural context of discrimination that helped to spawn the legend that surrounded Drew's death, see Spencie Love, *One Blood: The Death and Resurrection of Charles R. Drew* (Chapel Hill: University of North Carolina Press, 1996).

61. Felicia R. Lee, "Reclaiming a Black Research Scientist's Forgotten Legacy," *New York Times*, February 6, 2007.

62. In 1999 the American Chemical Society acknowledged Dr. Julian's synthesis of physostigmine to treat glaucoma as one of the top 25 achievements in the history of American chemistry. The 2007 Nova documentary, "Forgotten Genius," garnered wider public recognition for this remarkable scientist and his manifold contributions.

63. Darlene R. Stille, *Percy Lavon Julian: Pioneering Chemist* (Mankato, MN: Compass Point Books, 2009).

64. The African American millionaires of the early twentieth century had a nineteenth-century precursor. Jeremiah Hamilton was a notoriously merciless broker in New York who essentially operated a hedge fund in which white investors clamored to invest. At his death in 1875, his estate was valued at $2 million. Shane White, *Prince of Darkness: The Untold Story of Jeremiah G. Hamilton, Wall Street's First Black Millionaire* (New York: St. Martins Press, 2015).

65. Cookie Lommel, *Robert Church: Entrepreneur* (Los Angeles, CA: Melrose Square Publishing, 1995).

66. James Hollandsworth, Jr., *An Absolute Massacre: The New Orleans Race Riot of July 30, 1866* (Baton Rouge: Louisiana State University Press, 2001).

67. Donald R. Shaffer, *After the Glory: The Struggles of Black Civil War Veterans* (Lawrence: University Press of Kansas, 2004).

68. Cameron McWhirter, *Red Summer: The Summer of 1919 and the Awakening Black America* (New York: Henry Holt, 2011), 13.

69. *A Report by the Oklahoma Commission to Study the Tulsa Riot of 1921*, February 28, 2001.

70. Denis Fradin and Judith Fradin, *Fight On! Mary Church Terrell's Battle for Integration* (New York: Clarion Books, 2003), 57.

71. As of this writing, the Equal Justice Initiative has documented 4,384 racial terror lynchings in the United States between 1877 and 1950. See also Amy Louise Wood, *Lynching and Spectacle: Witnessing Racial Violence in America, 1890–1940* (Chapel Hill: University of North Carolina Press, 2009), for additional context.

72. Douglas Bristol, *Knights of the Razor: Black Barbers in Slavery and Freedom* (Baltimore: The Johns Hopkins University Press, 2009), 149.

73. Charlotte Ray had been admitted to the D.C. bar in 1872, making her among the first American women, and the first African American woman, to practice law in the United States.

74. Lia B. Epperson, "Alexander, Sadie Tanner Mossell (1898–1989) Economist, Lawyer" *African American National Biography*, eds., Henry Louis Gates, Jr. & Evelyn Brooks-Higgenbotham (New York: Oxford University Press, 2006), 15.

75. Henry Gates, et al., eds., *African American Lives* (New York: Oxford University Press, 2004), 45.

76. Rayford Logan, "James Weldon Johnson and Haiti," *Phylon* 32, no. 4 (1971): 396.

77. Martha Cobb, *Harlem, Haiti, and Havana: A Comparative Critical Study of*

Langston Hughes, Jacques Roumain, Nicholas Guillen (Washington DC: Three Continents Press, 1978).

78. Alberto, *Terms of Inclusion*, 171.

79. Alberto, *Terms of Inclusion*, 173.

80. J. Todd Moye, *Ella Baker: Community Organizer of the Civil Rights Movement* (Lanham, MD: Rowman and Littlefield, 2013), 11.

81. Barbara Ransby, *Ella Baker and the Black Freedom Movement: A Radical Democratic Vision* (Chapel Hill: The University of North Carolina Press, 2005).

82. Glenda Elizabeth Gilmore, "At Yale, a Right That Doesn't Outweigh a Wrong," *New York Times*, April 29, 2016.

83. Sarah Azaransky, *The Dream is Freedom: Pauli Murray and American Democratic Faith* (New York: Oxford University Press, 2011), 38. In 1989 the University of Tennessee Press posthumously published Murray's autobiography, self-titled, *Song in a Weary Throat: An American Pilgrimage*, as *Pauli Murray: The Autobiography of a Black Activist, Feminist Lawyer, and Poet.*

84. Kathryn Schulz, "The Many Lives of Pauli Murray," *New Yorker* (April 17, 2017).

85. Rustin and his mentor, labor leader A. Philip Randolph, had nineteenth-century predecessors like Isaac Myers. Myers worked as a caulker in antebellum Baltimore and established a cooperative grocery store in 1864. When post-Civil War labor competition led to the firing of 1000 black caulkers, Myers established another cooperative, the Chesapeake Marine Railway and Dry Dock Company, in 1866. After efforts to collaborate with the National Labor Union failed, Myers became the first president of the Colored National Labor Union in 1869, an organization founded with the help of George Downing. As noted at the start of the chapter, George Downing was a prolific nineteenth century civil rights activist whose nephew, Henry Francis Downing, attended the London Pan African Congress in 1900.

86. John D'Emilio, *Lost Prophet: The Life and Times of Bayard Rustin* (Chicago: University of Chicago Press, 2003).

87. Taylor Branch, *Parting the Waters: America in the King Years, 1953–63* (New York: Simon & Schuster, 1988); Wesley Hogan, *Many Minds, One Heart: SNCC's Dream for a New America* (Chapel Hill: University of North Carolina Press, 2009); Manning Marable, *Malcolm X: A Life of Reinvention* (New York: Viking, 2011); Stanley Nelson *The Black Panthers: Vanguard of the Revolution* (2015); Nancy Kates and Bennett Singer *Brother Outsider: The Life of Bayard Rustin* (2003); The American Experience Public Broadcasting Series, *Eyes on the Prize: America's Civil Rights Movement, 1954–1985* (1987–1990).

Conclusion

New World History

History has too often been misconstrued as something based on purity when it is, in reality, based on interaction. Many of us have been conditioned to think of Americans in binary terms: black or white, slave or free, North or South, us or them; but as it turns out we are, and always have been, completely intertwined. Arguably, the first documented slave owner in the United States was a black man—Anthony Johnson was certainly among the first in any case. On the other hand, the nation's earliest documented slave, John Punch, sired a long lineage of white Americans, one of whom begat the first black president of the United States. Historians may debate the paternity of fair-skinned slaves on the plantations of the nation's first presidents, but that they, along with innumerable enslaved Americans, had significant European ancestry is beyond question.

Black and white Americans not only share the same New World history, they share the same genealogy. Despite mythologies that suggest the contrary, racial mixing was pervasive throughout American history, even, and perhaps especially, where interracial unions were proscribed. The idea of discrete biological categories of white and black Americans is vitiated by the vast ranks of mixed-race Americans who were assigned blackness by social conventions that placed children with one white parent in the subordinate racial category, including iconic black personages like Frederick Douglass, Bob Marley, and Barack Obama, along with many of the Afro-Americans described throughout these pages. In other cases, people with less visible African ancestry could become recognized as white, like Bernadino Rivadavia, who became Argentina's first president in 1825, Patrick Francis Healy who became president of Georgetown University in 1874, as well as the descendants of slaves from Monticello who fought in white units for the Union. Norbert Rillieux, the engineer who invented the technology that revitalized the sugar industry was of African descent (and a relation of the painter Degas). The Confederate hero Robert E. Lee had two enslaved sisters-in-law (fathered by George Washington's step-grandson). That black and white Americans have such deeply entwined heritage illuminates a fundamental way in which the traditional distinction between American and African American history is deceptive.

Americans are the descendants of slaves and slave owners both literally and figuratively. Men and women of African descent have fundamentally shaped American history since its inception and made massive contributions to the formation of the Americas in every possibly way. Africans and their progeny were among the earliest explorers, settlers, and defenders of the New World. Black conquistadores founded a continuous tradition of Afro-American community and military service in alliance with the state. For some this entailed claiming freedom for themselves and their children in courts, through self-purchase, meritorious service, or kinship networks and expanding the ranks of the free population in a variety of roles. Afro-Americans were among the first landowners in cities like New York, Los Angeles, Chicago, Mexico City, Havana, and Lima, and formed substantial parts of colonial populations at large.

Many of the first Africans in the Americas immediately liberated themselves and formed independent maroon communities. Though several of the most powerful of these fugitive slave societies were ultimately officially incorporated into free black towns, maroons inaugurated a continuous tradition of Americans who realized liberty by challenging the state. Many Afro-Americans fought for freedom through organized rebellion, foreign military service, and colonization, sometimes forming free communities and institutions as expatriates. The first known permanent transatlantic settlers in the United States were Africans who liberated themselves from a failed Spanish settlement in the 1520s.

Until the early nineteenth century, the vast majority of Americans arrived in the New World as slaves. Enslaved men and women were paramount in the establishment of the Americas materially, culturally, socially, politically, and economically; at many times and in many places, they were the demographic majority. In the United States, we have been conditioned to think of black people as a minority, but roughly half of all Southerners in 1860 were black. Despite the inherent violence, oppression, and reach of slavery, slaves often had more autonomy and historical impact than is commonly recognized. Slaves were instrumental to the initiation and course of virtually every major historical event—until the abolition of slavery, itself a revolution in which enslaved individuals played multiple and decisive roles. From the revolts initiated on Columbus's son's plantation in 1522 to the freedom seekers of Bacon's Rebellion in 1676 to the ubiquitous armed uprisings across the Americas at the close of the 1700s, slave resistance was a continuous and considerable part of American life that shaped the politics and policies that paved the way for patriot revolutions.

During the Age of Revolution, as Enlightenment discourse grappled with the contradictions of slavery and freedom, so too did people of African descent. For some Afro-Americans this meant service against the colonial powers as patriots in the American Revolution, the Haitian Revolution, and the Latin American wars for independence; for others it meant allying with the colonial state. Black people participated not just as soldiers, which they did en masse, but also as leaders and statesmen. Mexico's Vicente Guerrero, Venezuela's José Padilla, and Cuba's Antiono Maceo, for example, were military heroes who led their countries to independence. As the stories of James Armistead, Harry Washington, Mary Bowser, Toussaint L'Ouverture, and Juana Ramírez show, slaves and former slaves not only understood the significance of elite political conflicts, they profoundly shaped them. Many tens of thousands of slaves challenged slavery during the American Revolution, on both sides the battlefield. The American Civil War can also be viewed as slave uprising whose events were shaped by black Americans at every turn.

Too many of us have, consciously or unconsciously, thought of emancipation as a gift that Lincoln offered to black people. Yet the abolition of slavery in the United States was a process pushed forward at every turn by black Americans. The brave and persistent actions of fugitive slaves and the free people of color who risked their lives to support them contributed greatly the political crises that led the South to secede. And like every war in American history, Afro-Americans capitalized on the political upheaval to challenge slavery and stake claims to citizenship as soldiers. The vast majority of the 200,000 black combatants who officially served the Union forces and the unknown numbers who, like Susie Taylor King, served unofficially, liberated themselves and then fought for the freedom of others. The legislation leading up to and including the Emancipation Proclamation was made exigent by the actions and intentions of African Americans. The very text of the Emancipation Proclamation itself—as well as Lincoln's correspondence—declared that it was a war measure designed to officially muster all of the black servicemen upon whose sacrifice the nation's victory relied.

Afro-Americans were not only instrumental to the revolts and revolutions that brought slavery to a decisive end throughout the hemisphere, they defined and defended the principles of democracy before and after legal slavery was abolished. It is precisely because enslaved as well as free black people were often denied rights that Afro-Americans were especially invested in establishing and protecting them. From the sixteenth century to the twentieth, men and women of African descent pursed the right to liberty, to work, to education, to serve in the military, to vote, and to equal access and protection, in petitions to legislatures and in courtrooms as well as in a variety of organizations, symposia, and media. Afro-Latins continually took up arms against slavery and for independence as well as established civic organizations, political parties, and newspapers and produced scholarship and art to advance democracy. Afro-Caribbean advocates like Vincent Ogé, Julien Fédon, and Paul Bogle gave their lives battling for the citizenship rights of others while others, like Henry Sylvester-Williams, Amy Jacques Garvey, and Aimé Césaire, created international forums to advance universal citizenship rights.

Despite obstacles, people of color cultivated businesses and schools, pursued professions and political careers, advanced medicine and technology, and their contributions and achievements benefited their wider societies as well as implicitly and explicitly refuted the antidemocratic logic of slavery and racism. Black Americans contributed to every aspect of American industry and modern life, from Lewis Temple's whaling toggle and Andre Rebouças's torpedo to Elijah McCoy's train innovations and Charles Drew's blood bank. From the medical advances fostered by José Manuel Valdéz and Percy Lavon Julian to the decisive impact on western law made by James Somerset and Pauli Murray, we are the beneficiaries of and indebted to the contributions of these American founders.

The men and women presented in these pages should encourage us to think more deeply about what we Americans mean when we say "we" or "Americans." Americans of African descent who fought for freedom helped liberate all Americans from circumscribed conceptions of citizenship. Seeking and defending the ideals of liberty and justice, even in the midst of slavery and discrimination, Afro-Americans were crucial to the founding of the modern world and the development of democracy.

We will not understand American history until we understand African American history and recognize that it is not solely a story of oppression—though oppression is a continuous and dangerous current against which people of African descent have had to contend—but also that black people were among the architects of our nation and principal founders of the Americas at large. Black Americans continuously encouraged the United States to live up to the ideals enshrined in its founding documents. Afro-Americans were also innovators and pioneers, visionaries and scientists, who overcame the constraints of racism to make enormous contributions not just to American history but to humanity.

It is my hope that the reader will come away with a deeper appreciation for how complex, variegated, and integrated American history is. Multiculturalism is not politically correct; it is historically accurate. Recognizing our interconnected past can expand and enrich conventional conceptions of American history and help us recognize the ways in which the traditional narratives, categories, and habits of thought associated with it are not benign. We undermine ourselves and our society with segregated frames of reference cultivated by traditional history—erroneous conventions that shape how we think about history and understand race that are not just the result of the obvious malevolent kinds of racism that are easy to identify. Perhaps more insidious are the assumptions shaped by the subtleties of how we consciously and unconsciously understand ourselves and how we fit into the world around us.

Eighteenth-Century Uprisings for Freedom

Afro-Americans initiated uprisings for freedom throughout American history; however, slave revolts peaked between 1700 and 1800. During this century, over 400 shipboard revolts were documented on ships carrying enslaved passengers. Additionally, countless uprisings against slavery took place on land. Small numbers of individuals achieved their freedom immediately with these efforts. Many, including Afro-Americans who did not directly participate in rebellions, were punished severely through public torture and executions or pervasive, oppressive legal prohibitions that attempted to quell the omnipresent threat of resistance. Still, these organizing efforts and networks point to a larger context where enslaved Americans continually championed liberty as they fueled apprehensions about the state's ability to maintain slavery. Even a cursory glance at the partial timeline of slave uprisings between 1700 and 1800 reveals the ubiquity of Afro-American resistance movements.

1701 Coromantee revolt in Antigua; Afro-Creole plot in Barbados

1712 Enslaved New Yorkers protest; quelled by militia

1725 Increased maroon activity in Grenada punished with fourteen executions;

1725 Afro-Mexicans initiate slave uprisings in Cordoba and Orizaba in 1725, 1735, 1741, and 1749 and establish 6 maroon settlements in Oaxaca, one of which, after a series of armed clashes and negotiations led by Fernando Manuel, is formally granted freedom and the right to establish a town, Amapa, in 1769

1726 Incipient slave and maroon revolts in Surinam

1727 Some 300 enslaved individuals rise up in Havana, requires military intervention

1728 Slaves rise up in western Colombia's Chocó region (which remains today a predominantly Afro-Colombian region); the Cauca Valley and Magdalena River further inland experience a series of rebellions in 1781

1729 Rebellious slaves in Antigua sentenced to be burned alive

1730 Captives overtake slave ship *Little George* and force its return to Sierra Leone

1731 Samba Rebellion quashed by military in New Orleans

1731 Slaves in western Cuba escape from copper mines in El Cobre into mountains (again) as a deliberate negotiation tactic with Spanish authorities

1731–1733 Slaves rebel in Venezuela's Yaracuy area and also in Yare in 1747; 1749 slaves rise up in Caracas; enslaved Venezuelans rise up again 1771-1774

1731–1739 Jamaica's First Maroon War, the formation of Jamaica's powerful maroon communities were themselves the result of numerous,continuous slave revolts

1733 Maroons and rebel slaves capture St. John for six months;

1759 slaves rise up again in St. John and neighboring St. Croix

1734 Widespread conspiracy for freedom discovered by Bahamian governor

1736 Approximately 132 enslaved "rebels" in Antigua convicted, most burned alive; leader of island-wide plot for collective resistance, Klass, broken on the wheel

1737 Slaves rise up in Guadeloupe, the first of several uprisings

1739 Some 200 enslaved individuals revolt in Maryland, conspiracies persist

1739 Stono Revolt in South Carolina pits freedom seekers against colonial militia

1741 Enslaved New Yorkers set fires throughout city

1742 Slaves rise up in Jamaica and again in 1745

1760 Tacky's War organizes many hundreds of enslaved individuals in a three-month series of rebellions in Jamaica, militia & maroons called up to quell, exiled slaves instigate revolt in British Honduras

1763 Major slave rebellion in Berbice (Guyana)

1763 Fifty enslaved Afro-Mexicans flee sugar plantation to seek officials in Mexico City to whom they could appeal for their rights

1765 In Grenada, slave uprising followed by increased maroon activity

1773 Black Caribs in St. Vincent negotiate treaty with British soldiers

1774 Major slave uprising in Tobago preceded by numerous smaller events, authorities burn or dismember many in retribution

1775 Dumore's Proclamation offering liberty to slaves who aid British forces during the American Revolution officially recognizes de facto revolt of tens of thousands of enslaved Americans who had already begun to flee slavery during this uprising

1784 Louisiana maroons under Juan San Maló defend settlement against colonial militia

1786 Slave revolt in Dominica reported in London Times (April 3, 1786); Dominica experiences maroon wars, led by Pharcel and others, from 1785 to 1790, slave revolts in 1791 and 1795, and additional maroon wars, led by Quashie and others, 1809-1814

1789   Slaves revolt in Martinique after learning of revolution in France, prompting a civil war between patriots and royalists, similar conflicts play out Guadeloupe over the next several years where enslaved and free people of color demand their rights

1790   Slaves rebel in Tortola, again in 1823, 1830, and 1831

1790   Vincent Ogé leads mulatto rebellion in Saint Domingue

1791   Massive slave rebellion in Saint Domingue, significant slave rebellions in Dominica, Martinique, and Grenada

1794   Enslaved and free colored individuals resist British assault on French Guadeloupe

1794–1795   Slave revolts in Dutch Demerara (Guyana) in conjunction with maroons

1795   (February) troops of newly freed St. Lucians known as Brigands, led by Frenchman Victor Hughes, defend their liberty and evict British forces (aka Brigands War)

1795   (March) Colored planter Julien Fédon leads massive uprising of thousands of slaves in Granada, British enlist 5000 extra troops and take two years to restore control (aka Fedon's War)

1795   (March) in St. Vincent, Joseph Chatoyer leads Black Caribs (maroons), slaves, free coloreds, and Frenchmen who hold the island against the British for six months (aka Second Carib War)

1795   (April) Pointe Coupée Conspiracy in Louisiana unites enslaved and free colored individuals as well as white revolutionaries (preceded by Mina Conspiracy of 1791)

1795   (May) Colihaut uprising in Dominica (aka Second Maroon War)

1795   (May) Coro revolt in Venezuela joins hundreds together in protest against slavery: slaves, free people of color and native people, forerunner of independence movement

1795   (July) Slave uprising instigated in central Cuba

1795   (July) Jamaica's Second Maroon War erupts for eight months

1795   (August) massive slave insurrection in Curaçao led by Tula, another in 1800

Bibliography

Abu-Lughod, Janet. *Before European Hegemony*. New York: Oxford University Press, 1991.

Adams, Catherine, and Elizabeth H. Pleck. *Love of Freedom: Black Women in Colonial and Revolutionary New England*. New York: Oxford University Press, 2010.

Aguirre, Carlos. *Agentes de su Propia Libertad: Los Escalvos de Lima y la Desintegración de la Esclavitud: 1821–1824*. Lima: Pontificia Universidad Católica del Perú, Fondo Editorial, 1993.

Alberto, Paulina L. *Terms of Inclusion: Black Intellectuals in Twentieth-Century Brazil*. Chapel Hill: University of North Carolina Press, 2011.

Alexander, Adele Logan. *Parallel Worlds: The Remarkable Gibbs-Hunts and the Enduring (In)Significance of Melanin*. Charlottesville: University of Virginia Press, 2010.

Alexander, William, Cassandra Newby Alexander, and Charles H. Ford, eds. *Voices from Within the Veil: African Americans and the Experience of Democracy*. Newcastle: Cambridge Scholars Publishing, 2008.

Allured, Janet, and Judith F. Gentry, eds. *Louisiana Women: Their Lives and Times*. Athens: University of Georgia Press, 2009.

Altoff, Gerard T., and Roby Opthoff Lilik. *Among My Best Men: African-Americans and the War of 1812*. Put-in-Bay: The Perry Group, 1996.

Anderson, Benedict. *Imagined Communities*. New York: Verso, 1983.

Anderson, John. *Night of the Silent Drums*. New York: Scribner, 1975.

Andrews, George Reid. *Blackness in the White Nation: A History of Afro-Uruguay*. Chapel Hill: University of North Carolina Press, 2010.

Andrews, George Reid. *Afro-Latin America, 1500–1800*. New York: Oxford University Press, 2004.

Andrews, George Reid. *The Afro-Argentines of Buenos Aires, 1800–1900*. Madison: University of Wisconsin Press, 1980.

Andrews, George Reid. "The Afro-Argentine Officers of Buenos Aires Province, 1800–1860." *Journal of Negro History* 64, no. 2 (Spring 1979): pp. 85–100.

Appiah, Kwame Anthony, and Henry Louis Gates, Jr., eds. *Africana: The Encyclopedia of African & African-American Experience*. New York: Oxford University Press, 2nd Edition, 2005.

Arana, Marie. *Bolivar: American Liberator*. New York: Simon & Schuster, 2013.

Archoa, Jaime. "Inclusion of Afro-Columbians: Unreachable National Goal?" *Latin American Perspectives* 25, no. 3 (May 1998): pp. 70–89.

Araujo, Ana Lucia. *Shadows of the Slave Past: Memory, Heritage, and Slavery*. New York: Routledge, 2014.

Ashley, Clifford. *The Yankee Whaler*. Mineola: Dover Publications, 1991 [1926].

Aslakson, Kenneth. *Making Race in the Courtroom: The Legal Construction of Three Races in Early New Orleans*. New York: New York University Press, 2014.

Azaransky, Sarah. *The Dream is Freedom: Pauli Murray and American Democratic Faith*. New York: Oxford University Press, 2011.

Baepler, Paul. *White Slaves, African Masters: An Anthology of American Barbary Captivity Narratives*. Chicago: University of Chicago Press, 1999.

Bacon, Jacqueline. *Freedom's Journal: The First African-American Newspaper*. Lanham: Lexington Books, 2007.

Baldwin, James. "On Being White and Other Lies." *Essence* (April 1984): pp. 80–82.

Baldwin, James. "The White Man's Guilt." *Ebony* (August 1965): pp. 47–48.

Baldwin, James. *The Fire Next Time*. New York: Dial Press, 1963.

Baldwin, James. *Notes of a Native Son*. Boston: Beacon Press, 1984 [1955].

Ball, Charles. *Slavery in the United States: A Narrative of the Life and Adventures of Charles Ball, a Black Man, Who Lived Forty Years in Maryland, South Carolina and Georgia, as a Slave Under Various Masters, and was One Year in the Navy with Commodore Barney, During the Late War*. New York: John S. Taylor, 1837.

Ball, Edward. *Slaves in the Family*. New York: Ferrar, Straus and Giroux, 1998.

Banat, Gabriel. *The Chevalier de Saint-Georges: Virtuoso of the Sword and Bow*. Hillsdale: Pendragon Press, 2006.

Banks, Taunya Lovell. "Dangerous Woman: Elizabeth Key's Freedom Suit—Subjecthood and Racialized Identity in Seventeenth Century Colonial Virginia." *Akron Law Review* (March 23, 2009): pp. 799–837.

Baram, Uzi. "A New Chapter in African Diaspora History in Southwest Florida: The Evidence for a Maroon Community on the Manatee River." Paper presented at the Southeastern Archeological Conference, Tampa, Florida, November 8, 2013.

Barcia, Manuel. *The Great African Slave Revolt of 1825: Cuba and the Fight for Freedom in Mantanzas*. Baton Rouge: Louisiana State University Press, 2012.

Barnes, L. Diane. *Artisan Workers in the Upper South: Petersburg, Virginia 1820–1865*. Baton Rouge: Louisiana University Press, 2008.

Basler, Roy B., ed. *The Collected Works of Abraham Lincoln*. Brunswick: Rutgers University Press, 1953.

Bass, Carole, and Mark Alden Branch. "Yale College's First Black Grad: It's Not Who You Think." *Yale Alumni Magazine* (February 28, 2014).

Beasley, Delilah. *The Negro Trailblazers of California*. Los Angeles: CA, 1919.

Beatty-Medina, Charles. "The Spanish-African Maroon Competition for Captive Indian Labor in the Region of Esmeraldas During the Late Sixteenth and Early Seventeenth Centuries." *The Americas* 63, no. 1 (2006): pp. 113–136.

Beckles, Hilary, and Verene A. Shepherd. *Saving Souls: The Struggle to End the Transatlantic Trade in Africans*. Kingston: Ian Randle Publishers, 2007.

Beckles, Hilary. "The Slave-Drivers' War: Bussa and the 1816 Barbados Slave Rebellion." *Boletín de Estudios Latinoamericanos y del Caribe* 39 (December 1985): pp. 85–110.

Bell, Carolyn Cossé. *Revolution, Romanticism, and the Afro-Creole Protest Tradition in Louisiana, 1718–1868*. Baton Rouge: Louisiana State University Press, 1997.

Bell-Scott, Patricia. *The Firebrand and the First Lady: Portrait of a Friendship, Pauli Murray, Eleanor Roosevelt, and the Struggle for Social Justice*. New York: Knopf, 2016.

Bellegarde, Dantes. "President Alexandre Pétion: Founder of Agrarian Democracy and Pioneer of Pan-Americanism." *Phylon* 2, no. 3 (1941): pp. 205–213.

Bender, Thomas. "The Age of Revolution: Founding Fathers Dreamed of Uprisings, Except in Haiti." *New York Times* (July 1, 2001).

Bendini, Silvio A. "Benjamin Banneker and the Survey of the District of Columbia, 1791." *Records of the Colombia Historical Society* 47 (1970): pp. 7–30.

Bennet, Herman L. *Africans in Colonial Mexico: Absolutism, Christianity, and Afro-Creole Consciousness, 1570–1640*. Bloomington: Indiana University Press, 2003.

Bennett, Herman L. *Colonial Blackness: A History of Afro-Mexico*. Bloomington: Indiana University Press, 2009.

Bennett, Lerone, Jr. *Before the Mayflower: A History of Black America, 1619–1962*. New York: Penguin, 1984 [1962].

Berlin, Ira, and Leslie Harris, eds. *Slavery in New York*. New York: The New York Historical Society and The New Press, 2005.

Berlin, Ira. *Many Thousands Gone: The First Two Centuries of Slavery in North America*. Cambridge: Belknap Press of Harvard University Press, 2000.

Berlin, Ira, Joseph Reidy, and Leslie S. Rowland. *Freedom's Soldiers: The Black Military Experience in the Civil War*. New York: Cambridge University Press, 1998.

Betts, Robert B. *In Search of York: The Slave Who Went to the Pacific With Lewis and Clark*. Boulder: University Press of Colorado, 2002.

Biddle, Daniel R., and Murray Dubin. *Tasting Freedom: Octavius Catto and the Battle for Equality in Civil War America*. Philadelphia: Temple University Press, 2010.

Billingsly, Andrew. *Yearning to Breathe Free: Robert Smalls of South Carolina and His Families*. Columbia: University of South Carolina Press, 2007.

Black, Clinton V. *The Story of Jamaica*. London: Collins, 1965.

Blackburn, Robin. *The American Crucible: Slavery, Emancipation, and Human Rights*. New York: Verso, 2011.

Blackburn, Robin. *The Making of New World Slavery: From the Baroque to the Modern, 1492–1800*. New York: Verso, 1997.

Blackburn, Robin. *The Overthrow of Colonial Slavery, 1776–1848*. New York: Verso, 1988.

Blackett, R. J. M. *Building an Antislavery Wall: Black Americans in the Atlantic Abolitionist Movement, 1830–1860*. Baton Rouge: Louisiana State University Press, 1983.

Blackmon, Douglas A. *Slavery By Another Name: The Re-Enslavement of Black Americans from the Civil War to World War II*. New York: Anchor Books, 2008.

Blakely, Allison. *Blacks in the Dutch World: The Evolution of Racial Imagery in Modern Society*. Bloomington: Indiana University Press, 1994.

Blanchard, Peter. "The Language of Liberation: Slave Voices in the Wars of Independence." *Hispanic American Historical Review* 82, no. 3 (August 2002): pp. 499–523.

Blanchard, Peter. *Under the Flags of Freedom: Slave Soldiers and the Wars of Independence in Spanish South America*. Pittsburgh: University of Pittsburgh Press, 2008.

Blight, David. *Race and Reunion: The Civil War in American Memory*. Cambridge: Harvard University Press, 2001.

Blouet, Olwyn M. *The Contemporary Caribbean: History, Life, and Culture Since 1945*. London: Reaktion Books, 2007.

Blumberg, Rhoda. *York's Adventures with Lewis and Clark: An African-American's Part in the Great Expedition*. New York: Harper Collins, 2004.

Blumrosen, Alfred. "The Profound Influence in America of Lord Mansfield's Decision in Somerset v. Stuart." *Texas Wesleyan Law Review* 13, no. 2 (2007): pp. 645–658.

Blumrosen, Alfred and Ruth. *Slave Nation: How Slavery United the Colonies and Sparked the American Revolution*. Naperville: Sourcebooks, 2005.

Bogen, David S. "Mathias de Sousa: Maryland's First Colonist of African Descent." *Maryland Historical Magazine* 96, no. 1 (2001): pp. 68–85.

Bolster, W. Jeffrey. *Black Jacks: African American Seamen in the Age of Sail*. Cambridge: Harvard University Press, 1997.

Bowser, Frederick P. "Africans in Spanish American Colonial Society." *Cambridge History of Latin America*, vol. 2. Leslie Bethell, ed., pp. 357–379. London: Cambridge University Press, 1984.

Bowser, Frederick P. *The African Slave in Colonial Peru, 1524–1650*. Stanford: Stanford University Press, 1975.

Bowser, Frederick P. "The African in Colonial Spanish America: Reflections on Research Achievements and Priorities." *Latin American Research Review* 7, no. 1 (Spring 1972): pp. 77–94.

Bowser, Pearl, Jane Gains, and Charles Musser, eds. *Oscar Micheaux and His Circle: African-American Filmmaking and Race Cinema of the Silent Era*. Bloomington: Indiana University Press, 2001.

Boyd, Antonio Olliz. *The Latin American Identity and the African Diaspora: Ethnogenesis in Context*. Amherst: Cambria Press, 2010.

Brana-Shute, Rosemary, and Randy J. Sparks. *Paths to Freedom: Manumission in the Atlantic World*. Columbia: University of South Carolina Press, 2009.

Breen, Patrick. *The Land Shall Be Deluged in Blood: A New History of the Nat Turner Revolt*. New York: Oxford University Press, 2015.

Breen, T. H., and Steven Innes. *Myne Owne Ground: Race and Freedom on Virginia's Eastern Shore, 1640–1676*. New York: Oxford University Press, 1980.

Bristol, Douglas Walter, Jr. *Knights of the Razor: Black Barbers in Slavery and Freedom*. Baltimore: The Johns Hopkins University Press, 2009.

Brock, Lisa, and Digna Castañeda Fuertes, eds. *Between Race and Empire: African-Americans and Cubans Before the Cuban Revolution*. Philadelphia: Temple University Press, 1998.

Brockington, Lolita Gutierrez. "The African Diaspora in the Eastern Andes: Adaptation, Agency, and Fugitive Action, 1573–1677." *The Americas* 57, no. 2 (October 2000): pp. 207–224.

Bronfman, Alejandra. *Measures of Equality: Social Science, Citizenship, and Race in Cuba 1902–1940*. Chapel Hill: University of North Carolina Press, 2003.

Brown, Christopher Leslie, and Philip D. Morgan, eds. *Arming Slaves: From Classical Times to the Modern Age*. New Haven: Yale University Press, 2006.

Brown, Jeannette E. *African American Women Chemists*. New York: Oxford University Press, 2012.

Brown, Kathleen. *Good Wives, Nasty Wenches, and Anxious Patriarchs: Gender, Race, and Power in Colonial Virginia*. Chapel Hill: University of North Carolina Press, 1996.

Brown, Vincent. *The Reaper's Garden: Death and Power in the World of Atlantic Slavery*. Cambridge: Harvard University Press, 2008.

Bruce, Dickson D., Jr. *The Origins of African American Literature, 1680–1865*. Charlottesville: University of Virginia Press, 2001.

Brunson, Takkara. "Constructing Afro-Cuban Womanhood: Race, Gender, and Citizenship in Republican-Era Cuba, 1902–1958." Doctoral dissertation, University of Texas, Austin (2011).

Bryant, Sherwin K. *Rivers of Gold, Lives of Bondage: Governing Through Slavery in Colonial Quito*. Chapel Hill: University of North Carolina Press, 2014.

Bryant, Sherwin K., Rachel Sarah O'Toole, and Ben Vinson III, eds. *Africans to Spanish America: Expanding the Diaspora*. Urbana: University of Illinois Press, 2012.

Bryant, Sherwin K. "Finding Gold, Forming Slavery: The Creation of a Classic Slave Society, Popayan, 1600–1700." *The Americas* 63, no. 1 (July 2006): pp. 81–112.

Buckley, Gail. *American Patriots: The Story of Blacks in the Military from the Revolution to Desert Storm*. New York: Ransom House, 2002.

Burkhardt, George S. *Confederate Rage, Yankee Wrath: No Quarter in the Civil War*. Carbondale: Southern Illinois University Press, 2007.

Burkholder, Mark, and Lyman Johnson, eds. *Colonial Latin America*. 4th Edition. New York: Oxford University Press, 2001.

Burnard, Trevor. *Mastery, Tyranny, and Desire: Thomas Thistlewood and His Slaves in the Anglo-Jamaican World*. Chapel Hill: University of North Carolina Press, 2004.

Burns, E. Bradford. "Bibliographical Essay: Manuel Querino's Interpretation of the African Contribution to Brazil." *Journal of Negro History* 59, no. 1 (January 1974): pp. 78–86.

Burton, Art T. *Black Gun, Silver Star: The Life and Legend of Frontier Marshall Bass Reeves*. Lincoln: University of Nebraska Press, 2006.

Bush, Barbara. *Slave Women in Caribbean Society, 1650–1838*. Bloomington: Indiana University Press, 1990.

Bush, M. L. *Servitude in Modern Times*. Malden: Blackwell Publishers, 2000.

Butler, Kim. "From Black History to Diasporan History: Brazilian Abolition in Afro-Atlantic Context." *African Studies Review* 43, no. 1 (April 2000): pp. 125–139.

Butler, Kim. *Freedoms Given, Freedoms Won: Afro-Brazilians in Post-Abolition Sao Paulo and Salvador*. New Brunswick: Rutgers University Press, 1998.

Byrd, W. Michael, and Linda A. Clayton. *An American Health Dilemma: A Medical History of African Americans and the Problems of Race, Beginnings to 1900*. New York: Routledge, 2000.

Candlin, Kit. *The Last Caribbean Frontier, 1795–1815*. New York: Palgrave Macmillian, 2012.

Cañizares-Esguerra, Jorge, Matt D. Childs, and James Sidbury, eds. *The Black Urban Atlantic in the Age of the Slave Trade*. Philadelphia: University of Pennsylvania Press, 2013.

Canny, Nicholas, and Anthony Padgen. *Colonial Identity in the Atlantic World, 1500–1800*. Princeton: Princeton University Press, 1987.

Campbell, Mavis C. *The Maroons of Jamaica, 1655–1796: A History of Collaboration, Resistance, and Betrayal*. Trenton: Africa World Press, 1990.

Caravantes, Peggy. *The Many Faces of Josephine Baker: Dancer, Singer, Activist, Spy*. Chicago: Chicago Review Press, 2015.

Carrera, Magali M. *Imagining Identity in New Spain: Race, Lineage, and the Colonial Body in Portraiture and Casta Paintings*. Austin: University of Texas Press, 2003.

Carretta, Vincent. *Phillis Wheatley: Biography of a Genius in Bondage*. Athens: University of Georgia Press, 2011.

Carretta, Vincent, and Philip Gould, eds. *Genius in Bondage: Literature of the Early Black Atlantic*. Lexington: University Press of Kentucky, 2001.

Carroll, John M., ed. *The Black Military Experience in the American West*. New York: Liveright Publishing, 1973.

Carroll, Patrick J. *Blacks in Colonial Veracruz: Race, Ethnicity, and Regional Development*. Austin: University of Texas Press, 1991.

Castillo, Elvia Duque. *Aportes del Pueblo Afrodescendiente: La Historia Oculta de América Latina*. Bloomington: iUniverse, 2013.

Chasteen, John. *Born in Blood and Fire: A Concise History of Latin America*. New York: W. W. Norton, 2001.

Childs, Matt D. *The 1812 Aponte Rebellion and the Struggle Against Atlantic Slavery*. Chapel Hill: University of North Carolina Press, 2006.

Chinea, Jorge L. "Race, Colonial Exploitation and West Indian Immigration in Nineteenth-Century Puerto Rico, 1800–1850." *The Americas* 52, no. 4 (April 1996): pp. 495–519.

Chisholm, Hugh, ed. *The Encyclopaedia Britannica*. Eleventh Edition, Volume 28. New York: The Encyclopaedia Britannica Company, 1911.

Christopher, Michael C. "Granville T. Woods: The Plight of a Black Inventor." *Journal of Black Studies* (March 1981): pp. 269–276.

Ciment, James, and John Radzilowski. *American Immigration: An Encyclopedia of Political, Social, and Cultural Change*. New York: Routledge, 2015.

Clark, Emily. *The Strange History of the American Quadroon: Free Women of Color in the Revolutionary Atlantic World*. Chapel Hill: University of North Carolina Press, 2013.

Clinton, Catherine. *The Black Soldier: 1492 to the Present*. New York: Houghton Mifflin, 2000.

Cobb, Martha. *Harlem, Haiti, and Havana: A Comparative Critical Study of Langston Hughes, Jacques Roumain, and Nicholas Guillen*. Washington, D.C.: Three Continents Press, 1978.

Coffman, D'Maris, Adrian Leonard, and William O' Reilly. *The Atlantic World*. New York: Routledge, 2015.

Cohen, David W., and Jack P. Greens, eds. *Neither Slave Nor Free: The Freedmen of African Descent in the Slave Societies of the New World*. Baltimore: Johns Hopkins University Press, 1972.

Collins, Patricia Hill. *Black Feminist Thought: Knowledge, Consciousness, and the Politics of Empowerment*. London: Harper Collins Academic, 1990.

Collison, Gary Lee. *Shadrach Minkins: From Fugitive Slave to Citizen*. Cambridge: Harvard University Press, 1998.

Conniff, Michael L., and Thomas J. Davis, eds. *Africans in the Americas: A History of the Black Diaspora*. Caldwell: Blackburn Press, 1994.

Conrad, Robert Edgar. *The Destruction of Brazilian Slavery, 1850–1888*. Berkeley: University of California Press, 1972.

Controvich, James T. *African Americans in Defense of the Nation: A Bibliography*. Lanham: Scarecrow Press, 2011.

Cooper, Frederick, Thomas C. Holt, and Rebecca Scott. *Beyond Slavery: Explorations of Race, Labor, and Citizenship in Postemancipation Societies*. Chapel Hill: University of North Carolina Press, 2000.

Cooper, Valerie C. *Word Like Fire: Maria Stewart, the Bible, and the Rights of African Americans*. Charlottesville: University of Virginia Press, 2011.

Cope, Douglas R. *The Limits of Racial Domination: Plebeian Society in Colonial Mexico City, 1660–1720*. Madison: University of Wisconsin Press, 1994.

Coppege, Michael. *Strong Parties and Lame Ducks: Presidential Patriarchy and Factionalism in Venezuela*. Stanford: Stanford University Press, 1994.

Coppin, Fanny Jackson. *Reminiscences of School Life and Hints on Teaching*. Nabu Press, 2012 [Philadephia: A.M.E. Book Concern, 1913].

Cordingly, David. *Under the Black Flag: The Romance and Reality of Life Among the Pirates*. New York: Harcourt, 1995.

Cornish, Dudley Taylor. *The Sable Arm: Negro Troops in the Union Army, 1861–1865.* New York: Longmans, Green, and Co., 1956.

Costello, Ray. *Black Salt: Seafarers of African Descent on British Ships.* Liverpool: Liverpool University Press, 2012.

Cottrol, Robert. "The Long Lingering Shadow: Law, Liberalism, and Cultures of Racial Hierarchy and Identity in the Americas." *Tulane Law Review* 76, no. 1 (2001): pp. 11–79.

Cottrol, Robert, ed. *From African to Yankee: Narratives of Slavery and Freedom in Antebellum New England.* Armonk: M.E. Sharpe, 1998.

Cox, Edward L. "Fedon's Rebellion 1795–96: Causes and Consequences." *Journal of Negro History* 67, no. 1 (Spring 1982): pp. 7–19.

Craton, Michael. *Testing the Chains: Resistance to Slavery in the British West Indies.* Ithaca: Cornell University Press, 2009 [1982].

Criales Alcazar, Hernan. *Un Heroe Negro en la Guerra del Chaco.* La Paz: Honorable Alcaldia Municipal de La Paz, 1991.

Curtin, Philip. "The Tropical Atlantic in the Age of the Slave Trade." Washington D.C.: The American Historical Association, 1990.

Curtin, Philip D. *The Rise and Fall of the Plantation Complex: Essays in Atlantic History.* New York: Cambridge University Press, 1989.

Dallas, Robert C. *The History of the Maroons from Their Origin to the Establishment of Their Chief Tribe at Sierra Leone.* Vols. 1 & 2. London: Longman and Rees, 1803.

Davis, Darien J., ed. *Beyond Slavery: The Multilayered Legacy of Africans in Latin America and the Caribbean.* Lanham: Rowman & Littlefield, 2007.

Davis, Darien J., ed. *Slavery and Beyond: The African Impact on Latin America and the Caribbean.* Wilmington: Scholarly Resources Inc., 1995.

Davis, David Brion. *The Problem of Slavery in the Age of Revolution, 1770–1823.* Ithaca: Cornell University Press, 1975.

Davis, Robert C. *Christian Slaves, Muslim Masters: White Slavery in the Mediterranean, The Barbary Coast, and Italy, 1500–1800.* New York: Palgrave Macmillan, 2003.

Da Costa, Emilia Viotti. *Crowns of Glory, Tears of Blood: The Demerara Slave Rebellion of 1823.* New York: Oxford University Press, 1994.

Davies, Carole Boyce. *Encyclopedia of the African Diaspora.* Santa Barbara: ABC-CLIO, 2008.

Day, Thomas Robert. "Jamaican Revolts in British Press and Politics, 1760–1865." M.S. Thesis, Virginia Commonwealth University (2016).

De la Fuente, Alejandro. *Havana and the Atlantic in the Sixteenth Century.* Chapel Hill: University of North Carolina Press, 2008.

De la Fuente, Alejandro. "Slaves and the Creation of Legal Rights in Cuba: Coartacion y Papel." *Hispanic American Historical Review* 87, no. 4 (2007): pp. 659–692.

De la Fuente, Alejandro. "Slave Law and Claims-Making in Cuba: The Tannenbaum Debate Revisited." *Law and History Review* 22, no. 2 (Summer 2004): pp. 340–369.

De la Fuente, Alejandro. *A Nation for All: Inequality, Race, and Politics in Twentieth-Century Cuba*. Chapel Hill: University of North Carolina Press, 2000.

De la Fuente, Alejandro. "Race, National Discourse, and Politics in Cuba." *Latin American Perspectives* 25, no. 3 (May 1998): pp. 43–69.

De la Roche, Roberta Senechal. *In Lincoln's Shadow: The 1908 Race Riot in Springfield, Illinois*. Carbondale: Southern Illinois University Press, 1990.

D'Emilio, John. *Lost Prophet: The Life and Times of Bayard Rustin*. Chicago: University of Chicago Press, 2003.

Dearinger, Ryan. "Interracial Roads to American Freedom." *Common-Place: The Journal of Early American Life* 16, no. 1 (Fall 2015).

Díaz, Maria Elena. *The Virgin, the King, and the Royal Slaves of El Cobre: Negotiating Freedom in Colonial Cuba, 1670–1780*. Stanford: Stanford University Press, 2000.

Diggs, Irene. "Color in Colonial Spanish America." *The Journal of Negro History* 38, no. 4 (October 1953): pp. 403–427.

Dinerstein, Joel. *Swinging the Machine: Modernity, Technology, and African-American Culture Between the World Wars*. Amherst: University of Massachusetts Press, 2003.

Doiuf, Sylvaine A. *Slavery's Exiles: The Story of the American Maroons*. New York: New York University Press, 2014.

Dixon, Anthony. "Black Seminole Involvement and Leadership during the Second Seminole War, 1835–1842." Doctoral Dissertation, Indiana University (2007).

Dodson, Howard. *Becoming American: The African-American Journey*. New York: Sterling, 2009.

Dodson, Howard, and Colin Palmer, eds. *Ideology, Identity, and Assumptions*. East Lansing: Michigan State University Press, 2007.

Dorsey, Jennifer Hull. "A Documentary History of African American Freedom: An Introduction to the Race, Slavery, and Free Blacks Microfilm Collection." *Slavery & Abolition* 30, no. 4 (December 2009): pp. 545–563.

Dorr, Gregory Michael. *Segregation's Science: Eugenics and Society in Virginia*. Charlottesville: University of Virginia Press, 2008.

Douglas, Ann. *Terrible Honesty: Mongrel Manhattan in the 1920s*. New York: Noonday Press, 1995.

Dray, Phillip. *Capitol Men: The Epic Story of Reconstruction Through the Lives of the First Black Congressmen*. New York: Mariner, 2010.

Dray, Philip. *At the Hands of Persons Unknown: The Lynching of Black America*. New York: Random House, 2002.

Drescher, Seymour. *From Slavery to Freedom: Comparative Studies in the Rise and Fall of Atlantic Slavery*. London: Macmillan Press, 1999.

Drescher, Seymour. *Capitalism and Antislavery*. Oxford: Oxford University Press, 1987.

Dubois, Laurent, and Julius S. Scott, eds. *Origins of the Black Atlantic*. New York: Routledge, 2010.

Dubois, Laurent. *Avengers of the New World: The Story of the Haitian Revolution.* Cambridge: Belknap Press of Harvard University Press, 2004.

Dubois, Laurent. *A Colony of Citizens: Revolution and Emancipation in the French Caribbean, 1787–1804.* Chapel Hill: University of North Carolina Press, 2004.

Du Bois, W. E. B. *The Suppression of the African Slave-Trade to the United States of America, 1638–1870.* Minneapolis: Fili-Quarian Classics, 2010 [1896].

Duhl, Olga Anna, and Diane Windham Shaw. *"A True Friend of the Cause:" Lafayette and the Antislavery Movement.* New York: The Grolier Club and Lafayette College, 2016.

Dunn, Marvin. *Black Miami in the Twentieth Century.* Gainesville: University Press of Florida, 1997.

Dunn, Richard S. *Sugar and Slaves: The Rise of the Planter Class in the English West Indies, 1624–1713.* Chapel Hill: University of North Carolina Press, 2000 [1972].

Dutras, Francis A. "A Hard Fought Struggle for Recognition: Manuel Gonçalves Doria, The First Afro-Brazilian to Become a Knight of Santiago." *The Americas* 56, no. 1 (July 1999): pp. 91–113.

Earle, T. F., and K. J. P. Lowe, eds. *Black Africans in Renaissance Europe.* New York: Cambridge University Press, 2005.

Edward, Paul, and James Walvin. *Black Personalities in the Era of the Slave Trade.* Baton Rouge: Louisiana State University Press, 1983.

Edwards, Paul, and David Dabydeen, eds. *Black Writers in Britain, 1760–1890: An Anthology.* Edinburg: Edinburg University Press, 1995.

Egan, Pierce. *Boxiana: Or Sketches of Ancient and Modern Pugilism From the Days of the Renowned Broughton and Slack to the Championship of Cribb.* Volume 1. Elibron Classics, 2006 [1830].

Egerton, Douglas R. *Death or Liberty: African Americans and Revolutionary America.* New York: Oxford University Press, 2009.

Egerton, Douglas R. *He Shall Go Out Free: The Lives of Denmark Vesey.* Lanham: Rowman & Littlefield, 2004.

Egerton, Douglas R. *Gabriel's Rebellion: The Virginia Slave Conspiracies of 1800 and 1802.* Chapel Hill: University of North Carolina Press, 1993.

Ehret, Christopher. *Sudanic Civilization.* Washington, D.C.: American Historical Association, 2003.

Ellis, Major A. B. *The History of the First West India Regiment.* Crystal Palace Press, 1885.

Eltis, David. *The Rise of African Slavery in the Americas.* Cambridge: Cambridge University Press, 2000.

Equiano, Oluadah. *The Interesting Narrative of the Life of Olaudah Equiano, Gustavus Vassa, The African.* Simon and Brown, 2012 [1789].

Esquemeling, John. *The Buccaneers of America.* New York: Dover, 1967 [1893].

Esguerra, Jorge Canizares. *How to Write the History of the New World: Histories,*

Epistemologies, and Identities in the Eighteenth-Century Atlantic World. Stanford: Stanford University Press, 2001.

Ewing, Adam. *The Age of Garvey: How a Jamaican Activist Created a Mass Movement and Changed Global Black Politics*. Princeton: Princeton University Press, 2014.

Fanon, Franz. *Black Skins, White Masks*. New York: Grove Press, 1967.

Feldman, Heidi Carolyn. *Black Rhythms of Peru: Reviving Musical Heritage in the Black Pacific*. Middletown: Wesleyan University Press, 2006.

Fergus, Claudius K. *Revolutionary Emancipation: Slavery and Abolition in the British West Indies*. Baton Rouge: Louisiana State University Press, 2013.

Ferrer, Ada. *Freedom's Mirror: Cuba and Haiti in the Age of Revolution*. New York: Cambridge University Press, 2014.

Ferrer, Ada. *Insurgent Cuba: Race, Nation, and Revolution, 1868–1898*. Chapel Hill: University of North Carolina Press, 1999.

Fiehrer, Thomas. "Slaves and Freedmen in Colonial Central America: Rediscovering a Forgotten Black Past." *The Journal of Negro History* 64, no. 1 (Winter 1979): pp. 39–57.

Fields, Barbara J. "Ideology and Race in American History." *Race, Region, and Reconstruction: Essays in Honor of C. Vann Woodward*. J.M. Kousser and J.M. McPherson, eds. New York: Oxford University Press, 1982.

Fleishchner, Jennifer. *Mrs. Lincoln and Mrs. Keckly: The Remarkable Story of the Friendship Between a First Lady and a Former Slave*. New York: Broadway Books, 2003.

Finch, Aisha K. *Rethinking Slave Rebellion in Cuba: La Escalera and the Insurgencies of 1841–1844*. Chapel Hill: University of North Carolina Press, 2015.

Finkelman, Paul, ed. *Encyclopedia of American Civil Liberties*. New York: Routledge, 2006.

Fischer, Sibylle. *Modernity Disavowed: Haiti and the Culture of Slavery in the Age of Revolution*. Durham: Duke University Press, 2004.

Fluehr-Lobban, Carolyn. "Anténor Firmin: Haitian Pioneer of Anthropology." *American Anthropologist* 102, no. 2 (September 2000): pp. 449–466.

Foner, Eric. *Gateway to Freedom: The Hidden History of the Underground Rail Road*. New York: W. W. Norton, 2015.

Foner, Eric. *The Fiery Trial: Abraham Lincoln and American Slavery*. New York: W. W. Norton, 2010.

Foner, Laura, and Eugene D. Genovese. *Slavery in the New World: A Reader in Comparative History*. Englewood Cliffs: Prentice-Hall Inc., 1969.

Foner, Philip S. *Antonio Maceo: The "Bronze Titan" of Cuba's Struggle for Independence*. New York: Monthly Review Press, 1977.

Forbes, Ella. *African American Women During the Civil War*. New York: Garland Publishing Inc., 1998.

Fouché, Rayvon. *Black Inventors in the Age of Segregation: Granville T. Woods, Lewis Latimer, and Shelby Davidson*. Baltimore: Johns Hopkins University Press, 2005.

Fradin, Denis and Judith. *Fight On! Mary Church Terrell's Battle for Integration*. New York: Clarion Books, 2003.

Franklin, John Hope. *From Slavery to Freedom: A History of African Americans*. New York: Knopf, 2000 [1947].

Franklin, John Hope. *The Free Negro in North Carolina, 1790–1860*. Chapel Hill: University of North Carolina Press, 1943.

Fredrickson, George M. *White Supremacy: A Comparative Study in American and South African History*. New York: Oxford University Press, 1981.

Frost, Karolyn Smardz. *I've Got a Home in Glory Land: A Lost Tale of the Underground Railroad*. New York: Farrar, Straus, and Giroux, 2007.

Furtado, Júnia Ferreira. *Chica da Silva: A Brazilian Slave of the Eighteenth Century*. New York: Cambridge University Press, 2009.

Gallay, Alan. *The Indian Slave Trade: The Rise of the English Empire in the American South, 1670–1717*. New Haven: Yale University Press, 2002.

Gaspar, David Barry, and Darlene Clark Hine. *Beyond Bondage: Free Women of Color in the Americas*. Chicago: University of Illinois Press, 2004.

Gaspar, David Barry, and Darlene Clark Hine. *More Than Chattel: Black Women and Slavery in the Americas*. Bloomington: University of Indiana Press, 1996.

Gates, Henry Louis, Jr., and Donald Yacovone. *The African Americans: Many Rivers to Cross*. Carlsbad: Smiley Books, 2013.

Gates, Henry Louis, Jr. *Black in Latin America*. New York: New York University Press, 2011.

Gates, Henry Louis, Jr. *Upon These Shores: Looking at African American History, 1513–2008*. New York: Knopf, 2011.

Gates, Henry Louis, Jr., and Evelyn Brooks Higgenbotham, eds. *African American National Biography*. New York: Oxford University Press, 2006.

Gates, Henry Louis, Jr., and Evelyn Brooks Higginbotham, eds. *African American Lives*. New York: Oxford University Press, 2004.

Gates, Henry Louis, Jr. *The Trials of Phillis Wheatley: America's First Black Poet and Her Encounters with the Founding Fathers*. New York: Basic Civitas Books, 2003.

Gates, Henry Louis, and Maria Wolff. "An Overview of the Sources on the Life and World of Juan Latino, the 'Ethiopian Humanist.'" *Research in African Literatures* 29, no. 4 (Winter 1998): pp. 14–51.

Garrigus, John. *Before Haiti: Race and Citizenship in French Saint-Domingue*. New York: Palgrave MacMillan, 2006.

Garrigus, John. "Catalyst or Catastrophe? Saint-Domingue's Free Men of Color and the Battle of Savannah, 1779–1782." *Revista/Review Interamericana* 22, no. 1–2 (1992): pp. 109–125.

Gaspar, David Barry, and David Patrick Geggus, eds. *A Turbulent Time: The French Revolution and the Greater Caribbean*. Bloomington: Indiana University Press, 1997.

Geggus, David, and Norman Fiering, eds. *The World of the Haitian Revolution.* Bloomington: Indiana University Press, 2009.

Geggus, David, ed. *The Impact of the Haitian Revolution in the Atlantic World.* Columbia: University of South Carolina Press, 2001.

Gelderman, Carol. *A Free Man of Color and His Hotel: Race, Reconstruction, and the Role of the Federal Government.* Dulles: Potomac Books, 2012.

Gerhard, Peter. "A Black Conquistador in Mexico." *Hispanic America Historical Review* 58, no. 3 (1971): pp. 451–459.

Gerzina, Gretchen Holbrook. *Mr. and Mrs. Prince: How an Extraordinary Eighteenth-Century Family Moved Out of Slavery and Into Legend.* New York: Amistad HarperCollins, 2008.

Gilbert, Alan. *Black Patriots and Loyalists: Fighting for Emancipation in the War for Independence.* Chicago: University of Chicago Press, 2012.

Gilmore, Glenda Elizabeth. "At Yale, a Right That Doesn't Outweigh a Wrong." *New York Times* (April 29, 2016).

Gilmore, Glenda Elizabeth. *Defying Dixie: The Radical Roots of Civil Rights, 1919–1950.* New York: W. W. Norton, 2009.

Gilroy, Paul. *The Black Atlantic: Modernity and Double Consciousness.* Cambridge: Harvard University Press, 1993.

Girard, Philippe. *The Slaves Who Defeated Napoleon: Toussaint Louverture and the Haitian War of Independence.* Tuscaloosa: University of Alabama Press, 2011.

Glasrud, Bruce A. *African American History in New Mexico: Portraits from Five Hundred Years.* Albuquerque: University of New Mexico Press, 2013.

Glasrud, Bruce A., and Michael N. Searles, eds. *Buffalo Soldiers in the West: A Black Soldiers Anthology.* College Station: Texas A&M University Press, 2007.

Gomez, Michael. *Reversing Sail: A History of the African Diaspora.* Cambridge: Cambridge University Press, 2004.

Gordon, John D. *The Fugitive Slave Rescue Trial of Robert Morris.* Clark: Talbot Publishing, 2013.

Gould, William B., IV. *Diary of a Contraband: The Civil War Passage of a Black Sailor.* Stanford: Stanford University Press, 2002.

Graden, Dale Torston. *From Slavery to Freedom in Brazil: Bahia 1835–1900.* Albuquerque: University of New Mexico Press, 2006.

Graham, Richard, ed. *The Idea of Race in Latin America, 1870–1940.* Austin: University of Texas Press, 1990.

Greene, Robert Ewell. *Black Defenders of America, 1775–1973: A Reference and Pictorial History.* Chicago: Johnson Publishing Company, 1974.

Greenburg, Kenneth S., ed. *Nat Turner: A Slave Rebellion in American History and Memory.* New York: Oxford, 2003.

Greenly, Larry. *Eugene Bullard: World's First Black Fighter Pilot.* Montgomery: NewSouth Books, 2013.

Griffin, Judith Berry. *Phoebe the Spy.* New York: Puffin Books, 1977.

Gross, Ariela, and Alejandro de la Fuente. "Slaves, Free Blacks, and Race in the Legal Regimes of Cuba, Louisiana, and Virginia: A Comparison." *North Carolina Law Review* 5 (2013): pp. 1700–1756.

Guasco, Michael. *Slaves and Englishmen: Human Bondage in the Early Atlantic World.* Philadelphia: University of Pennsylvania Press, 2014.

Gudmundson, Lowell, and Justin Wolfe. *Blacks and Blackness in Central America: Between Race and Place.* Durham: Duke University Press, 2010.

Guridy, Frank Andre. *Forging Diaspora: Afro-Cubans and African Americans in a World of Empire and Jim Crow.* Chapel Hill: University of North Carolina Press, 2010.

Haber, Louis. *Black Pioneers of Science and Invention.* New York: Harcourt Inc., 1992 [1970].

Hall, Carl W. *A Biographical Dictionary of People in Engineering.* West Lafayette: Purdue University Press, 2008.

Hall, Gwendolyn Midlo. *Slavery and African Ethnicities in the Americas: Restoring the Links.* Chapel Hill: University of North Carolina Press, 2005.

Hall, Gwendolyn Midlo. "The 1795 Slave Conspiracy in Pointe Coupée: Impact of the French Revolution." *Proceedings of the Meeting of the French Colonial Historical Society* 15 (1992): pp. 130–141.

Hall, Gwendolyn Midlo. *Social Control in Slave Plantation Societies: A Comparison of St. Domingue and Cuba.* Baton Rouge: Louisiana State University Press, 1971.

Hall, N. A. T. "The 1816 Freedman Petition in the Danish West Indies: Its Background and Consequences." *Boletín de Estudios Latinoamericanos y del Caribe* 29 (December 1980): pp. 55–73.

Hall, Stephen G. "A Search for Truth: Jacob Oson and the Beginnings of African American Historiography." *William and Mary Quarterly* 64, no. 1 (January 2007): pp. 139–148.

Handler, Jerome. "The Barbados Slave Insurrection of 1816: Can It Properly Be Called 'Bussa's Rebellion?'" *Sunday Advocate* (March 26, 2000).

Harman, Anastasia, Natalie D. Cottrill, Paul C. Reed, and Joseph Shumway. "Documenting President Barack Obama's Maternal African-American Ancestry: Tracing His Mother's Bunch Ancestry to the First Slave in America." *Ancestry.com* (July 15, 2012): pp. 1–45.

Harris, C. L. G. *The Chieftainess: Glimpses of Grandy Nanny.* Huntsville: Publishing Designs, 2009.

Harris, David M. "David Jones Peck, M.D.: A Dream Denied." *Journal of the National Medical Association* 102, no. 10 (October 2010): pp. 954–955.

Harris, Marvin. *Patterns of Race in the Americas.* New York: W. W. Norton, 1964.

Harte, Walter. *Sir Francis Drake.* New York: MacMillan, 1920.

Heinegg, Paul. *Free African Americans of North Carolina, Virginia, and South Carolina, From the Colonial Period to about 1820, Volume I.* Baltimore: Clearfield, 2005.

Helg, Aline. *Liberty and Equality in Caribbean Colombia, 1770–1835.* Chapel Hill: University of North Carolina Press, 2004.

Helg, Aline. "Simón Bolívar and the Spectre of *Pardocracia*: Jose Padilla in Post-Independence Colombia." *Journal of Latin American Studies* 35, no. 3 (August 2003): pp. 447–471.

Helg, Aline. "Race and Black Mobilization in Early Independent Cuba: A Comparative Perspective." *Ethnohistory* 44, no. 1 (Winter 1997): pp. 53–74.

Helg, Aline. *Our Rightful Share: The Afro-Cuban Struggle or Equality 1886–1912*. Chapel Hill: University of North Carolina Press, 1995.

Helg, Aline. "Race in Argentina and Cuba, 1880–1930." *The Idea of Race in Latin America, 1870–1940*. Richard Graham, ed. Austin: University of Texas Press, 1990.

Henderson, James D. "Mariana Grajales: Black Progenitress of Cuban Independence." *Journal of Negro History* 63, no. 2 (April 1978): pp. 135–148.

Hendrick, George and Willene. *The Creole Mutiny: A Tale of Revolt Aboard a Slave Ship*. Chicago: Ivan R. Dee, 2003.

Hening, William. *The Statutes at Large: Being a Collection of All the Laws of Virginia*. New York: Barlow, 1823.

Herrera, Robinson A. "'Por Que No Sabemos Firmar:' Black Slaves in Early Guatemala." *The Americas* 57, no. 2 (October 2000): pp. 247–267.

Hervieux, Linda. *Forgotten: The Untold Story of D-Day's Black Heroes, At Home and at War*. New York: Harper Collins, 2015.

Herzog, Tamar. *Defining Nations: Immigrants and Citizens in Early Modern Spain and Spanish America*. New Haven: Yale University Press, 2003.

Heywood, Linda, and John K. Thornton. *Central Africans, Atlantic Creoles, and the Foundation of the Americas*. Cambridge: Cambridge University Press, 2007.

Heywood, Linda M., ed. *Central Africans and Cultural Transformation in the American Diaspora*. New York: Cambridge University Press, 2002.

Higman, B. W. "The Sugar Revolution." *Economic History Review* LIII, no. 2 (2000): pp. 213–236.

Hine, Darlene Clark, William C. Hine, and Stanley Harrold. *The African-American Odyssey*. Upper Saddle River: Prentice Hall, 2011.

Hine, Darlene Clark, and Earnestine Jenkins, eds. *A Question of Manhood: A Reader in U.S. Black Man's History and Masculinity*. Volume 1. Bloomington: Indiana University Press, 1999.

Hoberman, Louisa, and Susan Soclow, eds. *Cities and Societies in Colonial Latin America*. Albuquerque: University of New Mexico Press, 1986.

Hodges, Graham. *David Ruggles: A Radical Black Abolitionist and the Underground Railroad in New York City*. Chapel Hill: University of North Carolina Press, 2010.

Hodges, Graham. *Root and Branch: African Americans in New York and East Jersey, 1613–1863*. Chapel Hill: University of North Carolina Press, 1999.

Hogan, Wesley. *Many Minds, One Heart: SNCC's Dream for a New America*. Chapel Hill: University of North Carolina Press, 2009.

Hollandsworth, James Jr. *An Absolute Massacre: The New Orleans Race Riot of July 30, 1866*. Baton Rouge: Louisiana State University Press, 2001.

Hollandsworth, James Jr. *The Louisiana Native Guards: The Black Military Experience During the Civil War*. Baton Rouge: Louisiana State University Press, 1995.

Holloway, Joseph E. *A History of Slave Resistance in the United States*. Porter Ranch: The New World African Press, 2016.

Honeck, Mischa, Martin Klimke, and Anne Kuhlman, eds. *Germany and the Black Diaspora*. New York: Berghahn Books, 2013.

Hotaling, Edward. *The Great Black Jockeys: The Lives and Times of the Men who Dominated America's First National Sport*. Roseville: Prima Lifestyles, 1999.

Hothschild, Adam. "Human Cargo." *New York Times* (March 4, 2001).

Horne, Aaron. *Brass Music of Black Composers: A Bibliography*. Westport: Greenwood Publishing Group, 1996.

Horne, Gerald. *The Counter Revolution of 1776: Slave Resistance and the Origins of the United States of America*. New York: New York University Press, 2014.

Horne, Gerald. *Black and Brown: African Americans and the Mexican Revolution, 1910–1920*. New York: New York University Press, 2005.

Howard, Philip. *Changing History: Afro-Cuban Cabildos and Societies of Color in the Nineteenth Century*. Baton Rouge: Louisiana State University Press, 1988.

Howard, Rosalyn. *Black Seminoles in the Bahamas*. Gainesville: Florida University Press, 2002.

Hudson, Lynn. *The Making of Mammy Pleasant: Black Entrepreneur in Nineteenth Century San Francisco*. Urbana: University of Illinois Press, 2003.

Imrie, Robert. "Discovery in Mexico Gives Clue to Slavery's Start in New World: Researchers Finds Remains of Slaves in Old Graveyard." *Associated Press* (January 31, 2006).

Ivory, Annette. "Juan Latino: The Struggle of Blacks, Jews, and Moors in Golden Age Spain." *Hispania* 62, no. 4 (December 1979): pp. 613–618.

Jackson, Andrew. *The Papers of Andrew Jackson, Volume IV, 1816–1820*. Harold Moser, David Hoth, and George Hoemann, eds. Knoxville: University of Tennessee Press, 1994.

Jackson, Luther P. "Virginia Negro Soldiers and Seamen in the American Revolution." *Journal of Negro History* XXVII, no. 3 (July 1942): pp. 247–287.

Jackson, Luther P. "Free Negroes of Petersburg." *Journal of Negro History* 12, no. 3 (July 1927): pp. 365–388.

Jackson, Maurice, and Jacqueline Bacon. *African Americans and the Haitian Revolution: Selected Essays and Historical Documents*. New York: Routledge, 2010.

James, C. L. R. *The Black Jacobins: Toussaint L'Ouverture and the San Domingo Revolution*. New York: Random House, 1963 [1938].

Johnson, James Hugo. *Race Relations in Colonial Virginia and Miscegenation in the South*. Amherst: University of Massachusetts Press, 1970.

Johnson, Robert Lee. *Notable Southern Californians in Black History*. Charleston: The History Press, 2017.

Johnson, Robert. "Black-White Relations on Nantucket." *Historic Nantucket* 51, no. 2 (Spring 2005).

Johnson, Sarah E. *The Fear of French Negroes: Transcolonial Collaboration in the Revolutionary Atlantic*. Los Angeles: University of California at Los Angeles Press, 2012.

Johnston, James H. *From Slave Ship to Harvard: Yarrow Mamout and the History of An African American Family*. New York: Fordham University Press, 2012.

Jones, James H. *Bad Blood: The Tuskegee Syphilis Experiment*. New York: Free Press, 1993.

Jones, A. Keith. *A View to Masonic Education: The Blue House Lodge*. Bloomington: AuthorHouse, 2010.

Jones, George Fenwick. "The Black Hessians: Negroes Recruited by the Hessians in South Carolina and Other Colonies." *South Carolina Historical Magazine* 83, no. 4 (October 1982): pp. 287–302.

Jones, Howard. *Mutiny on the Amistad*. Oxford: Oxford University Press, 1987.

Jordan, Winthrop. *White Over Black: American Attitudes Toward the Negro, 1550–1812*. Chapel Hill: University of North Carolina Press, 1968.

Jouve Martín, José R. *The Black Doctors of Colonial Lima: Science, Race, and Writing in Colonial Peru*. Montreal: McGill-Queen's University Press, 2014.

Kantrowitz, Stephen. *More Than Freedom: Fighting for Black Citizenship in a White Republic, 1829–1889*. New York: Penguin, 2012.

Kaminer, Ariel. "Discovery Leads Yale to Revise a Chapter of Its Black History." *The New York Times* (February 28, 2014).

Kaplan, M., and A. R. Henderson. "Solomon Carter Fuller, M.D. (1872–1953): American Pioneer in Alzheimer's Disease Research." *Journal of the History of the Neurosciences* 9, no 3 (2000): pp. 250–261.

Kaplan, Sydney. *American Studies in Black and White, Selected Essays, 1949–1989*. Amherst: University of Massachusetts Press, 1991.

Kaplan, Sidney, and Emma Nogrady Kaplan. *The Black Presence in the Era of the American Revolution*. Amherst: University of Massachusetts Press, 1989.

Karttunen, Frances Ruley. *Law and Disorder on Old Nantucket*. Nantucket: Nantucket Press, 2007.

Karttunen, Frances Ruley. *The Other Islanders: People Who Pulled Nantucket's Oars*. New Bedford: Spinner Publications, 2005.

Katz, Frederick, ed. *Riot, Rebellion, and Revolution: Rural Social Conflict in Mexico*. Princeton: Princeton University Press, 1988.

Keita, Maghan. "Deconstructing the Classical Age: Africa and the Unity of the Mediterranean World." *The Journal of Negro History* 72, no. 2 (Spring 1994): pp. 147–166.

Kelley, Robin D. G. *Freedom Dreams: The Black Radical Imagination*. Boston: Beacon Press, 2002.

Kelley, Robin D. G. "'But a Local Phase of a World Problem:' Black History's Global Vision, 1883–1950." *Journal of American History* 86, no. 3 (December 1999): pp. 1045–1077.

Kendrick, Steven, and Paul Kendrick. *Sarah's Long Walk: The Free Blacks of Boston and How Their Struggle for Equality Changed America*. Boston: Beacon Press, 2004.

Kennedy, James H. "Luiz Gama: Pioneer of Abolition in Brazil." *Journal of Negro History* 59, no. 3 (July 1974): pp. 255–267.

Kent, R. K. "An African State in Brazil." *Journal of African History* 6, no. 2 (1965): pp. 161–175.

King, Lovalerie, and Richard Schur, eds. *African American Culture and Legal Discourse*. New York: Palgrave Macmillan, 2009.

King, Stewart. *Blue Coat or Powdered Wig: Free People of Color in Pre-revolutionary Saint Domingue*, Athens: University of Georgia Press, 2001.

Klein, Herbert S., and Ben Vinson III. *African Slavery in Latin America and the Caribbean*. Second Edition. New York: Oxford University Press, 2007.

Klein, Herbert S. *African Slavery in Latin America and the Caribbean*. New York: Oxford University Press, 1986.

Klein, Herbert S. *Slavery in the Americas: A Comparative Study of Virginia and Cuba*. Chicago: University of Chicago Press, 1967.

Klooster, Wim, and Gert Ostindie, eds. *Curaçao in the Age of Revolutions, 1795–1800*. Leiden: KITLV Press, 2011.

Knight, Franklin, ed. *General History of the Caribbean, Volume III*. London: UNESCO Publishing/Macmillan Education, 1977.

Knight, Franklin W. *The African Dimension in Latin American Societies*. New York: MacMillan, 1974.

Knoblock, Glenn A. *African American Historic Burial Grounds and Gravesites in New England*. Jefferson: McFarland Publishers, 2016.

Kurlansky, Mark. *The Big Oyster: History on the Half Shell*. New York: Random House, 2007.

Landers, Jane. *Atlantic Creoles in the Age of Revolutions*. Cambridge: Harvard University Press, 2010.

Landers, Jane, and Barry Robinson, eds. *Slaves, Subjects, and Subversives: Black in Colonial Latin America*. Albuquerque: University of New Mexico, 2006.

Landers, Jane. *Black Society in Spanish Florida*. Champaign: University of Illinois Press, 1999.

Landers, Jane, ed. *Against the Odds: Free Blacks in the Slave Societies of the Americas*. London: Frank Cass, 1996.

Lanning, Michael Lee. *The African American Soldier*. New York: Citadel Press, 2004 [1997].

Lanning, Michael Lee. *African Americans in the Revolutionary War*. New York: Citadel Press, 2000.

Lasso, Marixa. *Myths of Harmony: Race and Republicanism during the Age of Revolution, Colombia, 1795–1831*. Pittsburgh: University of Pittsburgh Press, 2007.

Lasso, Marixa. "Race War and Nation in Caribbean Gran Colombia, Cartagena, 1810–1832." *American Historical Review* 111, no. 2 (April 2006): pp. 336–361.

Lee, Felicia R. "Reclaiming a Black Research Scientist's Forgotten Legacy." *New York Times* (February 6, 2007).

Lebsock, Suzanne. *The Free Women of Petersburg: Status and Culture in a Southern Town, 1784–1860*. New York: W. W. Norton, 1984.

Levine, Robert S. *Martin R. Delany: A Documentary Reader*. Chapter Hill: University of North Carolina Press, 2003.

Levy, Leonard W. "The 'Abolition Riot': Boston's First Slave Rescue." *New England Quarterly* 25, no.1 (March 1952): pp. 85–92.

Lewis, Bernard. *Race and Slavery in the Middle East: An Historical Enquiry*. New York: Oxford University Press, 1990.

Lindfors, Bernth, ed. *Ira Aldridge: The African Roscius*. Rochester: University of Rochester Press, 2007.

Linebaugh, Peter, and Marcus Rediker. *The Many-Headed Hydra: Sailors, Slaves, Commoners and the Hidden History of the Revolutionary Atlantic*. Boston: Beacon Press, 2000.

Lockhart, James. *Spanish Peru, 1532–1560: A Social History*. Madison: University of Wisconsin Press, 1994 [1968].

Lockley, Timothy James, ed. *Maroon Communities in South Carolina: A Documentary Record*. Columbia: University of South Carolina, 2009.

Logan, Rayford. "James Weldon Johnson and Haiti." *Phylon* 32, no. 4 (1971): pp. 396–402.

Lokken, Paul. "Useful Enemies: Seventeenth-Century Piracy and the Rise of Pardo Militias in Spanish Central America." *Journal of Colonialism and Colonial History* 5, no. 2 (Fall 2004).

Lokken, Paul. "Marriage as Slave Emancipation in Seventeenth Century Guatemala." *The Americas* 58, no. 2 (October 2001): pp. 175–200.

Lopez, Antonio. *Unbecoming Blackness: The Diaspora Cultures of Afro-Cuban America*. New York: NYU Press, 2012.

Lott, Eric. *Love and Theft: Blackface Minstrelsy and the American Working Class*. New York: Oxford University Press, 1993.

Love, Nat. *The Life and Adventures of Nat Love, Better Known in the Cattle Country as "Deadwood Dick," by Himself; a True History of Slavery Days, Life on the Great Cattle Ranges and on the Plains of the "Wild and Wooly" West, Based on Facts, and Personal Experiences of the Author*. Los Angeles: CA, 1907.

Love, Spencie. *One Blood: The Death and Resurrection of Charles R. Drew*. Chapel Hill: University of North Carolina Press, 1996.

Lusane, Clarence. *The Black History of the White House*. San Francisco: City Lights Books, 2011.

Lyderson, Kari. "Dental Studies Give Clues About Christopher Columbus's Crew." *The Washington Post* (May 18, 2009).

Maconde, Juan Angola. "Los afrodescendientes bolivianos." *Journal of Latin American and Caribbean Anthropology* 12, no.1 (2007): pp. 246–253.

Maggs, Sam. *Wonder Women: 25 Innovators, Inventors, and Trailblazers Who Changed History*. Philadelphia: Quirk Books, 2016.

Manning, Kenneth R. *Black Apollo of Science: The Life of Ernest Everett Just*. New York: Oxford University Press, 1983.

Mamigonian, Beatriz G., and Karen Racine. *The Human Tradition in the Black Atlantic, 1500–2000*. New York: Rowman and Littlefield, 2010.

Marable, Manning. *Malcolm X: A Life of Reinvention*. New York: Viking, 2011.

Marshall, Patricia Philips, and Jo Ramsay Leimenstoll. *Thomas Day: Master Craftsman and Free Man of Color*. Chapel Hill: University of North Carolina Press, 2010.

Martinez-Alier, Verena. *Marriage, Class, and Colour in Nineteenth-Century Cuba*. Ann Arbor: University of Michigan Press, 1989.

Massey, Sarah R., ed. *Black Cowboys of Texas*. College Station: Texas A&M University Press, 2000.

Mattos, Hebe. "'Pretos' and 'Pardos' Between the Cross and the Sword: Racial Categories in Seventeenth Century Brazil." *Revista Europea de Estudios Latinoamericanos y del Caribe* 80 (April 2006): pp. 43–55.

Méndez-Méndes, Serafín, and Ronald Fernández. *Puerto Rico Past and Present: An Encyclopedia, Second Edition*. Santa Barbara: Greenwood, 2015.

McCarthy, Kevin. *Black Florida*. New York: Hippocrene Books, 1995.

McDaniels, Pellom, III. *The Prince of Jockeys: The Life of Isaac Burns Murphy*. Lexington: University Press of Kentucky, 2013.

McDonough, Yona Zeldis. *Who Was Harriet Tubman?* New York: Grosset & Dunlap, 2002.

McGrady, Richard. *Music and Musicians in Early Nineteenth-Century Cornwall: The World of Joseph Emidy – Slave, Violinist, and Composer*. Exeter: University of Exeter Press, 1991.

McKivigan, John, and Stanley Harold, eds. *Antislavery Violence: Sectional, Racial, and Cultural Conflict in Antebellum America*. Knoxville: University of Tennessee Press, 1999.

McKnight, Kathryn Joy, and Leo J. Garofalo, eds. *Afro-Latin Voices: Narratives from the Early Modern Afro-Atlantic World, 1550–1812*. Indianapolis: Hackett Publishing, 2009.

McNeil, William. *Age of Gunpowder Empires*. Washington, D.C.: American Historical Association, 1990.

McPherson, James M. *The Negro's Civil War: How American Negroes Felt and Acted During the War for the Union*. New York: Vintage Books, 1965.

McWhirter, Cameron. *Red Summer: The Summer of 1919 and the Awakening of Black America*. New York: Henry Holt, 2011.

Merritt, Carole. *The Herdons: An Atlanta Family*. Athens: University of Georgia Press, 2002.

Mickens, Ronald E. *Edward Bouchet: The First African American Doctorate*. World Scientific Publishing Company, 2002.

Millett, Nathaniel. *The Maroons of Prospect Bluff and Their Quest for Freedom in the Atlantic World*. Gainesville: University Press of Florida, 2013.

Mintz, Sidney W. *Sweetness and Power: The Place of Sugar in Modern History*. New York: Penguin, 1985.

Mintz, Steven, ed. *African American Voices: A Documentary Reader, 1619–1877*. Malden: Wiley-Blackwell, 2009.

Michell, Kortiha. *Living with Lynching: African American Lynching Plays, Performance, and Citizenship, 1890–1930*. Champaign: University of Illinois Press, 2011.

Morgan, Edmund. *American Slavery, American Freedom: The Ordeal of Colonial Virginia*. New York: W. W. Norton, 1975.

Morgan, Edmund. *The Challenge of the American Revolution*. New York: W. W. Norton, 1976.

Morgan, Thomas M. "The Education and Medical Practice of Dr. James McCune Smith (1813–1865), First Black American to Hold a Medical Degree." *Journal of National Medical Association* 95, no. 7 (2003): pp. 603–614.

Morner, Magnus. *Race Mixture in the History of Latin America*. New York: Little, Brown, & Company, 1967.

Morrison, Karen Y. "Slave Mothers and White Fathers: Defining Family and Status in Late Colonial Cuba." *Slavery & Abolition* 31, no. 1 (March 2010): pp. 29–55.

Morrison, Toni. *Playing in the Dark: Whiteness and the Literary Imagination*. New York: Vintage, 1993.

Moye, J. Todd. *Ella Baker: Community Organizer of the Civil Rights Movement*. Lanham: Rowman and Littlefield, 2013.

Murphy, Jim. *Gone A-Whaling: The Lure of the Sea and the Hunt for the Great Whale*. New York: Clarion Books, 1998.

Mustakeem, Sowande' M. *Slavery at Sea: Terror, Sex and Sickness in the Middle Passage*. Urbana: University of Illinois Press, 2016.

Nash, Gary, and Graham Hodges. *Friends of Liberty: Thomas Jefferson, Thaddeus Kosciuszko, and Agrippa Hull: A Tale of Three Patriots, Two Revolutions, and a Tragic Betrayal of Freedom in the New Nation*. New York: Basic Books, 2008.

Nash, Gary. *The Forgotten Fifth: African Americans in the Age of Revolution*. Cambridge: Harvard University Press, 2006.

Nash, Gary. *The Unknown American Revolution*. New York: Penguin, 2005.

Nell, William Cooper. *The Colored Patriots of the American Revolution, With Sketches of Several Distinguished Colored Persons*. Boston: Robert F. Wallcut, 1855.

Newman, Richard S. *Freedom's Prophet: Bishop Richard Allen, the AME Church, and the Black Founding Fathers*. New York: New York University Press, 2008.

Nichols, Philip. *Sir Francis Drake Revived*. New York: Collier & Son Company, 1910 [1623].

Nunnally, Shayla C. *Trust in Black America: Race, Discrimination, and Politics*. New York: New York University Press, 2012.

Obi, T.J. Desch. "Black Terror: Bill Richmond's Revolutionary Boxing." *Journal of Sport History* 36, no. 1 (Spring 2009): pp. 99–114.

Olsen, Margaret M. "Marzano's *Zafria* and the Performance of Cuban Nationhood." *Hispanic Review* 75, no. 2 (Spring 2007): pp. 135–158.

Olsen, Steve. *Mapping Human History: Genes, Race, and Our Common Origins*. New York: Mariner Books, 2003.

Olwig, Karen Fog. *Cultural Adaptation and Resistance on St. John: Three Centuries of Afro-Caribbean Life*. Gainesville: University of Florida Press, 1993 [1985].

Oshinsky, David M. *Worse Than Slavery: Parchman Farm and the Ordeal of Jim Crow Justice*. New York: The Free Press (Simon & Schuster), 1997.

Pappademos, Melina. *Black Political Activism and the Cuban Republic*. Chapel Hill: University of North Carolina Press, 2011.

Paquette, Robert L. *Sugar Is Made with Blood: The Conspiracy of La Escalera and the Conflict between Empires over Slavery in Cuba*. Middletown: Wesleyan University Press, 1988.

Parfait, Claire, Helene Le Dantec-Lowry, and Claire Bourhis-Mariotti, eds. *Writing History from the Margins: African Americans and the Quest for Freedom*. New York: Routledge, 2016.

Parish, Helen Rand. *Estebanico*. New York: Viking Press, 1974.

Patterson, Tiffany Ruby, and Robin D.G. Kelley. "Unfinished Migrations: Reflections on the African Diaspora and the Making of the Modern World." *African Studies Review* 4, no. 1 (April 2000): pp. 11–45.

Peabody, Sue. *There Are No Slaves in France: The Political Culture of Race and Slavery in the Ancien Regime*. Oxford: Oxford University Press, 1996.

Pennell, C. R. *Bandits at Sea: A Pirate Reader*. New York: New York University, 2001.

Perkins, Kathy A. *Black Female Playwrights: An Anthology of Plays Before 1950*. Bloomington: Indiana University Press, 1989.

Perkins, Linda M. "Heed Life's Demands: The Educational Philosophy of Fanny Jackson Coppin." *Journal of Negro Education* 31, no. 3 (Summer 1982): pp. 181–190.

Plummer, Betty L. "Letters of James Durham to Benjamin Rush." *Journal of Negro History* 65, no. 3 (Summer 1980): pp. 261–269.

Porter, Kenneth. *The Black Seminoles: History of a Freedom-Seeking People*. Gainesville: University of Florida Press, 1996.

Pratt, Terry, and David McCallam, eds. *The Enterprise of Enlightenment*. Bern: Peter Lang Publishing, 2004.

Price, Richard. *Alabi's World*. Baltimore: Johns Hopkins University Press, 1990.

Price, Richard. *Maroon Societies: Rebel Slave Communities in the Americas*. Baltimore: Johns Hopkins University Press, 1996 [1979].

Pulis, John W. *Moving On: Black Loyalists in the Afro-Atlantic World*. New York: Garland Publishing, 1999.

Putney, Martha. *Black Sailors: Afro-American Merchant Seamen and Whalemen Prior to the Civil War*. Westport: Greenwood Press, 1987.

Pybus, Cassandra. *Runaway Slaves of the American Revolution and Their Global Quest for Liberty*. Boston: Beacon Press, 2006.

Quarles, Benjamin. *The Negro in the American Revolution*. Chapel Hill: University of North Carolina Press, 1996 [1961].

Queen-Lacey, Marlette. *From Slave to Water Magnate*. Lincoln: iUniverise, 2006.

Ransby, Barbara. *Ella Baker and the Black Freedom Movement: A Radical Democratic Vision*. Chapel Hill: University of North Carolina Press, 2005.

Ramold, Steven J. *Slaves, Sailors, Citizens: African Americans in the Union Navy*. De Kalb: Northern Illinois University Press, 2002.

Rasmussen, Daniel. *American Uprising: The Untold Story of America's Largest Slave Revolt*. New York: Harper Perennial, 2012.

Rediker, Marcus. *The Slave Ship: A Human History*. New York: Penguin, 2007.

Rediker, Marcus. *Villains of All Nations: Atlantic Pirates in the Golden Age*. Boston: Beacon Press, 2004.

Reis, Joao José. *Slave Rebellion in Brazil: The Muslim Uprising of 1835 in Bahia*. Baltimore: The Johns Hopkins University Press, 1993.

Reiss, Oscar. *Blacks in Colonial America*. Jefferson: McFarland, 1997.

Restall, Matthew. *The Black Middle: Africans, Mayas, and Spaniards in Colonial Yucatan*. Stanford: Stanford University Press, 2006.

Restall, Matthew. *Seven Myths of the Spanish Conquest*. New York: Oxford University Press, 2003.

Restall, Matthew. "Black Conquistadores: Armed Africans in Early Spanish America." *The Americas* 57, no. 2 (October 2000): pp. 171–205.

Rhodes, Jane. *Mary Ann Shadd Cary: The Black Press and Protest in the Nineteenth Century*. Bloomington: Indiana University Press, 1998.

Richardson, David M. *Denmark Vesey: The Buried Story of America's Largest Slave Rebellion and the Man Who Led It*. New York: Vintage Books, 2009.

Richardson, Marilyn, ed. *Maria W. Stewart: America's First Black Woman Political Writer*. Bloomington: Indiana University Press, 1987.

Roberson, Heather. "Black Venus and Her Rainbow Tribe." *California Magazine* (January-February 2008).

Robinson, Carey. *The Fighting Maroons of Jamaica*. Jamaica: Collins and Sangster, 1969.

Robinson, Henry S. "Who Was West Ford?" *Journal of Negro History* 66, no. 2 (Summer 1981): pp. 167–174.

Roediger, David. *Seizing Freedom: Slave Emancipation and Liberty for All*. New York: Verso, 2014.

Roediger, David. *The Wages of Whiteness: Race and The Making of the American Working Class*. New York: Verso, 1999.

Rogers, J.A. *World's Great Men of Color*. New York: Macmillon Publishing, 1972 [1946].

Rohter, Larry. "After a Century a Literary Reputation Finally Blooms." *New York Times* (September 12, 2008).

Romero, Fernando, and Mercer Cook. "José Manuel Valdéz, Great Peruvian Mulatto." *Phylon* 3, no. 3 (1942): pp. 296–319.

Rout, Leslie B., Jr. *The African Experience in Spanish America*. Cambridge: Cambridge University Press, 1976.

Rowell, Charles Henry. "'El Primer Liberador de las Americas'/The First Liberator of the Americas: The Editor's Notes." *Callaloo* 31, no. 1 (Winter 2008): pp. 1–11.

Rupert, Linda M. "Marronage, Manumission and Maritime Trade in the Early Modern Caribbean." *Slavery & Abolition* 30, no. 3 (September 2009): pp. 361–382.

Salvatore, Susan, et al. "Civil Rights in America: Racial Desegregation of Public Accommodations: A National Historic Landmarks Theme Study." National Parks Service, U.S. Department of the Interior, 2009 [2004].

Sanders, James E. *The Vanguard of the Atlantic World: Creating Modernity, Nation, and Democracy in Nineteenth-Century Latin America*. Durham: Duke University Press, 2014.

Sanders, James E. *Contentious Republicans: Popular Politics, Race, and Class in the Nineteenth Century Columbia*. Durham: Duke University Press, 2004.

Sanders, Mark A., ed. *A Black Soldier's Story: The Narrative of Ricardo Batrell and the Cuban War of Independence*. Minneapolis: University of Minnesota Press, 2010 [1912].

Sanders, Nancy I. *America's Black Founders: Revolutionary Heroes and Early Leaders*. Chicago: Chicago Review Press, 2010.

Sanneh, Lamin. *Abolitionists Abroad: American Blacks and the Making of Modern West Africa*. Cambridge: Harvard University Press, 2000.

Saunders, A. *A Social History of Black Slaves and Freedmen in Portugal, 1441–1555*. New York: Cambridge University Press, 1982.

Savage, W. Sherman. "The Influence of William Alexander Liedesdorff on the History of California." *Journal of Negro History* 38 (July 1958): pp. 322–332.

Sayers, Daniel O. *A Desolate Place for a Defiant People: The Archeology of Maroons, Indigenous Americans, and Enslaved Laborers in the Great Dismal Swamp*. Gainesville: University Press of Florida, 2014.

Schoelwer, Susan P., ed. *Lives Bound Together: Slavery at George Washington's Mount Vernon*. Mount Vernon Ladies Association, 2017.

Scott, Rebecca J., and Jean M. Hebrand. *Freedom Papers: An Atlantic Odyssey in the Age of Emancipation*. Cambridge: Harvard University Press, 2012.

Scott, Rebecca. "The Atlantic World and the Road to Plessy v. Ferguson." *Journal of American History* 94 (December 2007): pp. 726–733.

Scott, Rebecca. *Slave Emancipation in Cuba*. Pittsburgh: University of Pittsburgh Press, 2000.

Scott, William R., and William G. Shade. *Upon These Shores: Themes in the African American Experience, 1600 to the Present*. New York: Routledge, 2000.

Schmidt-Nowara, Christopher. *Empire and Antislavery: Spain, Cuba, and Puerto Rico, 1833–1874*. Pittsburgh: University of Pittsburgh Press, 1999.

Schwatrz, Philip J. *Migrants Against Slavery: Virginians and the Nation*. Charlottesville: University Press of Virginia, 2001.

Schwatrz, Philip J., ed. *Slavery at the Home of George Washington*. The Mount Vernon Ladies Association, 2001.

Segal, Ronald. *Islam's Black Slaves: The Other Black Diaspora*. New York: Farrar, Straus and Giroux, 2001.

Sensbach, Jon F. *Rebecca's Revival: Creating Black Christianity in the Atlantic World*. Cambridge: Harvard University Press, 2005.

Sesay, Chernoh M., Jr. "The Revolutionary Black Roots of Slavery's Abolition in Massachusetts." *New England Quarterly* 87, no. 1 (March 2014): pp. 99–131.

Shaffer, Donald R. *After the Glory: The Struggles of Black Civil War Veterans*. Lawrence: University Press of Kansas, 2004.

Shannon, Timothy. *Atlantic Lives: A Comparative Approach to Early America*. New York: Pearson Longman, 2004.

Shellum, Brian G. *Black Officer in a Buffalo Soldier Regiment: The Military Career of Charles Young*. Lincoln: University of Nebraska, 2010.

Shetterly, Margot Lee. *Hidden Figures*. New York: William Morrow (HarperCollins), 2016.

Sidbury, James. *Becoming African in America: Race and Nation in the Early Black Atlantic*. New York: Oxford University Press, 2007.

Sidbury, James. *Ploughshares into Swords: Race, Rebellion, and Identity in Gabriel's Virginia, 1730–1810*. New York: Cambridge University Press, 1997.

Salenius, Sirpa. *An Abolitionist Abroad: Sarah Parker Remond in Cosmopolitan Europe*. Amherst: University of Massachusetts Press, 2016.

Skidmore, Thomas. *Black into White: Race and Nationality in Brazilian Thought*. New York: Oxford University Press, 1974.

Slatta, Richard W. *Comparing Cowboys and Frontiers: New Perspectives on the History of the Americas*. Norman: University of Oklahoma Press, 1997.

Sluyter, Andrew. *Black Ranching Frontiers: African Cattle Herders of the Atlantic World, 1500–1800*. New Haven: Yale University Press, 2012.

Smallwood, Arwin D., and Jeffrey M. Elliot. *The Atlas of African American History and Politics: From the Slave Trade to Modern Times*. Dubuque: McGraw Hill, 1998.

Smedley, Audrey. *Race in North America: Origin and Evolution of a Worldview*. Boulder: Westview Press, 1993.

Smith, Abbott. *Colonists in Bondage: White Servitude and Convict Labor in America 1607–1776*. Chapel Hill: University of North Carolina Press, 1947.

Smith College Alumnae Oral History Project Smith College Archives, Northampton, MA, Evelyn Boyd Granville, Class of 1945.

Smith, Gene Allen. *The Slaves' Gamble: Choosing Sides in the War of 1812*. New York: Palgrave Macmillan, 2013.

Smith, J. Clay, Jr. *Emancipation: The Making of the Black Lawyer, 1844–1944*. Philadelphia: University of Pennsylvania Press, 1993.

Smith, John David, ed. *Black Soldiers in Blue: African American Troops in the Civil War Era*. Chapel Hill: University of North Carolina Press, 2003.

Smith, Mark Michael, ed. *Stono: Documenting and Interpreting a Southern Slave Revolt*. Columbia: University of South Carolina Press, 2005.

Smith, Venture. *A Narrative of the Life and Adventures of Venture, A Native of Africa: But resident above sixty years in the United States of America*. New London: Holt, 1798.

Socolow, Susan Migden. *The Women of Colonial Latin America*. New York: Cambridge, 2000.

Spicer, Joaneth, ed. *Revealing the African Presence in Renaissance Europe*. Baltimore: The Walters Art Museum, 2012.

Stanton, Lucia. *"Those Who Labor for My Happiness": Slavery at Thomas Jefferson's Monticello*. Charlottesville: University of Virginia Press, 2012.

Stevenson, Brenda, ed. *The Journals of Charlotte Forten Grimke*. New York: Oxford University Press, 1988.

Stewart, L. Lloyd. *A Far Cry from Freedom: Gradual Abolition (1799–1827), New York State's Crime Against Humanity*. Bloomington: Authorhouse, 2005.

Stille, Darlene R. *Percy Lavon Julian: Pioneering Chemist*. Mankato: Compass Point Books, 2009.

Stocking, George W. "The Turn of the Century Concept of Race." *Modernism/Modernity* 1, no. 1: pp. 4–16.

Streitmatter, Rodger. *Raising Her Voice: African-American Women Journalists Who Changed History*. Lexington: University Press of Kentucky, 1994.

Tannenbaum, Frank. *Slave and Citizen: The Negro in the Americas*. New York: Knopf, 1947.

Taylor, Chris. *The Black Carib Wars: Freedom, Survival, and the Making of the Garifuna*. Jackson: University Press of Mississippi, 2012.

Taylor, Alan. *The Internal Enemy: Slavery and War in Virginia, 1772–1832*. New York: W. W. Norton, 2013.

Taylor, Elizabeth Dowling. *A Slave in the White House: Paul Jennings and the Madisons*. New York: St. Martin's Press, 2012.

Taylor, Quintard, Jr. *From Timbuktu to Katrina: Readings in African American History*. Volumes I & II. Boston: Thomson Wadsworth, 2008.

Taylor, Quintard, and Shirley Ann Wilson Moore. *African American Women Confront the West, 1600–2000*. Norman: University of Oklahoma Press. 2003.

Taylor, Quintard. *In Search of the Racial Frontier: African Americans in the American West, 1528–1990*. New York: Norton, 1998.

Taylor, Eric Robert. *If We Must Die: Shipboard Insurrections in the Era of the Atlantic Trade*. Baton Rouge: Louisiana State University Press, 2009.

Taylor, Susie King. *A Black Woman's Civil War Memoirs: Reminiscences of my Life in Camp with the 33rd U.S. Colored Troops, Late 1st South Carolina Volunteers*. New York: Markus Weiner Publishing, 1988 [1902].

Taylor, Ula Yvette. *The Veiled Garvey: The Life & Times of Amy Jacques Garvey*. Chapel Hill: University of North Carolina Press, 2002.

Teal, Christopher. *Hero of Hispaniola: America's First Black Diplomat, Ebenezer D. Bassett*. Westport: Praeger Publishers, 2008.

Temperley, Howard, ed. *After Slavery: Emancipation and Its Discontents*. London: Frank Cass, 2000.

Thomas, Hugh. *The Slave Trade: The Story of the Atlantic Slave Trade: 1440–1870*. New York: Simon & Schuster, 1997.

Thomas, Lamont D. *Paul Cuffe: Black Entrepreneur and Pan Africanist*. Urbana: University of Illinois Press, 1986.

Thompson, Alvin O. *Flight to Freedom: African Runaways and Maroons in the Americas*. Kingston: University of the West Indies Press, 2006.

Thompson, Vincent Bakpetu. *The Making of the African Diaspora in the Americas, 1441–1900*. New York: Longman, 1987.

Thornton, John K. *A Cultural History of the Atlantic World 1250–1820*. New York: Cambridge University Press, 2012.

Thornton, John. *Africa and Africans in the Making of the New World*. New York: Cambridge University Press, 1998.

Tillis, Antonio D., ed. *Critical Perspectives on Afro-Latin American Literature*. New York: Routledge, 2012.

Tobin, Jacqueline L., with Hettie Jones. *From Midnight to Dawn: The Last Tracks of the Underground Railroad*. New York: Anchor Books, 2008.

Tuner, Lozenzo D. "Some Contacts of Brazilian Ex-Slaves with Nigeria, West Africa." *Journal of Negro History* 27, no. 1 (1942): pp. 55–67.

Twinam, Ann. *Private Lives, Private Secrets: Gender, Honor, Sexuality, and Illegitimacy in Colonial Spanish America*. Stanford: Stanford University Press, 1999.

Tyler-McGraw, Marie. *An African Republic: Black and White Virginians in the Making of Liberia*. Chapel Hill: University of North Carolina Press, 2008.

Van Cleeve, George. "Somerset's Case and Its Antecedents in Imperial Perspective." *Law and History Review* 24, no. 3 (Fall 2006): pp. 601–646.

Van Deuson, Nancy E. *The Souls of Purgatory: The Spiritual Diary of a Seventeenth-Century Afro-Peruvian Mystic, Ursula de Jesús*. Albuquerque: University of New Mexico Press, 2004.

Vincent, Ted. "The Blacks Who Freed Mexico." *Journal of Negro History* 79, no. 3 (Summer 1994): pp. 257–276.

Vincent, Theodore G. *The Legacy of Vicente Guerrero, Mexico's First Black Indian President*. Gainesville: University Press of Florida, 2001.

Vinson, Ben, III, and Matthew Restall, eds. *Black Mexico: Race and Society from Colonial to Modern Times*. Albuquerque: University of New Mexico Press, 2009.

Vinson, Ben, III. "Articulating Space: The Free-Colored Military Establishment in Colonial Mexico from the Conquest to Independence." *Callaloo* 27, no. 1 (Winter 2004): pp. 150–171.

Vinson, Ben, III. "The Racial Profile of a Rural Mexican Province in the 'Costa Chica': Igualapa in 1791." *The Americas* 57, no. 2 (October 2000): pp. 269–282.

Voelz, Peter M. *Slave and Soldier: The Military Impact of Blacks in the Colonial Americas*. New York: Garland Publishing, 1993.

Wade, Peter. *Race and Ethnicity in Latin America*. London: Pluto Press, 1997.

Wade, Peter. *Blackness and Race Mixture: The Dynamics of Racial Identity in Columbia*. Baltimore: Johns Hopkins University Press, 1993.

Walker, David. *David Walker's Appeal*. New York: Farrar, Straus and Giroux, 1995 [Hill and Wang, 1829].

Weik, Terry. "The Archaeology of Maroon societies in the Americas: Resistance, Cultural Continuity, and Transformation in the African Diaspora." *Historical Archaeology* 31, no. 2 (1997): pp. 81–92.

Weiss, John McNish. *The Merikens: Free Black American Settlers in Trinidad, 1815–1816*. Austin: University of Texas, 2002.

West, Elizabeth. *Sante Fe: Four Hundred Years, Four Hundred Questions*. Santa Fe: Sunstone Press, 2012.

White, Shane. *Prince of Darkness: The Untold Story of Jeremiah G. Hamilton, Wall Street's First Black Millionaire*. New York: St. Martins Press, 2015.

Whitten, Norman E., and Arlene Torres. *Blackness in Latin America and the Caribbean: Social Dynamics and Cultural Transformations*. Vols. 1 & 2. Bloomington: Indiana University Press, 1998.

Whitten, Norman E., Jr., ed. *Cultural Transformations and Ethnicity in Modern Ecuador*. Urbana: University of Illinois Press, 1981.

Widmer, Ted. "How Haiti Saved America." *The Boston Globe* (March 21, 2010).

Wiecek, William M. "Somerset: Lord Mansfield and the Legitimacy of Slavery in the Anglo-American World." *University of Chicago Law Review* 42, no. 1 (Autumn 1974): pp. 86–146.

Wiencek, Henry. *Master of the Mountain: Thomas Jefferson and His Slaves*. New York: Ferrar, Straus and Giroux, 2012.

Wiencek, Henry. *An Imperfect God: George Washington, His Slaves, and the Creation of America*. New York: Ferrar, Straus and Giroux, 2003.

Wiencek, Henry. *The Hairstons: An American Family in Black and White*. New York: St. Martin's Press, 1999.

Wiener, Leo. *Africa and the Discovery of America*. Philadelphia: Innes and Sons, 1922.

Wilder, Craig Steven. *In the Company of Black Men: The African Influence on African American Culture in New York City*. New York: New York University Press, 2001.

Wilkins, Roy, ed. "Distinguished Solider Passes, Major George W. Ford." *The Crisis* (October 1939): pp. 306.

Winch, Julie. *A Gentleman of Color: The Life of James Forten*. New York: Oxford University Press, 2002.

Wintz, Cary D., ed. *African American Political Thought, 1890–1930*. New York: Routledge, 2015.

Williams, David. *I Freed Myself: African American Self-Emancipation in the Civil War Era*. New York: Cambridge University Press, 2014.

Williams, Eric. *From Columbus to Castro: The History of the Caribbean*. New York: Vintage, 1970.

Williams, Eric. *Capitalism and Slavery*. Chapel Hill: University of North Carolina Press, 1944.

Williams, George Washington. *History of the Negro Race in America, 1619–1880, Negroes As Slaves, Soldiers, and Citizens*. New York: Putnam, 1883.

Williams, Jean Kinney. *Bridget "Biddy" Mason: From Slave to Businesswoman*. Minneapolis: Compass Point Books, 2006.

Williams, Raymond. *Culture and Society*. New York: Columbia University Press, 1983 [1958].

Wood, Amy Louise. *Lynching and Spectacle: Witnessing Racial Violence in America, 1890–1940*. Chapel Hill: University of North Carolina Press, 2009.

Wood, Peter. *Weathering the Storm: Inside Winslow Homer's 'Gulf Stream.'* Athens: University of Georgia Press, 2004.

Wood, Peter. *Strange New World: Africans in Colonial America*. New York: Oxford University Press, 2003.

Wood, Peter. *Black Majority: Negroes in Colonial South Carolina from 1670 through the Stono Rebellion*. New York: W. W. Norton, 1974.

Wood, William J. "The Illegal Beginning of American Negro Slavery." *The American Bar Association Journal* 56 (January 1970): pp. 45–53.

Woodward, C. Vann, ed. *Mary Chesnut's Civil War*. New Haven: Yale University Press, 1981.

Wright, Donald. *The World and a Very Small Place in Africa*. Armonk: M.E. Sharpe, 2004.

Wright, Donald. *African Americans in the Colonial Era*. Arlington Heights: Harlan Davidson, 1990.

Yee, Shirley J. *Black Women Activists: A Study in Activism, 1828–1860*. Knoxville: University of Tennessee, 1992.

Sources of Illustrations

page

INTRODUCTION

xx William Hinton. Harvard Medical Library in the Francis A. Countway Library of Medicine.

xxvi Jefferson Runaway Ad. *The Virginia Gazette*, September 14, 1769. The Virginia Historical Society.

xxvi William Monroe Trotter. Photograph of William Monroe Trotter, 1895. HUD 295.04 PF (Box 2), Harvard University Archives.

xxvii Frederick Madison Roberts. Frederick M. Roberts graduation portrait, *Roberts Family Papers*, African American Museum and Library at Oakland, Oakland Public Library, Oakland, California.

xxviii Washington Family. Courtesy of Mount Vernon Ladies' Association.

xxix West Ford. Courtesy of Mount Vernon Ladies Association.

CHAPTER ONE

12 Atlantic Map.

18 Tabula Rogeriana.

19 Cantino Planisphere.

CHAPTER TWO

28 Alessandro de Medici. Philadelphia Museum of Art, John G. Johnson collection, Cat. 83.

29 Juan de Pareja. Metropolitan Museum of Art.

31 Matthew Henson. Robert E Peary/National Geographic Creative.

41 Three Gentlemen of Esmereldas. *Three Gentlemen of Esmeraldas*, 1599, Ecuador. Andres Sanches Gallque. Courtesy of Museo de América, Madrid, Spain.

CHAPTER THREE

62 Free Black Militia. Joseph Hefter, *Artes de Mexico,* no. 102, Mexico City, 1968. Courtesy of JohnHorse.com.

Chapter Four

95   The Protten Family. Moravian Archives Herrnhut, GS.393

102   Phillis Wheatley. Library of Congress, Rare Books and Special Collections, LC-DIG-ppmsca-02947.

109   *Lafayette at Yorktown*, 1782, oil on canvas. Jean-Baptiste Le Paon (1738–1785). Gift of Helen Fahnstock Hubbard, 1938. Lafayette College Art Collection, Easton, Pennsylvania.

111   Washington and William Lee. Metropolitan Museum of Modern Art.

114   Vincent Ogé. Photographs and Prints Division, Schomburg Center for Research in Black Culture, The New York Public Library, Astor, Lennox, and Tilden Foundations.

116   Le Chevalier de Saint-Georges. Public Domain.

117   Jean-Baptiste Belley. RMN-Grand Palais / Art Resource, NY.

125   Olaudah Equiano. Courtesy of the Newberry Library, Chicago. [H 5832 .27].

133   Richard Allen. Photographs and Prints Division, Schomburg Center for Research in Black Culture, The New York Public Library, Astor, Lennox, and Tilden Foundations.

134   James Forten. Leon Gardiner collection of American Negro Historical Society records [0008], Historical Society of Pennsylvania.

Chapter Five

150   York. Charles M. Russell; Lewis and Clark on the Lower Columbia; 1905; watercolor on paper; Amon Carter Museum, Fort Worth, Texas; 1961.195

159   John Jefferson. Photographs and Prints Division, Schomburg Center for Research in Black Culture, The New York Public Library, Astor, Lennox, and Tilden Foundations.

160   Vicente Guerrero. Courtesy of Museo Nacional de las Intervenciones, el Instituto Nacional de Antropología e Historia.

163   Alexandre Pétion. Photographs and Prints Division, Schomburg Center for Research in Black Culture, The New York Public Library, Astor, Lennox, and Tilden Foundations.

173   Paul Bogle. Courtesy of the National Library of Jamaica.

176   Joseph Jenkins Roberts. Library of Congress DAG no. 1000 | LC-USZC4-4609.

Chapter Six

191   John Russwurm. Photographs and Prints Division, Schomburg Center for Research in Black Culture, The New York Public Library, Astor, Lennox, and Tilden Foundations.

202   Andre Rebouças. Public Domain.

205   James McCune Smith. Photographs and Prints Division, Schomburg Center for Research in Black Culture, The New York Public Library, Astor, Lennox, and Tilden Foundations.

206   Mary Ann Shadd Cary. Library and Archives Canada.

206   George Downing. Manuscripts, Archives, and Rare Books Division, Schomburg Center for Research in Black Culture, The New York Public Library, Astor, Lennox, and Tilden Foundations.

207   John Mercer Langston. Library of Congress, Brady-Handy Collection, LC-DIG-cwpbh-00690.

207   Robert Morris. Public Domain.

209   Mary Seacole. Amoret Tanner Collection/fotoLibra.

212   José Silvestre White. Bibliothèque Nationale de France.

213   Ira Frederick Aldridge. Billy Rose Theater Division, The New York Public Library for the Performing Arts, Astor, Lennox, and Tilden Foundations.

216   James W. C. Pennington. Jean Blackwell Huston Research and Reference Division, Schomburg Center for Research in Black Culture, The New York Public Library, Astor, Lennox, and Tilden Foundations.

223   Robert Smalls. Library of Congress, Brady-Handy Collection, LC-DIG-cwpbh-03683.

224   William Gould and Family. Courtesy of Professor William B. Gould, IV and the Robert Crown Law Library, Stanford University.

225   Susie King Taylor. Public Domain

225   Christian Fleetwood. Public Domain.

226   Elizabeth Keckley. The Virginia Historical Society.

229   Bass Reeves. The Western History Collections at the University of Oklahoma Library.

230   George McJunkin. Courtesy of Brenda Wilkinson and the Bureau of Land Management.

231   Spanish American War. Library of Congress.

233   Antonio Maceo. Library of Congress, Hispanic Division.

CHAPTER SEVEN

249   Anna Julia Cooper. Oberlin College Archives.

251   Ida Gibbs Hunt. Oberlin College Archives.

254   Josephine St. Pierre Ruffin. Manuscripts, Archives, and Rare Books Division, Schomburg Center for Research in Black Culture, The New York Public Library, Astor, Lennox, and Tilden Foundations.

254   Josephine Silone Yates. Library of Congress.

256   Charlotta Bass. Courtesy of the Southern California Library.

260   Quentin Bandera. Manuscripts, Archives, and Rare Books Division,

Schomburg Center for Research in Black Culture, The New York Public Library, Astor, Lennox, and Tilden Foundations.

261 Juan Gualberto Gomez. Manuscripts, Archives, and Rare Books Division, Schomburg Center for Research in Black Culture, The New York Public Library, Astor, Lennox, and Tilden Foundations.

262 Consuelo A. Serra Heredia. Manuscripts, Archives, and Rare Books Division, Schomburg Center for Research in Black Culture, The New York Public Library, Astor, Lennox, and Tilden Foundations.

267 U.S. Signal Corps. Library of Congress.

269 Louis Latimer. Courtesy of Queens Library.

271 George Franklin Grant. Courtesy of Harvard Medical Library in the Francis A. Countway Library of Medicine.

272 Evelyn Boyd Granville. Smith College Archives, Smith College.

276 Mary Church Terrell. Library of Congress, LC-USZ62-54722.

277 Sadie Tanner Mossell. From the Collections of the University of Pennsylvania Archives.

278 Tanner Family. From the Collections of the University of Pennsylvania Archives.

278 Mossell Family. From the Collections of the University of Pennsylvania Archives.

Index

A

Abele, Julian 145
Abele, Robert 145
abolition xix, xxi–xxiii, 3, 70, 101–107,
    113, 114, 118, 119, 121, 126–128,
    132, 134, 136, 138, 139, 145–148,
    153, 160–163, 166, 169, 171, 172,
    174, 175, 186, 191–197, 199, 201,
    202, 205–207, 214, 215, 217–220,
    225, 227, 233, 234, 236, 264, 295,
    296
Abubakari II 10
Acción Democrática 265
Action Committee of Veterans and Soci-
    eties of Color 261
Adams, John 99
Adams, John Quincy 215
Addams, Jane 250
Adelante 262
Afer, Publius Terentius 48
Afonso III 27
African Association 248
African Burial Ground 57
African Free School 86, 133, 204, 206,
    210, 213
African Grove Theater 213, 214, 257
African Methodist Episcopal Church
    134
African Missionary Society 175
African Union Societies 132
Africanus, Scipio 108
Afro-Americans
    and education xvii, xxvii, 24, 68, 80,
        86, 88, 95, 108, 130–133, 137, 140,
        144, 145, 149, 153, 175–178, 185,
        186, 189–194, 197, 199, 202–213,
        216, 225, 240, 245, 246, 248, 249,
        252, 255, 256, 258, 260, 262, 265,
        270–273, 277, 278, 280–282, 286,
        296
    and law xvii, xix, xxi, 26, 54, 65,
        68, 70, 71, 74, 79, 80, 95, 106,
        107, 130, 131, 138, 144, 153,
        178, 186–190, 195–203, 206, 207,
        211, 236, 246, 248, 265, 270, 271,
        279–284, 291
    and medicine xvii, xx, 24, 27, 52, 54,
        57, 80, 95, 104, 107, 130, 140, 145,
        154, 165, 176–178, 186, 194, 197,
        199, 202–206, 208, 209, 211, 218,
        220, 222, 225, 231, 234, 236, 244,
        248, 249, 264, 267–275, 278, 279,
        296
    and politics xxiii, xxx, 5, 58–60,
        75, 79, 80, 86, 90, 97, 105, 119,
        126–128, 130, 132, 134, 135, 147,
        153, 160–166, 175–177, 188, 191,
        192, 194, 201–204, 208, 210, 212,
        227, 235, 236, 244, 246, 248, 252,
        254, 256, 260–265, 268, 270, 271,
        277, 281–283, 296
    as artists 2, 24, 103, 105, 106, 116,
        118, 126–128, 132, 145, 155, 181,
        185, 187, 188, 194, 198, 201–204,
        206, 208, 210–214, 216, 231, 234,
        238, 244, 246, 248, 249, 257–259,
        277, 278, 280–283, 287, 296
    as athletes 37, 127, 144, 212, 230,
        251, 288
    as cowboys xvi, 32, 33, 37, 46, 48,
        161, 228, 230
    as explorers xvi, xxi, 13, 24, 30–35,
        40, 44–46, 80, 97, 146, 150, 285,
        294
    as law enforcement 186, 229, 271
    as pirates xvi, xxi, 66–68, 88

as rebels xvi, 25, 35–40, 58, 67, 68,
  86, 88, 89, 91–94, 96, 99, 118,
  121, 136, 147, 151, 158–160, 163,
  165–172, 178, 182, 183, 187, 195,
  201, 208, 210, 217, 236
as religious leaders xvi, 52, 68, 78, 80,
  85, 88, 95, 108, 133, 134, 172, 173,
  175–178, 191, 193, 204, 210, 252,
  255, 278, 284
as scientists 2, 128, 130, 180, 186,
  193, 202, 204, 205, 210–212, 230,
  244, 248, 250, 255, 269, 270,
  272–276, 288, 290, 291, 294, 296,
  297
as settlers xvi, 24, 25, 33, 34, 36–38,
  41, 43–46, 52–55, 57, 58, 63, 65,
  77, 80, 86, 91, 98, 128, 129, 157,
  158, 174, 175, 177, 192, 228–230,
  285, 294
as slaveholders xxiv, 33, 42, 46, 56,
  74, 78, 93, 110, 111, 114, 161, 178,
  293
entrepreneurship of xvi, xxiv, xxx,
  xxxiii, 24, 34, 41–43, 46, 54, 57, 61,
  78, 80, 88, 105, 106, 126–130, 135,
  141, 148, 153, 158, 162, 167–169,
  175–178, 181, 185, 186, 188–193,
  196–199, 201, 203, 204, 206, 209,
  226, 235, 236, 242, 246–248, 252,
  275–277, 279, 288, 291, 292, 296
military service of xvi, xxi–xxiv, xxvii,
  xxxii, 24–26, 31, 33, 34, 36, 39, 40,
  43, 45, 46, 52, 54, 59–63, 66–68,
  80, 86, 88–90, 92, 96, 98, 99, 104,
  106–126, 128, 129, 131, 133, 136,
  138–141, 144, 146–148, 151–157,
  159–166, 168, 169, 172, 175, 186,
  187, 189, 193, 197, 201, 202, 205,
  206, 208, 217–227, 232–234, 236,
  241, 244, 246–248, 250, 258–260,
  263–268, 270, 273–275, 277, 282,
  288, 289, 294–296
Aftermath (Burrill) 259
Alabama xxxii, 98, 158, 179, 181, 199,

220, 241, 278
Albuquerque, New Mexico 60
Alcindor, John 249, 286
Alcorn University 211
Alcott, Louisa May 211
Aldridge, Ira Frederick 213
Aleijadinho 181
Alexander, John 288
Alexander, Raymond Pace 244, 280
Alexander, Sadie Tanner Mossell
  278–280
Alexander the Great 7
Allen, Ethan 107
Allen, Richard 86, 133, 134, 136, 192,
  194
Allen, William 211, 213
Allyón, Lucas Vázquez de 36, 97
Almagro, Diego de 33, 34
Almagro, Margarita 24
Alvarado, Pedro de 32, 34
Al-Zahrawi 6
Alzheimer, Alois xx
American Anti-Slavery Society 145,
  197, 210
American Chemical Society 291
American Civil Liberties Union 284
American Civil War xxii, xxvii, xxxii,
  112, 128, 145, 147, 156, 159, 165,
  168, 182, 185, 187, 192, 198, 205,
  206, 208, 209, 211, 212, 214–219,
  221–223, 225–227, 229, 234–236,
  241, 246, 250, 258, 260, 266, 270,
  275, 277, 289, 292, 295
American College of Surgeons 270
American Colonization Society 172–
  176, 192, 198
American Geographical Society 205
American Missionary Association 215,
  216, 288
American Revolution xxi, xxii, xxiv,
  xxvi, xxviii, xxxiii, 3, 58, 61, 62,
  88, 91–93, 96, 98–100, 103–105,
  107–118, 123, 127, 129, 131–136,
  140–142, 148, 151–155, 169, 174,

188, 189, 192, 197, 208, 249, 288, 295
American Veterans Association 271
American Women's Suffrage Association 255
Amistad 186, 214, 215, 217, 240
Amo, Anton Wilhelm 86, 95
Andes Mountains 33, 38, 164
Andrade, Miguel Moreno de 69
Andrew, John 154
Andros Island 157, 158
Angola 52, 60, 64, 69, 91, 157, 249
Anthony, Susan B. 197, 250, 279
Antigua 96
anti-Semitism 72, 84
Antoinette, Marie 118
António, Maestre 24
Apache Indians 228, 288
Apalachicola River 156
Aparicio, Nicomedes Santa Cruz 259
Apex Company 276
Aponte, José Antonio 169, 170
Aponte Rebellion 146, 170, 172
Appeal (Walker) 186, 192
Appomattox Court House 222
A Raisin in the Sun (Hansberry) 287
Archer, John Richard 248
Arcía, Valentín 163
Argentina 32, 34, 146, 160, 164, 165, 202, 293
Aristotle 7
Arizona 44
Arkansas 221, 229, 288
Armistead, James xxi, 86, 109, 110, 112, 141, 295
Armstrong, Louis 268
Arnold, Benedict 110
Arobe, Francisco 41
Arthur, Chester 197
Artis, Billy 169
Ashworth, Aaron 229
Ashworth, Abner 229
Ashworth, Moses 229
Ashworth, William 229

Assis, Joaquim Machado de 244
Association Test 105
Astor, John Jacob 242
Athens, Greece 4
Atlanta, Georgia 252, 286
Atlanta Life Insurance Company 252
Atlanta University 252, 280, 288
Atlantic City, New Jersey 276
Atlantic Ocean xix, xxiii, 9–13, 21, 29, 89, 91, 100, 101, 103, 110, 113, 126, 170, 214, 217, 226, 245, 253, 282
Atlantic system xvii, xviii, xxiv, xxx, 2, 4, 10, 12, 14, 16, 17, 20, 21, 26, 87, 148
Attucks, Crispus 86, 99
Auba, Etienne 61
Augusta, Alexander T. 222
Auker, Katherine 138
Australia 267
Austriad (Latino) 48
Avery College 210, 211
A Voice from the South (Cooper) 250
Ayres, Louisa 276
The Azores 11, 12
Aztec 20, 32

B

Bacon, Nathaniel 58, 59
Bacon's Rebellion 52, 58, 295
Badin, Adolf 47
Báez, Buenaventura 146, 166, 183
Baghdad, Iraq 2, 6, 7, 16
The Bahamas 13, 113, 115, 155, 157, 217, 248, 258, 280
Bahia, Brazil 68, 201
Baja, California 32
Baker, David 108
Baker, Edward 231
Baker, Ella xxxiii, 283
Baker, Josephine 268
Baker, Lee D. 235
Baker, Newton 289
Baldwin, Maria 255, 256
Ball, Charles 152
Baltic Sea 9
Baltimore, Maryland 130, 195, 210,

255, 292
Bandera, Quentin 260
Banneker, Benjamin 86, 128
Banneker Literary Institute 212
Bantu language 37
Baptiste, John 56, 71
Baraguá, Cuba 233
Barbados 52, 54, 55, 71, 137, 138, 146, 155, 171, 248
Barbary pirates 2, 151
Barbosa, José Celso 264
Barcala, Lorenzo 166
Bardales, Juan 34
Barnett, F. L. 235
Baroque period 28
Barron, James 108
"Bars Fight" (Prince) 102, 105
Bass, Charlotta 244, 256, 257
Bassett, Ebenezer D. 211, 212, 255
Bass, Joseph 257
Batallas, Angela 165
Bates, Polly Ann 195
Bath, England 127
Batista, Fulgencio 184
The Battle of Lexington (Haynes) 108
Battle of Brandywine 107
Battle of Bunker Hill 104, 107, 131
Battle of Great Bridge 141
Battle of Mobile Bay 223
Battle of Monmouth 107
Battle of New Market Heights 222
Battle of New Orleans 154
Battle of New Orleans (Hudson) 154
Battle of San Juan 231
Battle of Saratoga 105
Battle of the Bulge 269
Battle of Trafalgar 163
Battle of Trenton 104, 107
Battle of Yorktown xxi, 86, 107, 109, 110
Battles of Lexington and Concord 86, 104, 107, 108, 152
Bayamo, Cuba 170
Bayamón, Puerto Rico 264

Beaufort, South Carolina 218
Belgium 270
Bell, Alexander Graham 270
Bellamy, Sam 67
Belle, Dido Elizabeth 127
Belley, Jean-Baptiste 86, 118, 142
Beltran, Juan 33
Benin 30
Bering Strait 10
Berlin Conference 247
Berlin International Congress of Women 279
Bermuda 156
Berry, Polly 198
Bethel Institute 255
Bethel Literary Society 251
Beverly Hills, California 129
Bibb, Henry xxxiii, 186, 194, 211
Bibliotheque Saint Genevieve 47
Bilal ibn Rabah 2, 16
Billy the Kid 229
Biograph Films 259
Bioho, Domingo 24
Birchtown, Nova Scotia 53, 86, 113, 129, 133
Bird, J. B. 182
The Birth of a Nation (Griffith) 257, 259, 273
Biscayne Bay 67
Blackbeard 67
Blackburn Riots 194
Blackburn, Robin 11
Blackburn, Ruthie 194, 195
Blackburn, Thornton 194, 195
Black Caesar 67, 80, 83
Black Carib 120
blackface 257, 287
Black History Month xv
The Black Jacobins (James) 244
Black National Convention 283
Black Pioneers 113
Black Power Movement 257
Black Rangers 122, 123
Blanchard, George 105

Bland, James 258
Bogle, Paul 146, 173, 296
Bogota, Colombia 24, 43
Bohio, Domingo 37
Boisrond-Tonnere, Louis 147
Bolívar, Simón xxii, 119, 146, 148, 161, 162, 164–166, 183
Bolivia 70, 160, 161, 164
Bolling, Fannie Meade 185
Bologne, Joseph 116–118
Bonaparte, Napoleon xxii, 29, 119, 148, 149
Bonetta, Sarah Forbes 47
Book of Medical Discourses (Crumpler) 209
Boston, Absalom 189, 190
Boston Gazette 91
Boston Guardian 250
Boston Herald 255
Boston Historical and Literary Association 250
Boston, Massachussetts 99–104, 107, 116, 131–133, 140, 186, 190, 195–198, 207, 209, 212, 219, 253, 254
Boston Massacre 86, 99, 103
Boston, Phebe Ann 190
Boston, Prince 189
Boston Slave Rescue 195
Boston University xx, 186
Bouchet, Edward 205
Bowdoin College 191
Bowser, Mary Elizabeth 218, 236, 241, 295
Braganza, Catherine de 17
Branham, Lucy xxix
Brazil xxiii, 10, 21, 35, 43, 46, 52, 54, 60, 64, 68–70, 78, 79, 83, 84, 87, 123, 148, 170, 171, 180, 181, 184, 187, 200–203, 236, 244, 245, 260, 263, 282, 283
Brazil Anti-Slavery Society 202
Breedlove, Sarah 275
Breton, André 181
British Labor Party 286

Brito, Sebastian Rodriguez 60
Brom and Bett v. Ashley 107
Brown, Henry "Box" 213
Brown, John 198, 271, 281
Brown v. Board of Education 284
Brown, William Henry 214
Brown, William Wells xxxiii, 194, 216
Brussels, Belgium 247
Bryan, Andrew 85
Bubonic plague 8
Bucks of America 104
Buenos Aires, Argentina 24, 29, 43, 53, 164
Buffalo, New York 210, 250
Buffalo Soldiers xxix, 99, 159, 186, 227, 231, 266, 288
Bulgaria 26
Bullard, Eugene 268
Bunche, Ralph xxx, 75
Bunch, John 75
Bunch, John, II 75
Bunch, John, III 75
Bunch, Paul 75
Bureau for Colored Troops 221
Burgess, Ezra 152
Burma 267
Burrill, Mary P. 259
Burwell, Armistead 79
Bush, George H. W. 274
Bussa (rebel) 171
Butler, Benjamin 220
Buzzard 214, 240
Byrd, William, II 91
Byzantium 2, 6, 15, 22

C

Cabeza de Vaca 30
Cabra, Spain 27
Caesar's Creek 83
Calhoun, John 215
California 34, 44, 79, 186, 197, 199, 208, 216, 256
California Eagle 257
California State Assembly xxvii
California State University 273

Camagüey, Cuba 232
Cambridge Massachusetts City Hospital xx
Cambridge, Massachussetts 256
Camejo, Pedro 162
Cameron, Simon 220
Camp Alexander 289
Campeche, Mexico 59
Campos, Pedro Albizu 244
Canada xvi, 30, 86, 113, 126, 129, 132, 144, 147, 149, 175, 191, 194, 206, 207, 215, 216, 271
Canary Islands 2, 10–13, 26
Cane River 78
Cantino, Alberto 19
Cantino Planisphere 19
Cape Fear River 225
Cape of Good Hope 8, 30
Cape Town, South Africa 255
Cape Verde 11, 12
Cap-Francais 61
capitalism xvii, xxii, 8, 14, 17, 87
Capitein, Jacobus 95
Caracas, Venezuela 59
Cardozo, Marcos 201
Carey, Lott 146, 175
The Caribbean xxiii, xxiv, 14, 21, 39, 43, 46, 54, 59, 63, 66, 67, 72, 76, 79, 86–88, 100, 101, 109, 112, 113, 118, 119, 124, 132, 136, 146–148, 155, 162, 166, 171, 172, 209, 214, 235, 236, 246, 248, 252, 253, 262, 263, 265, 296
Carleton, Guy xxviii
Carlisle, Cato 108
Carmouche, Pierre 234
Carneiro, Domingo Rodriguez 60
Carolina General Assembly 90
Carriére, Noel 154
"Carry Me Back To Old Virginny" (Bland) 258
Cartagena, Colombia 37, 59, 61, 64, 162–164
Carvajal, Juana 52, 78

Cary, Mary Ann Shadd 186, 206, 236
Casor, John 47, 52, 56, 74
Castellanos, Rosa 234
Castile 11, 69
Catholicism xviii, 51, 52, 55, 68, 69, 72, 80, 81, 84, 97, 160
Catto, Octavius 212
Central Park (New York) 81
Central University of Venezuela 265
Centro Cívico Palmares 264
Cervantes, Antonio "Pambelé" 37
Césaire, Aimé 282, 296
Céspedes, Carlos Manuel de 232, 233
Ceuta, Spain 18
Chaplin, Charlie 259
Charles II 59, 66
Charleston, South Carolina 90, 114, 130, 132, 168, 192, 223
Charlotte of Mecklenburg-Strelitz 27, 47
Chase, Abraham 153
Chase, Samuel 106
Chasseurs Volontaires de Saint-Domingue 115
Chatoyer, Joseph 86, 120
Chavannes, Jean-Baptiste 114
Chavis, John 133
Cherokee Indians 132, 229
Chesapeake-Leopard Affair 146, 151
Cheswell, Hopestill 104
Cheswell, Richard 104
Cheswell, Wentworth 86, 104, 105
Cheyney University 255
Chicago Defender 264
Chicago, Illinois 86, 129, 208, 209, 235, 250, 272, 275, 294
Childs, Matt 171
Chile xvi, 33, 34, 40, 70, 160, 164–166, 187
China 2, 5–9, 15, 22, 181, 216
Chirino, José 121
Christianity xviii, 6, 8, 29, 39, 44, 47, 65, 67, 69–71, 73, 75, 85, 95, 132, 134, 171, 175, 215, 216, 247

Christiansborg, West Africa 95
Christina, Queen of Sweden 68
Christmas Rebellion 146, 172
Christophe, Henri xxii
Churchill Downs 230
Church, Robert Reed xxxiii, 276, 277
citizenship xv–xvii, xxi, 53, 63, 108,
   115, 118, 131, 132, 136, 147, 148,
   169, 178, 179, 187, 188, 191, 201,
   202, 207, 208, 217, 233, 234, 247,
   253, 257, 259, 263, 273, 280, 283,
   296, 297
civil rights 86, 146, 189–192, 196–199,
   201, 206, 208, 210, 211, 214, 215,
   227, 247–252, 255, 272, 279–281,
   283, 284, 286, 292
Civil Rights Act of 1875 207
civil rights movement xv, xxiii, 53, 208,
   216, 245, 246, 260, 284, 285
Claasen, Franz 94
Clark, Lewis xxxiii
Clarkson, Thomas 102, 114, 126
Clay, Henry 186, 198, 238, 281
Clement VII 28
Cleveland Association of Colored Men
   269
Cleveland, Grover 249
Cleveland, Ohio 211
Cloise, Peter 66
Clovis II 23
coartacion 71, 101, 130, 200
Cobre, Cuba 52, 65, 70, 122
Cochrane, Alexander 155
Cocom, Mario de Valdez y 27
Code Noir 52, 72, 76
coffee 87, 115, 170, 200
Coincoin 78–80
Coker, Daniel 210
Cole, Bob 258
Cole, Rebecca 209
Coleridge-Taylor, Samuel 249
Colihaut rebellion 122
Collavechio, Simonetta da 47
College of William and Mary 66

Colombia 24, 35–38, 41, 43, 46, 52,
   54, 64, 67, 127, 146, 148, 160–166,
   179
Colon, Diego 35
colonialism xviii, xxi, xxiv, 11, 12, 31,
   36, 37, 40, 42, 44–46, 53–55, 57, 58,
   61–63, 65–67, 69–73, 75–81, 86–89,
   91, 93, 94, 96, 97, 99–101, 105,
   113–115, 119, 121–126, 130, 131,
   133, 135–137, 146–149, 152, 161,
   163, 165, 168–175, 178, 179, 186,
   189, 193, 195, 203, 204, 215, 219,
   220, 227, 228, 233, 234, 245, 247,
   248, 253, 294, 295
Colorado 44
Colored National Labor Union 292
Colson, James 185
Colson, James Major, III 185
Colson, William 176, 177, 185
Columbia University 276
Columbus, Christopher 10, 13, 18, 19,
   24, 25, 27, 29, 32, 35, 45, 295
Combahee Ferry Raid 218
Commonsense (Paine) 192
Compromise of 1850 196, 198
Compromise of 1877 227
Confederate States of America xxx,
   xxxiii, 74, 218–223, 241, 269, 294
Congress of Racial Equality 284, 285
Connecticut 107, 180
conquistadores 20, 30, 33, 45, 48, 294
Constantinople 2, 15
Continental Army 106, 110, 114
Contraband Relief Association 226
convict labor systems xix, xxxii
Cook, Pardon 189
Cooper, Anna Julia xxxiii, 249, 251
Coppin, Fanny Jackson 255, 256
Coppin, Levi Jenkins 255
Coppin State University 256
Cordoba, Mexico 6, 18, 92
Cornish, Samuel 186, 191
Cornwallis, Charles 110
Coronado expedition 80

Coro, Venezuela 121
Cortez, Hernan 24, 30, 32, 34
Costa, Mathieu da 30
Costa Rica 34, 234, 252
The Count of Monte Cristo (Dumas) 116
Covey, James 240
Cox, Edward 120
Craft, Ellen xxxiii
Crafus, Richard 153
Crawford, James xxxiii
Creed, Cortlandt Van Rensselaer 205
Creek Indians 98, 157, 181, 229, 268
Creole 78, 96, 263
Creole 217
Crespo, Juaquín 166
Crimean War 209
The Crisis 287
Cromwell, Oliver 107
Crumpler, Rebecca 186, 208, 236
The Crusades 8
Cuba xxiii, 13, 19, 24, 29, 32, 34–36,
    41–43, 46, 52, 54, 61, 65–69, 77, 104,
    114, 115, 120, 122, 131, 146–149,
    158, 159, 162, 166, 169–172, 179–
    181, 184, 186, 187, 200, 202, 203,
    210, 212–215, 232–234, 236, 243,
    245, 260–263, 265, 280, 282, 295
Cuban Liberation Army 232
Cuffe, John 188
Cuffe, Paul 186, 188, 189, 191
Cuffe, William 189
Cugoano, Ottobah 127
Cummings, E. E. 256
Curaçao 120, 121, 197
Custer's Last Stand 228
Custis, Daniel Parke xxix
Custis, Eleanor xxix
Custis, George Washington Parke xxix
Cuzco, Peru 20, 34
Cyprus 11

D

Damas, Léon 282
Dandridge, Ann xxix
Danube River 7

Dartmoor Prison 153
Dartmouth College 140, 185, 205
Dávalos, José Manuel 204
Davis, Benjamin O., Jr. 268
Davis, Benjamin O., Sr. 268
Davis, Edward 66
Davis, Jefferson 218, 226, 241
Davis, William 94
Day, John, Jr. 178
Day, John, Sr. xxxiii, 178
Day, Thomas 177, 178
Deagan, Kathleen 47
Decatur, Stephen 193
Declaration of Independence xix, xxv,
    xxviii, xxxiii, 192, 215, 251, 265
Declaration of Principles (Niagara Move-
    ment) 251, 265
The Declaration of the Rights of Man
    (Oge) 114
Deerfield, Massachussetts 105
Degas, Edward 180, 294
de La Fuente, Alejandro 77
Delany, Lucy 198
Delany, Martin 208
Delaware 135, 206, 209
Delaware River 107
Delhi, India 16
Demerara. *See* Guyana
Demerara Rebellion 146, 171, 172
democracy xv, xix, xxii, xxiii, xxx, xxxiii,
    4, 58, 98, 104, 134, 144, 147–149,
    153, 166, 174, 175, 178, 187, 188,
    194, 196, 197, 201, 204, 205, 208,
    213, 217, 225, 233–236, 244, 245,
    247, 250, 253, 257, 260, 263–265,
    268, 273, 277, 280, 282–286, 296,
    297
Denison, Peter 152
Denmark 46, 47, 93–96, 112, 138
Deslondes, Charles 146, 150, 178
Detroit, Michigan 152, 194
Dias, Bartolomeu 8, 30
Dias, Henrique 60, 84
Dickens, Charles 248

Dinerstein, Joel 257
discrimination xix, xxiv, xxxi, xxxii, 59, 62, 68, 73, 79, 81, 87, 90, 130, 132, 174, 180, 187, 189, 197, 203, 204, 222, 236, 244, 246, 250, 257, 259–262, 266, 280, 283, 290, 297
DNA 47, 84
Dodson, Jacob 219
Domesday Book 21
Dominica 120, 122
Dominican Republic 13, 25, 27, 32, 36–38, 46, 57, 119, 146, 166, 183
Don Quixote (Cervantes) 29
Dorantes, Esteban "El Negro" 24, 30
Doria, Manuel Gonzales 52, 60
Dorman, Isaiah 228
Dos Santos, Arlindo 264
Dos Santos, Isoltino Veiga 264
Douglas, Lewis Henry 227
Douglas, Robert 213
Douglass, Charles Remond 197, 227
Douglass, Frederick xxxiii, 168, 187, 188, 194, 197, 208, 213, 227, 242, 279, 293
Douglass, Laura 227
Downing, George Thomas 206, 248, 292
Downing, Henry Francis 206, 248, 292
Downing, Thomas 248
Draft Riot 205
Drake, Francis 24, 39
Drew, Charles 244, 274, 290, 296
Driggus, Emmanuel 56
Du Bois, W. E. B. xviii, xxix, 149, 244, 249–253, 256, 261, 286
Duke University 145, 235
Dumas, Alexandre 116, 118
Dummer Academy 105
Dunbar School 259, 268, 273, 279, 290
Duncanson, Robert S. 181
Dunham, Ann xxx
Dunmore Proclamation 86
Duplex, Prince 208
Dupuy, Charlotte 186, 198

Durham, James 140
Durham, North Carolina 279
Dutch Berbice 123
Dutch West India Company 57

E

East Africa 5, 8
Easterbrooks, Prince 86
Easterling, Ruth xx
Easter Plot 167
East Louisiana Railroad 235
Ecuador 24, 36, 38, 39, 41, 46, 54, 64, 70, 160–166
Edinburgh University 205
Edison Company 270
Edison Pioneers 270
Edison, Thomas 238, 242, 270
Egerton, Douglas 101, 113, 167
Eguia, Francisco de 32
Egypt 2, 5, 16, 26
Eisenhower, Dwight xxvii
Elaw, Zilpha 213
Elfrith, Daniel 67
Elizé, Raphael 268
Ellington, Duke 231
El Nuevo Criollo 263
El Paso, Texas 228
emancipation xxi, 65, 76, 79, 112, 118, 119, 156, 165, 168, 177, 182, 185, 187, 200, 204, 219–221, 224, 226, 228, 234, 241, 252, 264, 270, 295
Emancipation Proclamation xv, xxiii, 221, 266, 296
Emancipation Wars 146, 171, 172
Embargo of 1807 152
Emerson College 259
emigration 146, 208
Emory University xxxiii
Enclosure Acts 81, 174
England, English xvi, xxi, xxiii, xxv, xxviii, 2, 5, 10, 17, 21, 22, 27, 39, 45, 47, 52, 53, 55–59, 62, 63, 66–68, 71, 73, 74, 81, 86, 89, 91–95, 97–105, 107–115, 119–128, 131–133, 135, 137–141, 144, 146, 147, 151–157,

163, 164, 166, 171–174, 188, 189,
191, 195, 197, 209, 210, 212–215,
217, 240, 244, 248, 249, 252, 254,
258, 267, 281, 286
Enlightenment xviii, xxii–xxiv, 3, 52,
53, 68, 80, 86, 96, 115, 128, 131, 132,
147, 203, 204, 212, 234, 295
Episcopalianism 250, 284
equality 163, 165, 166, 173, 174, 192,
193, 212, 219, 226, 233–236, 250,
252, 253, 261, 263, 279, 285, 286
Equality 261
Equal Justice Initiative 291
Equal Rights League 209
Equiano, Olaudah 86, 126, 127, 146,
174
Esmeraldas 38, 39, 41
Espinar, José Domingo 166
Estenoz, Evanisto 244, 261
Ethiopia 2, 16, 26
Ethiopian Regiment 112
eugenics xxxii
Eurasia 2, 7
Evanston, Indiana 286
exogamy xix, xxv, 29, 72, 73, 75–79,
81, 116, 119, 211, 246, 293

F

Fabian Society 286
Fabulé, Francisque 65
Farragut, David 223
fascism 274
Federal Bureau of Investigation 256,
257
federalism 264
Federal Militia Act 219
Federation of Afro-American Women
279
Fédon, Julien 86, 120, 122, 296
feminism 262, 283
Femmes de France 251
Ferdinand II 29
Fergusson, William 205
Fermina (revolutionary) 171
feudalism 98

Fields, W. C. 259
Figueroa, Luis Beltrán Prieto 265
Firmin, Anténor 248
First African Baptist Church 85
First Confiscation Act 220
First Continental Congress 101
First Maroon Treaty 92
The Fish (Williams) 259
Fisk University 281
Fleetwood, Christian 225
Flipper, Henry 288
Flora, William 141
Florença, Domingo de 27
Florence, Italy 24, 28, 47, 197
Flores Pasageres (Manzano) 203
Florida 19, 30, 32, 34, 36, 41, 43–46,
51, 52, 54, 56, 59–62, 67, 68, 79, 86,
89, 90, 93, 97–99, 104, 113, 115, 121,
156–159, 172, 179–181, 220, 280
Florida A&M University 241, 251
Folsom, New Mexico 230
Foner, Eric 196
Ford, George xxix
Ford, West xxix, xxxiii
Fort Duncan 228
Fort Monroe 220
Fort Mosé 44, 86, 98
Fort Sumter 168, 219
Fort Wagner 227
Forten, Charlotte 145, 197, 213
Forten, Harriet 145
Forten, James 86, 135, 136, 145, 152
Fort Sill 288
Fossett, Edith 199, 250
Fossett, Joseph 199
France, French xviii, xxii, xxiv, xxvii, 4,
10, 11, 21–23, 29, 30, 43, 45, 47, 52,
61, 62, 65, 68, 71, 72, 76, 78, 84, 86,
93, 94, 100, 111, 115–124, 127–129,
133, 147–149, 153–155, 167, 180,
193, 194, 199, 216, 234, 235, 251,
255, 261, 268, 271, 282
Francés, Juan el 122
Frances, Mary 153

Francis, Nathaniel 169
Franklin, Benjamin 103, 106, 131
Franklin Institute 212
Franklin, Martha Minerva 267
Fratello, Benedict da San 69
Fraunces, Sam xxviii
Frederick I 95
Free African Society 86, 134
Freedman's Bureau 209
Freedom Rides 285
Freedom's Journal 186, 191–193
Freeman, Elizabeth 47, 86, 107
Freeman, Robert Tanner 208
Freemasons 86, 131–134, 193, 234, 268, 269
Freetown, Sierra Leone 210
Freidan, Betty 284
Frémont, John C. 219, 220
French and Indian War. *See* Seven Years' War
French Guyana 45, 282
French National Assembly 116
French National Convention 118
French Quarter 78
French Revolution xxii, 3, 61, 86, 88, 116–118, 120, 136, 151, 163, 234
Frenegal, Juan de 42
Frente Negra Brasileira 244, 264, 282
Frías, Hugo Rafael Chávez 184
The Fugitive Blacksmith (Pennington) 216
Fugitive Slave Act of 1793 86, 111, 238
Fugitive Slave Act of 1850 196, 207
Fuller, Meta 181
Fuller, Solomon Carter xx
Fuller, Thomas 128
Furtado, Júnia Ferreira 79

G

Gage, Thomas 67
Gaines, Edmund 98
Gainesville, Florida 98
Gainsboro, Thomas 127
Gálvez, Bernardo de 114, 154, 170
Gama, Luís 201, 236

Gambia River 9, 14, 113
Gandhi 284
Garay, Catalina 42
Garcia, Juan 34
The Garies and Their Friends (Webb) 213
Garnes, Thomas 177
Garnet, Henry Highland 186, 194, 210, 213
Garrido, Juan 19, 24, 31, 32, 43
Garrison, William Lloyd 136, 192, 197, 213
Garvey, Amy Ashwood 252, 253, 296
Garveyism 253
Garvey, Marcus xxvii, 244, 252, 253, 261, 264
Gaspee Affair 99
Gaulle, Charles De 289
genealogy 84, 293
Genoa, Italy 10
genomics 5
George, David 85, 175
Georgetown University 282, 293
Georgia 24, 36, 73, 91, 97, 98, 156, 157, 175, 179, 181, 182, 192, 199, 252, 268, 273
Germany 61, 86, 95, 113, 119, 126, 144, 216, 268, 289
Gerzina, Gretchen 106
Ghana 7, 93, 95, 127, 173
Gibbs, Mifflin Wistar 251
Gilder Lehrman Collection 139
Gil, Juan José Nieto 166
Gil, Madalena 27
Ginsburg, Ruth Bader 284
Gladstone, William 171
Glenn, John 273
Glidden Company 275
Gobineau, Arthur de 248
gold 9, 10, 13, 20–22, 32, 34, 38, 42
Gomez, Esteban 24, 30, 58
Gómez, Juan Gualberto 261, 263
Gonzales, Feliciano 166
Gonzales, José 121
Gonzales, Juan 32

Gordon, Dexter 231
Gould, William B. 224, 225
Gracia Real de Santa Teresa de Mosé 90
Graham, Elizabeth Jennings 197, 235
Grajales, Mariana 234
Granada, Nicaragua 208
Granada, Spain 24
Grant, George Franklin 272
Grant, Ulysses S. 222
Granville, Evelyn 273
Great African Slave Revolt of 1825 170
Great Awakening 95
Great Dismal Swamp 97, 113, 142
Greece 2, 4–8, 26
Greenland 9
Green Mountain Boys 107
Green, Petter 189
Green, Richard Henry 205
Greensboro, North Carolina 279
Greensburg, Indiana 286
Greenwich Village 57, 213, 214
Grenada 48, 86, 120, 122, 127
Griffin, Bessie Blount 270, 271
Griffith, D.W. 257, 259, 273
Grillo, Diego 66
Grimke, Angelina 136, 145
Grimke, Archibald xxxiii
Grimke, Francis 145
Grimke, Sarah 136, 145
Grinstead, John 74
Grito de Yara 232
Guadeloupe 32, 76, 117, 118, 124, 148, 210, 251
Guanches 26
Guatemala 33, 34, 40, 68, 77
Guerrero, Vicente 146, 148, 160, 161, 166, 179, 295
Guillén, Nicolás 263, 282
Guizot, Louis 116, 268
Gulf Coast 114, 157
Gutenberg Press 2
Guyana xxiii, 41, 46, 76, 104, 111, 120, 122, 123, 146, 171, 172
Guzman, Diego 37

H

Hadrian's Wall 5
Haiti xxii, xxiv, 13, 46, 66, 72, 86, 93, 115–119, 121, 122, 129, 140, 146–151, 154, 162, 166, 168, 170, 172, 177, 186, 191, 207, 210, 211, 219, 232–235, 248, 266, 268, 281, 282
Haitian Revolution xxii, 3, 86, 88, 112, 114, 119, 120, 124, 136, 147–149, 151, 154, 163, 167, 168, 170, 191, 200, 203, 210, 234, 280, 295
Hall, Gwendolyn 122
Hall, Lloyd 274
Hall, Prince 86, 131, 132, 134
Hamilton, Jeremiah 291
Hammon, Briton 86, 103
Hammon, Jupiter 103, 106
Hampton, Lionel 231
Hancock, John 104, 131
Hansberry, Lorraine 287
Harlem Hellfighters 244, 267, 268
Harlem Hospital 269, 273
Harlem (New York City) 283
Harlem Renaissance 207, 257, 281
Harper, Frances 210, 254
Harper's Ferry 281
Harrison, Benjamin 279
Harris, Samuel 189
Harvard Odontological Society 272
Harvard University xx, xxvii, 132, 145, 149, 208, 250, 254, 256, 272, 273, 275, 279, 280, 283
Havana, Cuba 42, 43, 50, 52, 54, 62, 67, 77, 78, 98, 156, 170, 203, 215, 243, 262, 263, 294
Hawley, Nero 107
Hayden, Lewis 196, 198
Hayden, Palmer 181
Hayes, Rutherford B. 227
Haynes, Lemuel 107
Healy, Patrick Francis 293
Helg, Aline 287
Hemings, Elizabeth xxv, xxvi, xxxii, xxxiii

Hemings, Harriet xxvii
Hemings, James xxvi
Hemings, Madison xxvii
Hemings, Sally xxv–xxvii, xxxiii, 78
Hemings, Thenia xxvii
Henry, Patrick 108
Henry Street Settlement House 270
Henson, Josiah 213
Henson, Matthew 31
Hercules (slave) 111
Heredia, Consuelo A. Serra 262
Herndon, Alonzo xxxiii, 252, 286
Herndon Foundation 286
Herndon, Norris Bumstead 286
Hessian 113, 144
Heureaux, Ulises 166
He, Zeng 8
Hidalgo, Miguel 160
Hidden Figures (Shetterly) 273
Hilton, John T. 193
Hilton, Lavinia 193
Hinduism 6
Hinton, William xx, 244
Hispaniola 13, 20, 24, 32, 34–38, 43, 59, 72
History of the Future (Vieira) 68
H.M.S. *Melampus* 152
Hobbes, Thomas 55
Holland 57, 68
Holocaust 268
Homer 2
The Homesteader (Micheaux) 244, 259
Honduras 24, 34, 35, 121, 234
Honoré, Isodore 154
Hope, John 110
Horse, John 158, 159, 178, 182
Howard University 206, 211, 258, 278, 282
Howe, Julia Ward 254
Hudson, Henry 58
Hudson, Julien 154
Hudson River Valley 24, 58
Hughes, Langston 207, 238, 268, 281, 282

Hughes, Victor 124
Hugo, Victor 216
Hull, Agrippa 106
Hunter College 262
Hunter, David 220
Hunt, Ida Gibbs 251
Hunt, William 251
Hyers, Anna 258
Hyers, Emma 258

I

Iberia. *See* Spain *and* Portugal
Iberian Peninsula 29
IBM 273
Iland, Anthony 52, 71
The Iliad (Homer) 2
Illescas, Alonso de 24, 39
Illinois 210, 274
immigration xvi, xviii, xxxiii, 37, 42, 57, 74, 87, 124, 127, 150, 170, 178, 210, 216, 262, 270
Imperial Constitution of 1805 119
imperialism 119, 234, 243, 247, 266
Impressionism 84
Inca 20
Incandescent Electric Lighting: A Practical Description of the Edison System (Latimer) 270
indentured servitude 52, 55, 56, 58, 59, 67, 72, 74, 113, 137, 174
independence xvi, 24, 70, 93, 98, 100, 101, 112, 146, 147, 152, 157, 159–165, 176, 186, 187, 203, 211, 232–234, 236, 243, 246, 247, 260–265
Independent Party of Color 262, 263
India xxiii, 5–8, 10, 13, 15, 17, 248, 284, 286
Indiana 199
Indian Removal Act of 1830 158
Indonesia 8
industrialization 17, 257
Industry 189
inequality xix, 264
Infante, Leonardo 162

Innocent XI 69
Institute for Colored Youth 211, 212, 255
integration 134, 186, 189, 197, 199, 206, 210–212, 222, 227, 244, 280, 283, 284
The Interesting Narrative of the Life of Olaudah Equiano (Equiano) 125, 126
Iola Leroy (Harper) 210
Iran 8, 15
Ireland 55, 81, 99, 137, 174, 196, 207
Isabel I 29
Islam 2, 6–9, 15, 16, 18, 22, 26, 33, 201
Italy 2, 10, 19, 22, 24, 26, 47, 68, 197
Ivonett, Pedro 261

J

Jablonowski, Wladyslaw 119
Jackson, Andrew 154, 155, 157, 158, 181, 230
Jackson, Elizabeth 144
Jackson, Luther 76, 244
Jacksonville, Florida 280
Jacobin 124
Jamaica xxiii, xxv, xxxiii, 17, 36, 41, 46, 54, 66, 86, 89, 91–93, 104, 113, 120, 123, 124, 129, 146, 148, 155, 172, 173, 191, 205, 209, 210, 213, 234, 244, 252, 253, 286
James, C. L. R. 244
James, Henry 242
James River 108, 176
Jamestown xvi, 36, 44, 53, 55, 58, 177
Janissary 16
Jarrett, Richard 177
jazz 257, 268
Jefferson, John 159, 266
Jefferson, Martha xxv, xxvi, xxxii
Jefferson, Thomas xix, xxv–xxvii, xxxii, 78, 93, 103, 106, 128, 150, 152, 172, 199, 241, 250
Jenné, Mali 2, 7
Jennings, Elizabeth 186
Jennings, Paul 128, 186

Jennings, Thomas 197
Jesús, Ursula de 69
Jim Crow xix, 186, 196, 227, 250, 289
Johannesburg, South Africa 276
John IV 68
Johnson, Anthony 52, 56, 80, 293
Johnson, Halle Tanner Dillon 278
Johnson, Henry 267
Johnson, James Weldon 280, 281
Johnson, John 56
Johnson, Joshua 181
Johnson, J. Rosamond 258
Johnson, Katherine 273
Johnson, Richard 56
Johnson, Robert 90
Johnson v. Parker 56
Jones, Absalom 86, 133, 134, 136, 145
Jones, Allen 271
Jones, Anna H. 271, 272
Jones, Charles 271
Jones, Frederick McKinley 244, 274
Jones, James Monroe 271
Jones, Jane Wright 274
Jones, John Paul 105, 108
Jones, Paul 108
Jones, Sophie Bethena 271, 272
Jordan, George 228
José, Antonio 170
journalism xvii, xxvi, xxvii, 91, 131, 144, 153, 186, 188, 191, 192, 194, 196, 201, 202, 204, 206, 208, 217, 218, 227, 235, 236, 246, 252, 254–257, 260, 261, 263–265, 270, 271, 278, 280–283, 296
Judaism 6, 33, 72, 84, 289
Judge, Ona xxvi, 111
Julian Laboratories 275
Julian, Percy Lavon 275, 291, 297
Julian Research Institute 275
July, Johanna 228
Just, Ernest 244
Justinian code xviii

K

Kansas xxx, 221

Kansas City, Kansas 255
Keckley, Elizabeth xxxiii, 79, 226
Kee, Salaria 269
Keiser Wilhelm Institute 244
Kennedy, John F. 284
Kenner, Harry 151
Kentucky 194, 198, 231, 266, 269
Kentucky Derby 230
Key, Elizabeth 52, 71, 74
Key, Elliot 67
Key, Francis Scott 227
Key, John 74
Key West, Florida 234
King, Martin Luther, Jr. 285, 289
King Philip's War 62, 139
King, Susie Taylor 296
King William's War 62, 139, 219
Knight, Jack 108
Kosciuszko, Tadeuz 106
Ku Klux Klan xxxii, 256, 257

L

La Cosa, Juan de 19
La Escalera 146, 171, 203
Lafitte, Pierre 154
Lagos, Nigeria 201
La Isabella 25, 47
Lake Champlain 30, 152
Lake Erie 269
Lake Michigan 129
La Liga 262
Lamson, David 104
Lam, Wilfredo 181
Lane, James H. 221
Langston, Charles Henry 281
Langston, John Mercer xxxiii, 79, 207, 227, 242, 282
Laredo, Texas 228
Larringa, José Pastor de 204
Las Trampas, New Mexico 60
Latimer Act 195
Latimer, George xxxiii, 47, 186, 195, 238, 270
Latimer Law 270
Latimer, Lewis Howard 238, 270

Latimer, Rebecca 186, 195, 238, 270
Latino, Juan 24, 27, 29, 48, 102
Leachy, William 71
Lebanon 26
Lee, Robert E. xxix, 222, 226, 241, 294
Lee, William xxviii, 111
Legion of the Americas 117, 118
Leile, George 85
Le Maniel 66
Lemba (freedom fighter) 37
Leon, Ponce de 19, 32
Leopard 152
Le Paon, John-Baptiste 109, 141
Lew, Barzillai 104
Lewis and Clark expedition 146, 150
Lewis and Clark on the Lower Columbia (Russell) 150
Lewis, Edmonia 181
Lewis, Oscar 230
Lewis, Robert 186, 193
liberalism 162, 164–166
liberation xvi, xx, xxiii, xxiv, xxvi, xxix, 35, 37, 38, 58, 76, 80, 88, 89, 105, 111, 129, 152, 156, 158, 162, 164, 166, 175, 187, 188, 190, 194–196, 214, 216–218, 220–223, 232, 245, 266, 281, 282, 294, 296, 297
The Liberator 186, 192
Liberia xx, xxx, 132, 146, 174–179, 191, 201, 210, 217–219, 251, 266, 267
liberty 70, 89, 91–93, 96, 106, 108, 110, 129, 130, 132, 147, 148, 155, 157, 162, 167, 174, 179, 188, 195, 196, 215, 217, 218, 234, 236, 241, 261, 294, 296, 297
Liberty Party 186, 194
Liedesdorff, William 144
"Lift Every Voice and Sing" (Johnson) 280
Light and Truth (Lewis) 186, 193
Lima, Peru 24, 32, 34, 38, 42, 54, 69, 294
Lincoln, Abraham xv, xxii, xxiii, 160,

161, 182, 219–221, 224, 226, 242, 295
Lincoln Hospital 279
Lincoln, Mary Todd 79, 226
Lincoln University 255
Lisbon, Portugal 26, 27, 29, 32, 68, 69, 113, 247
Livingston, Philip xxxiii
Llerena, Andres de 42
Locke, Alain 244
Locke, John 131
Lockhart, James 34
London, England xxviii, 100, 103, 113, 114, 127, 174, 206, 209, 244, 247–249, 252, 272
London School of Economics 286
Lone Ranger 186, 229
Longfellow, Henry Wadsworth 212
Lord Byron 213
Los Angeles, California 53, 86, 128, 144, 199, 257, 294
Los Angeles Herald 255
Louisa Ulrika of Sweden 47
Louisiana xxiv, 76, 78, 79, 88, 97, 114, 120, 122, 130, 146, 149, 151, 153, 154, 159, 170, 172, 179, 180, 192, 234, 235
Louisiana Purchase 149, 150
Louis XI 47
Louis XV 117
Louis XVI 109
L'Ouverture, Toussaint 118, 142, 146, 295
Love, Nat 228
Love, Vaughn 269
Love, Walter J. 269
Loyalists xxi, xxv, 86, 99, 112, 113, 124, 129, 133, 136, 140, 142, 155, 156, 174, 175
Lubolo, Juan 66
Lucas, Sam 258
Lucumí, Carlota 171, 178
Luís Gama Emancipation Fund 201
lynching xxxii, 186, 235, 259, 277, 281, 291
Lynch, John Roy xxxiii

M

Mabry, Godfrey 177
Maceo, Antonio 148, 166, 213, 232–236, 243, 295
Madagascar 251
Madeira, Portugal 2, 11–13
Madison, James 128, 186
Madrid, Spain 28, 33, 69, 230
Magellan, Ferdinand 30
Mahin, Luisa 201
Mahoney, Mary Eliza 244, 267
Maine 191, 193
Malé rebellion 201
Mali 2, 7, 9, 10
Malocello, Lancelotto 2, 10
Malone, Annie 275
Manchester, England 247, 253
Manhattan Medical Society 273
Manhattan (New York City) 52, 248
Manifest Destiny 266
Manly, Charles 134
Mann, Miriam Daniel 273
Mansa Musa 2, 9, 10
manumission xxi, xxiv, 38, 70, 75–77, 79, 90, 100, 105, 106, 108, 125, 126, 130, 133, 134, 139, 141, 153, 165, 175, 177, 199, 201, 202, 227, 271, 288, 294
Manzano, Juan Francisco 203
Maracaibo, Venezuela 146, 164
Marchena, Francisco de 42
Margarita, Venezuela 38
Margru, Sarah 240
Maria Theresa of Spain 47
Marie-Thérèse, Louise 47
Marinho, Amaro 201
Marley, Bob 293
maroons xvi, xxi, xxv, 24, 36–46, 52, 54, 59, 63–66, 70, 80, 86, 88, 91–94, 96–98, 113, 118, 120–126, 129, 136, 146, 156, 157, 173, 182, 264, 282, 294

Maroon Wars xxv, 37, 66, 86, 89, 91, 124, 129, 136
Marquetti, Campos 261
Márquez, Remigio 163
Marquis de Condorcet 128
Marquis de Lafayette 109, 110
Marrant, John 132
Marshall, Thurgood 284
Martel, Ana 41
Martí, José 232, 262
Martin, Daniel 152
Martín, Diego 67, 68
Martinet, Louis 235
Martinique 65, 76, 94, 118, 120, 254, 268, 282
Martín, José Jouve 204
Martín, José San 164
Maryland 52, 54–56, 58, 71, 73, 88, 181, 187, 216, 270
Maryland Gazette 132
Maryland General Assembly 58
Mashow, John 190
Mason, Bridget "Biddy" 144, 199
Mason, Henry 177
Mason, James W. xxxiii
Massachusetts 44, 73, 86, 101–107, 131–133, 145, 180, 186, 188–190, 192, 193, 195, 196, 207, 222, 254, 270
Massachusetts Anti-Slavery Society 190
Massachusetts General Colored Society 193
Matanzas, Cuba 171, 234
Matisse, Henri 181
Matthews, George 156
Matudere 52, 64
Mauritania 203
Mayans 44
Mayflower 37, 44
Mayo, Charlie 209
Mayo Clinic 209
Mazzini, Giuseppe 197
McCoy, Elijah 296
McDonough, Thomas 152

McJunkin, George 230, 244
Mecca 16
Medici, Alessandro de 24, 28, 47
Medici, Catherine de 22
Medici, Giulio de 47
The Mediterranean 2, 9, 11–13
Mehmet 15
Mejias, Francisco 32
Melrose Plantation 78
Memphis, Tennessee 235, 277
Mende 214, 215, 217
Mendez, Teresa de Jesus 183
Mendi Mission School 240
Mendonça, Lourenço da Silva de 52, 69
Mendoza, Carlos Antonio 184, 244, 265
Menendez, Francisco 59, 90, 97
Menezes, José Ferreira de 202, 236
Menses, Cristobal de 27
mercantilism 14
Mercy Hospital 145
Merida, Mexico 44
Merrick, John 263, 279
Mesopotamia 4
Methodism 133, 134, 168, 255
Metoyer, Louis 78
Metoyer, Nicolas Augustin 78
Mexican-American War 44
Mexican Revolution 159, 161, 266
Mexico 2, 5, 20, 24, 30, 32, 34–36, 38, 41–44, 46, 48, 52–54, 59, 60, 62, 64, 67–70, 77, 82, 114, 146, 148, 154, 158–160, 166, 170, 179, 187, 228, 230, 245, 266, 282, 288, 295
Mexico City, Mexico 20, 30, 32, 44, 48, 54, 294
Miami, Florida 67
Micheaux, Oscar 244, 259
Michigan 152, 194
Middle Ages 2, 4, 6, 7, 26
Middlebury College 108
Middle Passage xxx, xxxiii, 35, 103, 217, 271
Miguel I 38

Militia Act 221
Miller, Dorie 244
Milton, North Carolina 178
Minas Gerais, Brazil 78
Minerva 263
Minkins, Shadrach 196, 207
Minnesota 274
Minns, Allan Glaisyer 244, 248
Mirror of Liberty 188
miscegenation 73
Mississippi xxxii, 179, 199, 206, 211, 222, 289
Mississippi River 43, 114, 129, 149
Missouri 198, 220, 221
Missouri Compromise 105
Missouri River 150
mixed race xxvi, xxxi, 27, 29, 31, 33, 40, 42, 47, 48, 52–55, 58–60, 66, 68, 70–77, 79, 80, 90, 99, 105, 114, 115, 118, 123, 128–130, 141, 151, 153, 154, 160–162, 170, 177, 178, 188, 191, 194, 195, 211, 225, 226, 250, 252, 260, 276, 281, 283, 293
M.L. (Alcott) 211
modernization 257
Mogorán, Juan de Valladolid 29, 61
Mohammad 2, 6, 16
Mohammad al-Idrisi 18
Molineaux, Tom 128, 144
Mongols 2, 6–8, 15, 16
Monroe, James xxv, xxvii, 167, 172
Monrovia, Liberia 176
Montevideo, Uruguay 264
Montgomery, Alabama 275
Montgomery Bus Boycott 285
Montgomery, James 218
Monticello xxv, xxvi, xxxii, 78, 199, 250, 293
Montpellier, Virginia 128
Montreal, Canada 196
Moore, Aaron 263, 279
Moore, Lewis Baxter 278
Moors 2
Morales, Nicolas 170

Morant Bay Rebellion 173
Moravian Church 95
Morehead, Scipio 102
Morelos, José María 69, 160, 161
Moreno, Juan 52, 65
Morgan, Edmund 58
Morgan, Garrett xxxiii, 269
Morgan, Henry 66
Morgan, Sidney xxxiii
Morris, Robert 186, 196, 207, 236
Mossell, Nathan 278
Mossell, Sadie 244
Mount Vernon xxviii, xxix, 113, 175
Mozart, Wolfgang Amadeus 116
Mughals 15
Mulato, Diego el 67
multiculturalism 297
Murphy, Isaac 231
Murray, Anna Pauline xxxiii, 283, 284, 297
Murray, John, Lord Dunmore 112, 155
Murray, William, Earl of Mansfield 100, 127, 139
Museo del Prado 28
Myers, Isaac 292

N
Nanny Town 173
Nantucket, Massachussetts 189, 190, 197
Napoleonic Wars 152, 163
Narváez, Pánfilo 30
Nascimento, Abdias do 245, 282
Nash, Gary 112
Natchitoches, Louisiana 78
The Nation 281
National Academy of Science 275
National Advisory Committee for Aeronautics 272
National Aeronautics and Space Administration 272
National American Woman Suffrage Association 279
National Archives 241
National Association for the

Advancement of Colored People xxix, 235, 244, 250–255, 269, 271, 273, 275, 276, 279–281, 283, 287
National Association of Colored Graduate Nurses 267
National Association of Colored Women 186, 210, 251, 253–257, 272, 279
National Equal Rights League 207, 212
National Federation of African American Women 253
National Federation of Black Societies 263
National Inventors Hall of Fame 274
nationalism 148, 233, 247, 253, 262
National League of Colored Women 253
National Organization for Women 284
National Research Act (1974) xx
National Safety Device Company 269
Nation of Islam 253
Native Americans 20, 21, 30, 32, 33, 35, 38–41, 43, 45, 48, 53, 55, 57, 60–62, 64, 66, 68, 69, 72, 73, 77, 89, 97–99, 104, 105, 121, 129, 156–160, 174, 188, 193, 228, 229, 250, 266, 288
Natural Born Gambler (Williams) 259
The Nature and Importance of True Republicanism (Haynes) 108
Nebraska 288
Negro, Benito el 32
Negro Convention Movement 194
Negro Fort 146, 156–158
Negro People's Committee 274
Negro World 264
Nell, William Cooper 140, 213
Nelson, Sanford 272
The Netherlands 14, 21, 30, 45, 52, 57, 60, 62, 67, 74, 84, 92–95, 121–123, 126, 171
Nevada 44
New Bedford, Connecticut 190, 197
New Bedford's Union Society 190
New Brunswick, Canada 129, 156

New England Abolitionist Society 193
New England Conservatory of Music 280
New Guinea 267
New Hampshire 86, 104, 105, 111
New Haven, Connecticut 186, 214, 283
New Jersey 112
New London, Connecticut 214
Newmarket, New Hampshire 105
New Mexico 44, 52, 53, 60, 79, 80, 228, 244
New Orleans, Louisiana 78, 129, 140, 149, 151, 154, 166, 216, 234, 277
Newport News, Virginia 289
Newport, Rhode Island 103, 132, 133, 206
Newsome, Berry 169
New York 30, 52, 54, 57, 79, 84, 96, 112, 127, 132, 152, 186, 188, 191, 197, 199, 206, 210, 211, 213, 214, 234, 235, 247–249, 258, 259, 270, 273, 276, 280, 283, 291
New York African Society 103, 152
New York Central College 210, 211
New York Committee of Vigilance 188
New York, New York xxviii, 53, 57, 81, 86, 132, 133, 186, 187, 191, 197, 204, 211, 214, 252, 262, 286, 294
New York Philharmonic 212
New York Public Library 287
New York University 281
Niagara Movement xxix, 244, 250–252, 265, 286
Nicaragua 31, 67, 208, 281
Nicaraguan Civil War 208
Nigeria 47, 175, 202, 283
Niger River 9
Nightingale, Florence 209
Nina 13, 24
Nobel Prize 75
Norfolk, England 244
Norfolk, Virginia 100, 141, 152, 167, 176, 177, 270
Normandy, France 269

North Africa 2, 5, 6, 11, 15, 18, 26, 51, 151
Northampton County, Virginia 56
North Carolina 73–75, 97, 134, 145, 156, 157, 175, 178, 180, 192, 225, 271, 279, 283
North Sea 9
North Star 208
Northwestern University 274, 276
Notes on Virginia (Jefferson) xix
Nova Scotia 30, 124, 129, 133, 156, 175, 248
Nubia 2

O

Obama, Barack xxx, 52, 75, 184, 293
Oberlin College 207, 211, 240, 250, 251, 255, 258, 271, 281, 288
Ocampo, Diego 37
O Clarim 264
Odo, Jeanne 118
Of the Equality of the Human Races (Firmin) 248
Ogé, Vincent 114, 211, 296
Ohio 79, 207, 258, 266, 269, 281
Ohio Anti-Slavery Society 281
Oklahoma 159, 186, 229, 288
Olan, Nuflo de 24, 30
Oliveira, João Fernandez de 78
Olivier, Laurence 286
Olivier, Sydney 286
Olivier, Vincent 61
Olvera, Isabel de 48, 52–54, 60, 80
Oñate expedition 48
Oporto, Portugal 24
Order of Santiago 27, 60
The Origin and History of the Colored People (Pennington) 216
Ortiz, Licenciado 27
Oson, Jacob 186
Ottomans 2, 15, 16
Out of Bondage (Hyers) 258

P

Pacific Ocean 7, 30, 150

Pact of Zanjón 232
Padilla, Domingo 64
Padilla, José 146, 163, 164, 179, 295
Padilla, Juana 52, 64
Paine, Thomas 93, 103, 192
Palermo, Italy 18, 69
Palmares 52, 64, 264
Palos, Spain 13
Pamphlet, Gowen 85
Pan-African Conference 244, 247–249, 251, 253, 272, 286, 292
Pan-Africanism 248, 253
Panama 24, 30, 34–36, 39–41, 43, 46, 59, 64, 66, 160–162, 166, 184, 244, 252, 260, 265
Panama Canal 265
Panasco, João de Sá de 27
Paraguay 202
Paraguayan War 164, 202
Pardo, Adán 70
Pareja, Juan de 28
Paris, France 7, 78, 116, 118, 180, 181, 186, 205, 212, 216, 247, 248, 251, 268, 282
Parker, Richard 56
Parkinson, Leonard 124
Partido Autóctono Negro 264
Partido Democrático Nacional 265
Patriots xxi, xxii, xxiv, xxv, 61, 99, 104, 105, 107–113, 115, 136, 140, 141, 148, 151, 152, 170, 197, 199
Patrocínio, José Carlos do 202
Paul, Susan 193
Paul, Thomas 193
Pax Mongolica 2, 7, 8
Paxton, Edgar 150
Payne, Francis 56
Pearl Harbor 244
Peary, Robert 31
Peçanha, Nilo 184, 244
Peck, David Jones 208, 236
Pendarvis, Joseph 90
Pennington, James W. C. 186, 197, 213, 215

Pennsylvania 73, 144, 209, 244, 280
Penn, William 135, 273
Pensacola, Florida 140
Percival, John 91
Percy, Hugh, Duke of Northumberland 127
Peres, Luis 27
Perry, Oliver Hazard 153
Persia 5, 6, 11
Peru 5, 20, 24, 33–35, 42, 43, 54, 60, 64, 68–70, 160, 161, 164, 165, 186, 204, 259
Petersburg, Virginia 76, 85, 130, 167, 176–178, 185, 222
Peters, Thomas 175
Pétion, Alexandre 119, 146, 154, 162
Pharcell (rebel) 122
Phelps, Alvin 189
Philadelphia 86, 280
Philadelphia, Pennsylvania 103, 111, 116, 132–136, 140, 145, 152, 194, 206, 208, 211–213, 218, 255, 269
Philip, John Baptist 205
Philippine-American War 266
The Philippines 43, 159, 266, 267
Phillip III 69
Phillips, Wendell 197
Phillis 102, 103
Piar, Manuel 164
Picasso, Pablo 181
Picton, Cesar 127
Pieh, Sengbe 214
Pietro, Alonso 13, 24
Pinchback, P. B. S. xxxiii, 227
pirates xvi, xxi, 2, 36, 59, 61, 63, 66–68, 88, 151, 154, 188
Pissarro, Camille 84
Pittsburgh African Education Society 153
Pittsburgh Anti-slavery Society 153
Pittsburgh, Pennsylvania 153, 208
Pizarro, Francisco 34
plantations xv, xxi, xxiii, xxxi, 10–13, 17, 20, 24, 38, 40, 42, 55, 65, 72, 78,

87, 88, 90, 93, 111, 112, 123, 127, 137, 147, 151, 158, 159, 167–171, 175, 178, 187, 199, 203, 224, 232, 239, 293, 295
planters xviii, xxi, xxiv, 52, 55, 56, 58, 71, 74, 75, 80, 88, 90–92, 94, 100, 101, 110, 114–119, 122, 149, 154, 170, 177, 180, 186, 190, 198, 203, 211, 230, 232
Planter 223
Plato 7
Pleasant, Mary Ellen 144, 186, 197
Plessy, Homer 186, 234–236
Plessy v. Ferguson 196, 284
Poems on Various Subjects, Religious and Moral (Wheatley) 102, 103
Poesias Liricas (Manzano) 203
Point Coupée, Louisiana 122
Poland 106, 119
police brutality 257, 260
Polo, Marco 2, 7, 13, 22
Pompey, Edward J. 189, 190
Poor, Salem 107
populism 166, 283
Populus, Vincent 154, 181
Port Royal, South Carolina 220
Portugal xviii, 6, 8–14, 17, 19, 21, 24–29, 31, 32, 35, 45, 52, 54, 57, 58, 60, 62, 63, 65, 68–72, 77, 78, 84, 130, 251
Portuguese, Anthony 57
Potomac River 128
Powell, William 213
Pratt, Charles 240
prejudice 288
Price, Douglas 47
Prince, Caesar 105
Prince, Festus 105
Prince, Garshom 104
Prince Hall Grand Lodge 132
Prince Henry the Navigator 11, 14, 21
Prince, Lucy Terry 105, 106
Princeton University 107, 134
prison industrial complex xix

Progressive Party 257
Prosser, Gabriel xxii, 146, 167, 170, 172, 178
Prosser, Thomas 167
prostitution 174
Protestantism 84
Protten, Christian 95
Providence Island 67
Providence, Rhode Island 132, 219
Provident Hospital 210
The Provincial Freeman 186
Prussia 213
Puerto Príncipe, Cuba 122, 170
Puerto Rican Republican Party 264
Puerto Rico 32, 34, 35, 59, 244, 260, 264, 267, 287
Punch, John xxx, 52, 74, 75, 293
Purvis, Robert 145
Pyrenees Mountains 29
Pythian Baseball Club 212

Q

Quarles, Francis 281
Quarles, Lucy xxxiii
Quebec, Canada 191
Queen Anne's Revenge 67
Queen Anne's War 62, 139
Queen Nanny 173
Queen Victoria 47, 248, 258
Quejo, Domingo de 42
Querino, Manuel 244
Quilombo 282
Quintero, Luis 129
Quintor, Hendrick 67
Quito, Ecuador 24, 39, 43, 70

R

racism xvii–xix, xxv, xxxi, 22, 155, 165, 172, 174, 199, 222, 233, 245, 248, 257, 266, 296, 297
  codification of 75, 79
railroad 228, 235, 290
Raimond, Julien 86, 114, 116, 118
Raleigh, North Carolina 134, 249
Ralston, J.K. 150

Ramírez, Juana 146, 164, 178, 183, 295
Randolph, A. Phillip 285, 292
Rastafarianism 253
Ray, Charlotte 206, 236, 254, 291
Raynal, Abbé 68
Reason, Charles 186, 210, 211
Reason, Patrick 210
Rebouças, Andre 202, 203, 296
Recife, Brazil 10
Reconstruction 226, 227, 246, 257, 279
Red Cross 244, 249, 251, 275, 290
Reeves, Bass 186, 229
Remond, Charles 196, 197, 213
Remond, Sarah 186, 197, 213
Renaissance 6, 8
republicanism xvii, xxiv, 3, 86, 97, 116–122, 131, 148, 154, 160, 165–167, 197, 203, 204, 208, 212, 232, 234, 251, 263, 268
Republican Party 225
Restall, Matthew 30
Revere, Paul 105
Reyes, Frances 128
Rhode Island 62, 99, 206, 249
Rhodes Scholarship 244
Richardson, David 35
Richardson, Lewis 198
Richardson, Willis 259
Richmond, Bill 127, 144
Richmond Recorder 167
Richmond, Virginia 76, 91, 130, 167, 175, 177, 190, 209, 216, 218, 222, 254
The Rights of Moors in Europe (Amo) 95
Riguad, Tula 121
Riley, John xxviii
Rillieux, Norbert 180, 294
Rio de Janeiro, Brazil 54, 212
Rio Grande River 228
Rivadavia, Bernadino 146, 166, 293
Roanoke Colony xvi, 36
Roberts, Frederick Madison xxvii
Roberts, Joseph Jenkins xxx, xxxiii, 146, 176, 177

Roberts, Susanna Anthony 57
Roberts v. Boston 186
Robinson, Spottswood William, III 284
Roca, Vicente 166
Rocky Mountains 149
Rodin, Auguste 181
Rodriguez, Jan 30, 52, 57, 80
Roger II 18
Rogers, J. A. 160
Rojas, Diego de 42
Rollins, Ida Gray Nelson 272
Roman Empire xviii, 2, 4–6, 9, 15, 21, 25, 26, 48, 102, 240
Rome, Italy 26, 28, 69, 181
Romero, José 166
Romero, Pedro 162
Romualdo (slave) 170
Rondón, Juan José 162
Roosevelt, Eleanor 274, 284
Roosevelt, Franklin D. 244, 283, 285
Roosevelt, Theodore xxix, 231, 277, 279
Root, Barnabas 240
Roper, Moses xxxiii, 213
Roscius (actor) 240
Ross, Eunice 189, 190
Ross, Josephine Elizabeth 283
Rough Riders 231
Roumain, Jacques 282
Royal Albert Memorial Museum 125
Ruffin, George Lewis 254
Ruffin, Josephine St. Pierre 254, 256
Ruggles, David 186, 188, 236
Ruiz, Miguel 34
Rush, Benjamin 140
Russell, C. M. 150
Russia 11, 26, 119, 126, 213
Russwurm, John 186, 191
Rustin, Bayard 284, 285, 292

S

Sable, Jean Baptiste Pointe du 86, 129
Sablé sur Sarthe 268
Sacajawea 150
Safavids 15
Sahara Desert 9

Saint Augustine 51
Saint-Domingue xxii, xxiv, 54, 61, 65, 76, 114, 115, 118–119, 124, 129, 149, 150, 154, 170, 210
Salem, Massachusetts 197
Salem, Peter 107
San Antonio, Texas 228
San Basilio de Palenque, Colombia 24, 37
Sánchez, Maria G. 263
Sancho, Ignatius 127
Sancho (slave) 167
Sandy (slave) xxvi
San Francisco, California 129, 144, 197
San Lorenzo de los Negros de Cerralvo, Mexico 52, 63
San Martín, José de 148
San Miguel de Guadeloupe 36
Sanneh, Lamin 175
Santa Cruz la Real, Panama 40
Santa Cruz, Nicomedes 259
Santa Fe, New Mexico 48, 53, 60
Santa Marta 35
Santana, Maria Hidalgo 234
Santiago, Chile 24, 33, 41, 43
Santiago de Cuba, Cuba 234
Santiago del Principe, Panama 40
Santiago, Guatemala 41
Santo Domingo, Dominican Republic 32, 38, 39, 57, 65
Santomee, Lucas 52, 57, 80
Sarasota, Florida 157
Sardinia 26
Savage, Edward xxviii
Savannah, Georgia 85
Savary, Joseph 154, 178
Scandinavia 9
Schad, Hans 144
Schomburg, Arturo 287
Schroeder, Hannes 47
science xvii, 26, 238, 246
Scotland 2, 74, 205, 209, 210, 249
Scotland Yard 271
Scott, Dred 198

Scott, Harriet 198
Seacole, Mary 209
Second Confiscation Act 221
segregation xix, 133, 186, 190, 196, 197, 207, 227, 235, 261, 267, 273, 276, 279, 281, 284, 285, 289, 290, 297
Seminoles 98, 146, 156–158, 182, 228, 229, 266
Senegal 282
Senegal River 9
Senghor, Léopold 282
The Sentiments of the Nations (Morelos) 160
Separate Car Act 234
Sequoia National Park 266
serfdom 2, 21
Serra, Rafael 262, 263
Seven Part Code 71
Seven Years' War 86, 104, 105, 125, 126, 144
Severus, Septimius 2, 5
Seville, Spain 25, 29, 30, 32, 39
Shadd, Abraham W. 206
Shadd, Emaline 206
Shadd, I. D. 206
Shadd, Mary Ann 144
Shafer, Nathaniel 153
Shakespeare, William 212, 213
Sharpe, Samuel 172, 173, 178
Sharp, Granville 126
Shaw University 283
Sheels, Christopher xxviii
Shemin, William 289
The Shoo-Fly Regiment (Cole and Johnson) 258
Sicily 11, 18, 24, 69
Siege of Savannah 115
Sierra Leone 113, 124, 125, 174, 175, 186, 189, 201, 214, 215, 240, 249
Silone, Josephine 254
Silva, Chica da 78, 79
Silva, D. Pedro da 27
Silva, Pedro de 70

Silver Bluff, South Carolina 85
Six Nonlectures (Cummings) 257
slavery xv–xix, xxi–xxvi, xxviii–xxxi, xxxiii, 2–5, 8–21, 24–29, 31, 33–48, 52–56, 58–81, 85–94, 96–106, 108–114, 116, 118–136, 138–140, 145–153, 155–179, 181, 182, 184–196, 198–203, 209–223, 225–230, 232, 233, 235, 236, 238, 240–242, 245, 246, 248, 249, 251, 252, 255, 264, 266, 271, 279, 283, 288, 293–297
  descendants of xx, xxx, 69, 74, 105, 129, 135, 165, 176, 184, 192, 204, 208, 230, 241, 248, 250, 255, 259, 261, 268–270, 272, 273, 275, 276, 281, 283, 293, 294
  legality of xviii, xxi, xxiv, 26, 47, 54–56, 65, 70–74, 76, 100, 107, 126, 127, 132, 137–139, 174, 187, 188, 195, 196, 198, 200, 217, 227, 236, 239, 294
  reactions against xvi, xxi, xxiii, xxv, 24, 35, 36, 38, 40, 45, 55, 57, 58, 88–90, 92, 94, 96, 101, 112–118, 120–126, 136, 140, 151, 158, 166–172, 182, 200, 201, 211, 216, 217
Slavery Abolition Act 217
Slavs 11, 12, 16
Slayden, Sarah 75
Small, Eliza 195
Smalls, Robert 223, 224, 236
Smith College 273
Smith, Cuff 106
Smith, James McCune xxxiii, 197, 204, 213, 236
Smith, Stephen xxxiii, 191
Smith, Venture 106
Society of Colored Citizens 116, 118
Somerset, James xxi, 47, 86, 100–107, 127, 297
Sorbonne University 250
Soto, Catalina de 27
Sousa, Margarita de Castro y 27, 47

Sousa, Mathias de 52, 58, 80
South Africa xxiii, 248
Southampton, Virginia 169
South Carolina xxv, 54, 59, 74, 75, 86, 88–90, 93, 97, 101, 113, 126, 137, 146, 166, 168, 172, 178–179, 190, 192, 208, 212, 218, 220, 224, 225, 229, 237, 257, 259
Southern Christian Leadership Conference 283, 285
space race 272
Spain, Spanish xviii, 2, 4, 6, 7, 10, 13, 16, 20, 21, 24–31, 33–40, 42–45, 47, 48, 52, 53, 56, 58–67, 69, 70, 72, 77, 78, 84, 86, 89, 90, 93, 97, 98, 101, 102, 114, 115, 119–123, 128–130, 140, 146–149, 153, 154, 156, 157, 160–166, 170, 200, 203, 204, 212–215, 232, 261, 274, 294
Spanish-American War xxix, 224, 231, 232, 242, 266, 268, 272, 288, 289
Spanish Civil War 269
Spanish Colonial Army 62
Spelman College 271
Springfield, Illinois 252, 286
Springfield, Ohio 286
Stamp Act 103
Stanford University 242
Stanton, Lucia xxxii, 241
Starlins, Mark 108, 141
Staten Island (New York City) 127
States' Laws on Race and Color (Murray) 284
St. Augustine, Florida 29, 44, 53, 59, 78, 90, 97, 132, 156, 169
Staupers, Mabel Keaton 267
St. Benedict 24
St. Croix 47, 94, 138, 144
"The Star-Spangled Banner" (Key) 168, 199
Stevens, Christopher 177
Stewart, James 100
Stewart, John 76
Stewart, Maria 186, 193

Stewart, Mourning 178
Stewart, Thomas 177, 178
St. John 93, 94, 96, 112, 123, 138
St. John Historical Society 94
St. John Revolt 86
St. Louis, Missouri 198, 275
St. Lucia 120, 121
Stockbridge 106
Stone, Lucy 250, 254
Stono Rebellion xxv, 60, 89–91, 93, 137
Stono Revolt 86
Stono River 90
Stowe, Harriett Beecher 212
Strachin, John 152
Strait of Gibraltar 11, 29
Stratford-upon-Avon, England 213
St. Thomas 66, 84, 93–95, 168
Student Nonviolent Coordinating Committee 283
St. Vincent 86, 120
Sudan 2, 5
Suffolk, England 167
suffrage 145, 173, 189, 194, 197, 199, 205, 218, 244, 251, 277, 296
sugar 2, 8, 11–13, 17, 21, 36, 38, 42, 55, 64, 71, 72, 76, 87, 101, 115, 127, 151, 158, 170, 171, 180, 200, 232, 239, 294
Suleiman the Magnificent 15
Sumer 2, 4, 5
Sumner, Charles 242
Suriname 36, 41, 46, 89, 92, 122, 123, 171
Surín, Gregorio 261
Suwannee River 181
Sweden 47, 68
Sweeney, Robert Augustus 289
Switzerland 213
Sylvester-Williams, Henry 247, 296
Syphax, Maria Carter xxix
Syria 11, 26

T

Tabula Rogeriana 18
Tacky's War 86, 89, 92, 93

Taino Indians 35, 38
Tamarin, Mingo 94
Tampa, Florida 30
Tanner, Benjamin Tucker 278
Tanner, Henry Ossawa 181, 278
Tarrant, Caesar 108
Taylor, Daniel 249
Taylor, Eric Robert 35
Taylor, Susie King 225
Teal, Christopher 212
Teatro Nacional do Negro 282
Temple, Lewis 186, 190, 296
Tennessee 228, 281
Tenochtitlan 20, 44
Ten Years' War 232–234
Teotihuacan 2, 20
Terence the African 48
Terrell, Mary Church 227, 244, 251, 254, 276, 277, 279
Terrell, Robert 227, 279
Terrence the African 102
terrorism xix, 235, 236, 246, 291
Terry, Lucy Prince 102
Texas 32, 44, 154, 228, 229, 230
Thetford, Norfolk 248
Thirteenth Amendment 229, 242
Thoms, Adah 267
Thornton, John 9
Thoughts and Sentiments on the Evil and Wicked Traffic of the Slavery (Cugoano) 127
The Three Musketeers (Dumas) 116
Thurmond, Strom xix
Ticonderoga 107
Tiffany, Cyrus 153
Tilden, Samuel 227
Timbuktu, Mali 2, 7
Tinchant, Edouard 235
Tinsley, Charles 177
tobacco 21, 55, 65, 72, 87, 167, 175
Toral, Sebastian 44
Toronto, Canada 195
Trans-Atlantic Slave Trade Database xxxiii

Transylvania 15
Treaty of New York (1790) 86, 98
Treaty of Paris (1783) 152
Trelawny 123, 124
Trinidad 34, 156, 205, 244, 248, 249
Tristão, Nuño 14
Trollope, Anthony 242
Trotter, James Monroe xxvii, xxxiii, 250
Trotter, William Monroe xxvii, 250, 256
Truman, Harry 280
Trumbull, John 111
Truth, Sojourner 186, 199
Tubman, Harriet 186, 218, 224, 236, 254
Tucker, Thomas 240
Tucson, Arizona 60
Tufts University xx
Tulsa Race Riot 277
Turkey 16
Turks 2, 152
Turner, Nat 146, 169
Tuskegee Airmen 268
Tuskegee, Alabama xx
Tuskegee Syphilis Study xx, xxxii
Tuskegee University 261, 286
Tuskegee Veterans Administration Hospital xx
Tyler, John 215

U

Uncle Tom's Cabin (Stowe) 212
Underground Railroad 134, 153, 188, 195–197, 210, 217, 218, 274
UNESCO 37, 282
Union Missionary Society 216
United Negro Improvement Association 244, 252, 253
United States Colored Troops xxvii
United States Electric Company 270
University of California, Los Angeles xxvii
University of Cambridge 139
University of Chicago 274
University of Copenhagen, Denmark 47
University of Florida 47

University of Glasgow 204
University of Heidelberg 216
University of Leiden 95
University of Liberia 176
University of Maryland 256
University of Massachusetts 286
University of Michigan 264, 271, 272
University of Munich xx
University of North Carolina 283
University of Pennsylvania 280
University of Tennessee 292
University of Texas 182, 273
University of Vienna 275
University of Virginia 141
University of Wisconsin-Madison 47
University of Wittenberg 86, 95
Uruguay 160, 164, 165, 202, 260, 264
U.S. Board for the Certification of Gene-
    alogists 84
U.S. Congress xx, 86, 136, 145, 206,
    207, 220, 221, 225, 227, 277, 288,
    290
U.S. Constitution 133, 148, 190, 218,
    219, 238
U.S. military xxvii, 150–152, 157, 158,
    214, 227, 244, 267, 268, 270, 273,
    281, 288
U.S. Public Health Service xx
U.S.S. *Chesapeake* 151, 152
U.S.S. *Maine* 232
U.S. Supreme Court 186, 198, 214,
    215, 235, 244, 257, 284
U.S. Virgin Islands 93, 95
Utah 44

V

Valdéz, José Manuel 186, 204, 236, 297
Valdivia, Juana de 33
Valencia, Spain 16, 24, 26
Valiente, Juan 24, 33, 43
Valladolid, Spain 69
Valley Forge 104, 107
Valverde, Úrsula Coimbra de 263
Van Buren, Martin 198, 214, 215
Vaquero, Juan 37

Vasco de Gama 18
Vashon, George 153, 211
Vashon, John Bathan xxxiii, 153, 178,
    208
Vasquez, Tomé 24, 41
vaudeville 258
Velazquez, Diego 28, 43
Venezuela xxii, 32–35, 38, 46, 64,
    120, 121, 123, 146–148, 160–162,
    164–166, 171, 183, 184, 232, 260,
    281, 288, 295
Venice, Italy 7
Veracruz, Mexico 32, 52, 54, 59, 62, 63
Vermont 106
Vesey, Denmark 146, 168–170
Vidal, Ana Hidalgo 263
Vieira, Antonio 52, 68, 73, 80
Vienna, Italy 15
Vigilance Committee 186
Vikings 9
Villa, Maria Rita Valdez 129
Villa, Pancho 266
Virginia xviii, xx–xxii, xxiv, xxx, 52,
    54–59, 71, 73–75, 79, 88, 90, 97, 101,
    108–113, 126, 128, 141, 146, 147,
    151, 152, 166–169, 172–180, 195,
    196, 199, 200, 207, 211, 212, 222,
    226, 248, 258, 270, 276, 279, 284
Virginia Gazette 101
Virginia State University 207
Vivaldi brothers 2, 10
Vizzaneau, Mary 76
Voice of a Fugitive 194
Voltaire 103, 116, 131
Voorhees College 250
Vox Africanorum 132

W

Wales 132
Walker, David 186, 192, 193
Walker, Edwin 192
Walker, Quock 107
Walle, Jessie 153
Walpole, George 124
Ward, Samuel Ringgold 186, 194, 213

Ware, William 152
Waring, Laura Wheeler xxxiii, 181
War of 1812 99, 136, 146, 151–155, 175, 193, 219, 226
Warren, Earl xxvii
Washington and Lee University 134
Washington, Booker T. xxxiii, 286
Washington, D.C. xxvii, 86, 128, 198, 199, 206, 207, 212, 219, 224, 226, 242, 251, 255, 259, 273, 279, 281, 284, 285, 289, 291
Washington, George xxv, xxvi, xxviii, xxix, 93, 97, 98, 103, 106, 107, 110–114, 131, 142, 151, 160, 161, 294
Washington, Harry 111, 113, 124, 126, 129, 142, 175, 295
Washington, Madison 216
Washington, Margaret Murray 286
Washington, Martha xxv, xxvi, xxviii, xxix
Washington, Sarah Spencer 276
Washington Welfare Association 251
Watkins Academy 210
Watkins, James 213
Watkins, William 210
Watlings Island 13
Webb, Frank J. 212, 213
Webb, Mary 212
Webster, Daniel 242
Wells, Cuffee 104, 139
Wells, Gideon 223
Wells, Ida B. 186, 235, 236, 244, 254
West Africa 6, 7, 9–15, 17, 25–27, 33, 47, 59, 67, 74, 90, 95, 100–103, 106, 113, 126, 127, 175, 189, 214–216, 228, 249, 252, 285
Westminster Town Hall 247
West Point 266, 268, 288
Westport, Massachussetts 189
Wharton School 280
Wheatley, Phillis 103, 104
Wheeler, Barbara xxxiii
Whipper, William 191
Whitecuff, Benjamin 112

White House 128, 186, 199, 226, 227, 230, 279
White, José Silvestre 212
white supremacy xxxi, 77, 103, 151, 193, 219, 246
Whitfield, George 132
Whittier, John Greenleaf 213
Wilberforce University 271, 272, 288
William I 21
Williams, Bert 258, 259
Williamsburg, Virginia 85, 101, 185
Williams, Cathay 228
Williams College 106
Williams, Daniel Hale 186, 209
Williams, George Washington 99
Williams, Raymond 22
Williamson, Ansel 231
Wilmington, North Carolina 224, 286
Wilson, Henry 215
Wilson, Woodrow 289
Wisconsin 209
Women's Era Club 253–256
Women's International League for Peace and Freedom 251
Women's League 255
Wonderful Adventures of Mrs. Seacole in Many Lands (Seacole) 209
Wood, Frances 22
Wood, Nancy 123
Wood, Peter 80
Woods, Granville T. 270, 290
Woodson, Waverly 268, 289
World's Fair 250, 276
World War I 159, 224, 242, 244, 247, 249, 253, 259, 266–269, 274, 289
World War II xxxiii, 159, 208, 244, 247, 267, 268, 270, 272, 274, 282, 290
Wormley Hotel 227
Wormley, James 226, 227, 242
Wormley, Lynch 227
Wright, Ceah 273
Wright, Elizabeth Evelyn 250
Wright, Louis Tompkins 273, 274

Wyoming 44, 288

X

xenophobia xvii

Y

Yale College 108, 205, 211, 214, 216,
  273, 284
Yamasee War 86, 89, 93
Yanga, Gaspar 52, 63
Yanga, Veracruz, Mexico 82
Yates, Josephine Silone 254, 255
Yellow Fever 133, 134
York Islands 150
Young, Charles 244, 266–268, 289
Yucatan 44

Z

Zafria (Manzano) 203
Ziegfeld Follies 258
Zorita, Catalina de 42
Zoroastrianism 6
Zumba, Ganga 64
Zumbi dos Palmares International
  Airport 83
Zumbi (revolutionary) 65, 80, 83